ENEMIES OF PROMISE
AND OTHER ESSAYS

ENEMIES OF PROMISE AND OTHER ESSAYS: AN AUTOBIOGRAPHY OF IDEAS BY CYRIL CONNOLLY

Anchor Books, Doubleday & Company, Inc.

Garden City, New York, 1960

Library of Congress Catalog Card Number 60–5920

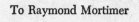

To Raymond Mortimer

ACKNOWLEDGMENTS

Enemies of Promise and *The Condemned Playground* were first published in this country by The Macmillan Company.

"Told in Gath" is reprinted from *Parody Party*, edited by Leonard Russell and published by Hutchinson's.

"Where Engels Fears to Tread" is reprinted from *Press Gang*, edited by Leonard Russell and published by Hutchinson's.

"A Baudelaire Conundrum" first appeared in the *Times Literary Supplement*.

"François Villon," "Addison Revisited," "Coleridge," "Stendhal's Letters," "Balzac in English," "Delacroix's Journal," "Arnold Bennett," "F. Scott Fitzgerald: The Last Romantic," and "Opposite Number: Edmund Wilson," are reprinted by permission of the London *Sunday Times*, in which they first appeared.

"America and Europe" is reprinted from *Vogue*, in which it appeared under the title of "A Bitter Britisher Praises America."

CONTENTS

II.   GERMANE STUDIES

III.   RECONSIDERATIONS

IV.   ENVOI

FOREWORD

Enemies of Promise is complete in itself, but I have added
two more sections which I believe to be relevant, one consisting of some pieces from *The Condemned Playground*
which were written at the time and in which the same ideas
appear in different treatment, the other being a group of
reconsiderations of the same authors. The idea of the book
was with me for a long period and I came to it largely
through my experience as a fiction reviewer which I also
expressed in parodies, beginning with "Ninety Years of
Novel-Reviewing" written when I was twenty-five. In 1935
a book about an Eton friend by his father set me thinking
about the literary formation of my school days and the germ
of "A Georgian Boyhood" (this title and its chapter headings were themselves a parody) will be found in this review
("The Fate of an Elizabethan"). The comments on Rimbaud ("Onus Vallis Visionis") appeared just after *Enemies
of Promise* and illustrate my final reaction against romanticism ("final" means, of course, "until the next time") while
"The Ant-Lion" tolls the quittance bell for the carefree expatriate who began his omelette under the plane tree two
years before. Judgment matures, memories ripen, vanity re-
cedes, large areas of consciousness collapse suddenly like
sand castles, leaving, we hope, stimulating voids, but middle age seldom enlarges the sensibility and when I returned
to Albi in 1948, I could feel nothing.

The Condemned Playground, from which the "Germane
Studies" of Part II are taken, signifies for me the literary
scene of the 1930's, the period of ebullience, mediocrity,
frivolity, and talent during which I wrote most of these essays and my first two books. I also chose the title to refer

in a more limited sense to that leafy tranquil cultivated
spielraum of Chelsea, where I worked and wandered. But
there is another sense in which *The Condemned Playground*
refers to Art itself; for Art is man's noblest attempt to preserve Imagination from Time, to make unbreakable toys of
the mind, mud pies which endure; and yet even the masterpieces whose permanence grants them a mystical authority
over us are doomed to decay: a word slithers into oblivion,
then a phrase, then an idea. *"Le mot vieillit,"* as Valéry puts
it, *"devient trés rare, devient opaque, change de forme ou
de role. La Syntaxe et les tours prennent de l'âge, étonnent
et finissent par rebuter. Tout s'achève en Sorbonne."*

This feeling of evanescence has always been with me as
a critic; I feel I am fighting a rear-guard action, for although each generation discovers anew the value of masterpieces, generations are never quite the same and ours are
in fact coming to prefer the response induced by violent
stimuli—film, radio, press—to the slow permeation of the personality by great literature. Like most critics, I drifted into
the profession through a lack of moral stamina: I wanted
to be a poet, and to revive the epic; I wanted to write a
novel about archaic Greece—but my epic and my novel fell
so short of the standards which my reading had set me that
I despaired of them and, despairing, slipped into the interim
habit of writing short-term articles about books. The habit
grew and conquered: many years later, and almost too late,
I set out to conquer it. That is how most of our critics are
formed. Not that I despise criticism: I wish only that I had
been a better critic—for I think that the distinction between
true criticism and creation, as Wilde pointed out in *The
Critic as Artist,* is non-existent and that many a novelist who
flatters himself that he is creative is hanging second-hand
ideas on lifeless puppets in a mechanical fashion of which
a conscientious critic would be ashamed. I have always
been heartened by the words of Sainte-Beuve, *"Le don de
critique . . . devient même du génie lorsqu'au milieu des
révolutions du goût, entre les ruines d'un vieux genre qui
s'écroule et les innovations qui se tentent, il s'agit de dis-
cerner avec netteté, avec certitude, sans aucune mollesse, ce*

qui est bon et ce qui vivra; si, dans une oeuvre nouvelle, l'originalité réelle suffit à racheter les défauts."

But I wish I had been a better critic and that I had not written brightly, because I was asked to, about so many bad books. What merits I have are somewhat practical and earthy. I stay very close to the text—no soaring eagle but a low-swung basset who hunts by scent and keeps his nose to the ground. I am not sure that a critic should have any opinions. Experience develops in the critic an instinct, which, like a water-diviner's, agitates him when near to treasure. He digs and explains afterwards. The authors I most enjoy writing about are first those great, lonely, formal artists who spit in the eye of their century, and after them the wild and exquisitely gifted young writers who come to an untimely end through passion, and lastly those wild epicureans who combine taste with the gossiping good sense of the world, and whose graceful books are but the shadow of their intimate communion with their friends or with nature. And sometimes I don't mind making fun of the pompous and pretentious, the second-rate best-sellers whose word in the thirties was literary law.

"Reconsiderations" consists of short pieces . . . all having some bearing on the favourite authors commented on in *Enemies of Promise.* Petronius and Villon I loved as a schoolboy and the glimpses of Coleridge, Stendhal, Balzac, Baudelaire, Delacroix portray my never-ending conflict with romanticism. Yeats called himself "the last romantic" —he had not read F. Scott Fitzgerald, but I am certainly the last and the most unwilling.

I should like to be able to conclude with a solution to the riddle of the universe which I believe to have been constructed by a mathematical genius who forgot to allow for the development of consciousness and spelt death with a small "d"—or at least with some impressive and final reflections on literature which certainly still elude me. It is, I still believe, the greatest of the arts, for by the mere arrangement of letters on a page it can move us to tears. Music requires performer and instrument, painting canvas and colour, sculpture, architecture, even more paraphernalia—but poetry alone has this sublime economy

ibi tu calentem
debita sparges lacrima favillam
vatis amici

"There may you sprinkle the still warm ashes of your poet
friend with the tears that are his due"—no, not even that—
"there you the warm with customary may you sprinkle tear
ashes of poet friend." A magic telegram, variations on a
theme of "a," "l" and "t" never to be pronounced, even
after two thousand years, with a dry eye. But supposing
we are unmoved? Supposing literature, like musk, has lost
its scent? I should like to think a Renaissance was abroad
but I cannot. Even when I charted the "enemies of promise" I did not consider radio worth mentioning and televi-
sion did not exist, now they loom so large that the spoken
word and visual personality destroy what is written. Literature should be what St. John of the Cross called a *soledad
sonora.*" It is not the writer but the reader who is to blame;
we read too fast and too much, we skip and forget. A
century ago a poem like *In Memoriam* could go anywhere;
it penetrated every home and was read aloud in the winter
evenings. Paintings remained in the great collections, music
in the opera houses. Now paintings circulate like *In
Memoriam,* a good Cézanne may visit every capital,
museums pullulate, reproductions abound, while music
pours from every chink and cranny. *In Memoriam* can also
be broadcast, televised, filmed—for literature shares in the
new facilities, but none of that amounts to being read.

If, therefore, such a book as this can justify the faith of
those who reissue it in a cheap edition, it must encourage
people to read as well as write and this is all I can hope
to do, for I believe that one gift I can truly claim to possess
is the ability to communicate enthusiasm. It does not matter if such a book dates, provided that it dates honorably,
though it so happens that my main contentions still apply.
The war saw the "Mandarin style" obtain an overwhelming
victory, at any rate in England, in protest against the drabness of life. But too often the pulleys creak and the donkey
engine rattles through the long sentence and now I am
bored with anxiety and complicated feelings; we need

Sappho and Archilochus, intensity, rapidity and the dazzling smile of archaic Greece. We must think out carefully
exactly what literature does best and uniquely, what it expressed that cannot be expressed as well in any other art
and how to say it so that it cannot be debased and exploited. Perhaps that quality is not emotional, since emotion may be better expressed in music (Debussy's faun
killed Mallarmé's), but intellectual. Literature remains the
supreme vehicle for thought. It also offers the only complete participation in another human personality. We can
never know Mozart as we know Montaigne. And this
participation is an extension of living and therefore its own
reward. Finally there is the matter of style—let us return to
that nine-word miracle with its arrangements of "a"s and
"l"s and "t"s. Is it not perhaps subtler than anything that
can be said by music? For even the order of the words
causes a little of their meaning to leak from one to another—
"*lacrima,*" the tear, communicates by proximity a little
moisture to the ash, "*favillam,*" even as our own later
knowledge links that word to the "Dies Irae"—"*solvet
saeclum in favilla.*" We have, of course, lines as beautiful in
English, like "Distasted with the salt of broken tears," but
not the same multiplicity of word order. And so farewell—
do not despise the scrappiness of my book. I work best in
scraps and, besides, a little of me goes a long way.

ENEMIES OF PROMISE

"Quando sovviemmi di contanta spemè"

To Logan Pearsall Smith

INTRODUCTION

Enemies of Promise was first published in 1938 as a
didactic enquiry into the problem of how to write a book
which lasts ten years. That limit is now reached and the
book has survived; the proof lying in the fact that it has
been republished. The original edition appeared in the
week of the Munich crisis and, despite some very favourable and some very offensive reviews, sold extremely badly.
One provincial reviewer attacked me for daring to eat
peaches for lunch on the first page, though in the South of
France that summer they were cheaper than potatoes. Another accused me of plagiarising Valéry who in an essay
which I had not read made use of the Mandarin image
for some kinds of writing. A more general criticism was
that the autobiographical section of Part III should precede
the rest of the book or alternatively be published separately,
since it had nothing to do with it.

The objection to beginning with Part III, aside from the
fact that I wrote it in the position which it now occupies, is
that a section dealing with life and living people would
make the ensuing literary criticisms seem dry and insipid.
And in fact there is a very intentional harmony, if not an
obvious one, between the last section and the others, to
which it stands in the relationship of illustrations to text.
Thus several writers who appear as text-book names in
Part I occur as people in Part III. Literary theories mentioned in Part I are seen originating from existence itself in
Part III. Romanticism is measured against a romantic education—and the autobiography is essentially an autobiography of ideas and one which deliberately leaves out all
those episodes in my life which do not further the growth
of those literary speculations on which the first part is
based. Even the title "A Georgian Boyhood" and the chap-

ter headings are meant to shed an ironical emphasis on
the Pater-Ruskin-Mackenzie autobiographical pastiche that
was the fashion of the day.

One more point: the enquiry into the nature of contemporary prose style and the recommendation towards a certain solution in Parts I and II is meant to be illustrated by
the style which emerges in Part III. The autobiography is
intended to be composed in a language which combines the
rapidity of the colloquial with an elasticity permitting in-
cursions into the Mandarin of prose poetry. It should be
felt evolving as it goes along. Were the first and second
halves of the book to be separated there would result a
very indifferent and incomplete work of criticism and a
very evasive and partial autobiography; the poisons in the
laurel would be segregated from its delights. I hope that
my readers of to-day will be more perceptive.

What is much more disturbing is that I should have
found it necessary to make so few alterations. On every
page I have retouched the writing itself (it was Edmund
Wilson who remarked that it was not a very well-written
book and put me on to this) and I have cut out one or two
rather dull passages and restored in their place one or two
from the original manuscript. But I have not altered or inserted a single opinion. I have retained all the engagingly
simple left-wing militancy since it breathes the air of the
period, but I have found it quite unnecessary to modify
any of my literary judgments. In other words I am unwilling to recognise any revolution in the reputation of
modern authors over the last ten years. Yeats, Joyce, Virginia Woolf, alas, are dead. The Sitwells have grown
enormously in stature, Aldous Huxley has made a brilliant
recovery, Auden and Orwell added new triumphs—but with
these modifications the literary values remain unaltered.
Unless it is I who have been stationary, time would seem
to have stood still—or rather literary time—for the effect of
wars and catastrophes is to slow up the movement (so
much more profound) of the human spirit. I would have
preferred to re-write the whole book in order to bring it
into line with a revolution in taste rather than be compelled only to revarnish it and send it forth into a stagnant

world and a moribund society. But there is one change. In the autobiography I wrote of the premature death of one of my schoolmates as a momentous and distressing event, but in a year or so after its appearance death was to take a heavy toll of my generation and now I find the later chapters inexpressibly sad for me through the deaths of Denis Dannreuther, my kind and loyal mentor, the gentle Peter Loxley, and the one whose friendship was the mainstay of my existence during the seven years after leaving Eton, Robert Longden, killed—the only casualty—by a bomb splinter in a raid on the great school of which he was headmaster. To these I would now like to dedicate the last portion. Several others mentioned in these papers were to follow and this presence of death now lends a remoteness to the chronicles of what I see to be a far more weird and privileged and threatened and vanishing society than I ever realised—a doomed seminary of humanism singled out for especial displays of carnage in the chaotic liquidation of the West.

Sometimes I meet people who think the autobiography is meant to be an attack on Eton and as I understand that it was thrown out with bell, book and candle on its appearance there, I expect the author would meet with the same fate. Of course it is not meant to be anything of the kind, it is an effort to tell the truth. The truth, I should have thought, emerges fairly clearly. It is possible to have a very bad time indeed in one's first year or so in a large public school if one's companions are bullies and there are bloody-minded people at the top. This would be avoided at a secondary school or an advanced school like Dartington. On the other hand my last two years at Eton, as I have tried to convey, were among the most interesting and rewarding of my whole life and I do not believe they could have been so at any other public school or in any other house than College. My criticism is not of Eton but of a system which tends to keep boys at school too late. I believe they should go at the age of twelve and leave at seventeen and go down from the university a year earlier, and I think that preparatory schools should be mostly for day-boys. And masters should all come up regularly before a psychiatrist. But parents who can send their children to Eton should at all costs do so; it may be their one chance of survival, and if they don't survive, their one moment of happiness. For, ten years after the threats of dictators and rumours of wars which toll through the opening and closing paragraphs of *Enemies of Promise*, the knell is heard again and when this reprint appears my subject may seem as trivial and superficial as in that terrible Munich week. But we must go on doing what we like doing best as if it were the illusions of humanism which are real and the realities of nihilism that prove a nightmare. *"Il faut tenter de vivre"* —we must try to live and that for many of us means we must try to write, and very difficult it is, as I found out during that Mediterranean summer, especially in those moments when one leaves off telling others how to:

> As Helluo, late dictator of the feast
> The nose of Haut-gout and the tip of taste
> Critiqu'd your wine, and analysed your meat,
> Yet on plain pudding deigned at home to eat.

PART ONE: PREDICAMENT

In vain do individuals hope for immortality, or any patent from oblivion, in preservations below the Moon.

SIR THOMAS BROWNE

CHAPTER I: THE NEXT TEN YEARS

This is the time of year when wars break out and when a broken glass betrays the woodland to the vindictive sun. Already the forest fires have accounted for a thousand hectares of the Var. We fight them by starting little manageable blazes which burn a strip to ashes before the main conflagration has had time to arrive. These flames in turn must be extinguished and isolated by setting fire to other and still more obedient strips till the last cinders expire in the garden where I am writing.

It is after lunch (omelette, vichy, peaches) on a sultry day. Here is the plane tree with the table underneath it; a gramophone is playing in the next room. I always try to write in the afternoon for I have just enough Irish blood to be afraid of the Irish temperament. The literary form it takes, known as the "Celtic Twilight," consists of an addiction to melancholy and to an exaggerated use of words and such good Irish writers as there have been exorcise the demon by disciplining themselves to an alien and stricter culture. Yeats translated Greek, while Joyce, Synge and George Moore fled to Paris. For myself I find Augustan Latin and Augustan English the best correctives. But they do not at all times function well and when I write after dark the shades of evening scatter their purple through my prose. Then why not write in the morning? Unfortunately in my case there is never very much of the morning, and it is curious that although I do not despise people who go to bed earlier than I, almost everyone is impatient with me for not getting up. I may be working in bed on a wet morning and they have nothing to do, yet they cannot conceal their feelings of superiority and ill will.

But between the dissipated bedridden morning and the dangerous night fall the cicada hours of afternoon so

pregnant in their tedium and these I now have free for the
problem that is obsessing me.

THE NEXT TEN YEARS

(1) What will have happened to the world in ten years'
time?

(2) To me? To my friends?

(3) To the books they write?

Above all to the books—for, to put it another way, I have
one ambition—to write a book that will hold good for ten
years afterwards. And of how many is that true to-day? I
make it ten years because for ten years I have written about
books, and because I can say, and this is the gravest warning, that in a short time the writing of books, especially
works of the imagination which last that long, will be an
extinct art. Contemporary books do not keep. The quality
in them which makes for their success is the first to go;
they turn overnight. Therefore one must look for some
quality which improves with time. The short-lived success of a book may be the fault of the reader, for newspapers, libraries, book societies, broadcasting and the
cinema have vitiated the art of reading. But the books of
which I am thinking have all been read once, and have
all seemed good to discriminating readers. They go bad
just the same.

Suppose we were describing English literature in 1928.
We would mention Lawrence, Huxley, Moore, Joyce,
Yeats, Virginia Woolf and Lytton Strachey. If clever we
would add Eliot, Wyndham Lewis, Firbank, Norman
Douglas and, if solid, Maugham, Bennett, Shaw, Wells,
Galsworthy, Kipling. Of these Strachey, Galsworthy, Bennett, Lawrence, Moore, Firbank are dead and also out of
fashion. They are as if they had never been. Suppose new
manuscripts were discovered, a *Five Towns* by Bennett, a
Forsyte by Galsworthy, even another novel by Lawrence,
it would be a nightmare. We can discount for this prejudice
as a natural reaction from the work of yesterday to that of
to-day but much of it is unnatural because during their
lifetime these writers were unnaturally praised. Since their

booms, the reputations of Shaw, Joyce, Firbank and Huxley and many others have declined; in fact, of the eminent writers of ten years ago, only the fame of Eliot, Yeats, Maugham and Forster has increased. And the young writers of ten years ago are also stringing out.

My own predicament is—how to live another ten years.

Living primarily means keeping alive. The predicament is economical. How to get enough to eat? I assume however that most people who read this will have made some kind of adjustment, in fact I am writing for my fellow bourgeois. A writer has no greater pleasure than to reach people; nobody dislikes isolation more than an artist, a difficult artist most of all—but he must reach them by fair means—if he flatters them, if he screams at them, begs from them, lectures them or plays confidence tricks on them, he will appeal only to the worthless elements, and it is they who will throw him over. Meanwhile the way I write and the things I like to write about make no appeal to the working class nor can I make any bridge to them till they are ready for it. So I greet you, my educated fellow bourgeois, whose interests and whose doubts I share.

Another way to keep alive is not to get killed. That is a political question. The official policy by which we are not to get killed is by keeping out of war, but in order to keep out of war it is necessary to avoid the rôle of the good Samaritan; we have to pass by on the other side.

To have to dispense with their ideals and thus support a cynical policy in which they do not believe is a humiliating position for idealists. They therefore cannot be said to remain spiritually alive and this necessity of choosing between the perils of war and physical extermination and the dangers of an ostrich peace and spiritual stagnation, between physical death and moral death, is another predicament.

Since at present our own expectation of life is so insecure, the one way to make certain of living another ten years is to do work which will survive so long. For the best work explodes with a delayed impact. There is E. M. Forster, who has only produced two books since the last war, yet he is alive because his other books, which are from twenty to thirty years old, are gaining ground among intelligent readers. Their pollen fertilises a new generation. There are reasons for this. To begin with, the novels of Forster state the general conflict which is localised in the political conflict of to-day. His themes are the breaking down of barriers: between white and black, between class and class, between man and woman, between art and life. "Only connect . . ." the motto of *Howard's End*, might be the lesson of all his work. His heroes and heroines, with their self-discipline, their warm hearts, their horror of shams and false emotion, of intellectual exclusiveness on the moral plane and of property, money, authority, social and family ties on the material one, are the precursors of the left-wing young people of to-day; he can be used by them as a take-off in whatever direction they would develop. Thus the parable form of Forster's novels may survive the pamphlet form of Shaw's plays, despite their vigorous thinking, because Forster is an artist and Shaw is not. Much of his art consists in the plainness of his writing for he is certain of the truth of his convictions and the force of his emotions. It is the writer who is not so sure what to say or how he feels who is apt to overwrite either to conceal his ignorance or to come unexpectedly on an answer. Similarly it is the novelist who finds it hard to create character who indulges in fine writing. This unemphatic, even style of Forster's makes him easy to re-read, for it contains nothing of which one can get tired except sprightliness. But there is another reason why the work of Forster remains fresh. His style has not been imitated.

What kills a literary reputation is inflation. The advertising, publicity and enthusiasm which a book generates— in a word its success—imply a reaction against it. The element of inflation in a writer's success, the extent to which it has been forced, is something that has to be written off. One can fool the public about a book but the public will store up resentment in proportion to its folly. The public can be fooled deliberately by advertising and publicity or it can be fooled by accident, by the writer fooling himself. If we look at the boom pages of the Sunday papers we can see the fooling of the public going on, inflation at work.

A word like genius is used so many times that eventually the sentence "Jenkins has genius. *Cauliflower Ear* is immense!" becomes true because he has as much genius and is as immense as are the other writers who have been praised there. It is the words that suffer for in the inflation they have lost their meaning. The public at first suffers too but in the end it ceases to care and so new words have to be dragged out of retirement and forced to suggest merit. Often the public is taken in by a book because, although bad, it is topical, its up-to-dateness passes as originality, its ideas seem important because they are "in the air." *The Bridge of San Luis Rey, Dusty Answer, Decline and Fall, Brave New World, The Postman Always Rings Twice, The Fountain, Good-bye, Mr. Chips* are examples of books which had a success quite out of proportion to their undoubted merit and which now reacts unfavourably on their authors, because the overexcitable public who read those books have been fooled. None of the authors expected their books to become best-sellers but, without knowing it, they had hit upon the contemporary chemical combination of illusion with disillusion which makes books sell.

But it is also possible to write a good book and for it to be imitated and for those imitations to have more success than the original so that when the vogue which they have created and surfeited is past, they drag the good book down with them. This is what has happened to Hemingway, who made certain pointillist discoveries in style which have almost led to his undoing. So much depends on style, this factor of which we are growing more and more suspicious, that although the tendency of criticism is to explain a writer either in terms of his sexual experience or his economic background, I still believe his technique remains the soundest base for a diagnosis; that it should be possible to learn as much about an author's income and sex life from one paragraph of his writing as from his cheque stubs and his love letters and that one should also be able to learn how well he writes, and who are his influences. Critics who ignore style are liable to lump good and bad writers together in support of pre-conceived theories.

An expert should be able to tell a carpet by one skein

of it; a vintage by rinsing a glassful round his mouth. Applied to prose there is one advantage attached to this method—a passage taken from its context is isolated from the rest of a book, and cannot depend on the good will which the author has cleverly established with his reader. This is important, for in all the books which become best-sellers and then flop, this salesmanship exists. The author has fooled the reader by winning him over at the beginning, and so establishing a favourable atmosphere for putting across his inferior article—for making him accept false sentiment, bad writing, or unreal situations. To write a best-seller is to set oneself a problem in seduction. A book of this kind is a confidence trick. The reader is given a cigar and a glass of brandy and asked to put his feet up and listen. The author then tells him the tale. The most favourable atmosphere is a stall at a theatre, and consequently of all things which enjoy contemporary success that which obtains it with least merit is the average play.

A great writer creates a world of his own and his readers are proud to live in it. A lesser writer may entice them in for a moment, but soon he will watch them filing out.

But darkness falls, frogs croak, the martins bank and whistle over the terrace and the slanting hours during which I can be entrusted with a pen grow threatening with night.

CHAPTER II: THE MANDARIN DIALECT

Before continuing with our diagnosis it becomes necessary to have a definition of style. It is a word that is beginning to sound horrible, a quality which no good writer should possess. Stephen Spender can even brashly say of Henry James:

> As always with great æstheticians there is a certain vulgarity in his work, and this vulgarity found its expression in violence. It is vulgarity of a kind that we never find in the work of coarser writers like Fielding, Smollett and Lawrence, but which we always are conscious of in writers like Flaubert, or Jane Austen, or Wilde.

The dictionary defines style as the "collective characteristics of the writing or diction or artistic expression or way of presenting things or decorative methods proper to a person or school or period or subject, manner of exhibiting these characteristics." This suggests a confusion since the word means both the collective characteristics and the manner of exhibiting them, and perhaps this confusion may account for the distaste in which the topic is held. For a surprising number of people to-day would agree in principle with Spender, or would argue that the best writers have no style. Style to them seems something artificial, a kind of ranting or of preening. "The best writing, like the best-dressed man," as Samuel Butler said, is sober, subdued and inconspicuous.

In point of fact there is no such thing as writing without style. Style is not a manner of writing, it is a relationship; the relation in art between form and content. Every writer has a certain capacity for thinking and feeling and this capacity is never quite the same as any other's. It is a capacity which can be appreciated and for its measurement there exist certain terms. We talk of a writer's integrity, of his parts or his powers, meaning the mental force at his disposal. But in drawing from these resources the writer is guided by another consideration; that of his subject. Milton's prose style, for example, is utterly unlike his verse. Not because one is prose and the other poetry; it reveals a quite different set of qualities. The Milton of *Paradise Lost* is an aloof and dignified pontiff who makes no attempt to enter into a relationship with the reader, whose language exhibits a classical lack of detail, whose blank verse is restrained, and whose sublime sentences, often ending in the middle of a line, suggest the voice of a man who talks to himself trailing off into silence. The Milton of the pamphlets is out to persuade the reader and confute his enemy, the style is forceful, repetitive and prolix; he bludgeons away at his opponent until he is quite certain that there is no life left in him, the magnificent language is remarkable for detailed exuberance and masculine vitality. The same distinction can be made between the prose and verse style of Marvell. The style of these writers varies with their subject and with the form chosen. One might say that the style of a writer is conditioned by his conception of the reader, and that it varies according to whether he is writing for himself, or for his friends, his teachers or his God, for an educated upper class, a wanting-to-be-educated lower class or a hostile jury. This trait is less noticeable in writers who live in a settled age, as they soon establish a relationship with a reader whom they can depend on and he, usually a man of the same age, tastes, education and income, remains beside them all their life. Style then is the relation between what a writer wants to say—his subject, and himself—or the powers which he has: between the form of his subject and the content of his parts.

Style is manifest in language. The vocabulary of a writer is his currency but it is a paper currency and its value depends on the reserves of mind and heart which back it. The perfect use of language is that in which every word carries the meaning that it is intended to, no less and no more. In this verbal exchange Fleet Street is a kind of bucket shop which unloads words on the public for less than they are worth and in consequence the more honest literary bankers, who try to use their words to mean what they say, who are always "good for" the expressions they employ, find their currency constantly depreciating. There was a time when this was not so, a moment in the history of language when words expressed what they meant and when it was impossible to write badly. This time I think was at the end of the seventeenth and the beginning of the eighteenth centuries, when the metaphysical conceits of the one were going out and before the classical tyranny of the other was established. To write badly at that time would involve a perversion of language, to write naturally was a certain way of writing well. Dryden, Rochester, Congreve, Swift, Gay, Defoe, belong to this period and some of its freshness is still found in the *Lives of the Poets* and in the letters of Gray and Walpole. It is a period which is ended by the work of two great Alterers, Addison and Pope.

Addison was responsible for many of the evils from which English prose has since suffered. He made prose artful, and whimsical, he made it sonorous when sonority was not needed, affected when it did not require affectation; he enjoined the essay on us so that countless small boys are at this moment busy setting down their views on Travel, the Great Man, Courage, Gardening, Capital Punishment, to wind up with a quotation from Bacon. For though essay-writing was an occasional activity of Bacon, Walton and Evelyn, Addison turned it into an industry. He was the first to write for the entertainment of the middle classes, the new great power in the reign of Anne. He wrote as a gentleman (Sir Roger is the perfect gentleman), he emphasised his gentle irony, his gentle melancholy, his gentle inanity. He was the apologist for the New Bourgeoisie who writes playfully and apologetically about nothing, casting a smoke screen over its activities to make it seem harmless, genial and sensitive in its non-acquisitive moments; he anticipated Lamb and Emerson, Stevenson, *Punch* and the professional humorists, the delicious middlers, the fourth leaders, the memoirs of cabinet ministers, the orations of business magnates, and of chiefs of police. He was the first Man of Letters. Addison had the misuse of an extensive vocabulary and so was able to invalidate a great number of words and expressions; the quality of his mind was inferior to the language which he used to express it.

> I am one, you must know, who am looked upon as a Humanist in Gardening. I have several Acres about my House, which I call my Garden, and which a skilful Gardener would not know what to call. It is a Confusion of Kitchen and Parterre, Orchard and Flower Garden, which lie so mixt and interwoven with one another, that if a Foreigner who had seen nothing of our Country should be conveyed into my Garden at his first landing, he would look upon it as a natural Wilderness, and one of the uncultivated Parts of our Country. My flowers grow up in several Parts of the Garden in the Greatest Luxuriancy and Profusion. I am so far from being fond of any particular one, by reason of its Rarity, that if I meet with any one in a Field which please me, I give it a place in my Garden. . . . I have always thought a Kitchen-garden a more pleasant sight than the finest Orangerie, or artificial Green-house [etc.].

Notice the presentation of the author (whose mind is also a *jardin anglais*): he is eccentric, unpractical, untidy, but glories in it and implies superiority over the foreigner; he prefers home-grown vegetables to exotic fruits and in short flatters the Little Man and also the city Soames Forsytes of his day. The court jester with his cap and bells is now succeeded by the upper middle-class with his "awkward-squad" incompetence, his armchair, carpet slippers, and gardening gloves.[1]

I shall christen this style the Mandarin, since it is beloved by literary pundits, by those who would make the written word as unlike as possible to the spoken one. It is the style of all those writers whose tendency is to make

[1] "For these reasons there are not more useful Members in a Commonwealth than Merchants. They knit Mankind together in a mutual Intercourse of good Offices, distribute the gifts of Nature, find Work for the Poor, add Wealth to the Rich, and Magnificence to the great." Compare Addison's attitude to the Merchants with Congreve's, for whom a decade earlier they were comic cuckolds.

their language convey more than they mean or more than
they feel, it is the style of most artists and all humbugs
and one which is always menaced by a puritan opposition.
To know which faction we should belong to at a given moment is to know how to write with best effect and it is to
assist those who are not committed by their temperament
to one party alone, the grand or the bald, the decorative
or the functional, the baroque or the streamlined that the
following chapters are written.

Here are two more examples by Lamb and Keats of its
misuse.

(I) My attachments are all local, purely local. I have
no passion (or have had none since I was in love, and
then it was the spurious engendering of poetry and
books) to groves and vallies. The rooms where I was
born, the furniture which has followed me about (like a
faithful dog, only exceeding him in knowledge) wherever
I have moved—old chairs, old tables, streets, squares,
where I have sunned myself, my old school—these are
my mistresses.

(II) I had an idea that a man might pass a very
pleasant life in this manner. Let him on a certain day
read a certain page of full Poesy or distilled Prose, and
let him wander with it, and muse upon it, and reflect
from it, and bring home to it, and prophesy upon it, and
dream upon it, until it becomes stale—but when will it
do so? Never! When Man has arrived at a certain ripeness in intellect any one grand and spiritual passage
serves him as a starting-post towards all the two and
thirty Palaces. How happy is such a voyage of conception, what delicious diligent indolence! A doze upon a
sofa does not hinder it, and a nap upon Clover engenders
ethereal finger-pointing. The prattle of a child gives it
wings . . . [etc., etc.].

Notice how untrue these sentiments are. Lamb's old
school is not a mistress, nor is an old bookcase. The bookcase has to be packed up and put on a van when it moves;
to compare it to a faithful dog is to suggest that Lamb is

beloved even by his furniture. The delicious middlers probably believe it, for Essayists must be lovable, it is part of
their rôle.

"Until it becomes stale—but when will it do so? Never!"
Now, Keats is lying. "I am often hard put to it not to think
that never fares a Man so far afield as when he is anchored to his own Armchair!" One could turn this stuff out
almost fast enough to keep up with the anthologies. "The
Man," "your Man," always occurs in these essayists. (Addison: "There is nothing in the World that pleases a Man in
Love so much as your Nightingale.")

Here are two recent examples (also from the *Oxford
Book of English Prose*). The authors are Compton Mackenzie and Rupert Brooke.

(I) Some four and twenty miles from Curtain Wells
on the Great West Road is a tangle of briers among
whose blossoms an old damask rose is sometimes visible.
If the curious traveller should pause and examine this
fragrant wilderness, he will plainly perceive the remains
of an ancient garden, and if he be of an imaginative
character of mind will readily recall the legend of the
Sleeping Beauty in her mouldering palace; for some en-
chantment still enthralls the spot, so that he who bravely
dares the thorns is well rewarded with pensive dreams,
and, as he lingers a while gathering the flowers or watching their petals flutter to the green shadows beneath, will
haply see elusive Beauty hurry past. *The Basket of Roses*
was the fairest dearest inn down all that billowy London
Road . . .

Heigh ho! Georgian prose! Notice the words, especially
the adverbs, which do not aid but weaken the description,
serving only to preserve the architecture of the sentence.
They are Addison's legacy. A catalogue of flowers follows.
I will begin at flower thirty-five.

There was Venus' Looking-glass and Flower of Bristol,
and Apple of Love and Blue Helmets and Herb Paris
and Campion and Love in a Mist and Ladies' Laces and
Sweet Sultans or Turkey Cornflowers, Gillyflower Carna-

tions (Ruffling Rob of Westminster amongst them) with
Dittany and Sops in Wine and Floramer, Widow Wail
and Bergamot, True Thyme and Gilded Thyme, Good
Night at Noon and Flower de Luce, Golden Mouse-Ear,
Prince's Feathers, Pinks and deep red Damask Roses.

It was a very wonderful garden indeed.

(II) He was immensely surprised to perceive that the
actual earth of England held for him a quality which he
found in A— and in a friend's honour, and scarcely anywhere else, a quality which, if he'd ever been sentimental
enough to use the word, he'd have called "holiness". His
astonishment grew as the full flood of "England" swept
him on from thought to thought. He felt the triumphant
helplessness of a lover. Grey, uneven, little fields, and
small, ancient hedges rushed before him, wild flowers,
elms, and beeches. Gentleness, sedate houses of red
brick, proudly unassuming, a countryside of rambling
hills and friendly copses. He seemed to be raised high,
looking down on a landscape compounded of the western
view from the Cotswolds, and the Weald, and the high
land in Wilshire, and the Midlands seen from the hills
above Princes Risborough. And all this to the accompaniment of tunes heard long ago, an intolerable number of
them being hymns.

"England has declared war," he says to himself, "what
had Rupert Brooke better feel about it?" His equipment is
not equal to the strain and his language betrays the fact
by what might be described as the "Worthington touch."
"If he'd ever been sentimental he'd have called it 'holiness,'" i.e. he calls it holiness. "Triumphant helplessness of
a lover" has no meaning. It is a try-on. "Little, small, grey,
uneven, ancient, sedate, red, rambling, friendly, unassuming"—true escapist Georgian adjectives. They might all be
applied to the womb.

Pope as an Alterer is a very different case. He is one of
the great poets of all time and the injury he did to English
verse consisted in setting it a standard to which it could
not live up. He drove lyricism out except from isolated
artists like Burns and Blake, and left his successors the task

of continuing in a form which he had already perfected, and for which they had neither the invention nor the ear.

> A waving glow the blooming beds display
> Blushing in bright diversities of day

After this plenty poetry had become by the time of the Romantics barren and pompous, once again the content of the poetical mind was unequal to the form. The first Romantics, Wordsworth, Southey and Coleridge, therefore, set themselves to write simply, to entice poetry away from the notion of the Grand Style and the Proper Subject; their language was monosyllabic, plebeian, their subjects personal or everyday. They wore their own hair.

CHAPTER III: THE CHALLENGE
TO THE MANDARINS

The quality of mind of a writer may be improved the more
he feels or thinks or, without effort, the more he reads and
as he grows surer of this quality so is he the better able to
make experiments in technique or towards a simplification
of it, even to its apparent abandonment and the expression of strong emotion or deep thought in ordinary language. The great speeches in *Lear* and *Samson Agonistes*
do not seem revolutionary to us because we do not recog-
nize them as superb and daring manipulations of the obvious. Any poet of talent could write: "The multitudinous
seas incarnadine" or "Bid Amaranthus all his beauty shed,"
but only a master could get away with "I pray you undo
this button," or Lear's quintuple "Never."

Style is a relation between form and content. Where the
content is less than the form, where the author pretends to
emotion which he does not feel, the language will seem
flamboyant. The more ignorant a writer feels, the more
artificial becomes his style. A writer who thinks himself
cleverer than his readers writes simply (often too simply),
while one who fears they may be cleverer than he will
make use of mystification: an author arrives at a good style
when his language performs what is required of it without
shyness.

The Mandarin style at its best yields the richest and most
complex expression of the English language. It is the diction
of Donne, Browne, Addison, Johnson, Gibbon, de Quincey,
Landor, Carlyle and Ruskin as opposed to that of Bunyan,
Dryden, Locke, Defoe, Cowper, Cobbett, Hazlitt, Southey
and Newman. It is characterised by long sentences with
many dependent clauses, by the use of the subjunctive and
conditional, by exclamations and interjections, quotations,

allusions, metaphors, long images, Latin terminology, subtlety and conceits. Its cardinal assumption is that neither
the writer nor the reader is in a hurry, that both are in
possession of a classical education and a private income.
It is Ciceronian English.

The last great exponents of the Mandarin style were
Walter Pater and Henry James, who, although they wrote
sentences which were able to express the subtlest inflexions
of sensibility and meaning, at the worst grew prisoners of
their style, committed to a tyranny of euphonious nothings.
Such writers, the devotees of the long sentence, end by
having to force everything into its framework, because
habit has made it impossible for them to express themselves in any other way. They are like those birds that
weave intricate nests in which they are as content to hatch
out a pebble as an egg. But the case of Henry James is
sadder still, for his best writing, that found in his later
books, charged with all the wisdom and feeling of his long
life, went unappreciated. As he reminded Gosse, he remained "insurmountably unsaleable," and of his collected
edition of 1908 he could say, like Ozymandias, "Look on
my *works* ye mortals and despair."

The reason for this failure of James to reach an audience
lay in the change that had come over the reading public, a
change to which he could not adapt himself. The early
books of James appeared as three-volume novels which sold
at thirty-one and sixpence. They reached a small leisured
collection of people for whom reading a book—usually
aloud—was one of the few diversions of our northern winters. The longer a book could be made to last the better,
and it was the duty of the author to spin it out. But books
grew cheaper, and reading them ceased to be a luxury;
the reading public multiplied and demanded less exacting
entertainment; the struggle between literature and journalism began. Literature is the art of writing something that
will be read twice; journalism what will be grasped at once,
and they require separate techniques. There can be no delayed impact in journalism, no subtlety, no embellishment,
no assumption of a luxury reader and since the pace of
journalism waxed faster than that of literature, literature

found itself in a predicament. It could react against journalism and become an esoteric art depending on the sympathy of a few or learn from journalism and compete with
it. Poetry, which could not learn from journalism, ran away
and so we find, from the nineties to the last war, desolate
stretches with no poets able to make a living and few receiving any attention from the public. The stage is held by
journalist-poets like Kipling and Masefield, while Hopkins,
Yeats, Bridges, de la Mare, Munro and a few others
blossom in neglect.

Prose, with the exception of Conrad, who tried to pep
up the grand style, began to imitate journalism and the
result was the "modern movement"; a reformist but not a
revolutionary attack on the Mandarin style which was to
supply us with the idiom of our age. Shaw, Butler and
Wells attacked it from the journalistic side—George Moore,
Gissing and Somerset Maugham, admirers of French realism, of the Goncourts, Zola, Maupassant, from the æsthetic.

Only Wilde belonged to the other camp, and the style
he created was his own variation of the introspective
essayist:

> On that little hill by the city of Florence, where the
> lovers of Giorgione are lying, it is always the solstice of
> noon, of noon made so languorous by summer suns that
> hardly can the slim naked girl dip into the marble tank
> the round bubble of clear glass, and the long fingers of
> the lute-players rest idly upon the chords. It is twilight
> also for the dancing nymphs whom Corot set free among
> the silver poplars of France. In eternal twilight they
> move, those frail diaphanous figures, whose tremulous
> white feet seem not to touch the dew-drenched grass
> they tread on.

Notice the amount of "romantic" words, now well-known
hacks, "solstice, languorous, eternal, frail, diaphanous,
tremulous," which help to date the passage, while Shaw,
who was the same age, was then writing:

> This is the true joy in life, the being used for a purpose
> recognised by yourself as a mighty one; the being

thoroughly worn out before you are thrown on the scrap-
heap; the being a force of Nature instead of a feverish
selfish little clod of ailments and grievances complaining
that the world will not devote itself to making you happy.
And also the only real tragedy in life is the being used by
personally minded men for purposes which you recognise to be base. All the rest is at worst mere misfortune or
mortality; this alone is misery, slavery, hell on earth;
and the revolt against it is the only force that offers a
man's work to the poor artist, whom our personally
minded rich people would so willingly employ as pander,
buffoon, beauty monger, sentimentaliser, and the like.

This sentence with its boisterous sentiments and creaking
gerunds might have been written to-day. It is not a question of subject. The beauty of the Giorgione picture is just
as alive as a sense of social injustice. Giorgione is not Sir
Alma Taddema. But while the first passage is dead, constructed out of false sentiment and faulty linguistic material, the second is in the idiom of our time. For the idiom
of our time is journalistic and the secret of journalism is to
write the way people talk. The best journalism is the conversation of a great talker. It need not consist of what people say but it should include nothing which cannot be said.
The Shaw passage could be talked; the Wilde passage
would hardly stand recitation.

Moore also was not to remain a realist for long—but
Moore, after his *Esther Waters* period, carried on his warfare against the Mandarin style from another position. In
his *Ave, Salve, Vale* books he describes the Irish rebellion
against the official literary language.

Alas, the efforts of the uneducated to teach the educated would be made in vain; for the English language is
perishing and it is natural that it should perish with the
race; race and grammatical sense go together. The English have striven and done a great deal in the world;
the English are a tired race and their weariness betrays
itself in the language, and the most decadent of all are
the educated classes.

He perceived, however, the increasing unreality of Anglo-Irish, of Yeats and Synge filling their notebooks with scraps of tinker's dialogue which could be used only in plays, and in plays only about tinkers, and instead he moulded for himself a simplified prose in which he could describe pictures, books, people, places, and complex sensations—yet always maintain an unassuming unsophisticated equality with the reader.

The artist should keep himself free from all creed, from all dogma, from all opinion. As he accepts the opinions of others he loses his talent, all his feelings and ideas must be his own.

    .   .   .   .

I never knew a writer yet who took the smallest pains with his style and was at the same time readable. Plato's having had seventy shies at one sentence is quite enough to explain to me why I dislike him.

Men like Newman and R. L. Stevenson seem to have taken pains to acquire what they called a style as a preliminary measure—as something that they had to form before their writings could be of any value. I should like to put it on record that I never took the smallest pains with my style, have never thought about it, and do not know or want to know whether it is a style at all, or whether it is not, as I believe and hope, just common, simple straightforwardness. I cannot conceive how any man can take thought for his style without loss to himself and his readers.

Here in the colloquial English of 1897 is Samuel Butler attacking the Mandarin style. The musing introspective attitude of Pater and of Wilde's essays is replaced by one more social and argumentative.[1] This *arguing* style (as opposed to the soliloquy) is typical of the new relationship with the reader which is to sweep over the twentieth century and

[1] "Mr. Walter Pater's style is, to me, like the face of some old woman who has been to Madam Rachel and had herself enamelled. The bloom is nothing but powder and paint and the odour is cherry blossom. Mr. Matthew Arnold's odour is as the faint sickliness of hawthorn."—Butler.

dominate journalism and advertising. It may be described as *you*-writing from the fact that there is a constant tendency to harangue the reader in the second person. It is a buttonholing approach. The Addison manner, on the other hand, has degenerated into whimsical *we*-writing. "We have the best goods. We like quality. We're funny that way," is one sort of advertising. "You realise the inconveniences of inadequate plumbing. Then why not of inadequate underclothing?" is the other.

Meanwhile, Wells, also, was not inactive (though it was not till 1915 that he attacked Henry James in *Boon*, a bogus autobiography). Henry James, in two magnificent letters (Vol. II, pp. 503–8, of his letters) answers Wells's criticism. Wells wrote:

> To you literature, like painting, is an end, to us literature, is a means, it has a use. Your view was, I felt, altogether too prominent in the world of criticism and I assailed it in lines of harsh antagonism. I had rather be called a journalist than an artist, that is the essence of it, and there was no antagonist possible than yourself.

James replied that his view can hardly be so prominent or it would be reflected in the circulation of his books.

> But I have no view of life and literature, I maintain, other than that our form of the latter [the novel] in especial is admirable exactly by its range and variety, its plasticity and liberality, its fairly living on the sincere and shifting experience of the individual practitioner . . . Of course for myself I live, live intensely and am fed by life, and my value, whatever it be, is in my own kind of expression of that . . . Meanwhile I absolutely dissent from the claim that there are any differences whatever in the amenability to art of forms of literature æsthetically determined, and hold your distinction between a form that is [like] painting and a form that is [like] architecture for wholly null and void. There is no sense in which architecture is æsthetically "for use" that doesn't leave any other art whatever exactly as much so; and so far from that of literature being irrelevant to the

literary report upon life, and to its being made as interesting as possible, I regard it as relevant in a degree that leaves everything else behind. It is art that *makes* life, makes interest, makes importance, for our consideration and application of these things, and I know of no substitute whatever for the force and beauty of its process. If I were Boon I should say that any pretence of such a substitute is helpless and hopeless humbug; but I wouldn't be Boon for the world, and am only yours faithfully, Henry James.

The justification for Wells's attack must lie in the defence it provoked, for these two majestic letters from the dying giant form a creed which he might not otherwise have left us. One is reminded of a small boy teasing an elephant which gets up with a noble bewilderment, gives him one look, and shambles away.

We are not concerned here with the people who prefer to be journalists rather than artists, but with those who have tried to make journalism into an art, and already it is possible to define the opponents of the Mandarin style, all those who tried to break it up into something simpler and terser, destroying its ornamentation, attacking its rhythms and giving us instead the idiom of to-day. Thus Moore's new language is somewhat lyrical, for his standards are æsthetic. Norman Douglas is intellectual, with a strong imaginative side. Maugham is also imaginative, though playwriting interferes with his literary development, but Butler, Shaw, Wells, Bennett, write as plainly as they can. If Henry James could have given up all hope of being read, had abandoned novels and written but a few magnificent pages about ideas that stirred him, he might have been happier and had greater influence. But he was obsessed with the novel to the neglect even of his long short stories; he still considered the novel the supreme art form, as it had been for Turgenev, Balzac and Flaubert. So he continued to write novels which came into competition with the journalistic novels of Wells and Bennett or the speeded-up Jamesian of Conrad, rather than take refuge in the strongholds of the leisurely style—memoirs, autobiography, books of criticism, or else venture out into the experimental forms of the short story. The younger writers whom he patronised—Rupert Brooke, Compton Mackenzie and Hugh Walpole[2]—were more remarkable for talent, personal charm and conventionality than for the "beginning late and long choosing" of genius, the crabwise approach to perfection.

[2] It is interesting to speculate on the effect Henry James might have had on, say, E. M. Forster, Virginia Woolf and Lytton Strachey had he bestowed on them the loving criticism which he lavished on his more personable disciples.

CHAPTER IV: THE MODERN MOVEMENT

Meanwhile Butler's dictum "A Man's Style in any art should be like his dress—it should attract as little attention as possible," reigned supreme, though only since Brummel had this stranglehold of convention been applied to what we wear.

> Here, on these remote uplands, I prefer to turn my back on the green undulations of Massa and Sorrento, on Vesuvius and Naples, Ischia and Phlegræan fields: all these regions are trite and familiar. I prefer to gaze towards the mysterious south, the mountains of Basilicata, and the fabled headland Licosa, where Leucosia, sister-siren of Parthenope, lies buried. At this height the sea's horizon soars into the firmament smooth as a sheet of sapphire, and the eye never wearies of watching those pearly lines and spirals that crawl upon its surface, the paths of silver-footed Thetis—a restful prospect, with dim suggestions of love and affinity for this encircling element that reach back, for aught we know, to primeval days of Ascidian-life. There is a note of impotence in the sea's wintry storms, for it can but rage against its prison bars or drown a few sailormen, an ignoble business: true grandeur is only in its luminous calm.

This is a good example of the reformed Mandarin. It is leisurely but not too leisurely, the syntax is easy, the thought simple, the vocabulary humdrum. The use of classical names takes for granted a reader who will accept this coin. The intellectual attitude is evident in the author's genial patronage of Nature and his calm analysis. It is readable, good-mannered and seems to-day a little flat, for the coins mean less to us, and yet it is redeemed by the lovely image of the patterns on the sea from a height—if

we know who Thetis is. It comes from Norman Douglas's
Siren Land (1911).

The poor little wife coloured at this, and, drawing her
handkerchief from her pocket, shed a few tears. No one
noticed her. Evie was scowling like an angry boy. The
two men were gradually assuming the manner of the
committee room. They were both at their best when
serving on committees. They did not make the mistake
of handling human affairs in the bulk, but disposed of
them item by item, sharply. Calligraphy was the item before them now, and on it they turned their well-trained
brains. Charles, after a little demur, accepted the writing
as genuine, and they passed on to the next point. It is
the best, perhaps the only way, of dodging emotion.
They were the average human article, and had they considered the note as a whole it would have driven them
miserable, or mad. Considered item by item, the emotional content was minimised, and all went forward
smoothly. The clock ticked, the coals blazed higher,
and contended with the white radiance that poured in
through the windows. Unnoticed, the sun occupied his
sky, and the shadows of the tree stems, extraordinarily
solid, fell like trenches of purple across the frosted lawn.
It was a glorious winter morning. Evie's fox terrier, who
had passed for white, was only a dirty grey dog now,
so intense was the purity that surrounded him. He was
discredited, but the blackbirds that he was chasing
glowed with Arabian darkness, for all the conventional
colouring of life had been altered. Inside, the clock struck
ten with a rich and confident note. Other clocks confirmed it, and the discussion moved towards its close.

To follow it is unnecessary. It is rather a moment when
the commentator should step forward. Ought the Wil-
coxes to have offered their home to Margaret? I think
not. The appeal was too flimsy.

This is a passage from E. M. Forster's *Howard's End*
(1910) and shows a great departure from the writing of
the nineteenth century. Extreme simplicity, the absence of
relative and conjunctive clauses, an everyday choice of

words (Arabian darkness is the one romanticism, for darkness in Arabia can be no different from anywhere else) constitute a more revolutionary break from the Mandarin style than any we have yet quoted. Twenty-two short sentences follow. How remote it is from James, Meredith, Conrad, Walter Pater whom one cannot imagine interpolating themselves into a novel to ask a question, and answer "I think not"! From a passage like this derives much of the diction, the handling of emotional situations and the attitude to the reader of such writers as Virginia Woolf, Katherine Mansfield, David Garnett, Elizabeth Bowen.

The hardest task in modern criticism is to find out who were the true innovators. Forster I think was one. Novels like *The Longest Journey* and *Howard's End* established a point of view, a technique, and an attitude to the reader that were to be followed for the next thirty years by the psychological novelists. Intellectual rebels against the grand style, such as Norman Douglas, who still wrote for Oxford and Cambridge graduates, for educated men, were but reformists. Forster wrote for men and women, chiefly women, of a larger though still cultured public, and evolved a more radically simplified, disintegrated, and colloquial form of art.

Now we are coming on the tracks of the writers of 1927–28. They are going to be judged by the contents of their minds and the form of their books and by what they make of them. From their failures and their successes we shall endeavour to learn how in the future to avoid failure, and so create that great book which will last a round ten years. This list forms the next stage in their pursuit.

SOME BOOKS IN THE MODERN MOVEMENT—1900–22

1900. Dreiser, *Sister Carrie; Oxford Book of English Verse*
1901. Gissing, *By the Ionian Sea*
1902. James, *The Wings of the Dove;* Yeats, *The Celtic Twilight;* Maugham, *Mrs. Craddock;* Belloc, *The Path to Rome*
1903. Butler, *Way of all Flesh;* Gissing, *Private Papers of Henry Rycroft;* James, *The Ambassadors*

1904. Baron Corvo, *Hadrian VII*
1905. Wilde, *De Profundis;* Forster, *Where Angels Fear to Tread;* Firbank, *Odette D'Antrevernes;* James, *The Golden Bowl;* H. G. Wells, *Kipps*
1906. Galsworthy, *The Man of Property*
1907. Forster, *The Longest Journey;* Beardsley, *Venus and Tannhäuser;* Gosse, *Father and Son;* James, *The American Scene;* Joyce, *Chamber Music*
1908. Conrad, *A Set of Six;* Forster, *A Room with a View*
1909. Stein, *Three Lives;* Beerbohm, *And Even Now*
1910. Forster, *Howard's End;* Bennett, *Old Wives' Tale;* Wedgwood, *Shadow of a Titan;* Saki's Stories; Wells, *Mr. Polly;* Shaw, *Plays Pleasant and Unpleasant*
1911. Beerbohm, *Zuleika Dobson;* Douglas, *Siren Land;* Lawrence, *The White Peacock;* Moore, *Ave;* Lytton Strachey, *Landmarks in French Literature;* Lowes Dickinson, *A Modern Symposium;* Hugh Walpole, *Mr. Perrin and Mr. Traill*
1912. Douglas, *Fountains in the Sand;* Samuel Butler, *Notebooks;* Beerbohm, *Christmas Garland;* Moore, *Salve;* Forster, *Celestial Omnibus;* Stephens, *Crock of Gold; Georgian Poetry* (to 1918)
1913. Conrad, *Chance;* Lawrence, *Sons and Lovers;* Mansfield, *In a German Pension*
1914. Wyndham Lewis, *Blast;* Moore, *Vale;* Imagists' *Anthology* (Aldington, H. D., Pound, etc.); Monro, *Children of Love;* James Joyce, *Dubliners;* Compton Mackenzie, *Sinister Street*
1915. Douglas, *Old Calabria;* Firbank, *Vainglory;* Somerset Maugham, *Of Human Bondage; Catholic Anthology* (includes Eliot's *Prufrock*); Virginia Woolf, *The Voyage Out;* Brooke, *1914,* etc.; D. H. Lawrence, *The Rainbow*
1916. Moore, *The Brook Kerith;* Firbank, *Inclinations;* Joyce, *A Portrait of the Artist; Ulysses* starts in the *Little Review*
1917. Douglas, *South Wind;* Eliot, *Prufrock; Wheels* (includes the Sitwells); Firbank, *Caprice*
1918. Strachey, *Eminent Victorians;* Lewis, *Tarr;* Pearsall-

Smith, *Trivia;* Bridges, *The Poems of Gerard
Manley Hopkins* and *The Spirit of Man;* Waley,
170 Chinese Poems

1919. Cabell, *Jurgen;* Firbank, *Valmouth;* Maugham, *The
Moon and Sixpence;* Daisy Ashford, *The Young
Visiters;* Barbellion, *Diary of a Disappointed Man;*
[Anderson, *Winesburg-Ohio*]; Beerbohm, *Seven
Men*

1920. Huxley, *Limbo* and *Leda;* Eliot, *The Sacred Wood;*
Wilfrid Owen, *Poems;* Henry James, *Letters*

1921. Huxley, *Crome Yellow;* Strachey, *Queen Victoria;*
Virginia Woolf, *Monday or Tuesday, Poems of To-
day*

1922. Housman, *Last Poems;* Mansfield, *The Garden
Party;* Garnett, *Lady Into Fox;* Strachey, *Books
and Characters;* Beerbohm, *Rossetti and His Circle;* Yeats, *Later Poems;* Gerhardi, *Futility;* Galsworthy, *Forsyte Saga;* James Joyce, *Ulysses;* Virginia Woolf, *Jacob's Room*

Not all of these books are of equal significance but they
reveal how long ago most of our well-known writers began,
how they overlap, how thick the field was before the
Armistice. There will be several new names to talk about
on our way to 1928.

I shall not group writers under movements, for the reason
that between the nineties and the present day they scarcely
exist. I recognise a complicating trend or inflation in the
nineties, a simplifying one or deflation (realism, Georgian
poetry) that followed. Then a further complicating process
(Bloomsbury) and a further deflation (Hemingway), and
I find the simplest guide the words used by writers themselves and the purposes for which they are employed. One
faith unites all the writers discussed (with the exception of
Shaw and Wells); whether realists, intellectuals or imaginative writers, from Pater to Joyce they believed in the importance of their art, in the sanctity of the artist and in his
sense of vocation. They were all inmates of the Ivory Tower.

An "ivory tower" is a vague image and those who adopt
it may take advantage of the vagueness. The image was

taken by Flaubert from Alfred de Vigny and all who accept it are to some extent his pupils; if they do not admire *Bouvard*, they admit *Bovary;* if they reject *Bovary* they will recognise the *Letters, Salammbô,* the *Tentation,* or the *Education Sentimentale.*

We write in the language of Dryden and Addison, of Milton and Shakespeare, but the intellectual world we inhabit is that of Flaubert and Baudelaire; it is to them, and not to their English contemporaries that we owe our conception of modern life. The artist who accepts the religion of the Ivory Tower, that is of an art whose reward is perfection and where perfection can be attained only by a separation of standards from those of the non-artist is led to adopt one of four rôles: the High Priest (Mallarmé, Joyce, Yeats), the Dandy (Firbank, Beerbohm, Moore), the Incorruptible Observer (Maugham, Maupassant) or the Detached Philosopher (Strachey, Anatole France). What he will not be is a Fighter or a Helper.

The tradition of dandyism is purer in France. Baudelaire was obsessed with "l'éternel superiorité, du Dandy" as were Nerval, Laforgue, D'Aurevilly. When the wit and lyricism are shallow the resulting dandyism will have a popular success—and we get Noel Coward and Paul Morand —when deep, we find the most delicate achievements of conscious art. Meanwhile there are one or two more contributions to the idiom of our time to be considered.

The period 1900–14 was that of the Dublin School— Yeats, Moore, Joyce, Synge and Stephens. The sentiment of these writers was anti-English; they found the Mandarin style the language of their oppressors for they were sufficiently interested in the National Movement to consider themselves oppressed. For them England was the Philistine and since they could not use Gaelic, their aim was to discover what blend of Anglo-Irish and French would give them an explosive that would knock the pundits of London off their padded chairs. All had lived in Paris, and all had absorbed French culture. Moore kept strictly to it, using his Irish background as an excuse for spiteful criticism and ponderous ancestor-worship, but always preferring simple and racy expressions and unforced sentences as the basis of his style. Yeats was engrossed in his mysticism and Gaelic legends; the French influence is more apparent in his verseforms, and in his cryptic utterances, sanctioned by Mallarmé. Synge went on from Villon to pick up peasant talk on the Aran islands and twine it into plays.

It isn't that I haven't prayed for you, Bartley, to the Almighty God. It isn't that I haven't said prayers in the dark till you wouldn't know what I'd be saying, but it's a great rest I'll have now, and it's time surely. It's a great rest I'll have now, and great sleeping in the long nights after Samhain, if it's only a bit of wet flour we do have to eat, and maybe a fish that would be stinking.

There could be no clearer example than this of the extent of that insurrection against the prose of the capital which was the Celtic movement.

James Stephens's *The Crock of Gold* was an attempt to reconcile Classical mythology with Celtic. It proved that the Irish could beat the English at whimsy and produce a rival to the *Wind in the Willows* and *Peter Pan*.

Of much greater importance are *Dubliners* and *A Portrait of the Artist*. These books are written in a reformed Mandarin, influenced by French Realism. The style is not as unconventional as Yeats's or Synge's, or even as Moore's, and fits in more with the English of Maugham (*Of Human Bondage*) and of the Lawrence of *Sons and Lovers*. The favourite epithet of all these writers at that time was "grey."

(I) The park trees were heavy with rain and rain fell still and even in the lake, lying grey like a shield. A game of swans flew there and the water and the shore beneath were fouled with their green-white slime. They embraced softly impelled by the grey rainy light, the shield-like witnessing lake, the swans.—Joyce, *Portrait of the Artist*.

(II) The day broke grey and dull. The clouds hung heavily, and there was a rawness in the air that suggested snow. A woman servant came into the room in which a child was sleeping, and drew the curtains.—*Of Human Bondage*, opening paragraph.

(III) I stood watching the shadowy fish slide through
the gloom of the mill-pond. They were grey, descendants
of the silvery things that had darted away from the
monks in the young days when the valley was lusty. The
whole place was gathered in the musing of old age. The
thick-piled trees on the far shore were too dark and sober
to dally with the sun; the weeds stood crowded and
motionless.—Lawrence, *The White Peacock*.

Nineteen fourteen-fifteen were important years in the
Modern Movement. Besides *Dubliners*, Joyce's first prose
book, we have *Of Human Bondage*, the first poems of
Eliot, Firbank's *Vainglory*, Lawrence's *Rainbow*, Douglas's
Old Calabria and Virginia Woolf's *Voyage Out*. Wyndham
Lewis edits *Blast*. The most serious artists among them con-
tinued to produce throughout the war. Joyce wrote *A Por-
trait of the Artist* and *Ulysses*. From his rooms in Oxford
Firbank let slip a novel a year. In 1918 Lytton Strachey,
a conscientious objector, was able to launch *Eminent Victorians* on a war-weary world. Moore produced *The Brook
Kerith* and Douglas *South Wind*, perhaps their two greatest books, Huxley appears in two slim volumes of poetry,
Eliot in *Prufrock*, while the Sitwells emerge in *Wheels;*
Lewis writes *Tarr*, and Pearsall-Smith publishes *Trivia* in
unashamed Mandarinese. Nineteen fourteen was also the
year of an important bad book, *Sinister Street*. It is a work
of inflation, important because it is the first of a long line
of bad books, the novels of adolescence, autobiographical,
romantic, which squandered the vocabulary of love and
literary appreciation and played into the hands of the
Levellers and Literary Puritans.

Three years afterwards came *South Wind*, a book which,
although one now recognises in it reiterations and longueurs,
remains a flower of the intellectual school, a book that was
to reform for a while Compton Mackenzie and which stated
for the first time the predicament (when anxious to be successful in love or at making a living) of the Petrouchka
of the twenties, the Clever Young Man. The plight of
Dedalus in revolt against the Jesuits is too particular;
Michael Fane of *Sinister Street* is a born success; it is Denis

of *South Wind* pursuing the Italian chambermaid and cut
out by the rough young scientist who is the hero of *South
Wind* and the years that follow, the Oxford Boy, the miserable young man on the flying trapeze.

CHAPTER V: ANATOMY OF DANDYISM

Dandies in literature have often begun by making fun of the Mandarin style, for it is the enemy of their qualities of wit and lyricism, though in the end they come round to it. Dandyism is capitalist, for the Dandy surrounds himself with beautiful things and decorative people and remains deaf to the call of social justice. As a wit he makes fun of seriousness, as a lyricist he exists to celebrate things as they are, not to change them. Moore's *Confessions of a Young Man* is a typical dandy book but one finds much dandyism in Wilde and some in Saki who, however, adulterated his Wilde to suit the *Morning Post* and to procure the immediate impact of journalism. In his work the reactionary implication of dandyism is very clear.

Of the young men of these years (1914–18) Firbank, Eliot and Huxley, the three most prominent, were dandies. Firbank followed Beardsley and Apollinaire, Eliot followed Laforgue, Huxley Eliot and Firbank. They were intellectuals, but in his writing Firbank took pains to conceal the fact and so can best be taken as an example of the type. He harked back to the dandyism of the seventeenth century; his play *The Princess Zoubaroff* is based on Congreve and among his few allusions are one to the Memoirs of Grammont and another to the acting of Betterton. He was an impressionist; his sentences are hit or miss attempts to suggest a type of character or conversation, or to paint a landscape in a few brush strokes. When something bored him, he left it out (a device which might have improved the quality of innumerable novelists). Firbank is not epigrammatic, he is not easily quotable, his object was to cast a sheen of wit over his writing. Like all dandies, like Horace, Tibullus, Rochester, Congreve, Horace Walpole and the youthful Beckford, like Watteau and Guardi, he was obsessed with the beauty of the moment, and not the beauty only, but the problem of recording that beauty, for with one false touch the description becomes ponderous and overloaded and takes on that unreal but sickly quality often found in modern paganism. Firbank, like Degas, was aware of this and, like Degas, he used pastel.

What is his contribution to modern literature? To what extent can we profit from him if we wish to write well ourselves?

One thing which we recognise not to have kept in him is an element of sexuality. Firbank was homosexual, which is not a factor of importance in the assessment of a writer's style but he was of the breed with a permanent giggle and the result is a naughtiness in his books, a sniggering about priests and choirboys, nuns and flagellation, highbrows and ostlers which shocks us because it does not come off. It is meant to be a joke but it actually betrays the author, his inhibitions and his longings and it is his capacity for not betraying himself that is the secret of his art. It is this element which looks back to the nineties, to Beardsley and Corvo, when so much more looks forward. For the "queen" or homosexual capon being usually a parasite on society, a person with an inherited income and no occupation, can criticise that society only in jest. When goaded by wars and slumps it will become unfriendly and any criticism, however frivolous, will seem impertinent. Firbank, like most dandies, disliked the bourgeoisie, idealised the aristocracy and treated the lower classes as his brothel.

It is customary to assume that Firbank was frivolous because frivolity was his only medium of self-expression. In fact he was no less serious than Congreve or Horace Walpole but he recognised frivolity as the most insolent refinement of satire. The things Firbank hated were the moral vices of the bourgeoisie, stupidity, hypocrisy, pretentiousness, greed and the eye on the main chance. What distinguishes the characters he writes about is their unworldliness and he believed that the most unworldly people are those who are born with everything. It was a complete vagueness about money, a warm erratic unjudging heart, a muddled goodness, an instinctive elegant disorder that he loved. The quality common to his characters is their impulsiveness; their virtue lies in their unawareness of evil. Where they are ambitious, their ambitions are preposterous. To be perpetuated by a stained-glass window, to shine in the highest circles of Cuna-Cuna, to go to Athens, to be a great tragic actress and yet to remain unconscious of the difficulty of attaining these ends, was what appealed to him. Whom he disliked were the schemers, the Becky Sharps, the Babbitts. Here is Mrs. Sixsmith, thinking of her dead friend, Sally.

> Those fine palatial houses, she reflected, must be full of wealth . . . old Caroline plate and gorgeous green Limoges: Sally indeed had proved it! The day she had opened her heart in the Café Royal she had spoken of a massive tureen *too heavy even to hold.*
>
> Mrs. Sixsmith's eyes grew big.

Or:

> And now a brief lull, as a brake containing various delegates and "representatives of English Culture" rolled by at a stately trot—Lady Alexander, E. V. Lucas, Robert Hichens, Clutton Brock, etc.—the ensemble, the very apotheosis of the worn-out *cliché.*

For what he hated was vulgarity and vulgarity of writing as much as vulgarity of the heart. Indeed, the writers with the most exquisite choice of words, those who take pains to avoid the outworn and the obvious to achieve distinction of phrasing, are equally susceptible to the fine points of the human heart. The world to Congreve is a sink out of which a few young people manage to drag themselves, to Horace Walpole an arena which friendship alone makes tolerable. They are strongly conscious of good and evil. "To write simply," explains Maugham, "is as difficult as to be good." Perhaps one requires the other. For Dandies are perfectionists and perfectionism involves disappointment and from the disappointments is built up the idea of an elect, of a few human beings gifted with distinction of mind and heart heaving themselves up from the general mud bath. Some are kept up for a few years by their

beauty, breeding or charm, but all those without moral
qualities and a courageous intelligence are bound to flop
back.

"Now that the ache of life with its fevers, passions,
doubts, its routine, vulgarity and boredom was over, his
serene unclouded face was a marvelment to behold. Very
great distinction and sweetness was visible there together
with much nobility and love, all magnified and commin-
gled," writes Firbank of the death mask of Cardinal Pirelli
and it was the last sentence but two he ever wrote; his most
serious, though not his most successful, for he is nervous of
his own seriousness and suddenly produces a word, "marvelment" out of his old 1890 past to reassure him. But it is
the sentence of an ascetic, as must be all those who are
dandies in the fullest sense.

The lesson one can learn from Firbank is that of incon-
sequence. There is the vein which he tapped and which
has not yet been fully exploited.

His method was to write in dialogue, and to omit what
would not fit in. Narrative prose as opposed to dialogue is
used only for vignettes of places or descriptions of characters when they first appear. It is the most brisk and readable
form of writing, making demands on the reader's intelligence but none on his eye or ear: and it is to Firbank that
we owe the conception of dialogue—not as a set-piece in
the texture of the novel, as are the conversations of Wilde
and Meredith—but as the fabric itself. A book by Firbank
is in the nature of a play where passages of descriptive
prose correspond to stage directions.

As a prose writer Firbank did not have a large or an interesting vocabulary and his work is full of spelling mis-
takes, but he wrote with a horror of the cliché and with a
regard for the words he used, achieving the freshness he
needed by grammatical inversion, and by experiments in
order. He also applied impressionism with startling results.

The mists had fallen from the hills, revealing old woods
wrapped in the blue doom of Summer.

Boats with crimson spouts, to wit, steamers, dotted the
skyline far away, and barques with sails like the wings

of butterflies, borne by an idle breeze, were winging more than one ineligible young mariner back to the prose of the shore.

It was the Feast night. In the grey spleen of evening through the dusty lanes towards Mediavilla, country-society flocked.

Do they come off? On the whole, yes, much better than his overloaded passages in *Cardinal Pirelli* and *Santal*, for it is one of the weaknesses of the dandy's position that the seriousness on which it is based must at all costs be concealed. The preoccupation of the dandy is with the moment.

Every moment some form grows perfect in hand or face; some tone on the hills or the sea is choicer than the rest; some mood or passion or insight or intellectual excitement is irresistibly real and attractive for us—for that moment only. Not the fruit of experience, but experience itself, is the end. A counted number of pulses only is given to us of a variegated dramatic life. How may we see in them all that is to be seen in them by the finest senses? How shall we pass most swiftly from point to point, and be present always at the focus where the greatest number of vital forces unite in their purest energy? To burn always with this hard gemlike flame, to maintain this ecstasy is success in life. . . . Not to discriminate every moment some passionate attitude in those about us, and in the brilliancy of their gifts some tragic dividing of forces on their ways, is, on this short day of frost and sun, to sleep before evening.

So wrote Pater, calling an art-for-art's-sake muezzin to the faithful from the topmost turret of the ivory tower. By leaving out the more affected "any stirring of the senses, strange dyes, strange colours, and curious odours, or work of the artist's hands, or the face of one's friend" it becomes one of the great passages of Mandarin writing, and as a text concentrates as much on the moment in personal relations, on the ethical moment as on the sensual one. Henry James spent his life in "discriminating passionate attitudes and tragic divisions in those about him" as thoroughly as Wilde

investigated his own moods or Moore and Yeats and Joyce
waited for "some tone on the hills or the sea." Pater, when
he realised its implications, suppressed the passage which
is but the philosophy of the refractory pupil of Socrates,
Aristippus of Cyrene, who believed happiness to be the
sum of particular pleasures and golden moments and not,
as Epicurus, a prolonged intermediary state between ecstasy and pain.

The artistic fault of the Cyrenaic philosophy is a tendency
to fake these golden moments, inevitable when they are regarded as the only ones worth living for; the artist becomes
like the medium who has to produce a psychic experience
to earn her money, and the result is that he leans too heavily
on the moment, and so produces that effect of satiety which
runs, for instance, through the translations of Mackail. Similarly if we examine the kind of poetry that we read and
appreciate when we are unhappy, we soon find that it is
not the best kind or, if the best, that we appreciate it for
the wrong reasons, we over-emphasize it to make it support a weight which it was not intended to bear. The perfectionists, the art-for-art's-sakers, finding or believing life to
be intolerable except for art's perfection, by the very violence of their homage can render art imperfect. This was
the danger of Firbank's growing seriousness, it is a danger
which besets all lyric poets, dandies and ephemerids although it is a danger which by emotional awareness and
technical discipline they can often avoid.

At the moment dandyism in its extreme form, perfectionism, is on the increase, for perfectionists, like the hermits
of the Thebaid, take refuge from the world in private salvation. I have known many perfectionists, all of whom are
remarkable for the intense stripping process which they
carry out. Their lives are balloons from which more and
more ballast has to be cast; they never have more than one
suitcase, wear no pyjamas or underclothes, travel constantly
and are the mystics of our time *"pressés de trouver le lieu
et la formule."* An element of guilt and expiation in their
activity awakens distrust in the complacent herd and certainly perfection has a bleaching, death-wishful quality. But

it is so seldom attained that a little respect for it would do no harm to its detractors.

It will be seen then that dandyism, despite its roots in the *status quo* and its tendency to pessimism, is a tenable position—since any position which can be shown to produce good writing is tenable—for as long as the writer can count on a natural constitutional gaiety to inform his lyricism. When that disappears as in Housman, the wit becomes bitter, the lyricism morbid. It is therefore suitable to young writers or to those with plenty of money. They have their roots in manure but the orchid blooms the richer for it, until ultimately the bloom dies down, and the manure is left. Tibullus, Rochester, Watteau and Leopardi—the greatest perfectionist of them all—died before this could happen. Congreve retired; Walpole and Beckford became ancestor-worshipping and reactionary antiquarians, only Horace and Degas, obedient always to the discipline of their art and intellectually agile, arrogant and tough, remained perfectionists to the last. Had he lived, Firbank would not have written worse, he would have written differently.

[NOTE: The debt of Firbank to Beardsley's *Under the Hill* is not here sufficiently stressed. It is the archetype of sophisticated butterfly impressionism in our tongue. Firbank perhaps was never quite so witty, vicious or well-informed as the adolescent of genius, however he was more radiantly preposterous, a humourist of wider calibre.]

CHAPTER VI: A BEAST IN VIEW

I have taken Firbank as the type of the writer Dandy but
what has been said of him is also true of the early Eliot
and the early Huxley. Eliot is the purest of the three, for a
lyric poet works in a more distilled medium than narrative
prose.

> Let us go then, you and I,
> When the evening is spread out against the sky,
> Let us go, through certain half-deserted streets . . .

I have often wondered what it must have felt like to discover these opening lines of *Prufrock* in *Blast* or the *Catholic
Anthology* in 1914–15 with the Rupert Brooke poems,
Kitchener's Army and *Business as Usual* everywhere. Would
we have recognised that new, sane, melancholy, light-
hearted and fastidious voice?

> There will be time, there will be time
> To prepare a face to meet the faces that you meet;
> There will be time to murder and create.

Surely we would have noticed it, would have "lingered"
in the chambers of the sea" and experienced that exquisite
sensation, the apprehension of the first sure masterful flight
of a great contemporary writer. But how few of us did!

What can one learn from Eliot? Not to be ashamed of
borrowing and to assimilate what we borrow. Yet his influence on young writers is disconcerting; Auden, I think,
is the one young poet to survive it. The reason I believe is
that Eliot, the purest artist and most austere critic in England to-day, is yet a writer whose background is unfamiliar
—the least like anyone else's. He is an American expatriate
who is escaping from a far more refined and cultivated,
though perfectly barren society, than any he can find here

—in other words, he is not running away from a rough
America to a cultured England but from an overpolite and
civilised humanism to the bellyworld of post-war London.
As a result his poetry is a struggle to break down inhibitions in himself by which the coarser Englishman is not
troubled and his solution, the Anglo-Catholic Church, one
that makes small appeal to his imitators.

Yet in spite of this he is a master; he has created for us
a world of his own. There are places where I miss Firbank,
in Knightsbridge or Rome, going over some Balkan palace
or in an autumnal cathedral city; there are remarks one
overhears or whole scenes between simple, fatuous, complacent people when one recognises that the artist who
could best have done them justice is no more. But there
exists a whole mood for whose expression we must thank
Eliot, the mood of dissatisfaction and despondency, of bar-
renness and futility—the noonday devil, the afternoon impotence which is curiously unpoetical and which no one
else has been able so adequately to render into verse.

The idea of futility is an important concept in the twenties and dominates the poetry of Eliot (up to *Ash Wednes-
day*), the novels of Huxley (to *Point Counter Point*) and
much of the work of Lawrence, Hemingway and Joyce. It
is an extension of the ivory-tower attitude which arises from
a disbelief in action and in the putting of moral slogans
into action, engendered by the Great War. Thus Henry
James and the authors who were killed in the war had no
such experience, it was left to those who survived beyond
1917 to make the discovery.

> Behold, behold, the goal in sight
> Spread thy fans and wing thy flight

sings Janus, in Dryden's *Secular Masque,* and Venus adds:

> Calms appear when storms are past
> Love will have his hour at last,

but the chorus is not taken in:

> All, all of a piece throughout:
> Thy chase had a beast in view;

Thy wars brought nothing about;
Thy lovers were all untrue.
'Tis well an old age is out,
And time to begin a new.

And that might well have been the device of the writers of
the early twenties.

I have said that futilitarianism is an extension of the
philosophy of the Ivory Tower because no writer of that
group pretended that art was futile; it is the men of action
who do that. Behind the concept of futility is a passionate
belief in art, coupled with a contempt for the subjects about
which art is made. This puts too great a strain on technique,
for even Flaubert, in *Bouvard and Pecuchet,* that Baedeker
of futility, has not been able to avoid unintentionally boring
the reader. But the novelists of the 1920's were not Flaubert's equal in construction. They knew that they had been
"had" and they were in a hurry to tell the world about it.
Those who had been fooled most were the young men who
had fought and survived the war; the literature of that time
in consequence is predominantly masculine, revolving round
a theme which may be called "The Clever Young Man and
the Dirty Deal." When I search for the most representative
work of the period, I am inclined to choose *Petrouchka,*
for though pre-war the ballet expresses the situation with
clarity. The people at the fair are the audience whom
Petrouchka, the introspective young masochist, wishes to
win over; the Magician who controls him is Fate, that cruel
deity of the Housman poems, or the Vile Old Man, the general, the father too old to fight, gleefully sacrificing his son.
Petrouchka's problem is how to keep alive, and have a successful love affair and his rival, the Moor, is the hated man
of action, the accomplished womaniser who has not been
to Balliol and has nothing of Hamlet in him, but in whom
vulgarity triumphs. This situation or relationship has a way
of turning up in many books.

The father-chorus in these books is not malignant, rather
is it wistful and friendly, in some books of the period he is
a priest. The lesson we can learn from this school is the
danger of allowing those literary vices, cleverness and self-

CHARACTERISTICS OF THE CLEVER YOUNG MEN AND THEIR DIRTY DEALS

Author	Man	Place of Education	Nature of Predicament	Solution
Douglas	Denis, *South Wind*	Oxford	Inability to seduce a woman. Rival, young scientist. Father, Keith	Acquires virility and self-respect instead by assisting drunken pseudo-father to sober up
Huxley	Denis, *Crome Yellow*	Oxford	Inability to seduce a woman. Rivals, painter and rich young peer. Father, Scogan	Flight to London ("and what on earth was he going to do in London when he got there?")
Huxley	Chelifer, Gumbril, Quarles	Oxford	Inability to seduce a woman. Rivals, all their friends. Father, Cardan, etc.	Expatriation (Mantua) the picture gallery and the reading-room
Eliot	Alfred Prufrock	?	General indecision and fear of experience. Rival, Sweeney. Runs away from women	Polite resignation
Joyce	Stephen Dedalus	Clongowes	Superiority to vulgar surroundings, yet at mercy of them. Rival, Buck Mulligan. Father, Bloom	"Silence, exile and cunning." Expatriation, discovery of pseudo-father (Bloom)
Hemingway	Jake *The Sun Also Rises*	?	War wound, hence inability to seduce a woman, general aroma of diffused alcoholism. Rivals, boxer, bullfighter, etc.	Trout-fishing, drink, the Catholic Church

pity, to come up too often for air. It was, however, the clever young men who were the first to see the vanity of the war and the greater vanity of the peace. They could not settle down to boring jobs and unprofitable careers with pre-war patience and their cleverness seemed a liability rather than an asset. Besides women did not like it. Nor were they yet sure whether they liked women, for they were still romantic enough to be appalled by the distinction between love and lust and to find the inevitable transition degrading.

Such a state of war between intellect and the senses, unless a genuine truce is made between them, can only end unhappily. Either the senses conquer the mind and we get the erudite sensualist, the Keith of *South Wind*, the Cardan of *Those Barren Leaves*, with their consciousness of wasted opportunities, or the mind is triumphant and we have what Huxley became, a moralist and a puritan. I have considered him in his early works as a dandy for it is only in them that he is an artist and in them that the irony and lyricism are unadulterated. *Leda*, *Limbo*, *Crome Yellow* and the stories of *Little Mexican* belong to this period, *Antic Hay* begins another.

I quote him often because he is the most typical of a generation, typical in his promise, his erudition, his cynicism and in his peculiar brand of prolific sterility.

CHAPTER VII: THE NEW MANDARINS

It is as difficult to foretell the weather in a language as in the skies, and as urgent. In our case the problem is to find out what sort of writing at this moment at the end of the thirties is likely to last. We have seen that there are two styles which it is convenient to describe as the realist, or vernacular, the style of rebels, journalists, common-sense addicts and unromantic observers of human destiny—and the Mandarin, the artificial style of men of letters or of those in authority who make letters their spare-time occupation.

The lyrical or dandy style matures with age into the Mandarin.

As in party government, there is an interaction between these two styles; each will seem in or out of office at a given moment; when one style is in abeyance it will receive new blood and be thrust forward, when the other is at the height of its success, it will wither away. The panjandrums of the nineteenth century, Ruskin, Arnold, Pater, Meredith, Henry James, Swinburne, Conrad, gave way to the realists, Gissing, Butler, Moore, Maugham, Bennett, Wells, and Shaw. It was now their turn to be driven from the temple. It was in 1906, I think, that the disheartened Conservative party, after being trounced in the general election, were elated by an attack made on their victors by young F. E. Smith. In the same year, in the pages of a dull review, another gifted young man, also a dark horse, was attacking the successful literary doctrine of the day, and the day's most eminent critic.

The study of Sir Thomas Browne, Mr. Gosse says, "encouraged Johnson, and with him a whole school of rhetorical writers in the eighteenth century, to avoid circumlocution by the invention of superfluous words, learned but pedantic, in which darkness was concentrated without being dispelled". Such is Mr. Gosse's account of the influence of Browne and Johnson upon the later eighteenth century writers of prose. But to dismiss Johnson's influence as something altogether deplorable, is surely to misunderstand the whole drift of the great revolution which he brought about in English letters. The characteristics of the pre-Johnsonian prose style—the style which Dryden first established and Swift brought to perfection—are obvious enough. Its advantages are those of clarity and force; but its faults, which, of course, are unimportant in the work of a great master, become glaring in that of the second-rate practitioner. The prose of Locke, for instance, or of Bishop Butler, suffers, in spite of its clarity and vigour, from grave defects. It is very flat and very loose; it has no formal beauty, no elegance, no balance, no trace of the deliberation of art. Johnson, there can be no doubt, determined to remedy these evils by giving a new mould to the texture of English prose; and he went back for a model to Sir Thomas Browne. . . . With the *Christian Morals* to guide him, Dr. Johnson set about the transformation of the prose of his time. He decorated, he pruned, he balanced; he hung garlands; he draped robes; and he ended by converting the Doric order of Swift into the Corinthian order of Gibbon. . . . Attacks of this kind—attacks upon the elaboration and classicism of Browne's style are difficult to reply to, because they must seem, to anyone who holds a contrary opinion, to betray such a total lack of sympathy with the subject as to make argument almost impossible. . . . The truth is that there is a great gulf fixed between those who naturally dislike the ornate, and those who naturally love it. There is no remedy; and to attempt to ignore this fact only emphasises it the more. . . . Browne's "brushwork" is certainly unequalled in English literature, except by the very greatest masters of sophisticated art, such as Pope and Shakespeare; it is the inspiration of sheer technique.

It was not till 1918, however, that the author, Lytton Strachey, became well known with *Eminent Victorians*.

Eminent Victorians is a revolutionary book. Through what at first sight seemed only biographical essays—on Arnold, Florence Nightingale, General Gordon and Cardinal Manning, dead for half a century—the author contrived to attack and undermine all that was most cherished in the morality of to-day. The public-school system, public service, philanthropy, the army, the empire, the Church, all were questioned in these sleek periods and skulking behind them, authority itself, the nature of the will, the hypocrisy by which good men climb and cling to power were in their turn examined and exposed. *Eminent Victorians* is the work of a great anarch, a revolutionary text-book on bourgeois society written in the language through which the bourgeois ear could be lulled and beguiled, the Mandarin style. And the bourgeois responded with fascination to the music, like seals to the Eriskay love-lilt. At first the suave tones brought nothing but pleasure: this was the civilisation they had been fighting to save: here were the restored humanities, the accent of the "studious cloisters of Trinity": too late they understood that four Victorian idols had been knocked off their pedestals in such a way that they have never been replaced, or deemed in any manner replaceable. And after they had dismissed the book as "clever, but unsound," worse was to follow, a questioning of the values the Victorians stood for and all reflected from the eyes of their own demobilised and disillusioned children.

The trial of Oscar Wilde was responsible for a flight from æstheticism which had lasted twenty years. He had himself done much to discredit it by the vulgar and insincere element which he had introduced; his conviction was the climax. From that moment the philistine triumphed and although there were still poets and critics who loved beauty, who were in fact romantic, their romanticism was forced to be hearty. Hence the cult of beer and Sussex, of walking and simplicity which ended with Masefield, Brooke, Squire and Gould; hence the leanest years in the history of English verse and the manly criticism of Quiller-Couch and Walter Raleigh. It was left to Lytton Strachey to lay the ghost of Reading Gaol, to proclaim *"un peu de faiblesse pour ce qui est beau—voilà mon défaut,"* and so make non-conformity again permissible.

With the success which his first two books gained him, Strachey's bitterness disappeared, he became a lion and settled down to a quiet life of private pleasure. His gifts appear as with all fine critics, when he is able to love and to admire and for this reason he is at his best when writing about the eighteenth century. As a critic he is admirable, as a biographer he is slightly vulgar. In his second book, *Queen Victoria,* his insurrectionary movement expired, he could not dislike Melbourne or Disraeli, or such a human bundle as his subject. By *Elizabeth and Essex* his style has become an elaborate experiment in cliché which, though rising to fine passages, contains not a little of the sniggering we have commented on in Firbank. It is his first book (*Eminent Victorians*), so admirably argued and constructed, original, polished and daring, to which we can profitably return together with his essays and criticism. There is much to be learnt from his gifts, from his intellectual pride, his forceful phrasing, his love of beauty and gesture, his grasp of character; "he is not dead but sleepeth" and one day these gifts will be rescued from the neglect into which, by his spectacular success, they were too soon precipitated.

Another Mandarin to emerge from his retreat in 1918 was Pearsall-Smith, whose *Trivia* was the preliminary bombardment in a long attack which is not yet exhausted against puritanism in English letters. His anthology of English prose (1919) which omits Dryden and devotes only twelve pages to the eighteenth century from Addison to Lamb, concentrating entirely on fine writing and the purple patch, continued the onslaught. He is with Professor Mackail the last of the old Mandarins, of the men of the eighties, and the most intransigent.

Meanwhile a new Mandarin was taking over the novel. In 1915 Virginia Woolf published *The Voyage Out.* This was followed by *Night and Day, Monday or Tuesday* (1921), *Jacob's Room* (1922), *Mrs. Dalloway* (1925), *To the Lighthouse* (1927) and *Orlando* (1928), one of the books in which, like *Elizabeth and Essex* or *Point Counter*

Point, the new Mandarin movement of the twenties culminates.

Virginia Woolf seemed to have the worst defect of the Mandarin style, the ability to spin cocoons of language out of nothing. The history of her literary style has been that of a form at first simple, growing more and more elaborate, the content lagging far behind, then catching up, till, after the falseness of *Orlando,* she produced a masterpiece in *The Waves.*

Her early novels were not written in an elaborate style. Her most significant early book is *Monday or Tuesday* (1921) and demonstrates the rule that Mandarin prose is the product of those who in their youth were poets. In short it is romantic prose. Not all poets were romantic-prose writers (e.g. Dryden) but most romantic-prose writers have attempted poetry.

The development of Virginia Woolf is the development of this lyrical feeling away from E. M. Forster, with his artlessness and simple, poetical, colloquial style, into patterns of her own. The reveries of a central character came more and more to dominate her books. In *The Waves* she abandoned the convention of the central figure and described a group of friends, as children, as young people and finally in late middle age. In a series of tableaux are contrasted the mystery of childhood, the promise of youth, the brilliance of maturity and the complex, unmarketable richness of age. If *The Years* seems an impressionist gallery with many canvases, landscapes, portraits, and conversation pieces, then *The Waves* is a group of five or six huge panels which celebrate the dignity of human life and the passage of time. It is one of the books which comes nearest to stating the mystery of life and so, in a sense, nearest to solving it.

In *Mr. Bennett and Mrs. Brown,* Virginia Woolf attacked Bennett, Wells and Galsworthy for their materialism, for the doctrine of realism which they had made all powerful in the 1900's.

For Mandarin prose is romantic prose and realism is the doctrine of the vernacular opposed to it. Thus among the new Mandarins of the twenties were several who began as

poets; besides Virginia Woolf and Lytton Strachey, it included the work of the Sitwells with their flowery periods
and predilection for highly coloured and sophisticated
settings.

But the greatest Mandarin was Proust, who has become
so familiar as almost to rank as an English writer. He exhibits, beyond all others, the defect of the Mandarin style;
the failure of the writer's intellectual or emotional content
to fill the elaborate frame which his talent plans for it. The
honeycombs continue to develop but fewer and fewer
pollen bags are emptied into them. There are many great
passages where the complexity is worthy of the emotion
expended on it, where very subtle and difficult truths are
presented in language that could only express them if difficult and subtle.

Notwithstanding, now that the element of novelty and
cult-snobbery has worn off, much of Proust, as of his master Ruskin, must stand condemned. He is often repetitive
and feeble; the emotions of envy, jealousy, lust, and snob-
bishness around which his book is built, though they gen-
erate an enormous impetus, are incapable of sustaining it
through twenty or thirty volumes; Swann's jealousy of
Odette is enough without Proust's jealousy of Albertine,
Saint-Loup's of Rachel and Charlus's of Morel and if the
emotions repeat themselves, so also do the stories, the situations, the comments, parentheses and clichés. Proust will
remain a great writer, but his titles to fame may have to
be reconsidered. His hatred and contempt for the life of
action suited the war-weary and disillusioned generation he
wrote for, his own snobbery offered them both a philosophy
and a remunerative career, he believed also in art for art's
sake. He was in no sense a new writer although it was the
illusion of novelty which contributed so much to his success. His models are pre-war, his artists are taken from the
haute bourgeoisie, they are members, like his politicians and
men of science, of the terrifying class which ruled in France
and which corresponded to the Forsytes in England; his
nobility are of the same period, so are his operas, his dinner parties; it is the world of the Dreyfus Case, the Victorian world. He was modern enough to attack the values

of this world but he had nothing to put in their place, for their values were his own, those of the narrator of the book who spends his life in going to parties and watching snobs behave but is never a snob himself.

In short, although he is preoccupied with time, his world is static because in all the movements of his book there is no movement of ideas. "Everything changes," he seems to say, "and I am the historian of that change," but what in fact he declares is that nothing changes except the small social set which he admired in his youth and which fell to pieces. How did they change? They grew older and went out less or got mixed up in anti-social love affairs or lost their money or died—but nothing else changed for him. There was a new face with an old title in a box at the opera —but the title and the box are always there, coveted and prized by the ruling class of six or seven countries; there are no new ideas, no revolution in wisdom, no reversals of taste, nobody to declare that they never want to see an opera again.

Proust was a reactionary writer so steeped in the lore of the high society which he envied in the nineties and with such a nostalgia for the emotions of his own childhood, he was so much the introspective masochist that he admitted no change in his world beyond the inescapable evidences of old age that confronted him. The aim of his book was how to revive his past and he discovered that by remembering everything that had happened, and by relying on intuitive visions produced by familiar smells and noises, such a revival was possible. And where he failed to revive it, his style, that blend of unselective curiosity with interminable qualification, would carry on like a lumbering, overcrowded, escaped tram that nobody can stop.

Proust lives rather through his extrovert satirical scenes, his balls and dinner parties, the great ironical spectacle of the vanity of human wishes displayed by the Baron de Charlus and the Duchesse de Guermantes and through the delightful pictures which he provides of the countryside and his neighbours, the plain of Chartres, the coast, the quiet streets which Swann climbed in the Faubourg St. Germain. Where his egocentric masturbatory self-analysis

begins to function and his anxiety neurosis about his grandmother or Albertine, love or jealousy, comes into play, then
all is tedious and unreal, like that asthma which his psychiatrist said he was unwilling to cure since something
more unpleasant would be bound to take its place.

There are two more of these new Mandarins worth ex-
amining. We have seen that Aldous Huxley is a writer particularly accessible to the spirit of his time and by the middle twenties his period of dandyism was over. The influence
of Mallarmé and Prufrock waned and he set himself to
moralise on the flux around him. Witty, serious, observant,
well-read, sensitive and intelligent, there can have been few
young writers as gifted as Huxley—as can be seen from his
early stories, *Happily Ever-After, Richard Greenow, Little
Mexican, Young Archimedes* or *The Gioconda Smile*.

Yet he had the misfortune to suffer from what he considered, quoting Buddha, to be the deadliest of mortal sins,
unawareness, for he was both unaware of his own nature as
a writer and of the temptations into which he was falling.
His nature was a very English one, that of the divided man,
the lover of beauty and pleasure dominated by the puritan
conscience. At first his dichotomy is apparent in his treatment of love. Love means everything to him but sex—and
sex, although he is obsessed by it, is disgusting. The conflict
is extended to become a warfare between the senses on one
side and the intellect, generously moralising in the moment
of victory, on the other until Huxley the intellectual pulls
the lower self along like a man pulling a dog by a leash;
there are glimpses of other dogs, lamp-posts, green grass,
trousers and tree trunks; then comes a jerk, "eyes look your
last" and a scientific platitude.

It is a question whether anyone so at war with himself
can be a novelist, for to the novelist a complete integration
is necessary; the proper medium for the split-man is the
Journal Intime or the *Dialogue*. *Ends and Means* owes its
success to being a complete break with the novel for as a
novelist, apart from being at war with himself, Huxley was
hampered by his inability to create character or see a character except in an intellectual way.

The greatness of a novelist like Tolstoy is that he creates

characters who being real creations are able to think and
behave unlike themselves, to be false to type. Proust also
had some of this greatness, and in English, Thackeray. But
weaker novelists can only sling a few traits on to the characters they are depicting and then hold them there. "You
can't miss So-and-so," they explain, "he stammers and now
look, here he comes—'What's your name?' 'S-s-s-so-and-
s-s-s-so.' There you see, what did I tell you!" Nearly all
English novels are written to this prescription. Huxley suffers from the intellectual's difficulty of communicating with
the people around him except through the intellect. In consequence the only people he can write about at length are
those with whom he can carry on an intellectual discussion.

But the consequences of Huxley's *artistic* unawareness
are more serious. He is a defaulting financier of the written
word, and nobody since Chesterton has so squandered his
gifts. A contract to produce two books a year forced him
to vitiate that keen sense of words with which he started
and as he had less to say, so, by a process which we have
noticed, he took longer in which to say it. For such a writer
who had to turn out two hundred thousand words a year,
the Mandarin style was indispensable.

By dinner-time it was already a Story—*the latest addition* to Mary Amberley's *repertory*. The *latest*, and as
good, it seemed to Antony's *critically attentive ear* as
the *finest classics of the collection*. Ever since *he received
her invitation*, he now realized, *his curiosity had been
tinged* with a *certain vindictive hope* that she would have
altered for the worse, either relatively in his own knowl-
edgeable *eyes, or else absolutely* by reason of the *passage of these twelve long years;* would have degenerated
from what she was, or what he had imagined her to be,
at the time when he had loved her. Discreditably enough,
*as he now admitted to himself, it was with a touch of
disappointment* that he had found her *hardly changed
from the Mary Amberley of his memories*. She was
forty-three. *But her body was almost as slim as ever, and
she moved with all the old swift agility*. With *something
more than the old agility indeed;* for he had noticed that

she was now agile on purpose, that she acted the part of
one who is *carried away by a youthful impulse* to break
into quick and violent motion—acted it, moreover, in circumstances where the impulse could not, if natural, pos-
sibly have been felt.

    •   •   •   •   •   •   •

After a lonely dinner—for Helen was keeping her room
on *the plea of a headache*—Gerry went up to sit with
Mrs. Amberley. He was *particularly charming that evening*, and so *affectionately solicitous that Mary forgot* all
her *accumulated grounds* of complaint and *fell in love*
with him *all over again*, and for *another set of reasons*
—not because he was so *handsome, so easily and inso-
lently dominating*, such a ruthless and *accomplished
lover*, but because he was *kind, thoughtful, and affectionate*, was everything, *in a word*, she had previously
known he wasn't.

I quote these as examples of Huxley's writing, of the
muse's revenge, but they also show the influence of Proust
in all its flatulence. Thus, although the clichés I have
italicised are examples of the lack of distinction in Huxley's
writing, as is the use of unnecessary adverbs or the dogged
repetition, the determination to hit the nail on the head and
then hit it on the head and then hit it on the head, that
vulgarity with which we are familiar yet there is also here
the Proustian note: ". . . either relatively . . . or else absolutely . . . what she was, or what he had imagined her
to be, etc." It is fake analysis and fatigued introspection, a
frequent combination in Mandarinism at its worst.

The last and strangest arrival among these new Mandarins was Joyce. *Work in Progress* is a Mandarin book
which demands, and demands in vain, complete leisure, the
widest education and devoted patience from the reader
who wishes to understand it. It could not be more remote
from colloquial English, from the spoken word. But on his
way there Joyce had experimented with both styles. Thus
Dubliners and *A Portrait of the Artist* are in reformed or
anti-Mandarin, and belong to the early years of Joyce's Irish
rebellion against the academic pundits and the literature

of the ruling class, while the value of *Ulysses* and its importance to this analysis of the trends in English prose lies
in the mixture of styles to be found there. In *Ulysses*, Joyce,
a sensitive stylist, is trying to make his mind up as to the
side he will take in the battle of the books. Thus we have
in the passages where Stephen Dedalus holds the stage the
Anglo-Irish lyrical mixture that we find in the *Portrait of
the Artist*. But whenever Bloom is on the scene the language
becomes the demotic journalese in vogue where people like
Bloom foregather, and corresponds to the French of Celine
who in his *Voyage au Bout de la Nuit* creates a Bloom-like
character. In the two long reveries, that of Mrs. Bloom and
the Cyclopean Nameless One, the style is petty bourgeois,
almost proletarian; in the lying-in hospital and the strange
penultimate chapter highly Mandarin.

The quality common to the Mandarins was inflation
either of language or imagination or of both and it was this
inflation which made inevitable a reaction against them.
For their success was enormous. In the history of literature
there can have been few books more talked and written
about; few names more mentioned than those of Proust,
Joyce, Lytton Strachey, Virginia Woolf, the Sitwells and
Paul Valéry. Their moment was propitious. After the post-
war disillusion they offered a religion of beauty, a cult of
words, of meanings understood only by the initiated at a
time when people were craving such initiations.

The world had lived too long under martial law to desire
a socialised form of art, for human beings in the mass had
proved but a union of slaughterers. There was more hope
and interest in extreme individuality. This romantic restatement of the individual was of value to the younger generation, since it enabled them to inflate their own lives and
gave them a depth and importance which they otherwise
lacked. Soon the universities were flooded with emotional
dud cheques, stumers on the bank of experience forged in
the name of Swann or Dedalus, Monsieur Teste or Mrs.
Dalloway. Proustians developed a wool-winding technique
in friendship, an indefatigable egotism in affairs of the
heart, combined with a lively social ambition. Valérians
made it clear that everything was a little more difficult than

it seemed and then more difficult again. The Dedalus young men were defeatist, proud and twisted, their rudeness was justified by the impact of some ancestral curse; the Waste Landers were more miserable still, while the young Huxleys found relief in epigrams and bawdy erudition.

> Oh yes, decidedly
> Having a sense of humour and a past
> One will amuse oneself, decidedly . . .

The Gidian immoralists were perverse and moody, the Stracheyites wore fringes and hooted with a dying pejorative fall, the Virginians were impulsive, the Mansfieldians very simple and "back-to-childhood," the Sitwellians went to the ballet in white ties and began their sentences with lingering sibilance: "I must say I do definitely think . . ." It was the golden age of Bloomsbury under the last long shadow of the Ivory Tower, a romantic, affected and defeatist epoch; action was discredited, it had caused the war; "And as for goodness—listen to Freud. Truth? But what about Einstein? History? Have you read the *Decline of the West?* Nothing remains but beauty. Have you read Waley's *170 Chinese Poems?* Beauty—and, of course, one's intellectual integrity and personal relations."

I have not dealt at length with these authors because I am assuming that the reader for whom this is written, the artist in his search for a relative immortality, will know the most important book about them: Edmund Wilson's *Axel's Castle* (Scribner's, 1931) which includes essays on Yeats, Valéry, Eliot, Proust, Joyce and Gertrude Stein. His summing up is against them, in so far as it is against their cult of the individual which he feels they have carried to such lengths as to exhaust it for a long time to come but it is a summing up which also states everything that can be said in their favour when allowance for what I have termed "inflation" has been made. Here is the last paragraph:

> The writers with whom I have here been concerned
> have not only, then, given us works of literature which,
> for intensity, brilliance, and boldness as well as for an

architectural genius, an intellectual mastery of their materials, rare among their Romantic predecessors, are
probably comparable to the work of any time. Though
it is true that they have tended to overemphasise the
importance of the individual, that they have been preoccupied with introspection sometimes almost to the
point of insanity, that they have endeavoured to dis-
courage their readers, not only with politics, but with
action of any kind—they have yet succeeded in effecting
in literature a revolution analogous to that which has
taken place in science and philosophy: they have broken
out of the old mechanistic routine, they have disintegrated the old materialism, and they have revealed to
the imagination a new flexibility and freedom. And
though we are aware in them of things that are dying
—the whole belletristic tradition of Renaissance culture
perhaps, compelled to specialise more and more, more
and more driven in on itself, as industrialism and democratic education have come to press it closer and closer
—they none the less break down the walls of the present
and wake us to the hope and exaltation of the untried,
unsuspected possibilities of human thought and art.

On this verdict we will leave them.

CHAPTER VIII: THE NEW VERNACULAR

The mass attack on the new Mandarins was launched in the late twenties. By that time these had squandered their cultural inheritance for their inflationary period coincided with the Boom and their adversaries were to come into their own with the Slump. In spite of their apparent success and publicity, the three great Mandarin books of 1928, *Orlando*, *Elizabeth and Essex*, *Point Counter Point*, were disappointing; they were not, except in America, popular successes and met also with considerable highbrow opposition.

This opposition may be said to have formed in three quarters. One quarter was that of the old realists, the remainder of those young men who had rejected Pater, Swinburne, Meredith and James. Of these Moore was too ill-read to be a good critic, Bennett too successful for he was anxious to conceal by his indiscriminate welcome to novelty the poverty of his own exhausted impulse; the opinion of Galsworthy, Shaw, Wells, Kipling was no longer of value in matters of art. It remained for Somerset Maugham, after his long excursion as a playwright, to return as the champion of "lucidity, euphony, simplicity, and the story with a beginning, a middle and an end," the doctrines of his French masters.

The second quarter was Paris, which held in the attack on the new Mandarins the line taken by Dublin against their predecessors thirty years before. It was here that conspirators met in Sylvia Beach's little bookshop where *Ulysses* lay stacked like dynamite in a revolutionary cellar and then scattered down the Rue de l'Odéon on the missions assigned to them. Here Gertrude Stein had launched her attacks on English culture by rinsing the English vocabulary, by a process of constant repetition, of all accretions of meaning and association. The prose style of Ezra Pound was hardly academic, and Joyce also, till he became the mandarin of *Work in Progress*, remained a king over the water for those who were discontented with the court of Bloomsbury. James Joyce, ambered in the Rue de Grenelle, and Gertrude Stein were the exiled royalties round whom centred the plots against Virginia Woolf and Lytton Strachey.

Any estimate of Miss Stein must largely depend on the pleasure derivable from her creations, but she applied to the writing of English as early as 1909 (*Three Lives*) a method which was to have far-reaching results. It was a simplification, an attack on order and meaning in favour of sound but of sound which in itself generated a new precision. Two young men were to be influenced by it, Sherwood Anderson and Ernest Hemingway, who each took Gertrude Stein's method and added to it his own quality of readability. The paper *Transition* was the court gazette of these kings in exile.

The third quarter in which opposition to the Mandarins arose was that of their contemporaries, Lawrence and Lewis. Lawrence, as the early lyricism of his pre-war books evaporated, became a master of the colloquial style. Though his work is marred by carelessness, repetition and want of ear and a tendency to preach and rant which ill-health accentuated, it is always vigorous, thoughtful and alive, the enemy of elaboration and artifice, of moral hypocrisy and verbal falseness. The poems in *Pansies* and *Nettles* are examples of the vernacular style at its best, as is the satire in his later books and stories such as *Lady Chatterley*. Around Lawrence centred Middleton Murry and his wife, Katherine Mansfield, who said in her diary that the greatest pleasure she had received from her stories was that they had given pleasure to the printer who set them up and also several younger writers of whom Richard Aldington, who also had one foot in Paris, and Robert Graves were the most important. A friend of Lawrence, though more influenced by George Moore, was David Garnett whose *Lady Into Fox* and *Sailor's Return* were excellent anti-Mandarin books, combining something of the dandyism of

Eliot and Firbank with a rustic basis, a fantasy logically worked out in language as simple as Defoe's.

The most dangerous enemy of the new Mandarins was Wyndham Lewis who after his realistic novel *Tarr* (1918) was preparing his onslaught on the citadels of literary culture; on the one hand Stein's simplicity and Joyce's complexity were to be attacked, with Hemingway, Faulkner and all other derivatives, while in England Bloomsbury was to tremble, Lawrence to be chastised for his worship of the black sun of the solar plexus and the Sitwells to be exterminated by an assassination five hundred pages long. Roy Campbell, in *The Georgiad*, brought up the rear. Since Lewis' style is that of a painter turned writer, it is difficult of analysis, being strongly marked by the visual quality of his imagination. His early books are full of fine onsets and satires and descriptions written in a technique of his own while his later ones are more colloquial or what he would call "informal."

To estimate his work is not easy. *The Art of Being Ruled, Time and Western Man, The Childermass, The Enemy* and *The Apes of God* contain some of the most vigorous satire, original description and profound criticism produced by the twentieth century; Lewis was unique in being a philosophical critic, who, attacking the modern conception of "time," was able to illustrate the workings of that conception by ranging up and down the whole of contemporary literature from the best poetry to the best-seller, the best-seller to the lowest kind of journalism or jazz.

As a constructive critic however he has little to offer, a belief in reason as opposed to metaphysical or sexual mysticism, a belief in Western civilisation, in the physical world, in the comic aspect of love, in the external approach to things (describing people via their personal appearance) and in the value of humour and satire. All this is not negligible, but it is not on a scale with the world he has set out to destroy or with his machinery of destruction.

What Lewis believes in most is himself and the measure he applies to his contemporaries is how far they differ from that yardstick and how far they stand in his way. His criticism also suffers from a lack of proportion. He will attack a

writer on philosophical, or moral grounds and then as violently for the most superficial and frivolous of errors or he
will turn from rending an important writer to maul an obscure and inconsiderable hack. He is like a maddened elephant which, careering through a village, sometimes leans
against a house and carelessly demolishes the most compact
masonry, trumpeting defiance to the inhabitants within,
sometimes pursues a dog or a chicken or stops to uproot a
shrub or bang a piece of corrugated iron. His writing can
be redundant and slovenly, his dialogue is often dull, his
novels begin with scenes worthy of a great master and
gradually lose themselves in unplanned verbosity. His last
volume of criticism, *Men Without Art*, while containing
brilliant glimpses of his mind, is unexpectedly trivial and
often bullying and unfair. His later books are ragged and
his style has become somewhat unbuttoned. From an article
of his in the Fascist quarterly, *British Union*, one gets the
impression that it is because he is writing now for a new
class of reader, the petty bourgeois, the philistine small
tradesman, the Fascist underdog.

What is necessary for Lewis is that some of his admirers
or he himself should make an omnibus Lewis, an anthology
of his best thought and finest passages, applying to his work
the selection and compression which in the spate of his
original creation have been wanting.

To go further it is necessary to bring the production chart
up to date and I have added after some of the more extreme
examples the letters (M) or (V) according as to whether
they are written in the Mandarin, or Vernacular or Colloquial style.

1923. Mansfield, *The Dove's Nest* (V); Huxley, *Antic Hay*
        (M); Firbank, *The Flower Beneath the Foot*
        (Dandy); Hemingway, *In Our Time* (V); Willa
        Cather, *A Lost Lady;* Elizabeth Bowen, *En-
        counters;* Eliot, *The Waste Land*
1924. Mansfield, *Something Childish* (V); Huxley, *Little
        Mexican;* Firbank, *Prancing Nigger;* Forster, *Pas-
        sage to India;* Garnett, *Man in the Zoo* (V);

Edith Sitwell, *The Sleeping Beauty* (M); Osbert Sitwell, *Triple Fugue* (M)

1925. Huxley, *Those Barren Leaves* (M); Dreiser, *American Tragedy* (V); Eliot, *Poems* (M); Compton-Burnett, *Pastors and Masters;* Garnett, *Sailor's Return* (V); Fitzgerald, *The Great Gatsby;* Loos, *Gentlemen Prefer Blondes* (V); Woolf, *Mrs. Dalloway* (M); Day Lewis, *Beechen Vigil;* Noel Coward, *The Vortex* (V); Geoffrey Scott, *Portrait of Zélide* (M)

1926. Huxley, *Two or Three Graces* (M); Hemingway, *Torrents of Spring* (V); Quennell, *Poems* (M); Lawrence, *Plumed Serpent;* Baring, *Daphne Adeane* (V); Cather, *My Mortal Enemy* (V); Fowler, *Modern English Usage;* V. Woolf, *To the Lighthouse* (M); Maugham, *The Casuarina Tree* (V)

1927. Bowen, *The Hotel* (M); Lehmann, *Dusty Answer* (M); Hemingway, *The Sun Also Rises* (V), *Men Without Women* (V); Lewis, *The Wild Body, Time and Western Man, The Lion and the Fox;* Mackenzie, *Vestal Fire;* Wilder, *Bridge of San Luis Rey* (M); Westcott, *The Grandmothers* (M)

1928. Sassoon, *Memoirs of a Fox-hunting Man;* Woolf, *Orlando* (M); Lawrence, *Lady Chatterley's Lover* (V); Nicolson, *Some People;* Edwards, *Winter Sonata* (V); Waugh, *Decline and Fall* (V); Isherwood, *All the Conspirators* (V); Lewis, *The Childermass;* Mackenzie, *Extraordinary Women;* Strachey, *Elizabeth and Essex* (M); Huxley, *Point Counter Point* (M); E. Sackville-West, *Mandrake Over the Water-Carrier* (M)

1929. Compton-Burnett, *Brothers and Sisters;* H. Green, *Living* (V); W. Faulkner, *The Sound and the Fury* (M); Hemingway, *Farewell to Arms* (V); Lawrence, *Pansies* (V); Joyce, *Fragments of Work in Progress* (M); Quennell, *Baudelaire and the Symbolists* (M); Graves, *Goodbye to All That* (V); Aldington, *Death of a Hero* (V)

1930. Kafka, *The Castle;* Dashiell Hammett, *Maltese
    Falcon* (V); O. Sitwell, *Dumb Animal* (M);
    Maugham, *Cakes and Ale* (V), *The Gentleman
    in the Parlour;* W. H. Auden, *Poems;* T. S. Eliot,
    Ash Wednesday (M); Evelyn Waugh, *Vile Bod-
    ies* (V); Spender, *Twenty Poems;* Lewis, *The
    Apes of God*

1931. V. Woolf, *The Waves* (M); Roy Campbell, *The
    Georgiad* (V); A. Powell, *Afternoon Men* (V);
    Edmund Wilson, *Axel's Castle*

1932. W. H. Auden, *The Orators*

There are, we know, many kinds of vernacular; the colloquial language of Hemingway is different from the colloquial language of Maurice Baring yet each believes in in-
formality and simplicity, they never use a word that they
would not in conversation—words like "nay," "notwithstanding," "pullulating," "mephitic," "sublunary," "Babylon,"
"lest," "corpulent," "futurity," "ecstasy," etc.

The outstanding writer of the new vernacular is Hemingway and he was aided by the talkies as were realists a generation before by journalism. The talking picture popular-
ised the vocabulary with which Hemingway wrote and
enabled him to use slang words in the knowledge that they
were getting every day less obscure, he surf-rode into fame
on the wave of popular American culture. Here, taken from
Death in the Afternoon, is a spat between him and a Mandarin which is in itself a defence of the new style:

Mr. Aldous Huxley writing in an essay entitled *Fore-
heads Villainous Low* commences: "In [naming a book
by this writer] Mr. H. ventures, once, to name an Old
Master. There is a phrase, quite admirably expressive"
[here Mr. Huxley inserts a compliment], "a single phrase,
no more, about 'the bitter nail-holes' of Mantegna's
Christ; then quickly, quickly, appalled by his own te-
merity, the author passes on (as Mrs. Gaskell might
hastily have passed on, if she had somehow been betrayed into mentioning a water-closet) passes on, shame-
facedly, to speak once more of Lower Things.

"There was a time, not so long ago, when the stupid

and uneducated aspired to be thought intelligent and cultured. The current of aspiration has changed its direction. It is not at all uncommon now to find intelligent and cultured people doing their best to feign stupidity and to conceal the fact that they have received an education"—and more; more in Mr. Huxley's best educated vein which is a highly educated vein indeed.

What about that, you say? Mr. Huxley scores there, all right, all right. What have you to say to that? Let me answer truly. On reading that in Mr. Huxley's book I obtained a copy of the volume he refers to and looked through it and could not find the quotation he mentions. It may be there, but I did not have the patience nor the interest to find it, since the book was finished, and nothing to be done. It sounds very much like the sort of thing one tries to remove in going over the manuscript. I believe it is more than a question of the simulation or avoidance of the appearance of culture. When writing a novel a writer should create living people; people, not characters. A *character* is a caricature. If a writer can make people live there may be no great characters in his book, but it is possible that his book will remain as a whole; as an entity; as a novel. If the people the writer is making talk of old masters; of music; of modern painting; of letters; or of science; then they should talk of those subjects in the novel. If they do not talk of those subjects and the writer makes them talk of them he is a faker, and if he talks about them himself to show how much he knows, then he is showing off. No matter how good a phrase or a simile he may have, if he puts it in where it is not absolutely necessary and irreplaceable, he is spoiling his work for egotism. Prose is architecture, not interior decoration, and the Baroque is over. For a writer to put his own intellectual musings, which he might sell for a low price as essays, into the mouths of artificially constructed characters, which are more remunerative when issued as people in a novel, is good economics, perhaps, but does not make literature. People in a novel, not skilfully constructed *characters*, must be projected from the writer's assimilated experience, from his knowledge, from his head, from his heart, and from all there is of him. If he ever has luck as well as seriousness and gets them out entire they will have more than one dimension and they will last a long time. A good writer should know as near everything as possible. Naturally he will not. A great enough writer seems to be born with knowledge. But he really is not; he has only been born with a quicker ratio to the passage of time than other men and without conscious application, and with an intelligence to accept or reject what is already presented as knowledge. There are some things which cannot be learned quickly, and time, which is all we have, must be paid heavily for their acquiring. They are the very simplest things and because it takes a man's life to know them the little new that each man gets from life is very costly and the only heritage he has to leave. Every novel which is truly written contributes to the total of knowledge which is there at the disposal of the next writer who comes, but the next writer must pay, always, a certain nominal percentage in experience to be able to understand and assimilate what is available as his birthright and what he must, in turn, take his departure from. If a writer of prose knows enough about what he is writing about he may omit things that he knows and the reader, if the writer is writing truly enough, will have a feeling of those things as strongly as though the writer had stated them. The dignity of movement of an iceberg is due to only one-eighth of it being above water. A writer who omits things because he does not know them only makes hollow places in his writing. A writer who appreciates the seriousness of writing so little that he is anxious to make people see he is formally educated, cultured or well-bred, is merely a popinjay. And this too, remember: a serious writer is not to be confounded with a solemn writer. A serious writer may be a hawk or a buzzard or even a popinjay, but a solemn writer is always a bloody owl.

The passage is an excellent example of Hemingway's style, notice the clumsy, facetious get-away, the admirable relation in the central passage between the language used and the thought to be conveyed, the polemical anti-climax at the end and notice also the slovenliness of such a phrase as "if the writer of prose knows enough about what he is writing about he may omit things that he knows." Like most writers of the thirties Hemingway seems terrified to blot a line.

Hemingway's difficulties as a writer arise from the limitations of realism. His style, derived from Huck Finn, Stein, Anderson with perhaps a dash of Firbank, is the antithesis of fine writing. It is a style in which the body talks rather than the mind, one admirable for rendering emotions; love, fear, joy of battle, despair, sexual appetite, but impoverished for intellectual purposes. Hemingway is fortunate in possessing a physique which is at home in the world of boxing, bull-fighting and big game shooting, fields closed to most writers and especially to Mandarins; he is supreme in the domain of violence and his opportunity will be to write the great book (and there have been no signs of one so far), about the Spanish war. Hemingway's tragedy as an artist is that he has not had the versatility to run away fast enough from his imitators. The talkies that facilitated his success brought on a flood of talkie-novels, the trick of being tough, the knack of writing entirely in dialogue interrupted only by a few sentimental landscapes caught on and with each bad copy the prestige of the original was affected. A Picasso would have done something different; Hemingway could only indulge in invective against his critics—and do it again. His colleagues in American realism, Dos Passos, O'Hara, Caldwell, have found the same difficulties and the Hemingway style is now confined to sporting journalists on the daily papers, advertising men with literary ambitions, cinema critics and the writers of thrillers. The first you-man sentence of the *Portrait of the Artist*, "when you wet the bed first it is warm, then it gets cold," a sentence intended to represent the simple body-conscious needs of early childhood, after dominating fiction for years, would seem to have had its day.

Lewis has attacked Hemingway for being a "dumb ox," for choosing stupid inarticulate heroes who are the passive victims of circumstance rather than active and intelligent masters of their fate. Yet at the period at which Hemingway wrote his best books it was necessary to be a dumb ox. It was the only way to escape from Chelsea's Apes of God and from Bloomsbury's Sacred Geese.

The most resolute and coherent of the opponents of fine writing has been Somerset Maugham although his hostility arises, he tells us, from his incapacity.

> I discovered my limitations and it seemed to me that the only sensible thing was to aim at what excellence I could within them. I knew that I had no lyrical quality, I had a small vocabulary and no efforts that I could make to enlarge it much, availed me. I had little gift of metaphors; the original and striking simile seldom occurred to me. Poetic flights and the great imaginative sweep were beyond my powers. . . . I knew that I should never write as well as I could wish, but I thought with pains I could arrive at writing as well as my natural defects allowed. On taking thought it seemed to me that I must aim at lucidity, simplicity and euphony. I have put these three qualities in the order of the importance I assigned to them.

Maugham (I am quoting from *The Summing Up*, though some of the arguments there are to be found in earlier books) then goes on to criticise Ruskin and Sir Thomas Browne with justice and to attack the influence of King James's Bible on English prose.

> Ever since, English prose has had to struggle against the tendency to luxuriance. When from time to time the spirit of the language has reasserted itself, as it did with Dryden and the writers of Queen Anne, it was only to be submerged once more by the pomposities of Gibbon and Dr. Johnson. When English prose recovered simplicity with Hazlitt, the Shelley of the letters, and Charles Lamb at his best, it lost it again with de Quincey, Carlyle, Meredith, and Walter Pater. . . .

> For to write good prose is an affair of good manners. It is, unlike verse, a civil art. . . . Poetry is baroque. I

cannot but feel that the prose writers of the baroque
period, the authors of King James' bible, Sir Thomas
Browne, Glanville, were poets who had lost their way.
Prose is a rococo art. It needs taste rather than power,
decorum rather than inspiration and vigour rather than
grandeur. . . . It is not an accident that the best prose
was written when rococo, with its elegance and modera-
tion, attained its greatest excellence. For rococo was
evolved when baroque had become declamatory, and
the world, tired of the stupendous, asked for restraint.
It was the natural expression of persons who valued a
civilised life. Humour, tolerance, and horse-sense made
the great tragic issues that had preoccupied the first half
of the seventeenth century seem excessive. The world
was a more comfortable place to live in and perhaps for
the first time in centuries the cultivated classes could sit
back and enjoy their leisure. It has been said that good
prose should resemble the conversation of a well-bred
man. Conversation is only possible when men's minds are
free from pressing anxieties. Their lives must be reasonably secure and they must have no grave concern about
their souls. They must attach importance to the refine-
ments of civilisation. They must value courtesy; they
must pay attention to their persons (and have we not
also been told that good prose should be like the clothes
of a well-dressed man, appropriate but unobtrusive?).
They must fear to bore, they must be neither flippant,
nor solemn, but always apt; and they must look upon
"enthusiasm" with a critical glance. This is a soil very
suitable for prose. It is not to be wondered at that it gave
a fitting opportunity for the appearance of the best writer
of prose that our modern world has seen, Voltaire. . . .
The writers of English, perhaps owing to the poetic nature of the language, have seldom reached the excellence
that seems to have come so naturally to him. . . . If you
could write lucidly, simply, euphoniously and yet with
liveliness you would write perfectly; you would write like
Voltaire.

I have quoted this passage because it is a typical defence

of vernacular prose, as also of much literary wish-fulfilment. Maugham thinks with pleasure of the civilised and wealthy society of the eighteenth century, he has made his own life wealthy and civilised and therefore would like to believe that the prose of the eighteenth century is the best. But supposing a new age of "great tragic issues" is now in being, then a prose of humour, tolerance, and horse-sense will seem frivolous and archaic! And what writer could have been more lucid and simple, more admired by Maugham, than Swift who living in the heart of that courteous and cultivated age contrived to go mad in it? Nor is the prose of Blake so negligible. Incidentally the defects of the colloquial style are well illustrated in this passage. The vocabulary is flat. "Sit back and enjoy," "pressing anxieties," "reasonably secure," "grave concern," "critical glance," "fitting opportunity," "it is not to be wondered at," while not yet officially clichés, are phrases so tarnished as to be on the way to them. They come from the vocabulary of political journalism; from the atmosphere where words deteriorate faster than in any other and the defect of the colloquial style, the breathlessness, the agitated dullness of the sentence which is too short for both eye and ear, becomes apparent. The phrases rattle like peas being shelled into a tin, the full stops bring the reader up short, the effect, owing to the absence of any relative clauses, is of reading a list of aphorisms and the best aphorists, even La Rochefoucauld, can be read only for a few pages. Again, the language of the Bible is more plain than complicated; its bad influence on English style has been in the direction of archaistic simplicity and is apparent in a writer like Kipling. It is no accident, as Maugham would say, that he goes on to praise American literature, ignorant, he claims, of the Authorised Version and to flatter American writers, galvanised by their journalism.

This concludes the case for the vernacular style. There remains one other argument often heard in its favour. "If culture is to survive it must survive through the masses; if it cannot be made acceptable to them there is no one else who will be prepared to guarantee it, since the liberal capitalist society who protected it will not be in a position to do so after another slump and a war. Much that is subtle in literature and life will have to be sacrificed if they are to survive at all; consequently it is necessary for literature to approach its future custodians in a language they will understand."

The old world is a sinking ship; to get a place in the boats that are pushing off from it not money nor leisure, the essayist's elegance nor the pedant's erudition will avail; the sailors are not impressed by courtesy or attention to one's person, nor even by good clothes and the conversation of a well-bred man; we cannot take our armchair with us. Nothing will admit us but realism and sincerity, an honest appeal in downright English. As far back as 1847 Tennyson said that the two great social questions impending in England were the "housing and education of the poor man before making him our master, and the higher education of women" and as the time for making him our master grows nearer, so his education becomes more necessary since on it depend the cultural values which he will choose to preserve.

For this reason left-wing writers have tended to write in the colloquial style while the Mandarins, the wizards and prose charmers remain as supporters of the existing dispensation. In England the ablest exponents of the colloquial style among the younger writers are Christopher Isherwood and George Orwell, both left-wing and both, at the present level of current English, superlatively readable. Here is an experiment:

The first sound in the mornings was the clumping of the mill-girls' clogs down the cobbled street. Earlier than that, I suppose, there were factory whistles which I was never awake to hear. There were generally four of us in the bedroom, and a beastly place it was, with that defiled impermanent look of rooms that are not serving their rightful purpose. One afternoon, early in Otcober, I was invited to black coffee at Fritz Wendel's flat. Fritz always invited you to "black coffee" with emphasis on the black. He was very proud of his coffee. People used to say it was the strongest in Berlin. Fritz himself was dressed in his usual coffee-party costume—a thick white yachting sweater and very light blue yachting trousers. You know how it is there early in Havana, with the bums still asleep against the walls of the buildings; before even the ice waggons come by with ice for the bars? Well we came across the square from the dock to the Pearl of San Francisco to get coffee. My bed was in the right-hand corner on the side nearest the door. There was another bed across the foot of it and jammed hard against it (it had to be in that position to allow the door to open), so that I had to sleep with my legs doubled up; if I straightened them out I kicked the occupant of the other bed in the small of the back. He was an elderly man named Mr. Reilly. He greeted me with his full-lipped luscious smile.

"'Lo, Chris!"

"Hullo, Fritz. How are you?"

"Fine." He bent over the coffee-machine, his sleek black hair unplastering itself from the scalp and falling in richly scented locks over his eyes. "This darn thing doesn't go," he added.

We sat down and one of them came over.

"Well," he said.

"I can't do it," I told him. "I'd like to do it as a favour. But I told you last night I couldn't."

"You can name your own price."

"It isn't that. I can't do it. That's all. How's business?" I asked.

"Lousy and terrible." Fritz grinned richly.

Luckily he had to go to work at five in the morning so I could uncoil my legs and have a couple of hours proper sleep after he was gone.

This passage is formed by adding to the first three sentences of Orwell's *Road to Wigan Pier* the first five sentences of Isherwood's *Sally Bowles* and then the first two sentences of Hemingway's *To Have and Have Not*. I have woven the beginning of the three stories a little further. Next three sentences by Orwell, then dialogue by Isherwood to "added," by Hemingway to "That's all," by Isherwood to "richly" and last sentence by Orwell again. The reader can now go on with whichever book he likes best, Orwell and his bed, Fritz and his coffee, or Harry Morgan and Havana. As Pearsall-Smith says of modern writers: "The diction, the run of phrase of each of them seems quite undistinguishable from that of the others, each of whose pages might have been written by any one of his fellows."

This, then, is the penalty of writing for the masses. As the writer goes out to meet them halfway he is joined by other writers going out to meet them halfway and they merge into the same creature—the talkie journalist, the advertising, lecturing, popular novelist.

The process is complicated by the fact that the masses, whom a cultured writer may generously write for, are at the moment overlapped by the middle-class best-seller-making public and so a venal element is introduced.

According to Gide, a good writer should navigate against the current; the practitioners in the new vernacular are swimming with it; the familiarities of the advertisements in the morning paper, the matey leaders in the *Daily Express,* the blather of the film critics, the wisecracks of newsreel commentators, the know-all autobiographies of political reporters, the thrillers and 'teccies, the personal confessions, the *I was a so-and-so,* and *Storm over such-and-such,* the gossip writers who play Jesus at twenty-five pounds a week, the straight-from-the-shoulder men, the middle-brow novelists of the shove-halfpenny school, are all swimming with it too. For a moment the canoe of an Orwell or an Isherwood bobs up, then it is hustled away by floating rubbish, and a spate of newspaper pulp.

It is interesting to notice the conflict between the two ways of writing in Auden. In the ballads he has lately been writing, excellent of their kind, he has attempted to reduce poetry to a record of simple and universal experience expressed in colloquial language.

> O plunge your hands in water
> Plunge them in up to the wrist
> Stare, stare in the basin
> And wonder what you've missed.

> The glacier knocks in the cupboard
> The desert sighs in the bed,
> And the crack in the tea-cup opens
> A lane to the land of the dead.

At the same time the bulk of his poetry has always remained private and esoteric.

CHAPTER IX: THE COOL ELEMENT OF PROSE

It is now time to express an opinion on the battle between the styles. I do not say that one is better than the other; there is much to admire in both; what I have claimed is a relationship between them, a perpetual action and reaction; the realists had it their way in the years before the war; from 1918 to 1928, the period of Joyce, Proust, Valéry, Strachey, Woolf, the Sitwells, and Aldous Huxley, the new Mandarins ruled supreme, while from 1928 to 1938 the new realists have predominated. The deflationary activities of the Cambridge critics (Richards, Leavis) have replaced the inflationism of Bloomsbury. But we have now had ten years of this new realism; ten years in which it has grown more popular and more tyrannical. Its vocabulary, never rich, has been worn away by the attrition of success; its exponents have been wearied by the enormity of their imitators.

It is possible to bring forward other causes for the silence or the deterioration of a writer than the weaknesses of his literary creed and the other causes are as likely to be correct. All we can say of the realists of the last ten years is that nothing in their technique seems to have insured them against the disastrously short term of the writer's life. Realism, simplicity, the colloquial style, would appear to have triumphed everywhere at the moment—yet where are their triumphant professors? With the exception of Isherwood among the young and Maugham among the old their prestige is already fading. The movement has passed out of their hands and sunk to wider and more anonymous strata, to the offices, the studios and the novelist's week-end cottages where is produced the great bulk of present-day commercial writing.

I have discussed the situation with Isherwood, whom I

regard as a hope of English fiction and I have suggested
how dangerous that fatal readability of his might become.
The first person singular of the German stories, Herr
Christoph, or Herr Issyvoo, is the most persuasive of literary
salesmen—one moment's reading with him and one is
tobogganing through the book, another second and one has
bought it—but he is persuasive because he is so insinuat-
ingly bland and anonymous, nothing rouses him, nothing
shocks him. While secretly despising us he could not at
the same time be more tolerant; his manners are charming
and he is somehow on our side against the characters—
confidential as, when playing with children, one child older
or less animal than the rest, will suddenly attach itself to
the grown-ups and discuss its former playmates.

Now for this a price has to be paid; Herr Issyvoo is not a
dumb ox, for he is not condemned to the solidarity with
his characters and with their background to which Hemingway is bound by his conception of art, but he is much
less subtle, intelligent and articulate than he might be. In
the little knitted skein from the three books it will be remembered that not only was the language almost identical
and the pace the same but the three "I"s of Isherwood,
Orwell and Hemingway were also interchangeable; three
colourless reporters.

In Isherwood's earlier *The Memorial* however, there is
no first person. The hero is a character who is more
favoured than the others, and in the Berlin diary (*New
Writing*, No. 3) the first person singular, unhampered by
the conventions of fiction, at once postulates a higher level
of culture and intelligence, and possesses a richer vocabulary. In conversation, Isherwood, while admitting the limitations of the style he had adopted, expressed his belief
in construction as the way out of the difficulty. The writer
must conform to the language which is understood by the
greatest number of people, to the vernacular, but his talent
as a novelist will appear in the exactness of his observation,
the justice of his situations and in the construction of his
book. It is an interesting theory, for construction has for
long been the weak point in modern novels. It is the con-

struction that renders outstanding *The Memorial, Passage to India,* and *Cakes and Ale.*

But will the construction, however rigid and faultless, of future books, if they are written in what will by then be an even more impoverished realist vocabulary, contribute enough to set those books apart from the copies made by the ever-growing school of imitators? At present it is impossible to tell; the path is beset by dangers; it is fortunate that Isherwood, who possesses the mastery of form, the imaginative content of a true novelist, is able to see them.

The most convincing attack on the realism of the thirties was made by Pearsall-Smith in his pamphlet on *Fine Writing* (reprinted in *Reperusals,* 1936). A Mandarin of the generation of the eighties, an admirer of Pater and Jowett and a friend of Henry James, he represents not a reaction against the new realism, but the old Adam, the precious original sinner, against whom the later realists took action. He, in return, attacks their austerity:

May it be accounted for by the fact that the spirit of Puritanism, having been banished from the province of moral conduct, has found a refuge among the arts? Do these critics of the art of writing, like certain critics of other arts, occupy themselves with the craft of literary composition because they think it wrong? . . . I shall make to our modern critics, especially of the Cambridge school, a few suggestions which are not amiable, and are perhaps unfair. The disconcerting fact may first be pointed out that if you write badly about good writing, however profound may be your convictions or emphatic your expression of them, your style has a tiresome trick of whispering, "Don't listen," in your reader's ears. And it is possible also to suggest that the promulgation of new-fangled æsthetic dogmas in unwieldly sentences may be accounted for—not perhaps unspitefully—by a certain deficiency in æsthetic sensibility; as being due to a lack of that delicate, unreasoned, prompt delight in all the varied and subtle manifestations in which beauty may enchant us.

He goes on to suggest that economic causes are also responsible:

> Are not the authors who earn their livings by their pens, and those who, by what some regard as a social injustice, have been more or less freed from this necessity—are not these two classes of authors in a sort of natural opposition to each other? He who writes at his leisure, with the desire to master his difficult art, can hardly help envying the profits of the money-making authors, since his own work at least till years, and often many years, have passed, has no appreciable market value. Unsaleability seems to be the hall-mark, in modern times, of quality in writing.

Puritanism in other people we admire as austerity in ourselves, yet there is much truth in Pearsall-Smith's accusation. Writing is a more impure art than music or painting. It is an art, but it is also the medium in which many millions of inartistic people express themselves, describe their work, sell their goods, justify their conduct, propagate their ideas. It is the vehicle of all business and propaganda. Since it is hard to paint or to compose without a certain affection for painting or music, the commercial element—advertisers, illustrators, are recognisable, and in a minority, nor do music and painting appeal to the scientific temperament.

But writing does. It is an art in which the few who practise it for its own sake are being always resented and jostled through its many galleries by the majority who do not. And the deadliest of these are the scientific investigators, clever young men who have themselves failed as artists and who bring only a passionate sterility and a dark, wide-focusing resentment to their examination of creative art. The aim of much of this destructive criticism, though not as yet publicly avowed, is entirely to eliminate the individual style, to banish imaginative beauty and formal art from writing. Prose will not only be as unassuming as good clothes, but as uniform as bad ones. For there is no use in Maugham arguing that a writer to be distinct from others must heighten his colloquial modern style by reading

Newman and Hazlitt; he is by now, if he is like any other
modern writer, moving too fast and such authors will seem
to him, if he has the patience to read them, so occupied
with unreal problems and so contaminated by a leisurely
attitude to life as to be hardly less archaic than their stylistic
rivals, Lamb, Ruskin, Pater, Matthew Arnold. The remedy
is proposed too late.

The one way by which a cure can be undertaken is to
persuade such writers to re-read their own books or those
contemporary books which, up to a year ago, they most
admired. Then, however jauntily they may protest—"Well,
it was what the public wanted at the time—it was in me
and it had to come out; it means no more to me now than
my old toenails—and, hell, who wants to read the same
book twice, anyway," a doubt will have arisen.

On the other hand Maugham expresses a truth when he
says that much writing of the kind he dislikes is the work of
"Poets who have lost their way." The defect of Mandarin
writing is not that it is poetical or imaginative prose, but
that much of it is not prose, but bad poetry. It is a fact of
importance that the prose of true poets is firm and muscu-
lar. Landor, Coleridge, Shelley, Donne, Shakespeare, Milton, Dryden, Blake, Hopkins, Yeats, Eliot, Gray, Cowper,
to name but a few, could write admirable prose—for poetry
is a more precise art than prose and to write it implies
qualities which prove valuable in the "other harmony."

The poetry of prose writers on the other hand is unworthy of them and very often they will have become prose
writers only after the failure of a slim volume of verse.
Since the decay of the Romantic Movement poetry has
gone through a bad patch and severe discipline has been
necessary to those who write it; consequently others who
start out with only facility, sensibility and a lyrical outlook,
rather than undergo the hardships of the training, have
allowed their poetical feeling to relax in prose. The result
has been to inflate and romanticise prose in its turn and
thus to bring about a philistine, puritan and pedestrian
reaction. The Tough Guy, of whose company we are now
growing tired, is the inevitable offspring of the androgynous
Orlando. There is no reason why prose should not be poeti-

cal provided that the poetry in it is assimilated to the medium and that its rhythms follow the structure of prose and not of verse—it is the undisciplined, undigested, unassimilated poetry written often in unconscious blank verse and bearing no relation to the construction, if any, of the book, which has discredited "fine writing."

At the moment the vernacular is triumphant. Damon Runyon sweeps the land. The you-men are everywhere victorious.

That is the situation. Is there any hope? Is there a possibility of a new kind of prose developing out of a synthesis of Orlando and the Tough Guy? Will the strong writers of the colloquial school heighten the form of their work or can the Formalists deepen their content? We must look to the poets for a lead, for there are signs that from them is coming a revival of imaginative prose. I like to detect a foreshadowing of it in Landor's description of the lioness with her young, which appears, like an oasis, in Richards' *Principles of Literary Criticism*.

> On perceiving the countryman, she drew up her feet gently, and squared her mouth, and rounded her eyes, slumberous with content, and they looked, he said, like sea-grottoes, obscurely green, interminably deep, at once awakening fear and stilling and suppressing it.

Such a phrase belongs to the real texture of prose, a texture now rarely seen, where syntax and a rich vocabulary are woven in a pattern to match the thought of the maker.

> I know that I am I, living in a small way in a temperate zone, blaming father, jealous of son, confined to a few acts often repeated, easily attracted to a limited class of physique, yet envying the simple life of the gut, desiring the certainty of the breast or prison, happiest sawing wood, only knowledge of the real disturbances in the general law of the dream; the quick blood fretting against the slowness of the hope; a unit of life, needing water and salt, that looks for a sign.

. . . .

From the immense bat-shadow of home; from the removal of landmarks, from appeals for love and from the comfortable words of the devil, from all opinions and personal ties; from pity and shame; and from the wish to instruct . . . in the moment of vision; in the hour of applause; in the place of defeat; and in the hour of desertion, O Holmes, Deliver us.

These two quotations from *The Orators* (W. H. Auden; Faber, 1932) show imaginative prose coming to life again by way of a young poet influenced by Rimbaud and the Prayer Book. And when the language comes to life, it ceases to be an imitation. The prose of Spender is also unusual and in his critical book, *The Destructive Element*, he makes a study of that great Mandarin, Henry James, which must affect the values of any contemporary who reads it, since he has restated for his generation the relationship between writing and ethics. The revival of the poetical drama and the group theater gives writers like Eliot, Auden, Isherwood, and MacNeice opportunities for declamatory and non-commercial prose.

Other glimpses of a revival in imaginative writing may be found in George Barker's *Janus* (Faber, 1935), Hugh Sykes-Davies' *Petron* (Dent), David Jones' *In Parenthesis* (Faber), Djuna Barnes' *Night Wood* (Faber), Henry Miller's *Tropic of Cancer* (Obelisk Press), and Henry Green's remarkable novel *Living* (Dent).[1]

One further question is raised by Maugham. "I have never had much patience," he states, "with the writers who claim from the reader an effort to understand their meaning." This is an abject surrender for it is part of the tragedy of modern literature that the author, anxious to avoid mystifying the reader, is afraid to demand of him any exertions. "Don't be afraid of me," he exclaims, "I write exactly as I talk—no, better still—exactly as you talk." Imagine Cézanne painting or Beethoven composing "exactly as he

[1] Readers who find the lioness quotation stirs them, like the memory of something of which they have been long deprived, may amuse themselves by searching for this quality in modern prose, this combination of imagination and accuracy into magic, and they will be fortunate if they can discover a single example.

talked!" The only way to write is to consider the reader to be the author's equal; to treat him otherwise is to set a value on illiteracy, and so all that results from Maugham's condescension to a reader from whom he expects no effort is a latent hostility to him as of some great chef waiting on a hungry Australian. As Richards says of the poet: "It is hard and, in fact, impossible, to deny him his natural and necessary resources on the ground that a majority of his readers will not understand. This is not his fault but the fault of the social structure."

At the present time for a book to be produced with any hope of lasting half a generation, of outliving a dog or a car, of surviving the lease of a house or the life of a bottle of champagne, it must be written against the current, in a prose that makes demands both on the resources of our language and the intelligence of the reader. From the Mandarins it must borrow art and patience, the striving for perfection, the horror of clichés, the creative delight in the material, in the possibilities of the long sentence and the splendour and subtlety of the composed phrase.

From the Mandarins, on the other hand, the new writer will take warning not to capitalise indolence and egotism nor to burden a sober and delicate language with exhibitionism. There will be no false hesitation and woolly profundities, no mystifying, no Proustian onanism. He will distrust the armchair clowns, the easy philosophers, the prose charmers. He will not show off his small defects, his preferences or his belongings, his cat, his pipe, his carpet slippers, bad memory, clumsiness with machinery, absentmindedness, propensity for losing things, or his ignorance of business and of everything which might make the reader think he wrote for money. There will be no whimsy, no allusiveness, archaism, pedantic usages, no false colloquialisms, or sham lyrical outbursts; there will be no "verily" and "verity," no "when all is said and done," no "to my way of thinking," "hardly of my own choosing," "I may be very stupid but," and no "If it be a sin to be half in love with the old days then I must aver," there will be no false relationship between art and experience; none of those dodges by which the sedentary man of letters is enabled to write about women, fighting, dancing, drink, by switching over to a prepared set of literary substitutes called Venus, Mars, Bacchus, and Terpsichore. References to infinity, to the remoteness of the stars and planets, the littleness of man, the charm of dead civilisations, to Babylon and Troy, "on whose mouldering citadel lies the lizard like a thing of green bronze" will be suspect. The adventurers "among their books," the explorer who never leaves his desk, will be required to live within their imagination's income.

From the realists, the puritans, the colloquial writers and talkie-novelists there is also much that he will take and much that he will leave. The cursive style, the agreeable manners, the precise and poetical impact of Forster's diction, the lucidity of Maugham, last of the great professional writers, the timing of Hemingway, the smooth cutting edge of Isherwood, the indignation of Lawrence, the honesty of Orwell, these will be necessary and the touch of those few journalists who give to every word in their limited vocabulary its current topical value. But above all it is construction that can be learnt from the realists, that discipline in the conception and execution of a book, that planning which gives simply written things the power to endure, the constant pruning without which the imagination like a tea-rose reverts to the wilderness.

He will not borrow from the realists, or from their imitators, the flatness of style, the homogeneity of outlook, the fear of eccentricity, the reporter's horror of distinction, the distrust of beauty, the cult of a violence and starkness that is masochistic. Nor will he adopt the victory mentality of those left-wing writers who imagine themselves already to be the idols of a conquering proletariat and who give their laws in simple matter-of-fact hard-hitting English to a non-existent congregation. That time is not yet; the artist to-day is in the position of a patient Mahomet towards whom the great art-hating mountain of the British public must eventually sidle.

This would seem the state of our literature. The battle between the schools I think has been proved to exist, but as with all civil wars, there are places where and moments when the fight rages with greater violence than at others. I have concentrated on those writers in the forefront of that battle, and any criticism I have made of them is intended only to relate them to it. Thus to call Proust a bad influence is not to deny that he is a great writer, but rather to consider his work in terms of what can be learnt from it to-day. It is the privilege of living in the twentieth century that one can take both sides in such controversies.

What I claim is that there continue action and reaction between these styles, and that necessary though it were and victorious as it may appear, the colloquial style of the last few years is doomed and dying. Style, as I have tried to show, is a relationship between a writer's mastery of form and his intellectual or emotional content. Mastery of form has lately been held, with some reason, to conceal a poverty of content but this is not inevitably so and for too long writers have had to prove their sincerity by going before the public in sackcloth and ashes or rather in a fifty-shilling suit and a celluloid collar. Now has come the moment when the penance is complete and when they may return to their old habit. It is no more a question of taking sides about one way or another of writing, but a question of timing, for the you-man writing of he-men authors is going out and the form must be enriched again. Our language is a sulky and inconstant beauty and at any given moment it is important to know what liberties she will permit. Now all seems favourable. Experiment and adventure are indicated, the boom of the twenties has been paid for by the slump of the thirties; let us try then to break the vicious circle by returning to a controlled expenditure, a balanced literary budget, a reasoned extravagance.

PART TWO: THE CHARLOCK'S SHADE

The Strongest Poison ever known
Came from Cæsar's Laurel Crown.

BLAKE

CHAPTER X: THE BLIGHTED RYE

We have seen how closely the style of a book may affect its expectation of life, passing through a charnel house in which we have observed the death and decomposition of many works confident ten years ago of longevity, hailed as masterpieces of their period and now equal in decay. A few only present an air of health and claim some immunity from the venom of time. It is necessary now to analyse the conditions which govern the high rate of mortality among contemporary writers, to enter a region, "where the thin harvest waves its wither'd ears . . ." a sombre but, to those for whom it is not yet too late, a bracing territory.

> There thistles stretch their prickly arms afar,
> And to the ragged infant threaten war;
> There Poppies nodding, mock the hope of toil,
> There the blue Bugloss paints the sterile soil;
> Hardy and high, above the slender sheaf,
> The slimy Mallow waves her silky leaf;
> O'er the young shoot the Charlock throws a shade,
> And clasping Tares cling round the sickly blade;
> With mingled tints the rocky coasts abound,
> And a sad splendour vainly shines around.

Let the "thin harvest" be the achievement of young authors, the "wither'd ears" their books, then the "militant thistles" represent politics, the "nodding poppies" day-dreams, conversation, drink and other narcotics, the "blue Bugloss" is the clarion call of journalism, the "slimy mallow" that of worldly success, the "charlock" is sex with its obsessions and the "clasping tares" are the ties of duty and domesticity. The "mingled tints" are the varieties of talent which appear; the "sad splendour" is that of their vanished promise. These enemies of literature, these parasites on

genius we must examine in detail; they are blights from
which no writer is immune.

Before making further use of Crabbe's description of the
heath with its convenient symbols we must answer a question sometimes put by certain literary die-hards, old cats
who sit purring over the mouseholes of talent in wait for
what comes out. "Is this age," they pretend to ask, "really
more unfavourable to writers than any other? Have not
writers always had the greatest difficulty in surviving? Indeed, their path to-day seems made much easier than it
was, to give an example, for myself!" The answer, if they
wanted an answer, is yes. Yes, because a writer needs
money more than in the ivory-tower decade since he can
no longer live in a cottage in the country meditating a
blank-verse historical drama and still get the best out of
himself. Yes, because he is more tempted to-day than at
any other time by those remunerative substitutes for good
writing: journalism, reviewing, advertising, broadcasting
and the cinema, but most of all because a writer to-day
can have no confidence in posterity and therefore is inclined
to lack the strongest inducement to good work: the desire
for survival.

For it is clear that "posterity" even to Samuel Butler,[1]
writing in the last century, meant the reading public of the
next few hundred years while since then the uncertainties
of fame have so increased that Maugham confines it to two
generations. A writer must grow used to the idea that culture as we know it may disappear and remain lost for ever
or till it is excavated, a thousand years hence, from a new
Herculaneum. Horace's boast of immortality, his *"non
omnis moriar,"* neither anticipated the hostility of the

---

[1] "All books die sooner or later but that will not hinder an
author from trying to give his book as long a life as he can get
for it. . . . Any man who wishes his work to stand will sacrifice
a good deal of his immediate audience for the sake of being
attractive to a much larger number of people later on. Briefly
the world resolves itself into two great classes—those who hold
that honour after death is better worth having than any honour
a man can get and know anything about, and those who doubt
this; to my mind those who hold this and hold it firmly, are the
only people worth thinking about."

church nor the ignorance of the Dark Ages. Of his two thousand years of posthumous life, a thousand slid by in a coma. One has but to consider the dearth of writers in Italy and Germany, the extinction of the cultural activity of the Weimar republic or the war waged by those countries against the intelligentsia of Spain to perceive how ephemeral are the securest literary reputations, the most flourishing movements. At any moment the schools of Athens may be closed, the libraries burnt, the teachers exterminated, the language suppressed. Any posthumous fame or the existence of any posterity capable of appreciating the arts we care for, can be guaranteed only by fighting for it and for many who fight, there will be no stake in the future but a name on a war memorial.

The love of posthumous fame is a common psychological substitute for the love of perfection, even as the love of perfection may prove a projection into the world of art of a sense of guilt. Thus astrologers find this love of perfection in those born under the sign of Virgo; it is to the artist as virginity to the nun and this love of purification they declare confined to those born between the end of August and the end of September. A writer should not be too conscious of such abstractions as perfection and posterity, "the cackle of the unborn about the grave," he should be above a flirtation with time, determined only to restore to the world in a form worthy of his powers something of what he has taken out of it. He must be a helping writer, who tells us what he sees through his periscope or there will be no writers and no readers left.

Otherwise Butler has stated the problem clearly. What ruins young writers is over-production. The need for money is what causes over-production; therefore writers must have private incomes. As he put it "No gold, no holy ghost." Genius is independent of money, but the world will always destroy it if it can. A writer, then, to avoid over-production, unless he acquires a private income, must either learn to make more money from his books or to earn money in other ways congenial to the writing of them.

To make more money from a book it is necessary either to potboil, to give way to the taste of the reading public

at the expense of the judgment of the author or to find
technical ways of improving sales. Other ways of earning
money and still finding time to write consist of journalism,
teaching, advertising, the civil service and the family business. Journalism will be discussed separately. Of the other
remedies, teaching provides long holidays and the work is
not such as to make inroads on the creative imagination
but not many people can teach or enjoy teaching and, in
spite of the long holidays, the work seems to make any
enlargement of the writer's experience awkward and un-
welcome. Of the dons at Oxford and Cambridge remark-
ably few attain literary eminence and the best known
among them are writers who have mixed in the world outside the universities. This is even more true of schoolmasters. Nor is the Civil Service the Parnassus which it
became in the nineties; its talent would seem to have run
dry with Humbert Wolfe. Since being a civil servant is a
static, arid and parasitic occupation, it is unlikely that anyone who is content with it will possess the imagination that
creates or the talent which will mature and ripen.

Most unsatisfactory is advertising for there is something
about copy-writing which so resembles the composition of
lyric poetry as to replace the process. When in order to
satisfy a corset manufacturer in search of a slogan, a writer
has to think of the rousing or the lapidary phrase, the as-
sonance of vowels and consonants, the condensation of
thought, the inflections of delicate meaning at his disposal,
he will be in no mood to write anything else. The family
business, if we have such a family and if it does no business,
is the best way out.

An outside job is harmful to a writer in proportion as it
approximates to his vocation. Thus reviewing poetry is the
worst profession for a poet, while broadcasting, advertising,
journalism or lecturing all pluck feathers from the blue bird
of inspiration and cast them on the wind. Living at home,
on the other hand, confines the writer's experience to the
family circle; rich marriages do not usually go with congenial tastes or a mutual love of the literary life and patrons
are capricious and hard to come by; besides, a relationship
with one in these days is open to imputation.

It is curious that while the brief-flowering and quick extinction of modern talent is everywhere so apparent, yet little should have been written on the subject. Our two sages, Pearsall-Smith and Maugham, croak their warnings but there is no sign that they are regarded.

As soon as any glimmering of talent, any freshness or originality, makes its appearance, it is immediately noted and exploited [Pearsall-Smith, *Prospects of Literature* (Hogarth Press, 1927)]. Editors of the weekly and even of the daily papers seize upon it; they have acquired, one may almost say of them, the habits of cannibals or ogres; they suck the brains of young writers, and then replace them by a new bevy of adolescent talent. Publishers also compete nowadays with editors in killing the goose whose golden eggs they live on. As soon as a young author makes a success his publisher urges him to repeat it at once; other publishers are eager to win his patronage, and he is not infrequently offered a fixed income on the condition that he shall regularly provide one or two volumes a year. It would be invidious to mention names, but in following the careers of the more recent writers whose first books have charmed me, I almost invariably find that their earliest publications, or at least their earliest successes, are their best achievements; their promise ripens to no fulfilment; each subsequent work tends to be a feeble replica and fainter echo of the first.

Maugham is more inclined to blame the talent that is so easily exhausted, and which he calls "the natural creativity of youth."

One of the tragedies of the arts is the spectacle of the vast numbers of persons who have been misled by this passing fertility to devote their lives to the effort of creation. Their invention deserts them as they grow older, and they are faced with the long years before them in which, unfitted by now for a more humdrum calling, they harass their wearied brain to beat out material it is incapable of giving them. They are lucky when, with what bitterness we know, they can make a living in ways, like journalism or teaching, that are allied to the arts.

The causes are interlocking. The trouble is that authors are not paid enough. If three hundred pounds were the normal advance on a book instead of fifty, a writer could take his time over it and refuse other work; that it is not is due to the intermediate profits and expenses of book production, and to the indifference of the reading public which is growing more impatient with books as it becomes more dependent on magazines. *The Reader's Digest* and its fellows will soon read the books for him.

The torpor of the reading public conditions the publisher; parsimonious to authors who fail to dispel that torpor, he is exacting and impatient with those who have succeeded. When publishers vacillate (and as repressed sadists are supposed to become policemen or butchers, so those with an irrational fear of life become publishers), the second villain, the editor, steps in—even Tennyson complained of him. "All the magazines and daily newspapers, which pounce upon everything they can get hold of, demoralize literature. This age gives an author no time to mature his work."

CHAPTER XI: THE BLUE BUGLOSS

Let us now tackle the problem of journalism—deadliest of the weeds on Crabbe's Heath—in its relation to literature. We have suggested that journalism must obtain its full impact on the first reading while literature can achieve its effect on a second, being intended for an interested and not an indifferent public. Consequently the main difference between them is one of texture. Journalism is loose, intimate, simple and striking; literature formal and compact, not simple and not immediately striking in its effects. Carelessness is not fatal to journalism nor are clichés, for the eye rests lightly on them. But what is intended to be read once can seldom be read more than once; a journalist has to accept the fact that his work, by its very to-dayness, is excluded from any share in to-morrow. Nothing dates like a sense of actuality, than which there is nothing in journalism more valuable. A writer who takes up journalism abandons the slow tempo of literature for a faster one and the change will do him harm. By degrees the flippancy of journalism will become a habit and the pleasure of being paid on the nail, and more especially of being praised on the nail, grow indispensable. And yet of the admirable journalism that has appeared in the literary weeklies, how little bears reprinting, how little even has been reprinted! The monthly and quarterly papers approximate more to literature and permit subjects to be treated at greater length, but they are few indeed! For brevity is all-important; it is the two-thousand-word look which betrays journalism, which makes the reader hurry on when he opens a volume of criticism and finds it to consist of jerky and disjointed essays, "The Prose of Keats," "Beddoes Revisited," "The English Hexameter," "Hazlitt's Aunt," "After Expressionism What?" "Miss Austen's Nephew," all with the fatal asterisk directing the reader to the title of some book once reviewed.

There are certain people who benefit from journalism. They are easily recognised and fall into two classes. The first are amateur writers who through lack of a public or through not having to consider a public, are verbose and obscure, who have acquired so many mannerisms or private meanings for the words they use or who employ such leisurely constructions that an editor alone, since they will not listen to their friends, can impatiently cure them. The other class who benefit are those well-stored minds who suffer from psychological sloth, and who can only reveal their treasures in short articles for quick returns. But this class includes few young writers and these would soon succumb to the atmosphere breathed with such impunity by a Hazlitt or by a wise old literary stager.

There is one other fortunate class: those who are masters of a literary style which so resembles journalism that they can make the transition from one tempo to the other without effort. Readers of *Abinger Harvest* by E. M. Forster will have found that there is about those essays nothing ephemeral since they are in the language of E. M. Forster the novelist. His literary style is cursive and no concession has to be made. The styles overlap; the tempos coincide. This is also true of Lytton Strachey who imposed his literary style on his editors. There are several writers in the same position as Forster. The danger for them is that, if their journalism is literature so is their literature journalism and Hemingway, for example, appears unable to distinguish between them, which accounts for the unevenness of such books as *Green Hills of Africa* or *Death in the Afternoon*.

Maugham detects another evil in journalism besides the vulgarisation of a writer's style.

There is an impersonality in a newspaper that insensibly affects the writer. People who write much for the press seem to lose the faculty of seeing things for themselves; they see them from a generalised standpoint, vividly often, sometimes with hectic brightness, yet never with that idiosyncrasy which may give only a partial picture of the facts, but is suffused by the personality of the observer. The press, in fact, kills the individuality of those who write for it.

Journalism for most writers means reviewing.

Let Walter Savage Shelleyblake be a young author. Let his book be called *Vernal Aires*. Soon will come the delicious summons from the literary editor of *The Blue Bugloss*. "Dear Shelleyblake, I was so interested to meet you the other night and have a chance to tell you what I think of *Vernal Aires*. I have been wondering if you would like to try your hand at a little reviewing for us. We are looking for someone to do the Nonesuch *Boswell*, and your name cropped up."

The Nonesuch *Boswell* alone is worth four guineas, and soon a signed review, "Expatriate from Auchinleck" by Walter Savage Shelleyblake, appears in the literary supplement of *The Blue Bugloss*. It is full of ideas and Mr. Vampire, the editor, bestows on it his praise. The next book which Shelleyblake reviews, on Erasmus Darwin, is not quite so good but his article "Swansong at Lichfield" is considered "extremely bright." Suddenly his name appears under a pile of tomes of travel; the secrets of Maya jungles, Kenya game-wardens and ricochetting American ladies are probed by him. In a year's time he will have qualified as a maid-of-all-work and be promoted to reviewing novels. It is promotion because the novel review is a regular feature, because more people read them and because publishers "care." If he is complimentary and quotable he will be immortalized on the dust wrapper and find his name in print on the advertisements. And eight or ten novels a fortnight, sold as review copies, add to his wage.

Certain facts must now be stated. However much Mr. Vampire admired *Vernal Aires* and however fond he is of Walter Shelleyblake, he is, before anything else, an editor. He is concerned with *The Blue Bugloss* and whether each number is bright enough to paint the sterile soil. In so far as he is developing in Walter latent gifts—competence, a turn for satire, lucidity, polish—his interests coincide; but they can never be identical, and the use Walter makes of these gifts is not his own concern but Mr. Vampire's. The competition for the best books, the Nonesuch *Boswells*, is fierce; Mr. Vampire is often lucky to get one of them himself and so if Shelleyblake is anxious to write several thousand words on the influence of Horace on English poetry or the psychological reasons for the retirement of Congreve, he will have to go on being anxious and hurry up with his copy on *Backstairs and Petticoats* (a chronicle of famous Royal Mistresses), or six more autobiographies, headed by *Fifty Years Down Under*.

Myself a lazy, irresolute person, overvain and overmodest, unsure in my judgments and unable to finish what I have begun, I have profited from journalism, owing to the admirable manipulation of my manager and trainer. Yet even so I would say to Shelleyblake, who clearly does not belong to the Hazlitt group, that any other way of making money would be better, that reviewing is a whole-time job with a half-time salary, a job in which the best in him is generally expended on the mediocre in others. A good review is only remembered for a fortnight; a reviewer has always to make his reputation afresh nor will he find time for private reading or writing, for he is too busy reading other people's books and this will disincline him to read when he is not working. The sight of his friends' books accumulating depresses him and he knows that, besides losing the time to write books of his own, he is also losing the energy and the application, frittering it away on tripe and discovering that it is his flashiest efforts which receive most praise.

There are not more than four or five posts in reviewing that carry with them money, freedom and dignity, whose holders can inherit the mantle of Arnold and Sainte-Beuve so that the most Shelleyblake can expect is that, by reading two books a day and writing for three papers, he may make about four hundred a year. During this time he will incur the hostility of authors, the envy of other reviewers and the distrust of his friends against whose books he will seem invariably prejudiced; the public will view him with indifference or accept him as an eccentric on whom they will launch their views and their manuscripts while old friends will greet him with, "Are you writing anything now?—apart of course from your articles," they will add. "I read you—but I don't say I agree with you," will be another approach, to which, "I know you, but I don't say I like you," is the correct answer.

No, if Walter Shelleyblake must be a journalist, there is but one chance for him. He must declare war on his employers and so manœuvre them that he never reviews a bad book, never reviews more than one at a time and never writes a review that cannot be reprinted, i.e. that is not of some length and on a subject of permanent value. He will know that the bad books he reads are like hours on a sun dial, *vulnerant omnes, ultima necat,* all wound, the last one mortally, neither will he spend himself on cheap subjects, nor put down his whole view of life in a footnote, for he will write only about what interests him. And whatever happens to him (and there are no pensions for literary hacks), he must realise that he is not indispensable.

> Brightness falls from the air,
> Queens have died young and fair . . .

but not *The Blue Bugloss,* and Mr. Vampire and his new young men will be perfectly able to get on without him.

CHAPTER XII: THE THISTLES

At the moment politics, the thistles

> . . . that stretch their prickly arms afar,
> And to the ragged infant threaten war

are more dangerous to young writers than journalism. They are dangerous because writers now feel that politics are necessary to them, without having learnt yet how best to be political.

Indifference to politics among artists has always been associated with a feeling of impotence. Thus those great non-politicals, the ivory-tower dwellers, flourished helpless, under the second Empire or in the Paris of 1870 after defeat in the Franco-Prussian war. English writers, in the late Victorian age, were equally helpless; only Kipling, who celebrated the jingoism and imperialism of the ruling class and the materialism of the time, and Shaw, who attacked them, obtained a political foothold. The "nineties" were a reaction of artists against a political world which they abhorred but could not alter. William Morris alone of the Victorian writers, combined poetry with socialism, while Tennyson's conception of the role of the poet as the supreme Endorser of new achievement in material progress was so forbidding as to deter younger writers from taking any interest in such subjects. This widespread indifference to politics crystallised into a theory that politics were harmful, that they were not artistic material of the first order, that an artist could not be a politician. Politics belonged to that realm of action which Proust and Strachey had discredited. A belief in action indicated a belief in progress, a belief in progress was Victorian and ridiculous.

Yet if we look at writers through the ages we see that they have always been political. Greek poets were political, they championed democracy or defended oligarchs and tyrants according to their sentiment. Pindar was political as were Aeschylus and Euripides, Plato and Aristotle, Catullus and Cicero, Virgil and Horace. Dante was engrossed in politics as were most of the artists of the Renaissance. Nobody told Byron he would be a better writer if he did not attempt *The Vision of Judgment* or Wordsworth not to bother with *Toussaint l'Ouverture;* Swift was not considered to have cheapened himself by *The Drapier Letters* or *The Conduct of the Allies,* nor Dryden to have let down poetry by *Absalom and Achitophel.* To deny politics to a writer is to deny him part of his humanity. But even from a list of political writers we can deduce that there are periods in the history of a country when writers are more political, or more writers are political than at others. They are not the periods of greatest political tension, they are those in which authors can do most, can be listened to, can be important, can influence people, and get their own way. Thus Roman poets ceased to be political after the Empire because they were powerless. A writer during the age of Augustus could not play the part of Catullus or Cicero. Writers flourish in a state of political flux, on the eve of the crisis, rather than in the crisis itself; it is before a war or a revolution that they are listened to and come into their own and it was because they were disillusioned at their impotence during the war that so many became indifferent to political issues after the peace.

It is clear that we are living now in a transition period as suited to political writing as were the days of Ship Money or the reign of Queen Anne. Writers can still change history by their pleading, and one who is not political neglects the vital intellectual issues of his time and disdains his material. He is not powerless, like the Symbolists of 1870, the æsthetes of the eighties and nineties, the beer-and-chivalry addicts of the nineteen hundreds or the demobilised Georgian poet on his chicken farm. He is not a victim of his time but a person who can alter it, though if he does not, he may soon find himself victimised. By ignoring the present he condones the future. He has to be political to

integrate himself and he must go on being political to protect himself. To-day the forces of life and progress are ranging on one side, those of reaction and death on the other.
We are having to choose between democracy and fascism,
and fascism is the enemy of art. It is not a question of
relative freedom; there are no artists in Fascist countries.
We are not dealing with an Augustus who will discover
his Horace and his Virgil, but with Attila or Hulaku, destroyers of European culture whose poets can contribute
only battle-cries and sentimental drinking songs. Capitalism
in decline, as in our own country, is not much wiser as a
patron than fascism. Stagnation, fear, violence and oppor-
tunism the characteristics of capitalism preparing for the
fray, are no background for a writer and there is a seediness, an ebb of life, a philosophy of taking rather than giving, a bitterness and brutality about right-wing writers now
which was absent in those of other days, in seventeenth-
century Churchmen or eighteenth-century Tories. There is
no longer a Prince Rupert, a Dr. Johnson, a Wellington,
Disraeli, or Newman, on the reactionary side.

We have seen that writers are politically-minded when
they are able to accomplish something; that these periods
are those of change, on the eve of revolutions and civil
wars and before the resort to arms takes matters out of
their control and we have seen that we are in such a period
now, and that unless writers do all they can it will be too
late; war will break out and the moment be past when
the eloquence of the artist can influence the destiny of
humanity.

If political writing is no more than the exercise of the
instinct of self-preservation, there can be no reason for class-
ing "politics" among the weeds that stifle writers. But there
are dangers about being political of which writers are unaware and so seldom avoid. Thus being political is apt to
become a whole-time job;

> To-day the expending of powers
> On the flat ephemeral pamphlet and the boring meeting,

writes Auden, though copies of his pamphlets are excessively rare. Canvassing, making speeches, and pamphleteering are not the best medium for sensitive writers. They involve much time and trouble and can be better performed by someone else. To command a listening senate, however, is a secret ambition of many writers and it is easy to justify it—to be "thankful that my words can be any comfort to these poor men," etc. The truth is that oratory is a coarser art than writing and that to become addicted to it is to substitute the ruses of the platform for the integrity of the pen. Neither is a writer improved by sitting on committees and cultivating the chairmanities.

Another effect of becoming too political is that such activity leads to disillusion. Thus writers become disheartened by the vulgarity of politicians. They find it hard to realise that the militants and executives of a movement may be narrow-minded, envious, ambitious and ungrateful, yet their cause remain fundamentally just and right. Their political judgment is often unsound for they refuse to allow for the slow motions of public opinion; they are disheartened by personal rebuffs and bored by drudgery. Defeatism is their occupational disease.

Politicians, on their side, can be unappreciative. Their favourite arts are those which are enjoyed in relaxation: light music or Mickey Mouse, *The Oxford Book of English Verse*, Edgar Wallace, Wodehouse, Webb. They do not like art to be exacting and difficult; they may envy the artists who collaborate with them because they do not understand their success, but with their idealism and their tender consciences they seem to them priggish and patronising. The enmities of highbrow and lowbrow, man of action and man of thought, classical side and modern side are not yet buried and reappear, over the ephemeral pamphlet or at the boring meeting, in unexpected forms.

In what way then should a writer be political? How can he make best use of his weapons?

Firstly, by satire. This is a satirical age and among the vast reading public the power of an artist to awaken ridicule has never been so great. To make the enemies of freedom look silly, to write like Low's cartoons or like

> I met murder on the way,
> He wore the mask of Castlereagh,

is the duty of any who can.

Then, if he is intelligent, he can analyse situations, draw attention to tendencies, expose contradictions and help his more active colleagues by cultivating lucidity, profundity and detachment. And lastly, he can help to contribute the idealism without which any movement fails. He must, in his serious writing, avoid propaganda and the presence in his work of lumps of unassimilated political material.[1] Like the termites who chew up the food for the fighters his rôle is to digest the experience they bring him. For this reason the poets are the best political writers for they have the best digestions, and can absorb their material. A poem like *Locksley Hall,* which has been so distilled, remains an alive and contemporary piece of thought.

> I must mix myself with action lest I wither in despair
> What is that which I should turn to, lighting upon days like
>   these?

[1] It is objectionable because it introduces into the form a lower level of workmanship, that of the pamphlet or the tract, and an imperfect fusion with the creative process. Propaganda is betrayed by an air of naïveté, as in, "Tomorrow he would canvas as he had never canvassed before," and "I had met the insidious power of Ann and defeated it, and now there was a splendid synthesis forming inside me," or "He was an admirable man and I felt warmed and happy when I looked at him. At Oxford he got up and stretched. I think he had read every word of the *Daily Worker* in the eighty minutes since we had left Paddington." Those are from a very young author. Here is an example from Upward:

" 'There will be a time of harshness and bitter struggle, but out of it will come flowers; splendour and joy will come back to the world. And life will be better than it has ever been in the world's history.'

" 'How soon can I join the worker's movement?'

" '. . . You can join some time within the next few days.'

" 'I don't want to wait.' "

This passage in a thoughtful novel brings a whiff of the Salvation Army. Right-wing propaganda, however, can be detected by an appeal to the reader to be "realistic."

Every door is barred with gold, and opens but to golden
 keys,
Every gate is thronged with suitors, all the markets overflow
I have but an angry fancy: what is that which I should do?

And so we find the best modern political writing in such
a book as Spender's *Trial of a Judge* or a poem like Day
Lewis's,

> Yet living here,
> As one between two massing powers I live,
> Whom neutrality cannot save
> Nor occupation cheer.

The novelists who feel their responsibilities are also
searching for something deeper and more universal than
superficial realism and are finding it in the allegory. A story
of Isherwood's like *The Novaks*, shows how political reality
can inform and deepen, can be informed and deepened, by
private experiences; and Spender's *Cousins* and his *Burning
Cactus* are also excellent illustrations. To strike deep and
keep general should be the maxim of the political artist,
and he should avoid describing any experience that he has
not first integrated and made part of him. He must take
pains with his vocabulary for political writing is honey-
combed with clichés; having been deadened to their meaning by oratory, politicians have no feeling for words; a
phrase which seems healthy at night will be on the sick-list
by morning. There is a tendency for left-wing journalists
to criticise left-wing poets for being obscure which is dangerous and stupid. The public are not expected to understand the formulas from which are evolved a new explosive
or a geodetic aeroplane. The poet is a chemist and there is
more pure revolutionary propaganda in a line of Blake than
in all *The Rights of Man*.

But if he wishes to be respected by politicians, to be
treated as an ally to whom a certain eccentricity is permitted, a writer must let them alone and refrain from taking
sides in political quarrels. There is a general left-wing position which has never been defined but which permits a
working agreement with the parties, as they now stand,

and which is well suited to a writer. To abandon this general position is safe for a militant journalist; for an artist, it may lead to a damaging retreat. There is so much side-choosing, heresy-hunting, witch-burning and shadow cabinet-making among the parties of the left, so much victory mentality among people for whom victory is most uncertain, that caution in a writer should be welcome. It is no time to quarrel with our own side.

I will conclude this excursion among the Thistles by quoting two points of view of left-wing writers, both communists, Upward and Stephen Spender. Upward, I find, is too logical for the times, his pronouncement on the only possible way for a writer to live is reminiscent of Tolstoy's socialist analysis of art which proved that Hugo's *Les Misérables* and Harriet Stowe's *Uncle Tom's Cabin* were the two great books of the nineteenth century. Spender lacks the narrowness and aridity of Marxist critics.

> A writer to-day who wishes to produce the best work that he is capable of producing, must first of all become a socialist in his practical life, must go over to the progressive side of the class conflict. . . . He must be told frankly that joining the workers' movement does mean giving less time to imaginative writing, but that unless he joins it his writing will become increasingly false, worthless as literature. Going over to socialism may prevent him, but failing to go over *must* prevent him from writing a good book (*The Mind in Chains*).

What is meant by "going over"? Upward thinks it must mean the abandonment of the bourgeois life and immersion in the work of the socialist parties. I do not think so. I think a writer "goes over" when he has a moment of conviction that his future is bound up with that of the working classes. Once he has felt this his behaviour will inevitably alter. Often it will be recognised only by external symptoms, a disinclination to wear a hat or a stiff collar, an inability to be rude to waiters or taxi-drivers or to be polite to young men of his own age with rolled umbrellas, bowler hats and "Mayfair men" moustaches or to tolerate the repressive measures of his class. He is like a caterpillar whose skin dulls and whose appetite leaves it before becoming a chrysalis. Often a writer is unable to go over. He approaches the barrier, shies, and runs away. Such writers will externalise their feelings and satirise those who have made the transition, who have jumped off the slowly moving train for the one which they believe leads towards life and the future. The angriest are the most frightened. But these fears can be surmounted by a moment of vision. It may be practical, a glimpse of the power of the writer in the socialist state or of his impotence in a capitalist one, going in perhaps, like Turgenev, sixty-first at a fashionable dinner or it may be a mystical feeling of release and emancipation. It is too early yet to say whether writers have done anything for Spain, but it is clear that Spain has done an immense amount for writers, since many have had that experience there and have come back with their fear changed to love, isolation to union and indifference to action.

This is a time then when anyone who is anxious to avert a protracted world war will have to work very hard to undermine the whole system of armed alliances. If we hope to go on existing, if we want a dog's chance of the right to breathe, to go on being able to write, it seems that we have got to make some choice outside the private entanglements of our personal life. We have got to try somehow to understand that objective life moving down on us like a glacier, but which, after all, is essentially not a glacier but an historic process, the life of people like ourselves, and therefore our "proper study".

Ultimately, however interested the writer may be as a person, as an artist he has got to be indifferent to all but what is objectively true. The road the future will tread may be the road of Communism, but the road of the artist will always be some way infinitely more difficult than one which is laid down in front of him.

These two quotations are from Stephen Spender's *Destructive Element*, and express a point of view that is sometimes forgotten. Political writing is dangerous writing, it deals not in words, but in words that affect lives, and is a weapon that should be entrusted only to those qualified to

use it. Thus a burst of felicitous militancy with the pen may
send three young men to be killed in Spain; for whose
deaths the author is responsible. If human beings have any
right they have the right to know what they are dying for.
"Better live an hour as a lion than a lifetime as a lamb" is
stencilled all over Italy—but supposing one is a lamb?

There is one last warning that must be given. In Blake's
words, "The eagle never lost so much time as when it submitted to learn from the crow"—and if we look back at the
political activities of artists, however necessary and satisfy-
ing they may have seemed at the time, now that time is
past it is not by them they are remembered. Milton's
poetry is read more than the *Areopagitica*. Marvell's pamphlets are read not at all, the political poems of Shelley and
Byron are not preferred to their lyrics, the Houyhnhnms are
more familiar to us than the *Conduct of the Allies. Robinson
Crusoe* means more than the *True Born Englishman, The
Lotus Eaters* than *Locksley Hall.* The writers who were
most political in the last war are not the most famous. Zola
too was more political than Flaubert, Lamartine than
Baudelaire and the truth is that the value of political experience to a writer's art is indirect. Not Milton's polemical
prose is the justification of his political life, but his character
of Satan, his great assemblages in Hell. And this is true to-
day, so that a writer whose stomach cannot assimilate with
genius the starch and acid of contemporary politics, had
better turn down his plate.

CHAPTER XIII: THE POPPIES

Let us now glance at the poppies, at the danger which is becoming known as "escapism." This is not a significant word, for in itself escaping cannot be right or wrong nor worthy of comment until we know from what danger the escapist is fleeing and whether flight is his best method of preservation. Escaping from a concentration camp or a burning building is admirable, escaping from responsibility, like the patient who wrote to his psychiatrist that he was "only happy when he had cast off every shred of human dignity" is sometimes not. We are all destroyed through that first escapist, Eve, and saved by the second who built an ark. The word is generally employed by realists to beat romantics with; thus it was "escapist" to live at Tossa or Torre Molinos till 1936, when the centre of actuality shifted, and Sir Peter Chalmers-Mitchell who had retired to end his days in the sun, found himself, for a few hours in Malaga, in the intenser glare of History.[1]

---

[1] Expatriation is often beneficial, as a stage in which the writer cuts adrift from irritating influences. It is a mistake to expect good work from expatriates for it is not what they do that matters but what they are not doing. It gives them a breathing-space in which to free themselves from commercialism, family and racial ties or from the "gentleman complex" which attacks public-school and university writers, just as the spectre of their "family business" haunts American ones. Only occasionally does a writer create a work out of his expatriation, Hemingway's *The Sun Also Rises* is such an exception. (Henry James was not an expatriate in so far as he repatriated himself as an Englishman —he exchanged American Society for international society and then settled down as an English man of letters.) It is important however to distinguish between the flight of the expatriate which is an essential desire for simplification, for the cutting of ties, the writer "finding" himself in the hotel bedroom or the café on the harbour and the brisker trajectory of the travel addict, trying not to find but to lose himself in the intoxication of

It is vain to accuse people of escaping from contemporary reality. Time is not uniform for all of us, neither is our imagination's food nor our artistic material. We cannot all do our best work with the sun in our eyes. There is but one crime; to escape from our talent, to abort that growth which, ripening and maturing, must be the justification of the demands we make on society.

At present the realities are life and death, peace and war, fascism and democracy; we are in a world which may soon become unfit for human beings to live in. A writer must decide at what remove from this conflagration he can produce his best work and be careful to keep there. Often a writer who is escaping from his own talent, from the hound of heaven, will run into what appears to be reality and, like a fox bolting into a farm kitchen, will seek sanctuary from his pursuers in group activities outside. And after a time the hounds will be called off, the pursuit weaken—a signal that the Muses no longer wish to avail themselves of his potentialities. Thus among the hardest workers in political parties will be found, like Rimbaud at Harar, those whom the God has forsaken.

The old-fashioned boltholes of writers who do not wish to undertake the responsibility of creating a work of art are no longer so easy of access. Drink is available and there are still artists who drink to excess out of the consciousness of wasted ability, for drunkenness is a substitute for art; it is in itself a low form of creation. But it is not drink which is the temptation, since that is but a symptom of the desire for self-forgetfulness, as is also the case with drugs which play small part in the literary life in England though among French writers opium has made such headway.

The harmless activities of daydreaming and conversation are more insidious. Daydreaming bears a specious resemblance to the workings of the creative imagination. It is in fact a substitute for it and one in which all difficulties are shelved, all problems ignored, a short cut ending in a blank wall. This is even more true of conversation; a good

motion. "How narrow is the line," as Nicolson wrote of Byron's last journey, "which separates an adventure from an ordeal, and escape from exile."

talker can talk away the substance of twenty books in as many evenings. He will describe the central idea of the book he means to write until it revolts him.

As journalism brings in quicker returns than literature, so the profits of conversation are more immediate than those of journalism. By the silence which he commands, the luxury of his décor, and by the glow from the selected company who have been asked to meet him, a good talker is paid almost before he opens his mouth. The only happy talkers are dandies who extract pleasure from the very perishability of their material and who would not be able to tolerate the isolation of all other forms of composition; for most good talkers, when they have run down, are miserable; they know that they have betrayed themselves, that they have taken material which should have a life of its own, to dispense it in noises upon the air.

Than good conversation nothing is sooner forgotten and those who remember it do so unconsciously and reproduce it as their own. Coleridge, Swinburne, Wilde, Harry Melville, Vernon Lee—not much survives now of the conversation of these mighty-mouthed international geysers. They were at the mercy of a few indolent, forgetful, and envious listeners. If we try to record the spoken word of one of these chrysostoms it becomes apparent that 30 per cent of their talk is a series of reassuring and persuasive qualifications, a buttonholing of the listener; it is the ardour of the talker's wooing which convinces the audience of the splendour of his talk. This is not true of talkers of the old school like Bernard Berenson who use their golden tongues for denunciation, but modern conversationalists make too free a use of the glad eye. They are apologetic, not only because they monopolise and individualise in an age opposed to these things, but because they are taking part in a ceremony of self-wastage and their audience knows it.

Sometimes when in flight from the demands of talent, from the bite of the gadfly, writers will seek refuge in gentility, in ancestor-worship or by becoming members of an unliterary sporting class. They will breed bulldogs, hunt, shoot, attend race-meetings and try to lose contact with all other writers except those whose guilt is of equal standing.

This instinct to hide themselves in a world where books are unheard of in no way resembles the artist's desire for *"luxe, calme, et volupté,"* for a lavish, ostentatious life, but is a particularly English affliction and it is no exaggeration to say that nearly every English author since Byron and Shelley has been hamstrung by respectability and been prevented by snobbery and moral cowardice from attaining his full dimensions. It is this blight of insular gentility which accounts for the difference between Dickens, Thackeray, Arnold, Tennyson, Pater and Tolstoy, Flaubert, Rimbaud, Baudelaire, Gide; it is the distinction between being a good fellow or growing up.

There remains one other major escape, religion. It is not so common now for writers to join a church. I know two Anglo-Catholic and one Roman Catholic convert among my contemporaries. All three are people of exceptional sensibility, poetically-minded writers for whom the ugliness of materialism is a source of horror. Are they escaping from their talent or from conditions which would have rendered impossible the use of it? We must wait and see. Religious faith involves the surrender of the intellect but not of the sensibility, which under its protection may long continue to develop. Yet for an intellectual, joining a church implies regression, it is a putting on of blinkers, a hiding under the skirts of one of the great reactionary political forces of the world and the poet drawn to the confessional by the smell of incense finds himself defending the garotte and Franco's Moors. Art becomes a means not an end to the churchman as to the politician. Churches are the retreat of artists with æsthetic appreciation, delicate humour, ethical sensibility and a sense of spiritual reality, who lack the enquiring mind, the constructive intellectual fearlessness which is the historic factor in Western civilisation and which has now moved far onwards from religion.

But in vain we discuss the nature of the poppies which put writers to sleep or try to restrict their use. Since those who are escaping from their talent employ them, let us find out why they are escaping. Many are in flight for psychological reasons which belong to their childhood and with which this book is not competent to deal. But in authors who have dried up, who have put their hobby before their vocation, who now are doing well in the city or who collect first editions or old dust-wrappers, who run chicken-farms or sit and solve Greek cross-word puzzles, who write detective stories or who have transferred their sensibility to cheese and old claret, there is one fact in common. They have all been promising.

Promise! Fatal word, half-bribe and half-threat, round whose exact meaning centred many tearful childhood interviews. "But you promised you wouldn't," "But *that* wasn't a promise," "Yes it was—you haven't kept your promise," till the meaning expands and the burden of the oath under which we grew up becomes the burden of expectation which we can never fulfil. "Blossom and blossom and promise of blossom, but never a fruit"—the cry first heard in the nursery is taken up by the schoolmaster, the friendly aunt, the doting grandmother, the inverted bachelor uncle. Dons with long reproachful faces will utter it and the friends of dons; the shapes and simulacrums which our parents have taken, the father-substitutes and mother-types which we have projected will accuse us and all await our ritual suicide. Whom the gods wish to destroy they first call promising.

Young writers if they are to mature require a period of between three and seven years in which to live down their promise. Promise is like the mediæval hangman who after settling the noose, pushed his victim off the platform and jumped on his back, his weight acting as a drop while his jockeying arms prevented the unfortunate from loosening the rope. When he judged him dead he dropped to the ground. Promise is that dark spider with which many writers are now wrestling in obscurity and silence. Occasionally they win and the load of other people's wish-fulfilments is cast off; they produce a book; more often after a struggle for breath they are stifled for ever. Let us listen in to them for a moment, poor wretches, on whom the executioner calls in the small hours.

Two o'clock. You won't accomplish anything now. Do you remember all the things you wanted to be? How Granny loved you! How we pinched and scraped to keep you at Oxford—and then those horrible bills! They killed Granny, you know, though we didn't tell you at the time. Now you're old enough to know. It wasn't that she minded the money—it was the thought you could ever do anything dishonourable. You did promise, you remember? That you could give all those bad cheques! Your father never got over it. Oh, we were all so proud of you. How could you, how could you, how could you!

Three o'clock. We always hoped you'd write. A serious book, I mean. We can't count the kind of stuff you're doing now. I know a high academic degree is not always the true justification for three years here. There are many people whose careers after leaving college bring us more distinction than anything they achieve while they are up. We take a long view. But I think you'll agree we were very patient with you and I doubt if the stuff you are turning out now will prove we were right. Still we must be tolerant. I had hoped great things for you and I dare say I was rather silly. Anyhow I shall always be glad to hear from you.

Why didn't you write to him? He would so have loved a letter. He often spoke of you before he died. I may say he was deeply hurt at what he considered, rightly or wrongly, your ingratitude. He had been fond of you in spite of everything. If you'd even troubled to send him a postcard! Why didn't you? Why didn't you? Why didn't you?

Four o'clock. Teeth hurt? I don't envy you at forty. Just as you're going to sleep you give a kind of twitch all over and wake up! H'm—a kind of noise like a clock makes before it strikes goes off at the back of your nose? That's bad! Your heart seems to miss a beat and you sit right up in bed with a jerk? Your blood beats too fast? Your mind races along? You can't breathe properly? Your bladder troubles you? A kind of dull aching pain somewhere in the side? You think it must be the spleen? H'm—— And a sharp searing pain in the oesophagus? That all? Oh yes—and a feeling like someone blowing up a balloon at the back of the nose? I wonder if you have some near relative or great friend whom I could talk to, just to check up on your family history. Your mother? Good. Well, Mr. Shelleyblake, if you don't mind waiting in here I think I'll try and get right through on the phone to her.

Five o'clock. *How old are you?* H'm, I see. Just about halfway. And you've done precisely what? H'm. Well, I must be off. Another patient. Sleep well, see you to-morrow, same time, same place.

·   ·   ·   ·   ·   ·   ·

Sloth in writers is always a symptom of an acute inner conflict, especially that laziness which renders them incapable of doing the thing which they are most looking forward to. The conflict may or may not end in disaster, but their silence is better than the over-production which must so end and slothful writers such as Johnson, Coleridge, Greville, in spite of the nodding poppies of conversation, morphia and horse-racing, have more to their credit than Macaulay, Trollope or Scott. To accuse writers of being idle is a mark of envy or stupidity—La Fontaine slept continually and scarcely ever opened his mouth; Baudelaire, according to Dr. Laforgue, feared to perfect his work because he feared the incest with his mother which was his perfect fulfilment. Perfectionists are notoriously lazy and all true artistic indolence is deeply neurotic; a pain not a pleasure.

CHAPTER XIV: THE CHARLOCK'S SHADE

Sex, the charlock's shade, is no more the danger that it was and seldom do we meet with a syphilitic Baudelaire, squandering his fortune, and ruining his health for a coloured mistress; the temptations of artists to-day are group-temptations in which the Cynaras and the Jeanne Duvals play little part. However for a writer to be too fond of women is not uncommon and the result may be found that they make crippling demands on his time and his money, especially if they set their hearts on his popular success. The charlock or wild mustard throws a more baleful shade on the young shoot when it is the love that dare not speak its name.

Many writers have been homosexual or gone through a homosexual period and, although from a literary standpoint it is enriching, they must grasp the limitations of homosexuality and plan production accordingly. Thus a male homosexual, if cut off by his attitude from experience with women, will have a certain difficulty in depicting them. This is not of consequence if he is, for example, a critic or a poet who works at that intense and sublimated level at which passion is general and the object of such passion without importance. But many writers are neither poets nor critics, and for novelists, short-story writers and playwrights, difficulties arise. Thus homosexual novelists who are able to create mother-types and social mother-types (hostesses) and occasionally sister-types (heroines) have trouble with normal women and may often make them out worse or better than they are. They are forced to describe things they know little about because so much of life is concerned with them. Courtship, marriage, childbearing and adultery play a major part in existence, a knowledge of the relations between men and women is essential to a novelist, and a comparison of, say, *War and Peace* with novels written by less normal authors will show how few acquire it. The heroine of *War and Peace*, Natasha, is a delightful creature, but she is capable of leaving her hero and running away with a man whom she does not love, after a single meeting, because he looked at her in a certain way. But she remains delightful because Tolstoy continues to find her lovable for being human. If Natasha had been one of Proust's heroines he would have turned her into a monster, she would have been analysed till nothing remained of her but lust and self-interest.

Nor is Proust's system of giving the male characters in his life girls' names and putting them as girls into his novels satisfactory. Their real sex protrudes and they have no plausible relationships with other characters in the books (Albertine is unreal when she confronts Charlus or Swann or the Duchesse de Guermantes; there is an ambiguous cloud over her relations with the author), and they are incapable of childbearing, home-making, husband-cheering or any of the drabber functions of woman. There is no solution for these problems. Nothing, for example, will make the two amorous young girls in *The Importance of Being Earnest* either young or amorous. The homosexual writer, until we can change society, must construct his books so as to avoid situations where a knowledge of such women is required, just as stammerers avoid certain words and substitute others. Otherwise the equipment of the homosexual writer: combativeness, curiosity, egotism, intuition and adaptability, is greatly to be envied.

The clasping tares of domesticity represent the opposite danger, and these too have grown less formidable. The harried author who sits in a garret surrounded by screaming children, with duns at the door and a sick wife nagging from the bed, is a thing of the past. But there remains some substance in the vision. The initial difficulty is in the sensitive writer's inability to live alone. The more he is alone the more he falls in love, if he falls in love he is almost certain to marry, if he marries he is apt to take a house and have children, if he has a house and children he needs more money, must do uncongenial work and so deny himself the freedom which may have inspired him.

The homosexual is unable to treat of a section of the life of human beings but in return he is free from the limitations of that life. He is apt to have a private income, he renews himself by travel, he has time for old friends and for the making of new ones and as he grows old remains isolated, free from responsibilities and ties and if he has been able to break free from the parasitism which is the weakness of homosexuals, he is detached. If he has joined the creative class, he is likely to become, like Gide, the "lonely old artist-man" that Henry James called himself.

In recent times the balance of literary success late in life is in favour of the childless writer. Children dissipate the longing for immortality which is the compensation of the childless writer's work. But it is not only a question of children or no children, there is a moment when the cult of home and happiness becomes harmful and domestic happiness one of those escapes from talent which we have deplored, for it replaces that necessary unhappiness without which writers perish. A writer is in danger of allowing his talent to dull who lets more than a year go past without finding himself in his rightful place of composition, the small single unluxurious "retreat" of the twentieth century, the hotel bedroom.

The fertility of the writer is often counterchecked by the happiness of the man. Each does not want the same thing and where their desires conflict, the writer-self will be the one to suffer. The "animal serenity," the "broad human touch" which Maugham envies in great writers, in Tolstoy and perhaps, in Thackeray and Dickens, can only be obtained by a series of experiences which have extinguished the lesser artists who have attempted them. As far as one can infer from observation it is a mistake for writers to marry young, especially for them to have children young; early marriage and paternity are a remedy for loneliness and unhappiness that set up a counter irritation. Writers choose wives, not for their money nor for their appreciation of art but for their beauty and a baby is even less capable of seeing the artist's point of view. As Tennyson put it—

O love, we two shall go no longer
To lands of summer across the sea;
So dear a life your arms enfold
Whose crying is a cry for gold.

Thus there would seem little to choose between the tares and the charlock. The homosexual avoids domesticity, he pays a price but pays it with his eyes open, the normal author walks into a trap. Most young writers are weak and know little about their weaknesses or their predicaments. They make a rush for the solution which promises them an immediate advantage and are not apprehensive of its after-effects. If they find the years when they come to London after the cosiness of the university unendurable then they marry the first person whom they can. They work hard to make money, grow torpid with domesticity and their writing falls off. After seven years or so they often divorce and their talent is given another chance which (it depends on how they marry again) may or may not be taken.

In general it may be assumed that a writer who is not prepared to be lonely in his youth must if he is to succeed face loneliness in his middle age. The hotel bedroom awaits him. If, as Dr. Johnson said, a man who is not married is only half a man, so a man who is very much married is only half a writer. Marriage can succeed for an artist only where there is enough money to save him from taking on uncongenial work and a wife who is intelligent and unselfish enough to understand and respect the working of the un-friendly cycle of the creative imagination. She will know at what point domestic happiness begins to cloy, where love, tidiness, rent, rates, clothes, entertaining and rings at the doorbell should stop and will recognise that there is no more sombre enemy of good art than the pram in the hall.

Some critics encourage a mystical belief in talent. They hold that in the nature of things it must come to fruition, that "if it is in you it's bound to come out," that true genius can neither be depressed by illness or poverty nor destroyed by success or failure. They go so far as to claim that people die at the right time, that Keats and Shelley had nothing more to say, that Marlowe or André Chénier met their violent deaths at the appropriate moment. This fatuous romantic fatalism is based on an optimistic nature and a refusal to face facts. If Milton had been drowned like *Lycidas*, there would have been people to say that he would never have written anything else. But talent is something which grows and which does not ripen except in the right kind of soil and climate. It can be neglected or cultivated and will flower or die down. To suppose that artists will muddle through without encouragement and without money because in the past there have been exceptions is to assume that salmon will find their way to the top of a river to spawn in spite of barrages and pollution. "If it's in you it's bound to come out" is a wish-fulfilment. More often it stays in and goes bad.

Fewer counsels and more money is what every artist must demand from society and it is the idiocy of society in refusing these demands, except to servile and indifferent performers, which is largely responsible for the present line-up of artists against that society.[1] Capitalism is expelling the artist as Spain expelled her Jews or France her Huguenots and the effects will soon be apparent; the French nobles who had Voltaire flogged acted with similar foresight.

[1] I should like to see the custom introduced of readers who are pleased with a book sending the author some small cash token: anything between half-a-crown and a hundred pounds. Authors would then receive what their publishers give them as a flat rate and their "tips" from grateful readers in addition, in the same way that waiters receive a wage from their employers and also get what the customer leaves on the plate. Not more than a hundred pounds—that would be bad for my character—not less than half-a-crown—that would do no good to yours.

CHAPTER XV: THE SLIMY MALLOWS

Of all the enemies of literature, success is the most insidious. The guides whom we have quoted, whose warnings
come through to us from various parts of the field, are unan-
imous against this danger. Pearsall-Smith quotes Trollope,
"Success is a poison that should only be taken late in life
and then only in small doses." Maugham writes,

> The common idea that success spoils people by mak-
> ing them vain, egotistic, and self-complacent is erroneous;
> on the contrary it makes them, for the most part, hum-
> ble, tolerant, and kind. Failure makes people bitter and
> cruel. Success improves the character of a man, it does
> not always improve the character of an author.

Success for a writer is of three kinds, social, professional
or popular. All three bring money but in none of them is
money all-important. Success is bad for a writer because
it cuts him off from his roots, raises his standard of living
and so leads to overproduction, lowers his standard of criticism and encourages the germ of its opposite, failure.

Social success was the variety which most appealed to
writers up to the Slump, for social success, besides gratify-
ing the snobbery which is inherent in romantic natures, also
provided them with delightful conditions, with the freedom
and protection of large country houses.

There are writers for whom such success is beneficial,
who find there the material they need and the leisure to
absorb it; their public is also found among the world of
fashion. Thus if Proust had been a social failure, if Pope
had never been asked to a ball nor Henry James presented
to a duchess, *The Rape of the Lock*, the *Côté de Guermantes*, *The Ambassadors*, could never have been written.
It is clear that a social success benefits some writers and is

bad for others; it is because we envy it more than other success that we denounce it so often. Writers are helped by it if they are dandies or lyricists; if they have suffered from poverty to the extent of being warped or weakened rather than braced or steadied by it; if they are homosexuals who need a frame to expand on, a beanstalk to climb up or the kind of backing which will impress and so free them from the domination of middle-class parents; it is good for satirists and playwrights, priests and poets. Congreve, Gay, Wilde were all the better for "being taken up" for they were whisked away to the field best suited for the flowering of their gifts, nor would Donne and Jeremy Taylor have written great prose had they delivered their wonderful sermons to a slum parish. It must be remembered that in fashionable society can be found warmhearted people of delicate sensibility who form permanent friendships with artists which afford them ease and encouragement for the rest of their lives and provide them with sanctuary. Lady Suffolk's friendship with Pope, Lord Sheffield's with Gibbon, Horace Walpole's for Gray, Lady Gregory's for Yeats, Lady Cunard's for George Moore, acted as conservatories where the artist's talents ripened at a suitable temperature, neither forced too quickly, nor exposed to the rigours of the Grub Street winter. That Milton or Blake or Keats or Hopkins did not require such friendships does not discredit those who do.

> Blest be the great for those they take away
> And those they leave me. . . .

But apart from these especial intimacies or from such a comfortable greenhouse as Holland House, there is little to be derived from an indiscriminating indulgence in fashionable society. That society is hard-hearted, easily bored and will exact from a writer either a succession of masterpieces or a slavish industry in providing amusement at its own level, while he in his turn acquires an appetite for external values, which, besides being hard to gratify, creates professional hostility and excludes him from a larger world in which he might be happily employed. The people for whom social success is most dangerous are the realists who have

no place among such unreality, the militants whose weapons rust in that atmosphere or writers like Bennett who
have already found their material, and can only deteriorate
when transplanted.[1] The best that can happen for a writer
is to be taken up very late or very early, when either old
enough to take its measure, or so young that when dropped
by society he has all life before him. Married writers in
particular are tormented by the contrast between the world
where they dine and the world in which they wake up for
breakfast, nor are the relations between writers' wives and
worldly hostesses renowned for cordiality.

Unfortunately the danger is past. Fashionable society is
no longer a temptation as when it maintained a cultural
standard. The singing birds nest no more in the great country houses; our Henry Jameses and Robert Brownings of to-
day are not met roaring for lunch in Belgrave Square.
"Cliveden's proud alcove" has no Pope to sing in it.
Maugham has shown that it is possible to possess and not
be possessed by society; Forster that it is quite easy to do
without it altogether, while Moore has summed it up:
"Well-mannered people do not think sincerely, their minds
are full of evasions and subterfuges . . . To be aristocratic
in Art one must avoid polite society." A young writer must
be careful not to pay the world more attention than it gives
him, he may satirise it but is not advised to celebrate it, nor
become its champion, for the moribund will turn on their
defenders.[2]

Professional success, the regard of fellow artists and
would-be artists is a true delight, for it is absurd to assume

[1] Thus a writer not intended for social success was Swift, and
it is interesting to notice what snobbish intoxication, what unpleasant vanity creep into the *Journal to Stella* at the height of
his "swingboat" or fashionable period. Johnson's comment on
Addison's marriage to Lady Warwick may also be considered:
"The marriage if uncontradicted report can be credited, made
no addition to his happiness, it neither found them nor made
them equal. . . . It is certain that Addison has left behind him
no encouragement of ambitious love."

[2] When suffering from social envy of other writers there is
only one cure—to work. Whatever consideration they are enjoying may then come your way and in any case by working you
are doing what they would most envy you.

that good writers cannot be famous in their lifetime. There
have always been a few thousand judges of good literature,
and these judges have recognised talent however unusual
and uncontemporary, even as they have accorded to masterpieces of the past an appreciation independent of fashion. Thus nobody could be more forgotten than the poet
Campbell yet the other day John Betjeman pointed out
three lines from *The Battle of the Baltic* which he admired.

> . . . When each gun
> From its adamantine lips
> Spread a death-shade round the ships
> Like a hurricane eclipse
> Of the sun.

Yet Tennyson, according to Palgrave, singled out the "death
shade" for praise when he was compiling the *Golden
Treasury,* even as he admired Marvell's *To His Coy Mistress*
or Cowper's *Poplars,* poems outside the general range of
Victorian sensibility. These celebrators of the unfashionable
best are the custodians of taste, the bodyguard of talent,
like Maurice Baring who has kept alive, in *Have You Anything to Declare,* French poetry that would be lost to English readers were it not for his impartial ear. In similar fashion Strachey wrote about Racine, Pearsall-Smith about
Sainte-Beuve and Madame de Sévigné, writers who tend
to be ignored owing to the cult of more violent sensations,
while Diderot, St. Evremond, Shenstone and Cowper have
all of late received sensitive homage.

If a professional success is painful in that it arouses the
envy of the ex-artists, a popular success is fatal. Much has
been written on the subject; I will try to summarise.

Success is a kind of moving staircase, from which an
artist, once on, has great difficulty in getting off, for whether
he goes on writing well or not, he is carried upwards, encouraged by publicity, by fan-mail, by the tributes of critics
and publishers and by the friendly clubmanship of his new
companions. The fan-mail gives the writer a sense of a mission. "Well, if I have made them forget their troubles for a
moment, my stuff may be some good." Publicity also seems
innocuous since once a writer is "news" he continues to be

so independently of his own wishes; besides it helps to sell his books. As for the critics' habit of praising a first book and damning a second, that can be put down to a personal grievance. "I regard every attack," a writer once told me, "as worth about sixpence a word."

A popular success may depend on the entertainment value of a writer or his political quality or his human touch. Those with the human touch never recover; their sense of mission grows overwhelming. Neither harsh reviews, the contempt of equals nor the indifference of superiors can affect those who have once tapped the great heart of suffering humanity and found out what a gold-mine it is. Writers who have a political success may keep their heads, for they may soon experience a political disappointment.

I myself had that experience. I went three times to Spain. The first time I returned with enthusiasm and wrote an enthusiastic and popular article. The second time I came back less hopeful but still militant and fire-eating and my articles were still successful. The third time I returned with a hopeless premonition of defeat; all I was certain of was the weakness of the Aragon front, the dissension (which broke out in the May fighting) among the Catalans and the enormous difficulties which faced the Government in procuring food and materials for war. Knowing Spanish (unlike the other fire-eaters) I had the misfortune to receive many confidences from people who already showed a personal weariness of the war. I came back with a septic throat, and the feeling that we experience when we see a tired fox crossing a field with the hounds and the port-faced huntsmen pounding after it. I could either conceal this feeling and try to write another fire-eater, or say nothing at all, or tell the truth. I thought the readers of my paper had the right to know the truth as I saw it and so I wrote a depressing article, recording the points of view of different people I had met and adding my own reflections. It was the time when Malaga and Bilbao fell and the article made me immensely unpopular. I had been unpopular before for saying *Journey's End* was a bad play and for criticising the deification of Housman, but literary unpopularity was very different from the political kind, from being called a coward, a Fascist, a stabber-in-the-back, etc., and, grateful to my escapism, I fled abroad. It is a mistake to exceed the artist's rôle and become political investigator.

The entertainer, on the other hand, suffers from no criticism whatever. No one has told P. G. Wodehouse which is his best book or his worst, what are his faults or how he should improve them. The fate of the entertainer is simply to go on till he wakes up one morning to find himself obscure.

For every admirer whom a writer gains by any means except the legitimate quality of his art he will gain an enemy. He will be an unconscious enemy, one who feels uneasiness at seeing the writer's name in the publisher's advertisements, who turns the other way from his picture in the Tube, one of those who voted against Aristides because he was tired of hearing him called "the just."

Every admirer is a potential enemy. No one can make us hate ourselves like an admirer—"*de lire la secrète horreur du dévouement dans des yeux*"—nor is the admiration ever pure. It may be *us* they wish to meet but it's themselves they want to talk about.

Popular success is a palace built for a writer by publishers, journalists, admirers, and professional reputation makers, in which a silent army of termites, rats, dry rot and death-watch beetles are tunnelling away, till, at the very moment of completion, it is ready to fall down. The one hope for a writer is that although his enemies are often unseen they are seldom unheard. He must listen for the death-watch, listen for the faint toc-toc, the critic's truth sharpened by envy, the embarrassed praise of a sincere friend, the silence of gifted contemporaries, the implications of the dog in the manger, the visitor in the small hours. He must dismiss the builders and contractors, elude the fans with an assumed name and dark glasses, force his way off the moving staircase, subject every thing he writes to a supreme critical court. Would it amuse Horace or Milton or Swift or Leopardi? Could it be read to Flaubert? Would it be chosen by the Infallible Worm, by the discriminating palates of the dead?

To refuse all publicity which does not arise from the

quality of his work, to beware of giving his name to causes, to ration his public appearances, to consider his standards and the curve of development which he feels latent within him, yet not to indulge in gestures which are hostile to success when it comes, must be the aim of a writer.

Failure is a poison like success. Where a choice is offered, prefer the alkaline.

There is a kind of behaviour which is particularly dangerous on the moving staircase—the attempt to ascend it in groups of four or five who lend a hand to each other and dislodge other climbers from the steps. It is natural that writers should make friends with their contemporaries of talent and express a mutual admiration but it leads inevitably to a succession of services rendered and however much the writers who help each other may deserve it, if they too frequently proclaim their gratitude they will arouse the envy of those who stand on their own feet, who succeed without collaboration. Words like "log-rolling" and "back-scratching" are soon whispered and the death-watch ticks the louder. Such writers must remember that they write for the reader—the most unloved person in the world. No jokes must be made which can't be explained to him, no relationships mentioned in which he is not asked to share. His capacity for being hurt, for feeling slighted and excluded, for imagining that he is being patronised, is infinite. And his capacity for revenge.

Success is most poisonous in America. According to Van Wyck Brooks, "The blighted career, the arrested career, the diverted career are, with us, the rule. The chronic state of our literature is that of a youthful promise which is never redeemed." He calls American literature "one long list of spiritual casualties." Hemingway gives an account of the diseases of American authors which is worth comparing with our own analysis of spiritual tares.

We do not have great writers. Something happens to our good writers at a certain age.

You see we make our writers into something very strange, we destroy them in many ways. First economically. They make money. It is only by hazard that a writer makes money, although good books always make money eventually. Then our writers when they have made some money increase their standard of living and they are caught. They have to write to keep up their establishments, their wives, and so on, and they write slop. It is slop not on purpose but because it is hurried. Because they write when there is nothing to say or when there is no water in the well. Because they are ambitious. Then once they have betrayed themselves, they justify it and you get worse slop. Or else they read the critics. If they believe the critics when they say they are great then they must believe them when they say they are rotten and they lose confidence. At present we have two good writers who cannot write because they have lost confidence, through reading critics. If they wrote, sometimes it would be good and sometimes not so good and sometimes it would be quite bad, but the good would get out. But they have read the critics, and they must write masterpieces. The masterpieces the critics said they wrote. They weren't masterpieces of course. They were just quite good books. So now they cannot write at all. The critics have made them impotent.[3]

It is not authors only who are killed by criticism but critics as well; they seem, like scorpions, able to destroy themselves with their own venom. But Hemingway's point is well-made. The praise from a critic is inflated by hope as often as his censure is distorted by envy since his longing for perfection or his desire to be a John the Baptist may drive him prematurely to recognise a Messiah and his disappointment thereby become correspondingly aggravated. Also, as Desmond MacCarthy has remarked, there comes a moment when every clever young man prefers to display his cleverness by exposing a writer's faults rather than proclaiming his virtues. That moment is most apt to occur in the early thirties which is a bad time all round both for creators and critics or it may occur when the critic is in his early thirties and the writer in his early forties. Butler

[3] Scott Fitzgerald? Thornton Wilder? Glenway Westcott? John O'Hara?

said an author should write only for people between twenty and thirty as nobody read or changed their opinions after that. Those are the years when the artists are promising and the admirers full of admiration; by the time the artist has ceased to be promising and become a good writer, the admirer is a critic whose judgments are flavoured by his own self-hatred or who, taking the author as a symbol of his own youth, refers all his later books back to his earliest. When an admirer says, "Ah, yes! But if only he would write another *Prufrock!*" he means, "If only I was as young as when I first read *Prufrock*." The sour smell of the early thirties hangs over most literary controversy.

The shock, for an intelligent writer, of discovering for the first time that there are people younger than himself who think him stupid is severe. Especially if he is at an age (thirty-five to forty-two) when his self-confidence is easily shaken. The seventh lustre is such a period, a menopause for artists, a serious change of life. It is the transition from being a young writer, from being potentially Byron, Shelley, Keats, to becoming a stayer, a Wordsworth, a Coleridge, a Landor. It would seem that genius is of two kinds, one of which blazes up in youth and dies down, while the other matures, like Milton's or Goethe's, through long choosing, putting out new branches every seven years. The artist has to decide on the nature of his own or he may find himself exhausted by the sprint of youth and unfitted for the marathon of middle age. A great many writers die between those years; some like Hart Crane, Harry Crosby, Philip Heseltine commit suicide; others succumb to pneumonia and drink or have nervous breakdowns. Others become specialists in the arts or in hobbies verging on the arts. Writers turn painters or painters writers or renew themselves through someone from whom they can obtain self-confidence and encouragement and a vicarious youth. Eventually, though critics are unfriendly, creation difficult and the future monotonous or uncertain, a new position is established and the young writer of promise becomes a master in his prime, one who can pass into old age as a sage, a prophet or a venerated, carefree and disreputable figure.

But English criticism, unless it proceeds from the indiscriminate malice of rotting ambition, is unfair only in that it is overkind—for a critic is subject to temptations of his own. Through praising their books, he gets to know more and more authors personally and once he has met them finds it embarrassing to alter his opinion. Critics in England do not accept bribes but one day they discover that in a sense their whole life is an accepted bribe, a fabric of compromises based on personal relationships and then it is in vain to remember that, like James's old man of letters, "our doubt is our passion, and our passion is our task."

CHAPTER XVI: OUTLOOK UNSETTLED

Such are the dangers and present temptations of writers. What consolations can be offered them? What positive advice will procure for a new book a decade of life and assure its author a patent from oblivion for another ten years? We have seen that realism, simplicity, the familiar attitude to the reader are likely to grow stale, that imagination, formality, subtlety, controlled by an awareness of the times we live in, are due to return. We can also learn something of the forms which have vitality and are assured of a future. Many writers who have no feeling for the live or the dead form still attempt those which are doomed to failure. The record of literature is that of great writers who perfect a form, imitators who bring into disrepute that perfection, and a new artist arising to perfect another.

Thus *Paradise Lost* dislocated the English language for a hundred years for it became impossible to write blank verse which was not an imitation of Milton. Ultimately Cowper broke away and after him Wordsworth and Tennyson. Since then poets have been trying to escape from Tennyson by returning to the blank verse of the Elizabethans. Coming after Milton, Pope was the first poet to elude blank verse and bring to perfection a new form, the couplet, and this couplet in its turn paralysed the poets of the eighteenth century till it was adapted by Crabbe and Byron. Blake and Collins meanwhile had broken free from the couplet and made possible the rebellion of the romantics who can be said to have held their own until *The Waste Land*.

A writer has to construct his shell, like the caddis worm, from the débris of the past, and, once there, despite the jostling of contemporaries, is safe till a younger generation dispossesses him or until the vicissitudes of taste crumble it about him. He may attempt a new form or he may revive an old one. But the revival, if it is to succeed, must not be too premature.

Which forms are available at the moment? The novel, the play, the poem, the article, the short story, the biography and the autobiography seem the most fertile.

From the novel, dominant literary form of the last hundred years, has emerged a succession of masterpieces. But there have been a number of bad novels and from them certain facts can be deduced. Firstly, that bad novels do not last; there is no point, therefore, in writing one unless it comes up to championship standard. And the novel is not a suitable form for young writers. The best novels (of Stendhal, Flaubert, Proust, James, etc.) are written from early middle age onwards. It is unsuitable because the construction of a long book is exacting for the young, whose novels generally begin well and go off and who lack staying power, and because to write a novel an author must have experience of people as they are, and have resolved the contradictions in his own nature; he must be integrated, a machine for observation.

Young writers force upon real people the standards, motives and behaviour which appeal to them in books; they are split-men, at war with themselves, and uncertain of their philosophy. I know of admirable young novelists but their development was difficult, for they began as lyricists or satirists; even *Wuthering Heights* is not so much a novel as a lyric flight of sublimated eroticism. The satire of Evelyn Waugh in his early books was derived from his ignorance of life. He found cruel things funny because he did not understand them and he was able to communicate that fun. But the predicament of the humorist is that his sensibility, if it should go on developing, causes him to find things less and less amusing, "for all our wit and reading do but bring us to a truer sense of sorrow." The English humorist must therefore either cease to be funny and thereby lose his entertainment status or abandon his integrity and, æsthetically stunted, continue to give his public what it wants. For this reason humorists are not happy men. Like Beachcomber or Saki or Thurber they burn while Rome fiddles, or, like P. G. Wodehouse, repeat themselves with profitable resignation.

The short story and the long short story are more fruitful. The short story avoids routine, it is the most fluid and experimental of forms, as Elizabeth Bowen says,

> Peaks of common experience soar past an altitude line into poetry. There is also a level immediately below this, on which life is being more and more constantly lived, at which emotion crystallises, from which a fairly wide view is at command. This level the short story is likely to make its own.

The long short story is one of the most rewarding and yet neglected forms in literature whose abandonment is solely due to the animosity of publishers. While short stories can be published in magazines and then in book form and so be paid for twice, long short stories of from twenty to fifty thousand words can be published nowhere. Yet *The Aspern Papers, Sylvie, Candide, The Alien Corn, A Lost Lady,* and *Death in Venice* show to what perfection it can be brought, and *Sylvie* and *Daisy Miller* prove it an ideal medium for youthful creation.

The play is another form whose revival seems possible, the length is right for young authors, the technical difficulties can be solved by good advice. There are in particular two forms of drama which can be reclaimed by art: the English comedy and the revue. The prose comedy of manners is one of the finest creations of English literature, the perfection of our native dandyism. In Congreve the English language reaches the farthest point to which it can be pushed in the direction of stylised, colloquial, contemporary elegance. It is the polished, racy talk of men in periwigs, with muffs and long waistcoats. From that moment people were to shorten their wigs and subdue their clothing, to begin the retreat to bald heads, sock-suspenders and undistinguished diction. The tragedy of Congreve was that although a young man, his mission was to bring an old form to perfection and then see it into its grave.

We know very little about Congreve. His predicament was that he belonged to the past, the form he perfected, the

comedy of manners belonged in spirit to the reign of
Charles II, and was haunted by that prince of dandies,
Wilmot, Earl of Rochester. Rochester had already been
taken by Etherege as the hero of his charming *Man of
Mode* and it was his habit of joking confidentially, almost
wistfully with his servant which, satirised here, established
the favourite relationship of hard-up young master and
wily, doting valet which has been a feature of the English
comedy down to *Jeeves*. But what appealed to contemporary writers in Rochester was his mixture of gaiety and
dignity, of the personal integrity of a man true to his own
thought and feeling with the disregard of all law and convention of the nobleman and the rake. Such a hero is pro-
foundly antipathetic to a bourgeois society, in which he is
a kind of enviable outlaw; he can only exist round a court.
His tradition retarded Congreve as much as that of Oscar
Wilde and the nineties retarded many young writers of the
1920's. How typical of the most classical dandyism for instance, was his reserve. "He is comparatively reserved; but
you find something in that restraint which is more agreeable
than the utmost exertion of talent in others" (Waller).
Congreve must have felt an obsession for a man of an earlier
generation so like what he himself would have wished to
be, just as even Pope felt a certain nostalgia for the small-
scale "little England" quality of Charles II's court. The diction of his heroes closely resembles that which Etherege
attributed to Rochester, one of Rochester's most favoured
mistresses was a prominent member of Congreve's cast and
Gosse mentions that Congreve bought a portrait of him.
The Restoration comedy, after all, belonged to the Restoration yet by a paradox it attained perfection in the 1690's.
The Way of the World appeared in 1700 and was a failure.
There is a rumour that Congreve went on the stage in a
fury and told the audience he would never write anything
for them again. Certainly he must have been conscious that
he had put the best of his genius into it. What he could
not have been conscious of in his disappointment was that
the audience of 1700 had changed; the merchants of the
reign of Anne, the Whigs, the new middle-class would not
stand for situations in which extravagant sons ruined selfish

and bestial old fathers, duped their humdrum creditors, seduced the wives of aldermen, made fun of country squires, got up in the afternoon and went out to see who they could pick up in the park after supper. London was becoming less and less like the Rome of Terence. It was a serious city. In the same year Addison's pompous *Cato* had a stupendous success.

There is room now for a revival of comedy. We have no dandyism of the Left. A play which is politically and socially true of its time and which yet achieves the elegance of *Love for Love* or the beginning of the *Importance of Being Earnest* would be secure of a future. Another likely form is the intelligent revue because short satirical sketches are easily written by young writers and because a revue which flattered the intelligence of the audience would present an element of surprise. Most creative writing to-day is Left in sentiment. It would gain by conquering those fields of comedy which are still feebly defended by Toryism in retreat, by dukes and butlers and people who think the word Epstein a joke in itself, by men of pleasure turned sour and baby blimps just cutting their water-wings.

The long article has a future, especially in the form of the critical essay, the analysis of times and tendencies, and the skilled "reportage." But articles which cannot be reprinted are not worth writing.

Poetry is highly explosive, but no poet since Eliot can but perceive the extreme difficulty of writing good poetry. The moment a poet forgets this, he will be superseded by a writer of prose. We have one poet of genius in Auden, who is able to write prolifically, carelessly, and exquisitely nor does he seem to have to pay any price for his inspiration. It is as if he worked under the influence of some mysterious drug which presents him with a private vision, a mastery of form and of vocabulary.

But poets have to keep in training. Poetry, to stand out, must be a double distillation of life that goes deeper than prose. It must be brandy as compared to wine, otherwise consumers will get their poetry from short stories and novels. This distillation of experience can be achieved only by a writer who maintains his sensibility and integrity at a high pitch and concentrates on the quality of his production. He must examine the meaning, weight, force, pace and implication of a word, he must calculate the impact of each line on the reader, know what concessions can be made to sound or sense, and deliver the finished poem only after a drastic trial. Otherwise prose will catch up on him. As things stand, inspiration is not enough, dreams have had their day, lucky shots miss the target. A poet, with the exception of mysterious water-fluent tea-drinking Auden, must be a highly conscious technical expert. Poetry is an instrument of precision. That is why societies in return must respect him as they respect scientists or all who have made greater sacrifices in their interest than they themselves care to. The poet is susceptible to the temptations which we have described by reason of his sensibility and we must not bully him.

> "Popular, popular, unpopular,
> You're no poet," the critic cried.
> "Why?" said the poet. "You're unpopular!"
> Then they cried at the turn of the tide,
> "You're no poet!" "Why?" "You're popular!"
> Pop-gun: popular and unpopular.[1]

A lyric poet has the advantage over a prose writer that he is entrusted with the experience of the ages; he is not a political conscript nor can he be accused of escapism if he confines himself to celebrating the changing seasons, memories of childhood, love or beauty. The tyranny of form to which he is subject is compensated by his free access to material. Literary history goes to prove that lyrical poetry is the medium which more than any other defies time. Didactic poetry becomes unreadable; epics are pillaged for a few similes; plays quarried for the songs in them; novels and essays crumble or ossify; but ten minutes' extra thought on the choice of a word or the position of a stress may make in the lyric a difference of a thousand years. There is no age or period at which great lyric poetry cannot be written. It is possible to argue that Homer and Virgil today would have written in prose, that Shakespeare would

[1] Not Lawrence: Tennyson.

have written novels—but Sappho, even after the international situation had been explained to her, would have remained true to verse.

One of the colophons of literature, one of those great writers who put full stop to a form of art, was Marcel Proust. The form whose consummation he brought about was the autobiographical novel. *The Way of All Flesh, Of Human Bondage, A Portrait of the Artist* preceded it; after 1922 they could not have been written, and such autobiographical novels as appear now are not by great writers. They are the green shoots which continue to put forth from a tree that has been cut down.

The result of the flight of all but the most obstinate from this dying form has been a return of emphasis to the autobiography which has an advantage over the novel in that it demands no fictional gifts from the writer and a disadvantage in that it permits no alibis; the characters are not imaginary and the hero is the one character with whom the author dare find fault. An interesting contribution was Harold Nicolson's *Some People*, which, disguised as short stories, is an autobiography where each episode represents a hurdle taken by the author on his way to maturity. Cowley's *Exile's Return* is another example of the planned autobiography (the one kind now worth writing), and in England I find it a temptation not to mention Orwell and Isherwood again. Closely related to reportage-autobiography is ideology-autobiography, in which an author looks back on himself in relation to the ideas of his time, a classic example of which is *The Education of Henry Adams*. There is room for many planned books of this sort by writers who can analyse themselves in relation to their environment and avoid padding, but all journalism must be kept out—so must the ideology, for the faults of these books are already apparent.[2]

[2] "A man scurried through the Chancellery. He moved too fast for me to get a glimpse of him—but I just discerned an ulster and a soft felt hat. 'That fellow's scared' I muttered. 'You bet he is' said Jeff Post. 'It's Schuschnigg (Schacht—Stresemann)'. It was the only time I saw him till I followed his coffin down the Siegenallee". Or (ideological): "All that year Lenin

To write well and to go on writing well depends on our sense of reality. There is such a thing as literary health and so far we have considered only literary diseases. If a writer is not writing as well as he would like to or as often as he would wish, he should give himself an examination. Is he satisfied with his reality? Is he *"dans le vrai"*? If not, when and how has he departed from it? Reality is a shifting thing. I take it to mean the nature of things as they are and as they will be. It is life and the future, however unpleasant, and not death and the past, however desirable. What people want to happen is real if it can be willed to happen, and there are realities of the imagination—such as the belief in a future life or in a perfectible human society which transcend at times the physical realities of death and annihilation. But for a professional writer it involves the realities of his time, the ideas and the actions which are changing the world and shaping history. The most real thing for a writer is the life of the spirit, the growth or curve of vision within him of which he is the custodian, selecting the experiences propitious to its development, protecting it from those unfavourable. When he fails to do this something seems to rot; he becomes angry, frightened, and unhappy, suffering from what Swift called "that desiderium which of all things makes life most uneasy."

The spiritual reality of the artist may come into conflict with the historical reality of his time and true to his own reality, he may even have to sacrifice himself by his opposition to the external world and so find that not life but premature death is required of him. There is no mysticism in this. We create the world in which we live; if that world becomes unfit for human life, it is because we tire of our responsibility. Genius is important in creating that world and therefore will be among the first things to suffer. There

was drinking café crèmes in Geneva. Trotsky was growing a beard, Kautsky was writing 'one step forward, two steps backward'; the Tennessee soapboilers' strike was repressed after twenty-nine days. Jaurés was fighting a municipal election but, obsessed with sex and education, my development was still experiencing a bourgeois time-lag of some two thousand years. I might have been talking with survivors of the 1905 revolution. I preferred to study Plato, Picasso and Proust".

are destructive elements—war, plague, earthquake, cancer and the dictator's firing squad are among them—which take no account of the unfinished masterpiece or the child in the womb. They are real and their reality must never be underestimated but there remains a reality of will and spirit by which within the unchanging limitations of time and death they can be controlled.[3]

Having satisfied himself of how he stands in relation to his time and whether his talent is receiving proper nourishment, an ailing writer will enquire about those other sources of creative happiness: health, sex, and money.

The health of a writer should not be too good, and perfect only in those periods of convalescence when he is not writing. Rude health, as the name implies, is averse to culture and demands either physical relief or direct action for its bursting energy. Action to the healthy man seems so desirable that literary creation is felt to be shaming and is postponed till action has engendered fatigue which is then transmitted to the reader. Also, in "this England where nobody is well," the healthy writer is communicating with a hostile audience. Most readers live in London; they are run-down, querulous, constipated, soot-ridden, stained with asphalt and nicotine and as a result of sitting all day on a chair in a box and eating too fast, slightly mad sufferers from indigestion. Except on holiday an author should not be fitter than his public or too well for reading and meditation. The relationship of an author with his reader is the barometer of his æsthetic health. If he flatters or patronises, is hostile or pleading, then something is amiss with him.

A preoccupation with sex is a substitute for artistic

[3] The Spanish poet Lorca was shot because he fell into the power of an element which detested spiritual reality. Yet Lorca fell into those hands because he lived in Granada. Had he lived in Barcelona or Madrid he would be alive to-day like Sender or Alberti. But he lived in reactionary Granada, a city of the past, of gipsies and bullfighters and priests, and he made his best poems about bullfighters and gipsies. That element in him which sought the past, which drew him to the mediævalism of Andalusia, contained the seed of his own death, placing him, who was no friend to priests or feudal chiefs, in a city where the past would one day come to life, and prove deadly.

creation; a writer works best at an interval from an unhappy love-affair, or after his happiness has been secured
by one more fortunate. So far as we can generalise it would
seem that the welling up of the desire for artistic creation
precedes a love-affair. Women are not an inspiration of the
artist but a consequence of that inspiration. An artist, when
his talent is uncoiling, has the desirability of any object fulfilling its function but he also enjoys a certain clearheaded-
ness. His habits become moderate, he drinks less because
drink has no longer a psychological appeal. He does not
lack confidence, he lives contentedly within his income and
he sees love and friendship as delightful things but without
their glamour. It is after creation, in the elation of success
or the gloom of failure that love becomes essential.

Solvency is an essential. A writer suffering from financial
difficulties is good only for short-term work, and will leave
all else unfinished. And if he has too much money, unless
he has had it all his life, he will spend it, which is also a
substitute for creation. Every writer should, before embark-
ing, find some way however dishonest of procuring with
the minimum of effort, about four hundred a year. Otherwise he must become a popular success or be miserable.
Success he will take in his stride for fewer writers are
marred by it than are discouraged by failure. It is wholesome magic.

> Gently dip, but not too deep
> For fear you make the golden beard to weep.

Failure on the other hand is infectious. The world is full
of charming failures (for all charming people have something to conceal, usually their total dependence on the appreciation of others) and unless a writer is quite ruthless
with these amiable footlers, they will drag him down with
them. More dangerous are those who are not charming—
the trapped foxes who bite the hand that would set them
free and worst of all the kibitzers, the embittered circle of
scoffing onlookers—

> The common rout
> That, wandering loose about,

Grow up and perish as the summer fly
Heads without name, no more remembered.

It is by a blend of lively curiosity and intelligent selfishness that the artists who wish to mature late, who feel too old to die, the Goethes, Tolstoys, Voltaires, Titians and Verdis, reach a fruitful senescence. They cannot afford to associate with those who are burning themselves up or preparing for a tragedy or whom melancholy has marked for her own. Not for them the accident-prone, the friends in whom the desire for self-destruction keeps blistering out in broken legs or threatening them in anxiety-neuroses. Not for them the drumming finger, the close-cropt nail, the chewed glasses, the pause on the threshold, the wandering eye or the repeated "um" and "er."

We create the world in which we live and the artist plays a dominant rôle in that creation. By extension he can live in any world which he has created. At present, some artists are creating a militant others a pacifist world, and it is not artists only who are creating worlds, but capitalists and dictators. There is doubt about which world is best as there is doubt about which world will triumph. If a fascist world wins we may expect a black-out of art as under Attila. A communist world may make experiments in intolerance and then grow tired of them. Or nothing may happen during our lifetimes and a few drops of patronage still be wrung from a barren capitalism. Honours will be conferred on the adroit, smart luncheon parties given, medals awarded. Or a world revolution may establish conditions in which artists will through their own merit reach the public from whom they have been isolated.

Within his talent it is the duty of a writer to devote his energy to the search for truth, the truth that is always being clouded over by romantic words and ideas or obscured by actions and motives dictated by interest and fear. In the love of truth which leads to a knowledge of it lies not only the hope of humanity but its safety. Deep down we feel that, as every human being has a right to air and water, so has he a right to food, clothing, light, heat, work, education, love and leisure. Ultimately we know the world will

be run, its resources exploited and its efforts synchronised
on this assumption. A writer can help to liberate that knowledge and to unmask those pretenders which accompany all
human plans for improvement: the love of power and
money, the short-sighted acquisitive passions, the legacies
of injustice and ignorance, the tiger instinct for fighting, the
ape-like desire to go with the crowd. A writer must be a
lie-detector who exposes the fallacies in words and ideals
before half the world is killed for them. It may even be
necessary for the poet to erect a bomb-proof ivory tower
from which he can continue to celebrate the beauty which
the rest of mankind will be too guilty, hungry, angry or
arid to remember. There is room in the arts besides the
militant novelists and journalists for the "necessary lovers,"
but the success worshippers, those for whom life is a Perpetual Party, a buffet where one swigs, if fortunate in the
draw, for eighty years and then grudgingly makes room,
are as out of favour as those who justify abuses as our
christian burden "in this Vale of Tears." The artist of to-day
must bear a wound—*"cette blessure,"* according to Gide,
*"qu'il ne faut pas laisser se cicâtriser, mais qui doit demeurer
toujours douleureuse et saignante, cette blessure au contact
de l'affreux réalité."* [4]

[4] "That wound which we must never allow to heal but which
must always remain painful and bleeding, the gash made by
contact with hideous reality."

PART THREE: A GEORGIAN BOYHOOD

Yet hark how through the peopled air
    The busy murmur glows,
The insect youth are on the wing
Eager to taste the honied spring
    And float amid the liquid noon.
Some lightly o'er the current swim
Some shew their gayly gilded trim
    Quick-glancing to the sun.

GRAY

"What sort of a thing is Tydeus?"
"Tydeus rose and set at Eton: he is only
Known here to be a scholar of Kings."
[West to Walpole: Walpole to West,
               October, 1735]

Altro dirti non vo'; ma la tua festa
Ch'anco tardi a venir non ti sia grave.

LEOPARDI

CHAPTER XVII: CREDENTIALS

Up to this point the function of this work has been entirely critical and performed with those privileges of the critic which allow him to assume equality with those whom he criticises and to take their books to pieces as if he were their equal in stature. But this equality is a fiction, just as it is a fiction that a juryman is superior to the temptations and stupidities of the prisoner he judges or qualifies to convict a company director on a point of corporation law. A critic is a product of his time who may affect impartiality but who while claiming authority over the reader projects his doubt and aspiration. Every critic writes as if he were infallible, and pretends that he is the embodiment of impartial intellectual sanity, a reasonable though omniscient pontiff. But without his surplice the preacher of the loftiest sermon is only human or subhuman, and now is the moment to step down from the pulpit, to disrobe in the vestry. The autobiography which follows is intended to be such a disrobing; it is meant to be an analysis of the grounding in life and art which the critic received, of the ideas which formed him in youth; the education, the ideals, the disappointments from which are drawn his experience, the fashions he may unwittingly follow and the flaws he may conceal.

A critic is an instrument which registers certain observations; before the reader can judge of their value he must know sufficient of the accuracy of the instrument to allow for the margin of error. We grow up among theories and illusions common to our class, our race, our time. We absorb them unawares and their effect is incalculable. What are they? In this case, I am trying to find out, hoping that all I discover, however personal, may prove of use. To do so I have to refer to something which I find intolerable, the early aura of large houses, fallen fortunes and county families common to so many English autobiographers. If the reader can stomach this, I will try to make it up to him.

CHAPTER XVIII: THE BRANCHING OGHAM

I have always disliked myself at any given moment; the total of such moments is my life.

The first occurred on the morning of the tenth of September 1903 when I was born at Coventry where my father had gone to look after a body referred to as "The Volunteers." My father was in the regular army. His father, Admiral Connolly, son of a General Connolly and nephew to various other veterans of the wars with France, belonged to a naval family long resident in Bath where he had married late in life the eldest daughter of the then Rector of Bath, Charles Kemble, who had restored the Abbey in the Victorian taste and who inhabited what is now the Spa Hotel. The Kembles of Overtown near Swindon were West Country squires who in the eighteenth century had gravitated to London and Bray and made a fortune in the tea trade. Charles Kemble had inherited the wealth of these nabobs and from his mother, a Miss Brooke, the estate of Cowbridge House, Malmesbury, which he had rebuilt in the baroque style with Italian workmen from the Great Exhibition. The vigorous, dominating millionaire Rector of Bath was said to be too Broad-Church in his views to be made a bishop, for from Wadham he had joined the Clapham Sect. The Connollys, however, were a frugal, blue-eyed, long-lived, quiet, tidy, obstinate race of soldiers and sailors; the Admiral's uncle, Captain Mathew Connolly, had been a kind of arbiter of Bath elegance in the reign of George IV. There was something eighteenth-century about the Connollys, while the Kembles were eminently Victorian. My grandfather, the Admiral, was born in 1816 and had done much of his sailing in the Mediterranean and the Pacific on wooden ships of which he was a great defender against the "ironclad." He was older than my grandmother, older than the Rector, his father-in-law, and died in 1901 at his house in Marlborough Buildings, Bath, with a great reputation for good looks of the genial, bearded, crusty, open sort, charm, gallantry, temper and bad language.

Meanwhile the Rector's fortune had vanished among his eleven children, his rectory had become a public school, his country houses all been sold. He left a book called *Memorials of a Closed Ministry* and a Victorian Gothic church he had built at Stockwell. The fifty thousand pounds he had contributed to the restoration of the Abbey was a bitter memory to his grandchild, whose frequent complaints about it to my mother afforded me at an early age a grudge against society. I never had a chance! Both my great-grandfather the Rector and my great-great uncle Mathew Connolly have their monuments in the Abbey and windows commemorate my great-uncle Brooke Kemble who was drowned off Tunis as a midshipman, and other members of the family. That quiet corner where are grouped in such incongruous harmony the Roman Bath, the Gothic Abbey and the eighteenth-century Colonnade is not the less sultry for enclosing my roots.

In 1900 when my father's regiment was on a visit to Ireland he met and married my mother, the daughter of Colonel Edward Vernon, D.L., J.P., of Clontarf Castle, outside Dublin. The Vernons of Clontarf were a branch of the Vernons of Haddon Hall and Tonge who had come over to Ireland with the Duke of Ormond in the reign of Charles II by whom John Vernon, Paymaster-General of the Royal Army, had been given Clontarf, then a castle of the Templars. They were a fiery race, proud of their Anglo-Norman descent, their sixty-three quarterings and their position among the sporting Church-of-England "Ascendancy," the landlords of the Pale.

My earliest memory is of a chemist's shop in Bath with coloured bottles in the window and a circular air-cushion with a hole in the middle. This mysterious rubber object excited me beyond words. What was it for? I never knew except that it must be for something quite unimaginably disgusting and horrible. I knew it and It knew it, and It knew that I knew it. It was vice made visible. And It was for Me!

Then my father's regiment was sent to South Africa, and all my memories became exotic; arum lilies, loquats, eucalyptus, freezias, are the smells which seem to me divine essences, balms of Eden remembered from another life. The freezias grew wild in the grass and those long thin stems with their wayward creamy blossom, and their fragrance, so strangely fresh and yet sophisticated, were my first clue to the vast riches of the universe. I remember also Cape Point, the walk to the sea through clumps of rushes and over white sand feathered with the tracks of lizard and all around me an indescribable irradiation of sun and wind and space and salt. And at Montagu there was an island in the mountain river on to which I used to be hoisted, clutching a stinking meercat's skin, lord of a rock on which a bird deposited the shells of crayfish, an Ithaca twelve feet long.

We lived at Wynberg; there were chameleons in the garden and squashed apricots; on Sundays the Regiment had church parades and there were smells of pine and eucalyptus paint blisters and hot tar. I had already grown accustomed to being an only child and enjoyed playing by myself. I had a dog called Wups, a cat called One-Eye and a crowd of other animals, some real and many imaginary. I derived enormous pleasure from animals and something approaching ecstasy from the smells of flowers and fruit and from the arid subtropical scenery.

Already my life was a chain of ecstatic moments; I invented happy families of tops and fir-cones or made overtures to the sacred personages whom I learnt about from *Line upon Line*: Isaac on his way up the mountain to be sacrificed, the infant Samuel, the other children David and Benjamin. But my deepest concern was the apprehension of visual beauty. To stand among arum lilies, faintly scented, thick in texture and to break off their leaves or among the brittle lines of sweet pea or with my wateringcan, by the rose-beds smelling of wet earth and to pour out the spraying water—these were experiences, like climbing a willow tree near the stables where the green and edible willow branches hung down like the reed curtains in Spanish doorways by which my existence was transformed! In vain Captain Scott shook hands with me on his last voyage to the South Pole, in vain I was shown the giant tortoises and the fleet at Simonstown or saw the Regiment parade on Minden Day—my relations, sadistic with One-Eye and Wups—æsthetic, with pale cones of silver fir and the gummy blue cups of eucalyptus, were all that concerned me.

I twice visited South Africa; at the age of five, and six. In between we went to Ireland and stayed at Clontarf, and then at Mitchelstown Castle in Cork which left a deep impression. This castle was an enormous eighteenth-century Gothic affair, which belonged with some thirty thousand acres to my great-aunt Anna, Countess of Kingston, who had once been besieged there by the Fenians; there was a lake in the grounds, and a wishing well. Now alas, not a stone remains. It was winter and there were icicles along the lake. I wore brown gloves on week-days and white ones on Sundays and held an icicle (the first I had seen) with its mysterious purposeful pointed whiteness, in my white glove. Of the rest of the visit I remember little. Lord Kingston descendant of Milton's Lycidas had long been dead, but my grandfather was there, terrifying. "Where is Grandpapa?" I asked my nurse one morning. "He's busy." "What's he doing?" "He's doing his duty." This answer, which would have covered the activities of all Irish landlords at that date, I took to mean that he was in the lavatory (Have you done your duty to-day?), and was more frightened of him than ever except when he would come in with his gun and a huge stiff dead grasshopper two feet long in his hand, waving it at me and saying "snipe, snipe."

This was my first visit to Ireland since babyhood and besides the love of the beautiful, it awoke in me a new passion. I became a snob. The discovery that I was an earl's great-nephew was important to me; I soon made another. My mother's favourite sister had married a rich man. Aunt Mab was very beautiful but she also had special smells, smells of furs and Edwardian luxe. Uncle Walter gave me a steam train and a watch for Christmas. Wherever we went with Aunt Mab there were presents and large houses and the appeal her wealth made to an imaginative child was irresistible. Bishopscourt, Loughananna, Roches-town, Marlay, the names of her houses (for she moved every six months) held a poetry for me. They went with security and romance, fires and potato cakes, footmen, horses and soft aquatinted Irish winter.

> Cold grew the foggy morn, the day was brief,
> Loose on the cherry hung the crimson leaf;
> All green was vanished save of pine and yew
> That still display'd their melancholy hue;
> Save the green holly with its berries red
> And the green moss upon the gravel spread.

In 1910 I was sent home from Africa for good. My parents stayed on while I went with my nurse to join my father's mother and sister in Corsica where they had a villa. By now I was an æsthete. I adored my mother, but lived otherwise in a world of my own. Sunsets were my pre-occupation. I saw all words, people, numbers and proper names in colours or notes of music and there was a different colour for every day of the week, which I tried to paint but failed. I remember being often ill with fever, and the taste of the orange-leaf tea I was given to bring my temperature down. I added the flavour of this infusion to my ecstasies, with walks in the "maquis" and sessions by the garden tank where I sailed my prickly-pear leaves in the evening.

Then there was the sea itself, though, like Petronius, I cared only for the seashore, for the beach by "les Iles Sanguinaires" where transparent "Venus' slippers" were thrown up by the sea. One evening I was taken out in a boat to see the French destroyers fire their torpedoes. The lurid Mediterranean sunset, the ships, the noise, the rolling, were not to my liking. I cried louder as each torpedo went off and from that evening I date a horror of battleships, bands playing, noises, displays of arms and all official functions.

I also discovered friendship in Corsica and fell in love with a child called Zenon, a Pole, three years older than myself. He had dark eyes, a fringe of brown hair and adored fighting. He made cardboard swords and shields for us on which he used to paint our coats of arms and we would hack at each other till our escutcheons were broken. From that moment I have seldom been heart-free and life without love for me has always seemed like an operation without an anæsthetic. I have been inclined to regard that condition as the justification of existence and one that takes priority over all other ideologies.

> Love the most generous passion of the mind,
> That cordial drop heaven in our cup has thrown
> To make the nauseous draught of life go down.

From Corsica we moved on to Tangier, where I was infatuated again, this time with a handsome bearded Moorish guide called Salem. We showered presents on each other and I still have a beautiful drum he gave me. Then we returned to Bath, where aged six I was sent to school as a day boy. It was the hot summer of 1910 and we wore dark blue cockades for the general election, except the dentist's son, who was a liberal. He seemed to me to smell quite different from the other boys. Oily.

I was now nearly seven and from this moment my character began to deteriorate. My grandmother spoilt me. I have since observed that it is a pleasure of grandparents to spoil their grandchildren. They revenge themselves in that way on their children for the insults they have suffered from them. My grandmother, lonely, religious and unselfish, was only playing her biological role. The tragedy was that I found it out and recognised my victim.

I remember being spoilt as an actual sensation, waking up early on Christmas morning and seeing the thrilling contours of my presents taking shape, the stocking bulging in the dark, afterwards unpacking the toy soldiers and setting them up in the new fort, going to church in my Eton jacket and suddenly, about three o'clock, being afflicted with a sensation of utter satiety and aggressive boredom. It was like eating—having been delicate and often feverish my appetite was most stimulated by invalid foods— the egg, the grape, the pat of butter, the cutlet, the tangerine, they were my highspots. In the winter afternoon

I would play by the fire with mines of matchboxes fired by
trains of torn paper in the grate, for I hated to leave the
fire for a moment, then tea would be brought in, my grandmother would cut the buttered toast into fingers, ready to
dip into the boiled eggs. Which tastes best? The first or the
second? The first finger of toast or the last little triangle dug
out from the bottom with a spoon? I don't know—but I do
know one should never have a third egg, and I remember
the unwilling sensation of not wanting to eat it yet hating
to let it go and finally forcing myself to dispose of it, and
then rounding on my grandmother—a vicious little golden-
haired Caligula.

To this period I trace my worst faults. Indecision, for I
found that by hesitating for a long time over two toys in a
shop I would be given both and so was tempted to make
two alternatives seem equally attractive; Ingratitude, for I
grew so used to having what I wanted that I assumed it as
a right; Laziness, for sloth is the especial vice of tyrants;
the Impatience with boredom which is generated by devotion; the Cruelty which comes from a knowledge of power
and the Giving way to moods for I learnt that sulking,
crying, moping, and malingering were bluffs that paid.

The people I had been in love with before, my mother,
my nurse Betty, Wups, One-Eye, Zenon, and Salem or
Selim (the spelling varied) were people who loved me, but
we loved as equals, conscious of each other's rights. Sufficiently provoked One-Eye would scratch, my mother
rebuke, Betty spank, Zenon, Wups and Salem slink away.
Now for the first time I learnt of unequal love. I was not
in love with my grandmother, she was in love with me, or
perhaps so ignorant and helpless with children as to seem
in love, and I took advantage. *Sic ego perire cœpi.*

At school I was popular for I had embarked on the
career which was to occupy me for the next ten years of
"trying to be funny." I was neither good nor bad at games;
my favourite exercise was to take a short piece of pointed
wood in my hand and meander for hours through the long
summer grasses round the playing fields, calling at imaginary ports, tunnelling through the hay, chewing sorrel and
following my faint tracks in the silver grass as a liner fol-

lows a trade route. Inside my desk a cardboard shoebox perforated with holes supported a brood of looper caterpillars. Who can forget that smell of caterpillars, the smell of wet cardboard, drying leaves and insect excrement, the odour of northern childhood? It was on one of these long summer cruises, in a patch of cow-parsley, that I realised my own identity; in a flash it came to me that my name and myself were something apart, something that none of the other boys were or could be, Cyril Vernon Connolly, a kind of divine "I am that I am" which I should carry all through life and at last deposit on my grave, like a retriever with a bit of stick.

I was still in love, as I had been since I first saw in *Little Arthur's History of England* the picture of the Princes in the Tower—those two royal princes, so sweetly embracing, so soon to be smothered—what only child could look at them without a disturbance or read of Prince Arthur himself, walking trustfully beside the gaoler on his way to have his eyes put out? Indeed, like many children, I had fixations on the early Plantagenets. With their remote grandeur and their drooping black moustaches these sad bad kings seemed like my great-uncles, huge brooding stylised figures who awoke a sense of guilt.

My great friend was a boy called Hubert Fitzroy Foley. I remember leaning out of the dormitory window with him to watch the fireworks on a summer night, while the rockets went off and we heard the inevitable Gilbert and Sullivan from the distant military band. That summer I seemed to be initiated into the secrets of preparatory school life. I came to know the smell of the classrooms, of slates, chalk and escaping gas, and to fear the green baize door which separated the headmaster's part of the house from the boys. On the one side, silence, authority, the smell of savouries; on the other noise and freedom.

At night we made "tabernacles" by stretching the sheets up over the tops of the beds and I would lie in the evening sunshine playing, flicking matches between the fingers of my right hand and my left or arching my hands into swan-like shapes that swooped up and down above my head. When I was ill there were cracks in the ceiling to map and explore and patterns in the wall-paper. I learnt the rhythm of the seasons: summer, which is the time for overdoing things, the recoil of creative autumn, the vibrant coma of winter and the lowering spring. I began to enjoy my work and to win prizes. I acted in a play and wrote facetious little Leacockian sketches. I declared a rebellion against the masters and returned a prize to one of them saying none of us would ever speak to them again. This was part of my insensitive teasing, but he took it seriously and looked hurt. I was so spoilt that I felt bored and disappointed with myself and tried to take it out on whom I dared. Otherwise I was a typical schoolboy, with a red cap, a belt with a snake (which I slept with under my pillow), a cricket bat, a knowledge of the tracks made by wapiti, skunk, raccoon and wolverine and a happy bitchiness which endeared me, as it was intended to, to my superiors. I went in brakes to watch matches and came home summertipsy in the dusk; I adored sausages and Sunday breakfasts, said my prayers, bickered with other boys on walks, cried "quis" and "ego," and was conceited and bright in the way in which so many small boys are, and which, alas, proves such a false dawn of intelligence.

I can never remember not being able to read and was already deep in "Natural History." I could reel off the habits of aardvarks, aye-ayes, and Tasmanian Devils, and I knew (from *The World of Wonders*) about the great Tun of Heidelberg, the deadly Upas Tree, and the Pitch Lake of Trinidad. I collected stamps, pressed flowers in blotters and adored chess. For lighter reading there were fairy stories and nonsense books. I enjoyed Burnand, Mark Twain and Stephen Leacock but wept at the humiliations of *Vice Versa* or the sufferings of the Yonghi Bonghi Bo. My thrill of the week was to visit a little shop on Landsdowne Hill in the early dusk of winter afternoon and receive a rolled-up bundle of "Comic Papers"; *Chips* and *Comic Cuts,* the *Rainbow,* the *Gem* and the *Magnet*—I hold them, as I did with everything, to my nose, the smell is excruciating—damp paper, newsprint; I feel I shall burst. Ahead of me stretches the evening with my grandmother; the gas lit, the fire burning, the papers unrolled and untied, the peace and security of the literary life though even then I am depressed by the knowledge that nothing I shall find inside will come up to the sensation of opening them. As with Leopardi's peasants, the eve of the Festival will always bring me more happiness than the Feast itself.

There was one other lesson I learnt, living with my grandmother. Hitherto I had been in exotic African surroundings or in Ireland. But my grandmother was poor and we lived in "rooms"; sometimes they were by the seaside in the isle of Purbeck, where balls bounced on the porphyry pavement, and a horse-drawn tumbril dragged the long-robed bathers far out into the string-coloured sea; sometimes they were in London, sometimes in Bath—but they were always middle class. While listening to tales of the Admiral's splendid dinner parties or of her childhood: the Rector's fine horses galloping the twenty-four miles from his country house at Malmesbury to his Palladian villa at Bath with its fourteen gardeners, the opulent safe Victorian saga, I yet was coming to know the world of the realist novel, those fuggy rooms with plush sofas and antimacassars, gas mantles, kettles on the hob, and their landladies, overfamiliar women with common voices and ripe bosoms sprayed with jet. I came into contact with the lower classes too, for we used to visit one or two old servants to whom my grandmother had made pensions. One, Old Sally, who lived in an alcoholic bed-ridden fug, distressed me particularly. Here were horrible things: illness, poverty, old age, and I felt I must make every effort to avoid coming into further contact with them.

I now made the comparison, as many a small boy would:

England = Grannie, Lodgings, School, Poverty, Middle Class.

Ireland = Aunt Mab, Castles, Holidays, Riches, Upper Class.

Ireland, therefore, became desirable and England sordid. This division, however unreal it may seem, had importance for me, it conditioned my homeless insecure lonely childhood, and made me a social hybrid. I could not consider myself entirely upper class; yet I was not altogether upper middle. I had fallen between two standards of living. With the upper class I felt awkward, dowdy, introspective and a physical coward. With the middle class I felt critical, impatient and sparkling. This class distinction, the line between Kensington and Belgravia, is a source of anguish. To consider oneself born into one and yet be slowly conditioned to the other was as uncomfortable as having one shoulder too low.

Meanwhile my mother returned and tried to repair the damages to my character. She disapproved of the school in Bath where I was always ill. I had whooped my way through the coronation summer, I had come out in measles and German measles, and chicken pox and, after a recurrence of malaria, I was removed. My mother came down to see me while I was ill and brought a trunk of toys, all the composition animals whom I adored in the holidays, with their house of parliament and the cricket elevens. I was ashamed of them and refused to play, for already my solitary only-child world seemed disgraceful to my social school world, even my mother's presence in it seemed incorrect. She took me away to Ireland and so Bath—that beautiful, relaxing town where the Abbey chimes played *The Harp that once through Tara's Halls* with morbid sweetness as we watched the county cricket matches—knew me no more.

Clontarf was a paradise for up in the musicians' gallery of its Gothic hall was a pitch for the kind of cricket I played, bowling a marble with my left hand to my right hand which held a toy animal as bat. A book standing up was the wicket. When an animal was out another took its place. Animals that were solid like the elephant or streamlined like the seal, made the best bats; animals like the giraffe, whose legs broke when they hit out, were less successful. Books were filled with their batting averages and my celluloid seal, besides being the best cricketer, was also a potent voice in my animals' parliament, and taken every night to bed with me.

My grandfather tried to give me real fielding practice on the lawn but I was frightened. There is a two-handed sword in the castle, reputed to have been used by Brian Boru in his battle there against the Danes, with which my grandfather and my great-uncle Granville Vernon would pretend to chop off my head. Their sombre jesting accentuated my cowardice, but I became interested in Brian Boru, and so was led to cultivate my "Irish" side. I wanted to learn Gaelic and I read history books from the nationalist standpoint. Shane O'Neill, Owen Roe O'Neill, Wolfe Tone, Lord Edward Fitzgerald were my heroes and I learnt to sing the Shan Van Vocht. The last intellectual to stay at Clontarf had been Handel, whose bedroom was my nursery, and I began to be considered "Queer." The introduction—"This is cousin Cyril [my nephew Cyril]. (*p*) He's supposed to be very clever. (*pp*) His grandmother's spoilt him," depressed me. I responded as usual by showing off and "trying to be funny."

I went on "trying to be funny" till I was seventeen. This grisly process was my defence mechanism. It was the shell I was secreting as a protection from the outside world: by making people laugh I became popular, and I ultimately became feared as well. "Go on, be funny!" some boy would command, and I would clown away or recite my poems and parodies, with their echoes of Mark Twain and Stephen Leacock. "Connolly's being funny," the word would go round and soon I would have collected a crowd. I revelled in this and would grow funnier and funnier till I passed quite naturally into tears. "Connolly's not funny now. He's gone too far," and the group would break up and leave me, except for some true friend who remained to puzzle over the psychology of the manic-depressive. "But you were being quite funny a moment ago." "Oh, Boo-Hoo-Hoo. I wish I was dead." "Oh, shut up, Connolly." "Oh, go away. I hate you." Then a master would come by and comfort me. I would be handed, still hysterical, to the matron, and the inevitable case-history would be gone over. (*p*) "It's his grandmother. (*pp*) She spoils him."

But I could not be so funny in Ireland. My wit was the opposite of the native sense of humour, my jokes, a combination of puns and personal remarks interlarded with the wisecracks of the day ("Oh, go and eat soap" was a favourite), were beyond the Anglo-Irish, who saw only the humour of situations, and could not appreciate a *calem-*

bour. They began to tease me about being English, which I gathered meant possessing a combination of snobbery, stupidity, and lack of humour and was a deadly insult. There were many stories of social triumphs at the expense of parvenu England—especially against unpopular viceroys, like Lord Aberdeen. The Anglo-Irish were a superior people. Better born, but less snobbish; cleverer than the English and fonder of horses; they were poorer no doubt but with a poverty that brought into relief their natural aristocracy. And, above all, they were loved (for "being Irish" meant belonging to the Protestant Landed Gentry) by about four million devoted bog-trotters, who served them as grooms, comic footmen, gardeners and huntsmen.

And the real Irish—what had happened to them? They were my first lost cause, and I worshipped them with passion, reciting the *Dead at Clonmacnois* to myself in a riot of grief.

> In a quiet watered land, a land of roses,
> Stands Saint Kieran's city fair
> And the warriors of Erin in their famous generations
> Slumber there.
>
> There beneath the dewy hillside sleep the noblest
> Of the Clan of Conn,
> Each below his stone with name in branching Ogham
> And the sacred knot thereon.
>
> Many and many a son of Conn the Hundred Fighter
> In the red earth lies at rest;
> Many a blue eye of Clan Colman the turf covers,
> Many a swan-white breast.

Even to-day such verses typify Ireland, the soft constipating weather, the unreality of that green cul-de-sac turned away from Europe where the revolutions lead backwards and the Present is invariably the victim of the Past.

In the meanwhile what of Clan Colman? Great-Uncle Granville obligingly made a list of chieftains for me. They were not all extinct; behind the Anglo-Norman families of the Pale, the Fitzgeralds, de Burghs, Tristrams, Talbots, Vernons and Plunkets, lurked the remnant of an older race

—the O'Grady of Killyballyowen, the O'Gorman, the O'Connor Don, the Magillicuddy of the Reeks, the O'Reilly and the Fox! These were the legitimate rulers, downtrodden heirs of Shane and Owen Roe. I begged Uncle Granville to point them out to me. To serve the O'Gorman! To speak Gaelic, wear a saffron Irish kilt, and sing the Shan Van Vocht!

> In the curragh of Kildare
> And the boys will all be there

with the O'Connor Don! The parliament of animals became supporters of the movement and the great seal himself, a fine cricketer and a generous statesman added the letters D.A.I. (Dublin and Irish), after his name. I planned a restoration of the monarchy and pestered my Uncle Granville about the claims of various families. Who should be considered the rightful King of Ireland, the successor of Brian Boru? Naturally all Connollys, O'Connors, and O'Connells, through Conn, the King of Connaught. That pointed to Edward Conolly of Castletown. But his family had taken the name Conolly and were really Pakenhams. Besides, his Gaelic . . . ? The O'Briens were Uncle Granville's candidates for the vacant throne. They had a Gaelic motto and were descended from Brian Boru himself through the kings of Thomond. Lord Inchiquin had the best right to the crown of Tara. For my own part I had no personal ambition, nothing to hope for from the Restoration.

> It was friends to die for
> That I would seek and find.

And my daydreams ended in my being sacrificed for the new King, like little Arthur.

This Irish nationalism may seem an extraordinary phase but it must be remembered that there are still several million who believe in it. Gaelic is now compulsory in Ireland, and I believe Lord Cullen of Ashbourne even wore a saffron kilt in Richmond Park. Monarchy has lost ground there since 1912, but at that time the revolutionary movement was unknown to me. My own feelings were romantic and literary, in fact English.[1] Ireland represented glamour and luxury, and I tried to make a religion out of them. Of course, I was a failure with the Irish. I never could learn the Gaelic alphabet, nor for that matter could I talk with an Irish brogue and the only Irish people I knew were the housekeeper at Clontarf and her husband.

All my cousins were healthy, destructive, normal children. I was lonely, romantic and affected and already the friction between extrovert and introvert was set up. I was extremely shy, for the effort to accommodate my inner life to my outer one was proving harder and harder. I was sentimental at night and facetious in the morning. Between morning and evening my personality would swing from one mood to the other as I watched my wisecracking morning self with its defiant battle-cry, "Oh, go and eat soap," turn by degrees into the tearful Celtic dreamer who believed in ghosts and at night would go into a trance over a line of poetry. My appetite for Gaelic and ghosts waxed and waned with my craving for titles. There were evenings when I wanted to kill myself because I was not the O'Grady of Killballyowen. Why had not my father got a title? Why was I not the heir to Castletown? It was heartless, anguishing—why be born, why live at all if I could not have one? Nobody understood me. Nobody cared, and I would scream and scream with real tears and screams that grew more and more artificial as I had to raise my voice to carry to the dining room. Nobody loved me, nobody understood me, nobody would give me what I wanted, there was an Elemental under the bed. I could die for all They cared. Wur! Wur! Wur! till at last my mother appeared in evening dress and would sit with me and stroke my head, smelling of chocolates.

The fever I got from time to time was a recurrence of African malaria, and was just enough to cause anxiety—

---

[1] The surnames of my eight great-grandparents were Connolly, Hall, Kemble, Catley, Vernon, Bowles, Graves and Brinkley. The Vernons had no Irish blood, the Connollys, at any rate since the early eighteenth century, had never been there and now despite my early infatuation nothing infuriates me more than to be treated as an Irishman.

the anxiety enough to procure me privileges. Nobody could be quite certain that I was shamming. And in the morning, when my night fears had been discussed and I would come down to an atmosphere of sympathy it was "Oh, go and eat soap," or "Stick him with a fork."

Such were these early excesses that to-day I cannot listen to any discussion of titles or open a peerage without feeling sick, as from the smell of rubber steps and stale whisky on the stairway of a Channel boat. I shall never be able to breathe till they are abolished. Nor has "being understood" proved reassuring.

In the end I compromised on the brogue. I pretended that I had got rid of it except in moments of great excitement and I would even affect to lose my temper so as to try out a few phrases, though I was careful to do this when no Irish boys were in the room. My new history books taught me to abominate England for I read *Tales of a Grandfather* at the same time and it never occurred to me that the England I hated, the oppressor of the Celt and the Gael, the executioner of Fitzgerald, Emmet and Wolfe Tone, was made manifest in my grandfather, who owned a thousand acres of suburban Dublin, and a shoot in Kerry; that the Anglo-Irish were themselves a possessor class whose resentment against England was based on the fear that she might not always allow them to go on possessing.

CHAPTER XIX: WHITE SAMITE

The new school my parents chose for me was on the coast.
At first I was miserable there and cried night after night.
My mother cried too at sending me and I have often wondered if that incubator of persecution mania, the English
private school, is worth the money that is spent on it or the
tears its pupils shed. At an early age small boys are subjected to brutal partings and long separations which undermine their love for their parents before the natural period
of conflict, and are encouraged to look down on them without knowing why. To owners of private schools they are a
business like any other, to masters a refuge for incompetence, in fact a private school has all the faults of a public
school without any of its compensations, without tradition,
freedom, historical beauty, good teaching or communication between pupil and teacher. It is one of the few tortures confined to the ruling classes and from which the
workers are still free. I have never met anybody yet who
could say he had been happy there. It can only be that our
parents are determined to get rid of us!

Yet St. Wulfric's where I now went was a well-run and
vigorous example which did me a world of good. We called
the headmistress Flip and the headmaster Sambo. Flip,
around whom the whole system revolved, was able, ambitious, temperamental and energetic. She wanted her venture to be a success, to have more boys, to attract the sons
of peers and to send them all to Eton. She was an able
instructress in French and History and we learnt with her
as fast as fear could teach us. Sambo seemed a cold, busi-
nesslike and dutiful consort. The morale of the school was
high and every year it won a shooting trophy and the Harrow History Prize from all the other preparatory schools.
Inside the chapel was a chaplain, inside the gym a drill-

sergeant and there were a virid swimming pool, a cadet corps, carpenter's shop and riding class.

The school was typical of England before the last war; it was worldly and worshipped success, political and social; though Spartan, the death rate was low, for it was well run and based on that stoicism which characterised the English governing class and which has since been underestimated. "Character, character, character," was the message which emerged when we rattled the radiators or the fence round the playing fields and it reverberated from the rifles in the armoury, the bullets on the miniature range, the saw in the carpenter's shop and the hoofs of the ponies on their trot to the Downs.

> Not once or twice in our rough island's story
> The path of duty was the way to glory

was the lesson we had to learn and there were other sacred messages from the poets of private schools: Kipling or Newbolt.

Muscle-bound with character, the alumni of St. Wulfric's would pass on to the best public schools, cleaning up all houses with a doubtful tone, reporting their best friends for homosexuality and seeing them expelled, winning athletic distinctions—for the house rather than themselves, for the school rather than the house and prizes and scholarships and shooting competitions as well—and then find their vocation in India, Burma, Nigeria and the Sudan, administering with Roman justice those natives for whom the final profligate overflow of Wulfrician character was all the time predestined.

After I had spent one or two terms at St. Wulfric's, blue with cold, haunting the radiators and the lavatories and waking up every morning with the accumulated misery of the mornings before, the war broke out. My parents had taken a house in London in Brompton Square and the holidays had become an oasis after St. Wulfric's austerity. In the big room at the top of the house with my grandfather's sea chest and the animal books by Ernest Thompson Seton, a fire and the view of the sea-green limes of the Brompton Oratory or in the drawing room with its vine-clad balcony

and rosewood furniture from Cowbridge I could be happy.
The square abounded with looper caterpillars, tight in the
shallow earth wriggled the pupæ of the privet moth (in
those that did not wriggle the ichneumon was at work).
On Sundays people made jokes about not going to church
but went and the churches disgorged their top-hatted con-
gregations into the Park from whence they strolled back,
myself in top hat and Eton jacket moving in an Anglo-
Irish phalanx and imagining I was Charles Hawtrey,
through gates and squares and crescents aromatic with
Sunday luncheons, the roast beef, the boredom, the security
of 1913. At night my fear of the dark was still acute. I
had to have night-lights and I had a terror of anything
"going out"—I could not bear a dying fire or a guttering
candle, or even a clock to run down—it seemed a kind of
death-agony.

The rest of my time at St. Wulfric's was spent on a war-
time basis. The school throve; its *raison d'être* apparent
in the lengthening Roll of Honour. Old boys came down in
uniform and retired generals lectured to the corps while
the boys stuck flags into maps, gave Woodbines to the
wounded soldiers and learned to knit; doing without more
and more, as Flip's organising genius found its expression.

The master who first took me in hand was Mr. Ellis.
He was gruff and peppery with an egg-shaped bald head.
He and Mr. Potter, the high-priest of the shooting trophies,
were professional teachers, the rest makeshifts thrown up
by the war. Ellis was pro-German; the Germans deserved
to win the war, he thought, because of their superior efficiency. The boys respected his point of view; to them, a
German victory would have seemed natural, a chastisement
on England for neglecting duty and discipline, and not
listening to "Lest we forget." He made me enthusiastic over
algebra and as my enthusiasm grew I became good at it.

From that moment Daddy Ellis befriended me. He called
me Tim Connolly and built up a personality for me as the
Irish Rebel, treating me as an intelligent and humorous
person, an opponent to respect. When the Germans conquered our decadent country through their discipline and

the superiority of their general staff I should be one of the first elements to be shot.

My new personality appealed to me. I changed my hand-writing and way of doing my hair, jumped first instead of last into the fetid plunge-bath, played football better and became an exhibit: the gay, generous, rebellious Irishman, with a whiff of Kipling's McTurk. Flip also admired the transformation and began to introduce me to parents as "our dangerous Irishman," "our little rebel." At that time I used to keep a favour chart in which, week by week, I would graph my position at her court. I remember my joy as the upward curve continued, and as I began to make friends, win prizes, enjoy riding and succeed again at try-ing to be funny. The favour charts I kept for several terms; one's favour began at the top and then went downwards as term wore on and tempers.

When angry Flip would slap our faces in front of the school or pull the hair behind our ears, till we cried. She would make satirical remarks at meals that pierced like a rapier and then put us through interviews in which we bellowed with repentance—"It wasn't very straight of you, was it, Tim? Don't you *want* to do me credit—don't you *want* to have character—or do you simply not care what I think of you as long as you can get a few cheap laughs from your friends and shirk all responsibility?" The example of brothers or cousins now in the trenches was then pro-duced to shame us. On all the boys who went through this Elizabeth and Essex relationship she had a remarkable effect, hotting them up like little Alfa-Romeos for the Brooklands of life.

The one thing that would bring our favour back (for, womanlike, Flip treated the very being-out-of-favour as a crime in itself, punishing us for the timid looks and under-dog manner by which we showed it) was a visit from our parents and many a letter was sent off begging for their aid. I was restored, after a low period during which I had been compared before the whole school to the tribe of Reuben because "unstable as water thou shalt not excel," by an enquiry for me from Lord Meath, the founder of Empire Day. Sometimes we could get back by clinging to

friends who were still "in favour." It might drag them down
or it might bring us up and the unhappiness of these little
boys forced to choose between dropping a friend in his
disgrace or risking disgrace themselves was most affecting.

I had two friends whose "favour" was as uncertain as my
own, George Orwell, and Cecil Beaton. I was a stage rebel,
Orwell a true one. Tall, pale, with his flaccid cheeks, large
spatulate fingers, and supercilious voice, he was one of those
boys who seem born old. He was incapable of courtship
and when his favour went it sank for ever. He saw through
St. Wulfric's, despised Sambo and hated Flip but was in-
valuable to them as scholarship fodder. We often walked
together over the downs in our green jerseys and corduroy
breeches discussing literature, and we both won, in con-
secutive years, the inevitable "Harrow History Prize."
There was another prize for having the "best list" of books
taken out of the library during the term, the kind which
might have been invented only to create intellectual snobs
and to satiate boys with the world's culture at a time when
they were too young to understand it. The books were
given out in the evening by Flip herself and a way by
which it was sometimes possible to get back into "favour"
was by taking out or returning one which caught her eye.
Old boys who came down promptly enquired, "What sort
of favour are *you* in?" and letters to those who had gone
on always ended up, "I am (touch wood) still in good
favour"—"I shall have to do something, I'm losing favour"
—or "I am in the most awful favour"; unjust at the time
as this feminine tyranny seemed it was a valuable foretaste
of the world outside; even the nickname Flip suggested
some primitive goddess of fortune. Thus, although I won
the prize through heading my list with "Carlyle's *French
Revolution*"—and Orwell won it next, we were both caught
at last with two volumes of *Sinister Street* and our favour
sank to zero.

We both wrote poetry. At sunset or late at night in the
dark, I would be visited by the Muse. In an ecstasy of flush-
ing and shivering, the tears welling up as I wrote, I would
put down some lines to the Night Wind. The next morning
they would be copied out. Although the process of com-

position always seemed an authentic visitation, the result
was an imitation of Stevenson or Longfellow or my favourite, Robert W. Service. I would compare them with Orwell's and be critical of his, while he was polite about mine,
then we would separate feeling ashamed of each other.

The remarkable thing about Orwell was that alone
among the boys he was an intellectual and not a parrot for
he thought for himself, read Shaw and Samuel Butler and
rejected not only St. Wulfric's, but the war, the Empire,
Kipling, Sussex, and Character. I remember a moment under a fig tree in one of the inland boulevards of the seaside town, Orwell striding beside me and saying in his flat,
ageless voice: "You know, Connolly, there's only one remedy for all diseases." I felt the usual guilty tremor when sex
was mentioned and hazarded, "You mean going to the
lavatory?" "No—I mean Death!" He was not a romantic, he
had neither use for the blandishments of the drill sergeant
who made us feel character was identical with boxing nor
for the threats of the chaplain with his grizzled cheektufts
and his gospel of a Jesus of character who detested immorality and swearing as much as he loved the Allies. "Of
course, you realise, Connolly," said Orwell, "that, whoever
wins this war, we shall emerge a second-rate nation."

Orwell proved to me that there existed an alternative to
character, Intelligence. Beaton showed me another, Sensibility. He had a charming, dreamy face, enormous blue
eyes with long lashes and wore his hair in a fringe. His
voice was slow, affected and creamy. He was not good at
games or work but he escaped persecution through good
manners, and a baffling independence. We used to mow
the lawn together behind an old pony, sit eating the goose-
berries in the kitchen garden or pretend to polish brass in
the chapel; from Orwell I learnt about literature, from
Cecil I learnt about art. He occupied his spare time drawing and painting and his holidays in going to the theatre.

On Saturday nights, when the school was entertained in
the big schoolroom by such talent as the place could offer—
when Mr. Potter had shown lantern slides of *Scrooge* or
Mr. Smedley, dressed up like a pirate at a P. & O. gala,
had mouthed out what he called "Poethry"—there would be

a hush, and Cecil would step forward and sing, "If you were the only girl in the world and I was the only boy." His voice was small but true, and when he sang these sentimental songs, imitating Violet Loraine or Beatrice Lillie, the eighty-odd Wulfricians felt there could be no other boy in the world for them, the beetling chaplain forgot hell-fire and masturbation, the Irish drill-sergeant his bayonet practice, the staff refrained from disapproving and for a moment the whole structure of character and duty tottered and even the principles of hanging on, muddling through, and building empires were called into question.

On other Saturday nights gramophone records were played; when we came to "I have a song to sing O, sing me your song O" I would open a book which I had bought in the Charing Cross Road, at the prepared place and read:

Far out at sea when the evening's dusk is falling you may often observe a dark-coloured bird with white under-plumage flit by just above the waves—another and another make their appearance, and you soon find out that a party of Manx Shearwaters have paid your vessel a passing call. They are nocturnal birds for the most part, spending the hours of daylight in their burrows, and coming out in the gloom to speed across the frowning waters in quest of food. There is something very exciting about the appearance of this singular bird. The noisy gulls which have been playing about all day drop slowly astern as the sun nears the west; the parties of Razorbills and Guillemots and Puffins have sped away to their distant breeding colonies; and the wide waste of waters seems unusually destitute and dreary as the night approaches, and the evening breeze fluttering in the sails, and through the rigging, is the only sound that breaks the oppressive stillness. But the hour of the Manx Shearwater's ghostly revelry has come, he holds high carnival over the waste of gray waters, flitting about in most erratic manner in his wild impetuous course, following the curve of every wave, dipping down into the hollows, where he is almost invisible, and then mounting the foamy crests, where you catch a brief glimpse of his hurried movements.

The combination of the music with this passage was intoxicating. The two blended into an experience of isolation and flight which induced the sacred shiver. The classroom disappeared, I was alone on the dark seas, there was a hush, a religious moment of suspense, and then the visitation—the Manx shearwaters appeared, held their high carnival, etc., and vanished. At length the schoolroom where each boy sat by his desk, his few possessions inside, his charted ink channels on top, returned to focus. This experience, which I repeated every Saturday, like a drug, was typical of the period. For those were the days when literature meant the romantic escape, the purple patch; when none of our teachers would have questioned the absolute beauty of such a line as "clothed in white Samite, mystic, wonderful!" We were still in the full Tennysonian afterglow and our beliefs, if the muse of St. Wulfric's could have voiced them, would have been somewhat as follows.

"There is a natural tradition in English poetry, my dear Tim, Chaucer begat Spenser, Spenser begat Shakespeare, Shakespeare begat Milton, Milton begat Keats, Coleridge, Shelley, Wordsworth, and they begat Tennyson who begat Longfellow, Stevenson, Kipling, Quiller-Couch and Sir Henry Newbolt. There are a few bad boys we do not speak about—Donne, Dryden, Pope, Blake, Byron, Browning, FitzGerald, who wrote *The Rubá'iyát of Omar Khayyám*, and Oscar Wilde who was a criminal degenerate. Chaucer is mediæval but coarse, Spenser is the poet's poet, Shakespeare you will remember from your performance as the witch ('aroint thee, witch, the rumpfed runion cried her husbands to Aleppo gone the master of the tiger, but in a sieve I'll thither sail and like a rat without a tail I'll do I'll do and I'll do'). Precisely. Milton was a great poet, he wrote *L'Allegro, Il Penseroso* and *Paradise Lost;* Keats wrote *The Ode to a Nightingale;* and Tennyson wrote *The Lady of Shalott*—and what else? *Morte d'Arthur, Locksley Hall, In Memoriam, Break, Break, Break,* and *Crossing the Bar.* Longfellow wrote *Hiawatha,* Stevenson *Under the*

Wide and Starry Sky, Kipling *Sussex* and *If* and *Gunga Din,*
Quiller-Couch is a Good Influence and *Drake's Drum* and
Lyra Heroica are by Sir Henry Newbolt.

"There are other good poems, *Chevy Chase, John Gil-
pin, The Armada, The Ancient Mariner, Grayselegy.* A
poem is good either because it is funny (Ingoldsby Legends, Bab Ballads) or because it makes you want to cry.
Some funny poems make you want to cry (the Jumblies,
the Dong with a Luminous Nose); that is because you are
not a healthy little boy. You need more Character. The
best poems have the most beautiful lines in them; these
lines can be detached, they are purple patches and are
Useful in Examinations. Gray's *Elegy* is almost all Purple
Patch and so is the *Ode to a Nightingale,* especially

> Magic casements, opening on the foam
> Of perilous seas, in faëry lands forlorn.

When you come to a purple patch you can tell it by an
alarm clock going off, you feel a cold shiver, a lump in the
throat, your eyes fill with tears and your hair stands on end.
You can get these sensations for yourself when you write
poems like your *Ode on the Death of Lord Kitchener* or *To
the Night Wind.*

"Nobody wrote so many purple patches as Tennyson,
and he had character too (*Bury the Great Duke, Charge of
the Light Brigade, The Revenge*). Kipling is the only great
poet alive to-day. Poetry is romantic, purple—a help in time
of trouble—or else it is clever and funny, like Calverley—or
has Character. (Life is real, Life is earnest, And the grave
is NOT its goal.) It is also something to be ashamed of, like
sex, and (except with the chaplain) religion."

My experience with the Manx shearwater fulfilled these
conditions. It was prose, so could not become poetry and
truly purple, till heightened by music. It was romantic;
something out of the ordinary, remote, and false, for in real
life I should hate tossing about the Hebrides in a small boat
—and escapist, since I imagined myself away from my present surroundings, alone on the northern waters, and yet
not alone, a Manx shearwater, playing with others of my
kind. The twilight was "my" time of day (the time I felt

most the poetical thrill), the waste of grey waters my weepy Celtic spiritual home. Because poetry was associated with emotional excess, night and unhappiness, I felt disgusted with it by day as by a friend in whom when drunk one has unwisely confided and I never exhibited the Manx shearwater even to Orwell.

It will be seen that the thread running through this autobiography is an analysis of romanticism, that romanticism in decline under whose shadow we grew up. Romanticism I would call the refusal to face certain truths about the world and ourselves, and the consequences of that refusal. It is a refusal which can be both splendid and necessary, this pretence that truth is beauty and beauty truth, that love is stronger than death, the soul immortal and the body divine—but in the hundred years that have elapsed since the romantic revival we have had too much of it. By the twentieth century the best work has been done and those of us who thought we were angels or devils have had a long struggle to free ourselves from such ideology. We have been the dupe of words and ideas, we have been unable to know when we are well off, we have expected too much from life, too many treats and we have precipitated crises to satisfy the appetite for sensation acquired in childhood; the womb world of the hot bath and the celluloid duck has been too near us. The romantic's artillery is always bracketing over the target of reality, falling short into cynicism or overreaching it into sentimental optimism so that, whatever the achievements of romanticism in the past, to be a romantic to-day, knowing what we know about the nature of man and his place in the universe, is the mark of a wilful astigmatism, a confession of cowardice and immaturity.

If but some of us lived in the world of romantic poetry, we all lived in the world of romantic love; there was no sentiment in *Maud* or *In Memoriam* that to us seemed exaggerated, we accepted "being half in love with easeful death" as a matter of course, like the psychology of the *Belle Dame Sans Merci*. Love was a recurrent ecstasy which drove us to make sacrifices for an object which might or might not be aware of them. Reciprocation killed love

faster than anything, then came Ridicule; it was only
Ignorance in the Beloved that could permit the emotion
to last. The prosaic Sambo seemed to have a flair for de-
tecting our romances and he would try to expel the
Cyprian by taps on the head from his heavy silver pencil.

> Always I long to creep
> Into some still cavern deep,
> There to weep and weep, and weep
> My whole soul out to Thee.

Such was my ideal, and if it met with any opposition I
would reply in the romantic's way with a spiteful poem.

The boy whom I loved for the last three years I was at
St. Wulfric's was called Tony Watson. He was small,
brown, wiry, good at games, untidy and silent, with a low
brow, green eyes and a fringe of rough short hair. I describe him because he is a type that has recurred through
my life and which gets me into trouble. It is that faunlike,
extrovert creature with a streak of madness and cruelty,
not clever, but narcissistic and quick to adapt itself to
clever people. In appearance it is between colours with a
small mouth, slanting eyes and lemon-yellow skin.

By the time I was twelve all four types to which I am
susceptible had appeared. I do not know whether it is
glands, numerology, the stars or mere environment which
dispose one to these fierce sympathies, inherited as if from
another life, but by now I recognise my kindred forms with
some familiarity; the Faun, the Redhead, the Extreme
Blond and the Dark Friend.

The Fauns well know their fatal power which a series of
conquests have made obvious and they derive a pleasure
that I mistake for reciprocation, from the spectacle of its
workings. Age is often unkind to these charmers and the
world is apt to turn against them. With the other types my
relations are happier. I supply them with vitality and intensive cultivation, they provide me with affection, balance, loyalty, good taste. The Extreme Blonds are quiet,
intelligent, humorous, receptive; they have an impressive
reserve against which I roll, like the Atlantic Ocean on the
Cornish cliffs, confident that they will be able to withstand

me. The Dark Friends are the most sympathetic, they have brown eyes and oval faces; they like my jokes and look after me when I am ill, but it is one of the hardships of romantic love that rarely is it bestowed on people like ourselves and the Dark Friends end by being Consolers. The Redheads have some of the quieting effect of the Extreme Blonds but they may suddenly become as deleterious as the Faun. They are a special type, not the dreamy, brown-eyed, long-faced auburn, nor the aggressive albino, but the gay, thin, dashing green-eyed variety.

Being an only child I romanticised sisterhood, I wanted an Electra and longed for a relationship with sister types of the same age. I liked health and equality in women, an implicit friendship. I desired the same for my imaginary brothers. The Dark Friends and the Extreme Blonds supplied this, the Redheads added an excitement which raised it to perfection. And then the exotic Faun would reappear and all peace of mind would vanish. As with other only children my desire for a brother or a sister was so strong that I came to see existence in terms of the couple; in whatever group I found myself I would inevitably end by sharing my life with one other, driven by an inner selection through a course of trial and error till after forming one of a group of four or five and then of a trio, I achieved my destiny as one half of a pair.

I christened this search for the *"dimidium animae meae"* the Pair System, and I was fascinated, when later I read the *Symposium* of Plato, to come across his theory that human beings had once been double and were for ever seeking the counterpart from whom they had been so rudely forced. We were all one half of a Siamese Twin.

> The brothered one, the not alone
> The brothered and the hated.

But it is a romantic theory and it is part of the romantic's misfortune that in the search for his affinity he is not guided by a community of interests but by those intimations which are the appeal of a mouth or an eye, an appeal which is not even private so that the spectacle is presented of half-a-dozen Platonic half-men trying to unite with the same in-

different alter ego. Love at first sight—and the first sight is
the supreme consummation for romantics—is an intuition
bred by habit of the person who can do us harm.

Yet Tony Watson let me down lightly. He was a wild
little boy with plenty of character but not of the right kind.
He taught me to smoke (which I hated); to rag in the
corridors at night, fighting among the coats hanging from
their pegs and to take part on the downs in gang warfare,
which I adored. He moved in a fast set of hard-smoking
and hard-swearing cronies from whom he protected me.
Our unlikeness made us over-polite. He accepted my devotion, even to a poem beginning, "Watson, the silent, Watson, the dauntless" and showed me, in return, an extraordinary drawing, a Parthenon Frieze on sheets of paper stuck
together that unfolded like a concertina, to reveal a long
procession of soldiers—cavalry, infantry, artillery, wounded
and dying, doctors, nurses, ghurkas, staff-officers and en-
gineers on their way to the war.

For most of us the war was skin-deep. The *Titanic* had
gone down, the passengers all singing "Nearer My God to
Thee"—that was terrible—and now the war: pins stuck in
maps, the Kaiser dying of cancer of the throat, Kitchener
drowned, ration cards, Business as Usual, a day when we
were told of the Battle of Jutland and another when we
heard that a terrible thing had happened, a revolution in
Russia with a monster called Kerensky now in power. None
of us, except perhaps Orwell, believed that England could
lose the war or that we would grow up to fight in it nor were
we old enough to understand the peril of our elder cousins
or the tragedy when—like Uncle Granville's only son, they
were killed on the first day of the Gallipoli slaughter. And
meanwhile Watson's exact and bloodthirsty pageant grew
fuller, a page at a time, till it stretched, by 1917, the whole
length of the schoolroom.

Tony shared my love of animals and drew for me pictures of foxes in lonely postures barking to the moon. I had
several excruciating moments with him. Once we vowed
blood-brotherhood in the Albanian fashion. Tony cut a
cross on each left hand and we held the bleeding scratches
together. Another time, left in the bathroom alone, he came

up to me, wrapped in his bath towel, and pursed his lips for a kiss. My spinster modesty made me flinch. He turned away and never did it again while for weeks I lay awake angry and miserable. He slept in a dormitory called the Red Room; I was in a two-bedded one across the passage with the Dark Friend, his cousin, Frankie Wright. Tony would come over in the morning after a night of pillow fighting, gang reprisals and smoking on the roof, and get into my bed where my innocence hung round my neck like an albatross. Then the eight-o'clock bell would ring and we would troop down to the ghastly plunge-bath. There was a smell of gooseflesh and slimy water. One by one, under the cold eye of Sambo and to the accompaniment of such comments as "Go on Marsden, you stink like a polecat," we dived or jumped in until it was the turn of the group of water-funks who shrank down the steps, groaning wer-wer-wer, while the sergeant-major waited to haul them out from the stagnant depths by a rope attached to a pole. When the last had been towed it was time to dress and go on the asphalt for "gym."

Year by year the air, the discipline, the teaching, the association with other boys and the driving will of Flip took effect on me. I grew strong and healthy and appeared to be normal for I became a good mixer, a gay little bit who was quick to spot whom to make up to in a group and how to do it. I knew how far to go in teasing and responding to teasing and became famous for my "repartee." I had a theory that there was one repartee effective for every situation and spent weeks in elaborating it. At that time the magic phrase seemed, "Dear me, how very uninteresting!" If I had to choose one now it would be "This is a very bad moment for both of us." I kept a Funny Book which contained satirical poems and character sketches. I became good at history, that is to say I learnt dates easily, knew which battle was fought in the snow and who was "the little gentleman in black velvet." I read Dickens, Thackeray, Carlyle and Scott and got marks for them and for pleasure John Buchan. It was time for me to go up for a scholarship. I had crammed Watson energetically for the common entrance which he just managed to pass and when

I saw him again in the holidays he was a dapper public schoolboy with his hair brushed back, a felt hat and a cane and we had nothing to say to each other.

My first attempt at a scholarship was at Wellington with Orwell. I hated every moment: the blue-suited prefects bustling about the dismal brick and slate, the Wellingtonias and rhododendrons, infertile flora of the Bagshot sand. It was winter and an old four-wheeler bore me from the examinations to my great-aunts with whom I was staying. The musical groaning of the wheels and springs in the winter stillness had a profound effect and I felt like Childe Roland, mystical and Celtic. Pines and heather, the whortle-bearing ridges, seemed to have a message for me, to be the background for some great event as I trundled over them after the afternoon paper. Orwell got a scholarship which he did not take. I failed but the experience was considered good practice.

A year later I went up for Eton, which was very different. Sambo took charge of us; he knew many people there and we had tea with old Wulfrician boys and masters. I had a moment on Windsor Bridge; it was summer, and, after the coast, the greenness of the lush Thames Valley was enervating and oppressive; everything seemed splendid and decadent, the huge stale elms, the boys in their many-coloured caps and blazers, the top hats, the strawberries and cream, the smell of wistaria. I looked over the bridge as a boy in an outrigger came gliding past, like a waterboatman. Two Etonians were standing on the bridge and I heard one remark, "Really that man Wilkinson's not at all a bad oar." The foppish drawl, the two boys with their hats on the back of their heads, the graceful sculler underneath, seemed the incarnation of elegance and maturity.

There was no doubt that this was the place for me, for all of it was, from the St. Wulfric's point of view, utterly and absorbingly evil. I got in twelfth on History and English as Orwell, after Wellington, had done the year before. In case there was no vacancy I went up for one more scholarship, this time at Charterhouse where we did the examination in a cellar during an air raid.

My last year at St. Wulfric's was rosy. I was in sixth form, which had its own sitting room, with Ned Northcote, the captain of the school (Extreme Blond), Frankie Wright (Dark Friend) and Nigel Kirkpatrick (Faunlike). We were about as civilised as little boys can grow to be. We were polite and we hardly ever caned anyone. We wrote to each other in the holidays, we got on with each other's parents, we went to theatres together and took tea at Rumpelmayer's. Ned was captain of the eleven and Nigel of the football team. I was head of the sixth.

My lack of character was now a permanent feature. I was *unreliable*. For that reason I was head of the sixth but not captain of the school; I occupied already the position I was so often to maintain in after life, that of the intellectual who is never given the job because he is "brilliant but unsound." I was also a physical coward, though I learnt how to conceal it, a natural captain of second elevens, and a moral coward by compensation, since, in an English community, moral cowardice is an asset.

Already I had accepted the theory that (1) Character is more important than intellect. (2) Intellect is usually found without character (Oscar Wilde). (3) Intellect, when found with character, is called Nous. (Intellect plus character = Nous plus gumption.) Character is desirable because it makes for success at school (winning colours and reporting best friend for homosexuality), prepares boys for the university and is the foundation of success in business, politics, the army, the navy, the Indian and Egyptian civil services, and the African Police. But my analysis of success had disclosed another quality which seemed, in school life at any rate, to go as far. It might be called Prettiness. In the matriarchy of St. Wulfric's, it was not Character, but Character plus Prettiness that succeeded; Colin and Nigel Kirkpatrick in their green kilts, even the outlawed Tony Watson or Roy Brown with his fine treble voice; they were the favoured of fortune, petted when others were scolded, permitted to wait on parents and old boys at Sunday-night supper in their blue suits, introduced to the guests when they brought the food into the room and in a position to stuff their pockets with potato salad when they took it out. Prettiness alone (Cecil) was suspect like intellect alone

(Orwell) but prettiness that was good at games meant "Character" and was safe. Since I was not pretty I worked hard to be charming and the four of us grew so civilised that we became inseparable. We were a little clique at the head of the school, a kind of "Souls" of St. Wulfric's, gay, powerful, introspective and absorbed in each other's impressions. We took to visiting in our cubicles at night. One evening, after lights out, Ned Northcote, and Frankie Wright were talking in mine when we heard the matron pass along.

> Stalk and sneak, stalk and sneak,
> Maud of the rubbery shoes.
> Sneak sneak every week,
> Maud of the rubbery shoes.
> Over the cubicle wings you go
> Hearing the Red Room whispering low . . .

I had once written to please Tony, and now it was my turn to be caught.

Maud went into Northcote's cubicle. No sign of him. She called out in a terrible voice, "Where's Northcote?" I answered from my cubicle, "I think he went to the lavatory." We heard her go along to open the door and lost our heads, like rabbits chased by a ferret. Ned bolted the latch of my cubicle with a toothbrush, and started to climb over the partition into his own. But Maud came and rattled it. "Why is this door locked? Open it this instant." I was afraid to. Silence. At last, with white face, Frankie opened it and she burst in. There was an eternity of waiting while our crime was reported, and then the three of us were taken down and caned by Sambo in our pyjamas. The locked door was evidence which our being a trio instead of the usual compromised pair could not palliate. It was Oscar Wilde over again.

The caning was only the beginning; next day our sergeant's stripes were removed, we were turned out of sixth form and a period of miserable disfavour started from which there seemed no hope of escape. But my scholarship was needed, like Ned's bowling, for propaganda; gradually we were forgiven, and our disgrace forgotten except by ourselves. For we never felt quite the same; we grasped that since we were all completely innocent there must be a pitch of civilisation which, once reached, brought down a Nemesis. Character was safest: we had seen the writing on the wall.

Before I went to Eton I had spent the Christmas of 1917 in Ireland, in my aunt's house at Rathfarnham. The Easter Rebellion had taken place since I was last there and to be pro-Irish, pro-Celt, pro-Gaelic was no longer a harmless eccentricity. I used to go riding with a groom over the Wicklow mountains and for the first time the Sinn Feiner of St. Wulfric's met his equal. Frank the groom was supposed to command a company of the Irish republican army whom he drilled in the glens of Kilmashogue and up by the Hell Fire Club. I afterwards pretended that I had been present at these parades but never met anyone with him except an old hermit. We went to the Abbey Theatre and saw Synge acted, and heard "God Save the King" hissed and to Clontarf for a pink-coated Christmas dinner at which everyone told hunting stories in the brogue. I felt dowdy, awkward, and English again.

Otherwise my holidays had been uneventful. My great moment at home had been the purchase of a bicycle with three speeds which I called the Green Dragon. I rode it over to where we lived at Crondall and a few days later was allowed to go away for a night by myself. My mother and my favourite Great-uncle Granville saw me off. I bicycled that day from Farnham to Winchester, stayed at the George and went over the school and the Cathedral. The hotel people thought I had run away from somewhere and were suspicious, for the sight of a tourist of thirteen booking a room and dining by himself, with a guidebook propped up was unusual. It was the first welling up of the passion for travel that was to dominate my spare time for the next twenty years.

I was still ignorant of anything which I had not read in a book but just before I went to Eton a concerted attack was made on my modesty. My father struggled to explain the facts of life and the chaplain at St. Wulfric's gave the boys who were leaving a seedy exhortation. Sambo was

184 ENEMIES OF PROMISE

more precise. We were going into a world full of temptations, he said, especially the Etonians; we must report any boy at once who tried to get into our bed, never go for a walk with a boy from another house, never make friends with anyone more than a year and a half older (eventually it would be younger), and above all, not "play with ourselves." There was an old boy from St. Wulfric's who became so self-intoxicated that when he got to Oxford he had put, in a fit of remorse, his head under a train. That miserable youth, I afterwards learnt, had attended all the private schools in England.

Sambo gave a few examples of Wulfricians who had made good and mentioned cases where those who were doing well and were now heads of their houses had been able to lend a helping hand to those floundering amid the sexual difficulties due to lack of character. The other boys leaving looked at me curiously, for I was warned to be careful, my literary temperament rendering me especially prone to "all that kind of poisonous nonsense" and I was told that the boy with "character" in my election at Eton who would, although not an old Wulfrician, keep an eye on me, was called Meynell. The Easter term over, we bade a tearful farewell to each other, Flip turned suddenly into a friend, and Nigel Kirkpatrick, Ned Northcote, Frankie Wright, promised to exchange letters with me from Marlborough, Repton and Radley. But it was three years before I wrote another letter.

CHAPTER XX: DARK AGES

If we had written, all our letters would have told the same story. The lively aristocrats of the cubicles and the sixth-form room were reduced to serfdom, cultivated Greeks pitched into the Carthaginian slave market. We began to adapt ourselves to our new indignity; C. V. Connolly, Esq., K.S., New Buildings, Eton College, Windsor.

The seventy Eton scholars lived together in a house, part Victorian, part mediæval where they were governed by the Master in College who had under him the Captain of the School and nine other members of Sixth Form, who wore stick-up collars, could cane, and have fags. All boys were divided into elections according to the year in which they won their scholarship; the elections moved slowly up the school *en bloc* and each represented a generation.

Below the top twenty came another thirty boys or so who formed the bulk of college and then the bottom twenty about fifteen of whom were doing their compulsory year of fagging, and who, while all the others had rooms, lived in wooden cubicles in Chamber.

The whole school, ruled in theory by Sixth Form and the Captain of the School, was governed by Pop or the Eton Society, an oligarchy of two dozen boys who, except for two or three *ex officio* members, were self-elected and could wear coloured waistcoats, stick-up collars, etc., and cane boys from any house. The masters could not cane. They punished by lines, detentions, and "tickets" or chits of misbehaviour which had to be carried to the housemaster for signature. Serious offences, or too many tickets, meant being complained of to the headmaster and might end in a birching.

This system makes Eton the most democratic of schools, for it is a school where all the prefects except the Sixth

Form (who are only powerful in College) are self-elected. The boys get the government they deserve.

In practice Eton was not a democracy for the system was feudal. The masters represented the Church, with the headmaster as Pope; the boys, with their hierarchy of colours and distinctions, were the rest of the population, while the prefects and athletes, the captains of houses and the members of "Pop" were the feudal overlords who punished offences at the request of the "Church" and in return were tacitly allowed to break the same rules themselves. Thus a boy had two loyalties, to his tutor and to his fagmaster or feudal overlord. Sometimes the "Church" could protect a young clerk, making the lot of a serious little boy more bearable, in other houses the housemaster was powerless, the "Church" weak and unable to control the feudal barons. At other times there were struggles between master and boy which ended in Canossa.

On the whole the feudal system worked well. The boys elected to Pop, those who combined goodness at games with elegance, vitality and a certain mental alertness, were urbane and tolerant; it was among the house-barons that bullies and stupid types were to be found.

A fag in Chamber I was in the lowest ranks of serfdom. Though fagmasters were usually chivalrous to their own slaves, mine was not, nor had we privacy, for our spare time was at the mercy of our rulers, who could send us far into Windsor to buy them food and beat us if we made a mistake over it. I had not often been beaten at St. Wulfric's, at Eton it became a hideous experience for even the little boy who was "Captain of Chamber" could beat us, not with a cane but with a piece of rubber tubing. There was a "Chamber Pop" who also could beat one in a body for a breach of privilege.

I felt quite lost and friendless in this world and sought out Meynell, the boy selected by Sambo to keep an eye on me. An eye was a euphemism for here was the familiar blend of character and prettiness, a tousled wire-terrier of a boy, tough, humorous, a natural leader and political commissar. We were all unhappy and had such a feeling of persecution that we bullied each other to forget it. I was

sixty-ninth in college order and among the most bullied
boys in my election where Meynell was ringleader. He invented tortures as a perpetual inquest to see if we had
"guts" and was much liked in the elections above him who
considered him a "good influence."

Nobody would have believed that he could make me
stand on a mantelpiece and dance while he brandished a
red-hot poker between my feet and said: "What is your
name?" "Connolly." "No—what is your real name? Go on.
Say it." "Ugly." "All right, Ugly, you can come down." He
was aided by a few boys who hoped that their sycophancy
would save their skins and by another bully called Highworth. Highworth was not a torturer like Meynell, but a
conceited, rakish, conventional boy who could not bear anyone to be eccentric or untidy. He should never have been
in College, he was a natural Oppidan.[1]

I spent much of my spare time in School Library, shel-
tering among the poets. I had discovered the Celtic Twilight and in proportion as I was unhappy, I took it out on
the *Lake Isle of Innisfree*, the *Little Waves of Breffny*,
Glencullen and other escapist poems, to which I added the
Golden Journey to Samarcand. I tried to make friends with
one other bullied boy but he reciprocated too violently,
showed me his own poems, and sniffed at the back of his
nose. Instead I fell for a boy called Wilfrid, the faun type
over again with green eyes, nectarine colouring, who was
quick to divine in the little black-gowned, dirty colleger a
potential admirer, even as a beautiful orchid accepts the
visits of some repulsive beetle. He was an Oppidan, good
at games and older than I. It was only possible to see him
leaving his classroom about once a week or sometimes coming out of Chapel or at Absence when the whole of our
feudal society assembled in School Yard. If he was with
anyone important he would cut me; if not he would make
a joke or two at my expense while I grinned like a waiter.
My daydreams centred round him. I looked up his home

[1] Oppidans were the thousand other boys not in College who
paid the full fees. Oppidans could be brilliant scholars but they
could never experience the advantages and disadvantages of the
intensive intellectual forcing-house which College was.

address, found out about his family, and copied his initials on to bits of paper. It was something to be in love at last.

The beatings were torture. We were first conscious of impending doom at Prayers when the eyes of Sixth Form would linger pointedly on us. They had supper in a room of their own and a special fag, "Senior," who was excused ordinary duties, like other police spies, was sent from there to fetch the "wanted" man. From Upper Tea Room "Senior" set out on his thrilling errand, past the boys chatting outside their rooms. "Who's 'wanted'?" "Connolly." "What, again?" At last he reached the fags, who were shivering with terror—for this was always an agonising quarter of an hour for them—in their distant stalls in Chamber. Those who were sitting in their tin baths paused with the sponge in the air—they might have to get out again to dress. The talkers ceased their chorus simultaneously, like frogs, even the favoured who were being tickled in their stalls by the Master in College stopped giggling and fear swept over the wooden partitions. "It's Connolly." "Connolly, you're 'wanted.'" "Who by?" "Wrangham." "That's all right. He won't beat me, only tick me off. He's my fagmaster." "He's going to beat someone. He's got the chair out."

The chair was only put in the middle of the room when beatings were to take place and sometimes the fag was sent beforehand to get the canes with which he would himself be beaten.

The worst part was the suspense for we might make a mistake the day before and not be beaten for it till the following evening. Or we could get a day's grace by pleading a headache and getting "early bed leave" or by going out to the shooting range, the musical society or to a mysterious evening service, held once a week to expedite the war, which was much frequented by guilty consciences, called Intercession. The huge chapel was dark and deserted, the gas mantles plopped, the stained-glass windows glittered, the headmaster droned the prayers from the altar. I too was praying. "Please God may Wrangham not 'want' me, please please God may Wrangham not 'want' me or may he forget about it by to-morrow, and I will clean my teeth. And make me see Wilfrid. Amen."

Often mass executions took place; it was not uncommon for all the fags to be beaten at once. After a storm of accusation to which it was wiser not to reply since no one, once the chair was out, had been known to "get off," the flogging began. We knelt on the chair bottoms outwards and gripped the bottom bar with our hands, stretching towards it over the back. Looking round under the chair we could see a monster rushing towards us with a cane in his hand, his face upside down and distorted—the frowning mask of the Captain of the School or the hideous little Wrangham. The pain was acute. When it was over some other member of Sixth Form would say "Good night"—it was wiser to answer.

These memories are associated for me with the smell of Sixth Form supper and with the walk back through the spectators to the bed that pulled down from the wall, with the knowing enquiries of the vice-haunted virginal master in college, a Jesuit at these executions and the darkness that prisoners long for.

The Captain of the School, Marjoribanks, who afterwards committed suicide, was a passionate beater like his bloody-minded successors, Wrangham and Cliffe. Meynell began to receive anonymous notes which made certain suggestions, and showed "character" by taking them straight to his fagmaster. The Captain of the School was told and the culprit was ordered to confess; nothing happened. Then another note arrived. The sender, clearly very high in the school, was never discovered, but in one satisfactory evening Marjoribanks had beaten all the lower half of college. Thirty-five of us suffered. Another time we were all flogged because a boy dropped a sponge out of a window which hit a master, or we would be beaten for "generality" which meant no specific charge except that of being "generally uppish."

The result of these persecutions, combined with Chamber beatings and bullyings, was to ruin my nerve. My work went off, and I received several "tickets" which I had to present my tutor, in itself a torture. To this day I cannot bear to be sent for or hear of anyone's wanting to see me about something without acute nervous dread.

My own election was broken under the strain of beatings at night and bullying by day; all we could hope for was to achieve peace with seniority and then become disciplinarians in our turn. But there was one ray of hope. The election now in power was a reactionary one which would be succeeded as it passed on by a gentler crowd, and our own senior election, the year above us, whom as yet we hardly knew, contained heroic fighters for liberty and justice. It bristled with Pyms and Hampdens and the feudal system was powerless there.

I had another stroke of luck. After a "Chamber Pop beating" from Meynell and four other boys, he began a heart-to-heart—"Ugly, why are you so filthy, what is the matter with you?" After the tears which followed I succeeded in making him laugh, and revealed my capacity as a wit. I was able to expand it and soon I could make not only Meynell laugh, but Highworth: they began to leave me alone, bullying me only when they could not find anyone else, but even then sparing me, if I seemed unsuspecting and confident and did not smell of fear. At last I made them laugh at the expense of their victims and my sarcasm became useful. One evening in my second term, after the Armistice had been signed, Meynell asked me to call him Godfrey. From then I was safe, my prayers at "intercession" were answered. I had become a bully too.

Highworth's father and Meynell's and my own had all been professional soldiers who had employed the methods of the parade ground for the disciplining of their sons. We now became the rulers of Chamber, in which Godfrey Meynell was the Hitler, Highworth the Goering, and I the Goebbels, forming a Gestapo who bullied everyone we could and confiscated their private property.

After two terms of being bullied, I had, with occasional relapses, a year of bullying until, owing to some bad tactics, I let both Godfrey and Highworth combine against me. Yet we were fond of each other and our triumvirate was racked with jealousy. Highworth was a big neat handsome boy, good at games, a fast bowler, fond of girls and dirty stories. Godfrey was untidy, lazy, yet energetic, sentimental and self-reproachful, a puritan with a saving grace of humour,

a border baron half-converted to Christianity whose tur-
bulent life fitted exactly into the pattern of Eton feudalism
for he was an example of character and prettiness in authority; his courage was tremendous, to play football under
his captaincy, on a losing side, was a sensation. For an hour
and a quarter he blamed, praised and appealed to our feelings, leading rush after rush against boys bigger than himself, poaching any kicks he could get and limping off the
field with his arm round my neck. "My God, you went
badly to-day, Nolly—haven't you any guts—to think we lost
to those bastards by three to one" and tears of rage would
roll down his cheeks. "Next time we've got to win—we've
just got to—understand, Flinchface?"

His personality dominated us because it was the strongest
and because it was the incarnation of schoolboyness; the
five hundred years of Eton life had gone to make it, the
Gothic windows, the huge open fireplace, the table in the
middle of Chamber round which our life centred, had been
brought into being for him. He was emotional and as Captain of Chamber would "beat" me for untidiness, half miserable at having to flog his best friend, half pleased at
fulfilling a Roman duty, only to suffer remorse at the condition of his own belongings. "God knows what I'm to do—
I can't let you beat *me*—I haven't the authority—if I ask
you to hit me as hard as you can I might lose my temper
and knock you down. We'll have to make Wayne and
Buckley tidy our stalls for us in future."

Godfrey's relaxation was reading Homer, he adored the
Odyssey, for the Homeric world was one in which he was
at home and the proverbs of "the wily Odysseus," to the
disgust of the able but philistine Highworth, were never off
his lips. "Oh, babababarbaba babababarbaba," he would
storm; "for God's sake stop spouting Greek—I can't understand a fellow with guts like you, Godfrey, wanting to
quote that filthy Greek all the time—and as for you, Cyril,
you're worse—nine bloody beanrows will I have there and
a hive for the honey bloody bee—my God it makes me crap."

Between two such personalities it seemed that I never
would have a chance to develop, or find room to reach
out to the sun, but I had two pieces of good fortune. High-

worth always sexually precocious laid hands on a confirmation candidate in the confessional stage and was sent away for two terms and Godfrey got pneumonia. He was in the sick-room for a month and while he was ill his trampled satellites plucked up their courage. I made friends with three of them and when he came back, we presented a united front against further bullying. Godfrey himself was deeply altered by his illness, his mischievous restlessness left him; being ill for so long and perhaps discovering how little he was missed and how well people got on without him, how transitory was power, had changed his character. For the rest of his time at Eton (he left early for Sandhurst), he was hardworking and modest. He never recovered his leadership but became liked by all those who once had gone in fear of him. The border baron, the prince of the dark ages, had undergone a change of heart, a genuine conversion.

Godfrey afterwards joined his father's regiment, went out to India and had himself transferred to the Indian Army, for he disliked the social side of army life and wanted to be in closer contact with the men he loved. From there he went with his ghurkas to Waziristan, still reading Homer and was killed in action on the frontier, winning a posthumous V.C.

> Liquenda tellus et domus et placens
> Uxor . . .

Encased in the shell secreted by my cowardice, I have thought about his death on that untenable hillside, outnumbered, putting heart into his troops by assuring them that help would reach them, though well aware that help could not, and dying covered with wounds after fighting all day.

Such an end seems remote from the literary life, yet it was the end of one my own age, with whom for four years I had been shaken about like stones in a tin. To a parent passing through College there must have seemed nothing to choose between Godfrey and myself, two small boys in Eton jackets cooking their fagmaster's sausages, both untidy, noisy, and mouse-coloured and yet in each a fate was at work; two characters, reacting differently to the same environment, were shaping their lives. The qualities I admire are intellectual honesty, generosity, courage, and beauty. Godfrey was brave. I was not.

Such was the reward of leadership, the destiny of character—not the position of business responsibility which St. Wulfric's had promised us but a premature and lonely death with the barren glory of a military honour.

The boys in my election with whom I now made friends were Charles Milligan, Kit Minns, and Jackie O'Dwyer. Charles became of morbid interest through being caught smoking which made him seem romantic and subversive. He was the Extreme Blond with delicate features and an air of neatness and languor. Minns, a peaceable Oriental-looking boy, surprised the Gestapo by refusing to be bullied. He was quiet and good-natured but when threats or force were employed he would not move. The Gestapo were puzzled; we felt like hunters up against a new animal for Minns was invincible, not through his badgerlike strength, but because he knew he was right. For the first time we felt guilty, aware that our bullying proceeded from a sense of inferiority deepened perhaps by sexual ignorance, and confined ourselves henceforth to the official victims.

O'Dwyer was nearly always in tears but he was affectionate, witty and genial and I secretly made friends with him. We arranged that if he publicly stood up to the Gestapo in my presence I would try to prevent him being punished. The moment came. Godfrey, as usual, was late in changing for afternoon school. "My God, I've lost my braces." He looked round, then marched up. "O'Dwyer, give me your braces." "No." "Take off your braces and give them me at once." "No." This was unheard of: Godfrey glowered at O'Dwyer, who stood rooted to the spot with the tears streaming down his face. After a silence, Godfrey turned away and claimed some braces elsewhere. Another serf was on the road to emancipation. Not unnaturally our election had a bad name though no one quite knew what was going on in it.

I was now fifteen, dirty, inky, miserable, untidy, a bad

fag, a coward at games, lazy at work, unpopular with my masters and superiors, anxious to curry favour and yet to bully whom I dared. The rule of the election system was that we spoke only to the boys of our own year; we could be beaten for speaking first to a boy in an election above and were expected to enforce the same discipline on those below. All our election were most formal with the year that had arrived beneath us. I got a bad report and was described as "cynical and irreverent" "*tu ne cede malis,*" wrote Mr. Stone, "*sed contra audentior ito.*"

My parents were upset, heads were put together, and the blame was thrown on Orwell, who was supposed to be my "bad influence" though now I hardly ever saw him. We had been for walks on Sundays but we belonged to two different civilisations. He was immersed in *The Way of All Flesh* and the atheistic arguments of *Androcles and the Lion,* I in the Celtic Twilight and Lady Gregory's resurrected Gaelic legends. His election found us (Meynell excluded) brutish and savage. They were anxious to talk to their junior election and subvert in that way the reactionary "election" system but they did not know how to begin for we were hardly the material on which liberal opinions could be tested.

The moral leaders of my senior election, known as "the caucus," were Denis Dannreuther, Roger Mynors, Robert Longden, Gibson and Cazalet. Orwell was rather extreme and aloof, and Farlow, the most original and vigorous member, too rough and cynical for the lofty inner ring of whiggery. These two precocious boys were bosom friends: Farlow a boisterous sceptic who applied "*cui bono*"—"who benefits by it" as a criterion to the whole school system and Orwell perpetually sneering at "They"—a Marxist-Shavian concept which included Masters, Old Collegers, the Church and Senior reactionaries. This did not prevent him knocking Highworth down once when he found him tormenting me. One day at the end of my sixth term I found myself "staying out" in the sick-room with Roger Mynors. Day by long day we made friends, discovering in each other the inevitable passion for the Isle of Purbeck, for chalk streams and geography and for the first time I underwent the civilising influence of my senior election. They were a most remarkable set of boys, and included a batch of five scholar athletes, animated, unlike the rulers of college, by post-war opinions. They hated bullying, beating, fagging, the election system, militarism, and all infringements of liberty and they believed in the ultimate victory of human reason. They were polite to each other and formed an oasis of enlightenment, with one set of baby reactionaries underneath them and another, more dangerous, in the year above.

Mynors did not drop me when we came out of the sickroom and an epidemic of mumps thinned out my own election, enabling Charles Milligan, Jackie O'Dwyer and myself to push forward together. Jackie was clever, lazy, good at games and attractive. He represented a type which is found in every school, the affable genial kind of boy whose life is a succession of enthusiasms; for dab cricket, for learning all the peers by sight, the variations of the house colours, the results of the Harrow matches or the batting averages of the eleven. He was sunny and tolerant, suspected of "not going hard" in the more painful sports and like myself, greedy. We ate quantities of bananas and cream and all day played a game called "passage fives" under a white fused light in the echoing mump-stricken corridor. Roger Mynors walked about with me and called me the "little ray of sunshine." The affectionate and civilised head boy of St. Wulfric's tentatively reappeared and that Easter, after my fourth term, I wrote O'Dwyer a letter. The dark ages were over.

CHAPTER XXI: RENAISSANCE

It was now the summer of 1920. I was no longer a fag and had a room of my own. Neither ruler nor serf, I now formed part of the central bourgeoisie of College. I first saw Nigel by the letter slab and from that moment I was as much changed as Godfrey by pneumonia. The "pair system" reappeared in my life, the faun, the dream brother. That afternoon we played in a knock-up cricket match and each made twenty-five. Nigel had all the familiar features, dark hair, green eyes, yellow skin and a classic head with the wistfulness of a minor angel in a Botticelli, but, being a colleger, he was not stupid like Wilfrid or Tony; in spite of the year and a half between our ages, companionship was possible.

To say I was in love again will vex the reader beyond endurance, but he must remember that being in love had a peculiar meaning for me. I had never even been kissed and love was an ideal based on the exhibitionism of the only-child. It meant a desire to lay my personality at someone's feet as a puppy deposits a slobbery ball; it meant a non-stop daydream, a planning of surprises, an exchange of confidences, a giving of presents, an agony of expectation, a delirium of impatience, ending with the premonition of boredom more drastic than the loneliness which it set out to cure. I was now entering adolescence and for long was to suffer from that disfiguring ailment. My sense of values was to be affected, my emotions falsified, my mind put out of focus, my idea of reality imposed on reality and where they did not tally, reality would be cut to fit.

Nigel was in my sub-junior election. This meant that although I could be seen about with my junior election, I could not be seen alone with him. One way I could talk to him was by availing myself of co-ordinated visits to the shooting gallery, glimpses on the way to meals, leaving chapel, at absence or other ceremonies of the community. The other was to frequent my junior election and make use of the etiquette by which they were allowed to go about with him. This meant altering my ideas about the election system, in fact, ceasing to be a reactionary. The change in emotional life led, as is often the case, to a new political alignment.

I first made friends with the two civilised members of my junior election, Peter Loxley and Walter Le Strange, and through them was able to see something of Nigel and his red-haired friend Freddie Langham. At the same time, growing more liberal, I became more acceptable to the election above. Denis Dannreuther and Robert Longden took me up and afterwards King-Farlow and George Wansbrough. At the end of the term I sat next Nigel at a housematch. (I could not give a picture of Eton if I did not emphasise how much time was devoted to planning meetings with people of another year or in another house; the intrigues were worthy of Versailles or Yildiz.) At the housematch I asked Nigel who he liked best in the school. Langham? "Second best," Loxley? "Fourth best," and so on. He also asked me. We realised that we had both omitted "first best" and that the only people we had not mentioned had been each other. I experienced the thrill not untinged with apprehension by which the romantic recognises reciprocated love.

Then came Camp, where my parents, who lived near, gave dinner parties for Godfrey and my new friends, Mynors, Runciman, Wansbrough, Longden, and Dadie Rylands. Our house was a refuge from Camp and, making up my little dinner parties, I tasted the joys of being a political hostess and laid my plans for the future.

The Christmas term of 1920 I was launched. Looking back at my school days I am conscious of a rhythm about them, every year culminated in the summer term; it was the term when things happened, the climax of emotions, successes, and failures. I never felt well in the summer term. The Thames Valley climate was lowering, I was enervated by the profusion of elms and buttercups and sheep-turds, the heat and the leisure. The summers at Eton were too pagan, one collapsed half-way through. Those hot afternoons punctuated by the "toc toc" of bat hitting ball when I sat with a book in the shade of Poets' Walk, a green tunnel that has etiolated so many generations of poets, or wandered through the deserted college buildings, where the chalky sunbeam lay aslant the desk, were deleterious. Christmas terms meant consolidation and new beginnings; Easter was a season of promise; the games that I was good at were fives and squash; I liked the Easter terms best. Christmas was a primitive, Easter the quattrocento, and summer the decadence.

To this day I can tell whether a person is school-minded: whether they are cowardly, gregarious, sensitive to pupil-teacher relationships, warm, competitive and adolescent— or whether they are schoolproof. The art of getting on at school depends on a mixture of enthusiasm with moral cowardice and social sense. The enthusiasm is for personalities and gossip about them, for a schoolboy is a novelist too busy to write. Orwell, for example, with his *"non serviam,"* or Steven Runciman who divided the world into two groups, the stupid and the sillies, lack the ape-like virtues without which no one can enjoy a public school. I possessed them, and from now on was happy and successful. I joined the College Literary Society for which we wrote poems, and criticism.

Two of my new friends in super-senior election belonged, Dadie Rylands and Terence Beddard, whom I called, as one was so much more censorious than the other, the Old and the New Testament. Dadie was a charming, feline boy; he lent me modern poetry to read in the chapbooks which were then coming out. He liked Rupert Brooke and introduced me to the Georgians. My possession of these chapbooks awoke in Highworth envy tinged with incomprehension. "My God, Cyril—if I'd known you were going to turn into a bloody æsthete and go bumsucking after people like Rylands! There's Godfrey turned pi as hell and all the rest of our election without any guts—and now you start letting your hair grow long and reading those bloody chapbooks. Rupert Brooke! Ow boo-hoo boo-hoo, stands the church

clock at ten to bloody three and is there honey still for
bloody tea!" After this I lost my temper and for the next
year never spoke to him. Handsome and neat as ever, with
several cricket colours and many Oppidan friends, he had
hopes of getting into Pop, and yet was bewildered, isolated
from the rest of us by his lack of adolescence.

One day I wrote a pines-and-heather poem myself for
the Literary Society which was favourably criticised. The
last couplet was:

> And, winging down the evening sky,
> The herons come to the heronry.

Dadie said that by accident I had written a couplet as good
as anything in Rupert Brooke. Godfrey took me aside and
said that he wished he could have written the poem, that it
expressed everything he felt and that he did not know anyone else could feel. Even Terence Beddard, a dandy with
a romantic side and a gift for satire, was impressed—but
Highworth never saw it.

Terence and I did classics up to Mr. Headlam in the
same division, we satirised Georgian poetry and the literary
society in our spare time and invented a Georgian poet
called Percy Beauregard Biles. Terence was a Byronic
character, the first one I had met; he was a Mercutio, a
foppish, melancholy and ironical dandy. I used to go along
to talk in his room and we discovered a common interest
in Nigel. By then I liked Freddie Langham almost as much;
he was more engaging, intelligent, and whole-hearted than
Nigel who could embarrass me by displaying a sentimentality which I shared. He was also inclined to grow weepy,
and religious. We sometimes walked across School Yard at
night and lay on our backs looking up at the buttresses of
the chapel for it was a discovery of mine that the height
of the Gothic could be appreciated in that way.

"I suppose we are the only people in College," said Nigel,
"who ever look at the stars. The others are all fools. We
are the only two who are humble."

By the next term Terence had left. He had had great
influence on me, bringing out a side—Don Juan with a touch
of Wilde—whose development made my life more interest-

ing but also more theatrical and egocentric. For years afterwards I wrote to him, about "Le Rouge et Le Noir" as I
called Freddie and Nigel. Nigel sulked that term and grew
more religious than ever. My friends were Denis Dannreuther (the head of my senior election), Charles Milligan
and Freddie Langham; the Dark Friend, the Extreme
Blond and the Redhead were rallying.

Denis was an exquisite classical scholar, one of those rare
people who combine a brilliant and logical mind with genuine moral feeling and who become more than a careerist.
We talked ethics and College politics, for the political situation was fascinating. There was party government in the
struggle between pre-war and post-war—between right and
left. The armistice and the end of the war had released a
wave of scepticism and revolutionary feeling over Eton
where a book like *Eminent Victorians* made a particular
sensation. The Left Wing or Liberals, as we called ourselves,
in opposition to the Reactionaries, had a clear view of the
situation.

(1) The war and the corresponding increase of militarism had affected the freedom of Eton boys. Emergency
measures had been enforced and not repealed, lights went
out earlier, discipline was stricter and privileges had been
given up in the crisis which had never been restored. The
tightening up of discipline involved a cynical view of boy
nature, which, especially in College, was to be deplored.
Those responsible were the ushers, among whom were certain Vile Old Men who wished to wrest from the boys all
liberty and independence and who were aided by our
vacillating Master, a sex-obsessed prude who extorted information about boys' morals from hysterical confirmation
candidates and practised other jesuitical abuses. Behind
him was that fine casuist the headmaster and of course the
Old Tugs—old collegers who belonged to the stoic pre-war
generations, the pillars of the *ancien régime*.

(2) The corner-stone of this régime was the election
system which did not exist in the houses, was of quite recent
origin, and harmful in that it created a false authority,
separating people who ought to be mixing with each other,
preventing a "bad" election being improved by a "good"

one and creating a sense of guilt in those who had innocent
relationships outside. The theory that the election system
prevented bullying was untrue, since bullying, like immorality, was commonest among boys of the same age. The
election system therefore must be abolished from the top,
and boys be allowed to talk to whom they liked. In this
daylight the danger of immorality would be less than in the
present atmosphere of privilege and intrigue.

(3) Corporal punishment was a relic of barbarism. It
was as bad for those who administered as for those who
received it. That torture also must be abolished from the
top while mass floggings and generality beatings of the kind
we had been subjected to were inexcusable.

(4) The fagging system must be modified. The sum-
moning of boys from Chamber to distant parts of College,
the last one to arrive being sent off to Windsor for a walnut cake, made too great inroads on their time and the
knight-and-squire relationship between fagmaster and fag
was sentimental.

(5) The privileges of College Pop or Debating Society
were invidious. There was too much canvassing and blackballing, the elections made too many people unhappy.

(6) Games and colours were over-important. Their influence was exaggerated and must be fought. They should
not be competitive or compulsory.

(7) The Corps was a joke; it had no business to be compulsory and any tendency to increase militarism among a
war-weary generation must be exposed and ridiculed.

(8) Boys must be appealed to through reason. They
must be given the benefit of the doubt; their fundamental
goodness and good sense must be believed in, however contrary to appearances.

To this the reactionaries replied as they always have;
that human nature could not be changed, give people an
inch and they would take an ell, that "one must draw the
line somewhere," that if games and discipline were relaxed
orgies would break out, that corporal punishment was the
only check on self-satisfaction and answered a bully in his
own coin, that boys were conservative and hated giving up

any of their hard-won privileges, that life was a Vale of Tears in which liberalism did not work.

At that time College Pop, unlike School Pop, still had debates and some of my senior election had been elected members of it. There had been two classic debates, on the "election system" and on corporal punishment that had almost ended in blows. The liberals at the bottom, Denis, King-Farlow, Roger Mynors, Bobbie Longden and Gibson had been supported by Miles Clausen and Christopher Hollis, the liberals at the top. The election in between that would shortly be coming into power was reactionary, except for Rylands and for one or two others who were non-political.

As the last liberals left the top of the school and my reactionary super-senior election came into office, the position of the liberals in senior election, and the few others, like myself, Charles Milligan, Le Strange, and Loxley grew unpleasant. Reprisals were due and our few protectors were leaving. Without Beddard and Rylands I had no friends among those coming into power and at the advanced age of seventeen I received a beating for "uppishness." Here are two letters of the time.

Easter, 1921

My dear Terence,

Home and Morbid. Since I wrote I have become clean gone on Nigel again. It's really too awful. I told you his attitude this half has been sulky with flashes of niceness —well, Monday I lectured him about it, and got out from him—A, the fact that he despised me. B, that his ideal was to be completely indifferent—this he kept up continually till on Thursday afternoon I got him alone in Lower Tea Room and discovered that "he was aiming at obtaining spiritual perfection, and that he regarded me as a distraction to be avoided, that I brought along other distractions (Loxley and Le Strange) and tried to talk about nothing with him and Langham."

All of which is true. I spent the last three days trying not to show him (Freddie) that I liked N. more (which I did since last Monday). N. told me that he thought it

impossible to like everyone and that he wanted to cut
down his acquaintances to a small but select circle and
he did not want me to be one but he was afraid my personality was too strong. Well, I then had him on toast.
I said that he must have a pretty rotten sort of perfection
if it had to be guarded from plausible antichrists like me
(that is his unexpressed idea of me), that he treated me
like a muck-heap in the corner of his room which he
shunned instead of trying to clear up—that he was running away from temptation instead of fighting it, that he
was completely selfish, and instead of trying to make
others better was only trying to safeguard himself—as for
his beastly set, he, I suppose, believed in the parable of
the good Shepherd? Yes he did—Well, which did the
shepherd admire most, the 99 good sheep or the wandering one? He had to admit he would admire the 99
more. But which did he like most and take most steps
over? Moreover who did he suppose liked the shepherd
best, the 99 good sheep or the wandering one?

He had to give in and admit he was quite wrong and
unchristian . . . I showed him that, temporarily at any
rate, I preferred him to Langham. This morning I found
him in Lower Tea Room and said goodbye, he asked me
to write to him and seemed to have forgiven me. Now I
can think of no-one else. Do you know the Greek epigram
"delicate are the fosterlings of Tyre but Myiscus out-
shines them as the sun the stars"; it seems to me that
suits him, there is a husky look about him which the
name Myiscus brings out and his good looks are typical
sun products, not rosy or effeminate. Langham is now
very nice and attractive but relegated to second place,
and now I am not glad at getting home but sorry at not
seeing N. I am altogether rather fed with last half—I
talked exclusively to a set consisting of Dannreuther,
Minns, Milligan, Eastwood, Langham and N., with no
one else have I talked anything but trivialities. I got on
badly with N. and quarrelled with Highworth. However
I got my first "stinker" [Distinction in Trials] the story
of which I must tell you when I have more time. I never

dreamt I could go clean gone on the *same* person. Wish
me luck in my new venture. I hope I can get him gone
on me again but I dread lest I should then cool myself.
N. despises you I think even more than me. χαῖρε.

Tuesday
My dear Terry,
    I wrote you two letters lately. Re N. I think it was
being treated the right way set me gone on him again.
What I like is a winning fight—well at first I got that,
then nothing to fight for, then a losing one. Now I am
straight again. It is not true to say the unattainable is
the spice of life, it is attaining the unattainable. I never
enjoy doing a thing until I have made sufficient difficulties
—given that I am colossally conceited, I only realised it
lately. Tuppa (Headlam) and Crace both saying I was
v. able bucked me up enormously. I used to think I could
never do more than obtain a superficial knowledge of a
few things. Now I think there is *nothing* I cannot do,
though very few things worth taking the trouble to (don't
end sentences with prepositions).
    You ask how life is? Chaos. I am in the state of mind
of not being able to get at anything, the only thing that
is true is that (*a*) *every*thing is true (*b*) everything is
false.
    Tuppa's formula of Some People . . . Others . . .
seems to be the only generality worthy of acceptance. I
am house-hunting for a way of life, it is fun in a way
but the agents do not know what I want and the houses
that sound most attractive are hideous to look at close,
others are beyond my income.
    I wrote to N. and sent him my photo, with a lot of
explanation of my present state, which seems to worry
him. I said I thought I lived for the best form of happiness: learning to appreciate the first rate and know the
sham, learning to look for beauty in everything, sampling
every outlook and every interest (bar stinks and maths),
trying to stop people being lukewarm and liking the second rate, trying to make other people happy, but not

doing so at the cost of my own happiness, or concealing it when I am being generous. Publishing all the good I do. I suppose I am too cautious to risk investing in treasure in heaven. Roughly these are my ideals. I said how much more I liked him than I used to, and that he must treat me as a nice dog, not worship or despise, but sympathise. I said I really had no aim in life (by the way I am trying to analyse after doing anything my motives for doing it and so deduce what my outlook is—unwilling to accept my own introspective failure). I think the fact that one does things and cannot analyse motives or reconcile them to averred principles goes a long way to proving fatalism. I love extremes, either I would be a Catholic fatalist, or an atheist. (I did not say that to N. at the time.) I began "Dear Nigel" and signed my photo "Cyril." I got:

Dear Conolly, I feel very honoured that you (*then in pencil*) consider me worthy of ink. You see that I don't think you are. I did not ask for the picture, but as you have sent it there remains no other course for me than to say "Thank you" (*you notice the improvement in style on the last letter!*). By the way I wish you would leave paragraphs in your so-called letters.

I want you to understand that I consider your spiritual welfare a thing that it is my duty to improve. I will allow that I have felt a certain amount of pitying affection for you. I saw last half that you were a waste paper basket for wrong ideas and that something ought to be done for you. I should have tried to do this had I had a chance of seeing you alone and discussing. But you, quite blindly and utterly incapable of putting yourself in my position, always brought company with you and went into Langham's room, where your frivolity, barely keeping within the bounds of decency, was to me so utterly despicable and repulsive to my principles, that I was bound to adopt the attitude which you called a pose. If it hadn't been for Langham I might have quarrelled with you quite nastily—but of course you are not appre-

ciating anything I say. Think of all the millions of times
last half you came into MY stall ALONE.

If you come next half alone I shall not generally consider you a distraction, but you must be quite prepared
to be sent away, and I want you to understand you are
are not going to come before either my work or my religion and I want you to realise that anything in the nature of company or popularity is quite repugnant to me.
Langham is quite nice and sociable, but as yet I do not
know much about him and am beginning to wonder if
there is much beneath the surface. Be it far from me to
worship you! You state that you have no aim in life as
yet and are trying to find one, well why not take the plain
one with which you have been fed from your youth up.
(*A. Because it is plain. B. Because I have been fed with
it from my youth up.*) I.E. The Christian One. You
can form a pretty average good ideal from this I should
have thought. Of course you must know all about it and
you can do this by systematic bible reading. Form your
principles on what you read, and do everything on principle. Imagine your ideal, which after all is set down in
the N.T. You need not call it God, if you dislike the word,
but think of it and act on it always. If you like, take
it as a matter of interest. Think how frightfully dull your
present aimless life is (*is house-hunting dull?*) compared
with what it might be. If you have an aim in everything
you do you will find you have an extraordinary pleasure
at every success achieved, renewed confidence, and
firmer principles. For instance I can assure you I gain
real genuine pleasure in turning you out of my stall when
I want to talk to you, but have some work to do. In your
condition you are perfectly lonely and whenever you are
in trouble you have nothing to fall back on, no one to
help you, and you act on inspiration. When I am in trouble I always know what to do through my principles. I
consult with God and so am acting definitely, and not
in an aimless helpless way.

Try this, will you? Call it imagination at first if you
like, but if you are sincere you will soon be convinced
that it is more than that.

You must see for yourself how thoroughly unsatisfactory your present state is.

Now I am sure you will laugh at me for all this.

N.

A wonderful letter for a boy of fifteen and I think he means it. I wonder why he is so deliberately rude and impersonal. I don't think his ideal is so very good, he says God is his principle while the Christian idea of God is Love. His is more Petrine than Joannine Christianity. I think unless I can make him take an interest in poetry, painting, etc. he will become an awful Puritan. If he cares only about religion he will become narrow-minded too. I know he does despise all popularity, but then he is good-looking enough to be able to. The only respectable Christianity is Broad Church or R.C., and here we have a modern P. father in embryo. Moreover he talks as if he will drop Freddy as soon as he is sure there is nothing in him, though Langham likes him best in the election. I want to make Langham interesting and wrote to him telling him to go to the National Gallery before he answered. He has not answered but I think he is too young to enjoy writing letters.

I am becoming quite a Socrates in the lower half of college. I do want people to like talking religion and morals, to read good books, like poetry and pictures, and think for themselves. N. merely retires further into his shell as when he wouldn't answer my questionnaire for my religion chart. You see I think my ideals are superior to his. Of course they are founded on the assumption that there is no conscious immortality, that happiness is the mean between good and evil (in their usual sense) that the greatest happiness is to be found in novelty. I think self-sacrifice is the greatest happiness when you are at an age to appreciate it, at present it must be ostentatious and announced to everyone. I think in Art it is at first necessary to accept the decisions of others. I have to go before a picture and say "that is a great picture, I must learn to like it," till, aided by my own good taste, I do like it. I think my ideals have deteriorated. I used to think Perfection the aim of life, now I think it is Perfection in Happiness. Adversity is like a purge, it is good for you at the time and you are the more able to enjoy life when you have done with it, and it gives me a chance to demonstrate my atheism. I think I must try and be a stoic in adversity, and Epicurean in prosperity. Baudelaire says somewhere:

> From the crude ore of each minute
> Draw the pure gold that is in it.

Gangue is the word for "ore."

I would love to have tea with you at Rumpelmayer's when you come back on the 24th when I go to stay with Loxley in town. I am so hard up for a sufficiently debauched confidant that you must excuse these long rambling epistles. Biles has written a bawdy ballad in exile. It begins—

> O to be back at school again
> To gossip and laugh and swear—

I must go to bed now. A Riverderci.
PS.

Is it so small a thing to have enjoyed the sun
To have lived light in the spring
To have loved, to have thought, to have done,
To have advanced true friends, and beat down baffling
    foes?
That we must feign a bliss
Of doubtful future date
And in pursuit of this
Lose all our present state
And relegate to worlds yet distant our repose?

The summer of 1921 my life was once again changed by Nigel. At first we got on well. We agreed that I should introduce him to art while he would convert me to religion. But the relations between adolescents are variable, and Nigel, who had perhaps over-reached himself with religion, cared that summer only for cricket, and despised all who were not cricketers. One day we quarrelled. I said our friendship must be All or Nothing; he said, "Very well, I choose nothing," and I left his room. After a day I tried to make it up. "Nothing" was not having the effect I hoped for. Nigel was brutal and called me a dirty scug (boy without a colour). I left him in a hysterical mood and went and broke a chair in Upper Tea Room. Then I rushed to Freddie and Denis for sympathy. I was fond of Nigel and fond of myself, and he had injured both these idols.

The rest of the half I kept on making overtures to him which he rudely ignored. Sometimes I was rude too and used to seek him out in order to cut him. He would make loud personal remarks and kick Walter Le Strange if he was walking with me for he had now got a cricket colour and made Oppidan friends. The effect of this quarrel on me was threefold. I was unhappy and for the first time in my life rebuffed; the guardian angel who looked after my relationships had forsaken me. My one ambition was to get over my feeling for Nigel and avenge myself by making him regret having quarrelled with me. I wanted to become the most useful and desirable person in his world, indispensable to his vulgar ambitions which I would help him to gratify as contemptuously as Lord Steyne assisted Becky Sharp to a new necklace. In my daydreams I acquired all the colours under the sun. I put him up for Pop.

The three results were that I became more social, that I worked harder, that I grew sceptical and pessimistic about the world. I was determined that Nigel must see me only with people he would himself like to know. I hugged closer to Denis and to King-Farlow, who was my fellow history specialist. He was robust, tough, cynical, good at games, energetic, and vulgar. We were both absorbed in Renaissance history and translated everything we learnt into our own lives; after reading Machiavelli I practised Machiavellianism, drawing up analyses of whom I should sit next, whom make friends with; of how to separate So-and-so, how to win over somebody else. Every man had a price. It was ncessary to discover his ruling passion and play on it. The test of action was whether it led to one's own advantage, i.e. was justified by political necessity. One must learn to keep "one's thoughts secret in an open face."

Thus all College must be cultivated for I could never

tell who might prove an asset in the humiliation of Nigel—that humiliation which was to consist in giving him the things he valued and which I despised and in being the only person who could give them him. He now went around with my enemy Highworth. They talked invariably of cricket and cast black looks in my direction so I made friends with Highworth again. Machiavelli would have approved. Highworth, outwardly successful, was still bewildered, and oppressed, I discovered, by the thought of the *Vale* or official leaving poem he would be expected to write at the end of the term and to which his attitude to poetry could scarcely contribute. I offered to compose it for him. I tried to make Nigel jealous by cultivating Freddie Langham whom I liked more and more; I could not make friends with cricketers as College did not possess any but I made up to our rowing men, two of whom were in the Eight. Farlow also had some rowing and football colours, and I felt less of a scug as I swaggered with him past Nigel's room.

It was the fashion to have photographs of our friends signed and installed on the mantelpiece. I had sent Nigel mine. He refused to give me his. I took one and he said that I had stolen it. I collected photos after that like an old hostess collecting celebrities. I cultivated anyone who was a rarity or who had not been taken, persuading them to get done for me and rushing off with the new scalp. Machiavelli functioned. I found I could charm people merely by asking them questions, and seeming interested in them, and at the end of the term I was elected to College Pop.

The election had been stormy and it was through my friendship with the rowing men that I got in for had I been put up by any of the liberals I would certainly have been blackballed. The political situation was now acute. Supersenior election were in power and beatings were frequent. To our indignation they beat Orwell for being late for prayers, then another member of senior election whom they considered uppish, finally and on the most flimsy pretexts, Whittome and myself. Orwell and Whittome were boys of eighteen; they were just outside Sixth Form, and were beaten by boys of the same age in their own senior election, as if they were fags.

The feeling ran so high against the Captain of the School, the odious Cliffe, and the six other reactionaries in his election that they were cut to a man. Denis's speeches at College Pop debates were reinforced by the contempt of Mynors, the intransigence of Farlow, the indignation of Cazalet and Gibson. At the end of the term it was customary to pass votes of thanks on those who were leaving from College Pop, on the President, Treasurer and Secretary, the Keepers of College Wall and Field. For the first time in history these votes of thanks were blackballed. The genial ceremony collapsed; Cliffe the Captain of the School, Lea the Cadet officer of the Corps, Babington-Smith and the boys who beat Farlow and Orwell and Whittome on trumped-up charges for political reasons faced the unprecedented verdict. Name after name was read out, the vote of thanks proposed and seconded, the ballet box passed, the blackballs counted, and the transaction noted down in the annals. At Farlow's "leaving tea" a day or two afterwards a lampoon of mine which drew attention to the idiosyncrasies of the seven blackballed reactionaries was sung with rapture. The Master in College protested against the breach of tradition, the Old Tugs got to hear of it, the Vile Old Men took it up, and there were whispers about Bolshevism which almost reached the newspapers.

Meanwhile I had succumbed to the disease of scepticism. My health was excellent but I could not get rid of ideas of mortality, futility, and death. What was the use of existence? Why did one do anything? All was vanity. Stupidity governed the world and human life was a blot on creation. I searched the classics for confirmation of my scepticism and found an overwhelming support. Job and Ecclesiastes and the author of the Wisdom of Solomon agreed with me; the Greek lyric poets and philosophers proclaimed it, Horace confirmed them as did Voltaire and Gibbon and Villon and Verlaine. I wrote a paper on Pessimism for the Essay Society. Only two kinds of thought existed, a pessimism which anticipated better things (Christianity) and my own—which did not. But if one believed this then one should kill oneself, which, of course, I was not prepared to do. Why not? Because of the consolations of friendship and learning, because suicide played into the hands of the Jealous God. One lived on to spite him.

For years I throve on this black doctrine for although it originated with me owing to a rebuff from Nigel and a Thames Valley summer more virulent than usual, it happened that I had caught the fashionable malady of the period. Futility was the rage. With Farlow I concocted a play which was to expose history. We had been set a "work of the imagination" to show to housemaster and history tutor, and we collaborated on a revue about the Renaissance, interspersed with songs and satirical sketches which showed knowledge and reading, vast cynicism and an unsuspected talent for horseplay. The Popes, the Emperors, the Medici, the Doges, the Kings of France and England, the Constable of Bourbon, Calvin, Luther, Zwingli and Savonarola, the King of Spain, the Borgias, Leonardo and Michelangelo were treated to the same knock-about. It was the first creation of my new-born scepticism and the most important. Nobody liked it but ourselves, least of all our tutors, who refused to sign it, Mr. Gow making only the ambiguous comment *"perveni ad umbilicum"* and I had instead to write a little purple essay "On a Crucifixion attributed to Antonello da Messina." But in the Specialists examination called the "Grand July" I did well and came out eleventh in the whole school. My gloom was not proof against this although my philosophy withstood it. What did it matter, eleventh or eleven hundredth? Was death deferred a day? Would anyone care in a hundred years? *Cui bono?* "Can I forget Myiscus, who is in all beautiful things?"

> Now years three and "halves" ten
> Have hastened by and flown
> And soon there will be other men
> But I shall be forgotten then
> My very name unknown.

And no more careless evening hours
Of slippered armchair ease
No glimpse of tea things in the towers,
No cans, no steam, no shouts from showers,
No shorts, nor mudded knees

as I made Highworth protest, echoing Mimnermus, in his commissioned *Vale*. At Camp that year my depression was entire, Nigel was not there nor Freddie nor Denis; I was glad to be able to get away on a motor-bicycle and drink a glass of port with one of my rowing friends at Ludgershall. I could only bear to talk to Jackie O'Dwyer; like some mad monarch with his favourite; even Farlow, in whose tent I was, lost patience with me, for like many Etonians, although cynical, he detested inefficiency. Nothing was worth doing but it was not worth doing badly. We argued till he used to yell, "Here, Private Connolly, you who appreciate the beauty of our English hedgerows, you who claim that pleasure and pain are the same thing, go and empty this bucket." I kept a volume of Gibbon in my uniform and read it when I could. My other bible was La Rochefoucauld whom I remember reading when the victorious Eight came back drunk from Henley. I found his opinions most reasonable for I was one to whom the existence of good seemed already more mysterious than the problem of evil.

In an old French exercise book of mine during this summer Walter Le Strange, my Anglo-Irish æsthetic friend in junior election was keeping a diary, a valuable contemporary document.

June 9th. In the afternoon repaired with Satyr and Apollo to the Stoa.[1] Pride was leading forth his chorus of Athleticism's devotees. "Ora pro nobis," he cried. "No anglo-catholicism" thought Man. Satyr fed him on strawberries while he read *Wuthering Heights,* and, that fin-

[1] The Stoa was the group of lookers-on at College cricket. They read and talked under the elms, which constituted "taking exercise." Pride is a boy called John Carter who leads his side out to field. I am Apollo, Man is the author, Tyrannus the Master in College, Satyr Clutton-Brock, Cato Farlow, Rome Gibson, and Cynicus Orwell.

ished, *The Newcomes*. Discussions on Socialism and Tyrannus followed. Yesterday Man and Calm and Conservation and Calculus discussed Slavery and Fagging. Both are utterly foul. Everybody here seems to think

(a) White men are better than others.

(b) England is everything.

(c) A "gentleman" is *the* thing. Also all or mostly all worship Athleticism.

Cynicus and Man listened to a revue—"The Renaissance" —by Apollo and Cato, Apollo good, especially the lyrics, Cato inclined to drag but his horseplay satire superb. The conversation in Hall turned on the peerage. How ignorant they all are, even Pride.

June 11th.

> Barnaby bright
> Barnaby bright
> The longest day
> And the shortest night.

A bright day indeed. The trees along the field and by Jordan looked splendid from the Stoa where I lay throughout the afternoon, near the Ball Alleys. Apollo was on my right. He too knows my loved acacia and has apostrophised it, he says, in verse. I am glad I did not try Shaw before. I am just in the state to understand him. Two years ago the preface to Androcles would have shocked me and upset me. A year ago I should have fallen too easy a prey to it. To-day I rejoice. Shaw wants just what I want. An equalising philosophy of life—politically and intellectually, morally, and socially a panacea, in fact an elixir. Stevenson's Velasquez is very interesting. I looked at the Prado reproductions with Apollo again to-day. How *ravissant* is *Mercury and Argus*. An English hamlet may be pretty, the country here—take Chamber Field overstrewn with buttercups and clover, or Fellows Eyot with its poplars—is beautiful. But O, for the Wicklow hills. I never realised till now the true glory of the sugar loaf—of Gilt Spear's top, or of the heights between Glencullen and the Scalp.

Evening full of the linnet's wings.

Sunday. Tea with the Alabasters. Then talk turned on the *Beggar's Opera*, which I have not seen. Apollo—with whom I walked in the evening—talked of introspection and confidences. Is introspection a good thing? I think it is. Why, I wonder, does one always feel a superiority to others? Not always, but frequently at least. Apollo, I fear, does it too much. Yet I like him.

June 13th. Apollo, Beatrice d'Este, Rome[2] and I argued most of the afternoon about religion. Very interesting. The result: "Man must worship something by an inborn instinct." Surely he can drive this instinct out of him. Later on Satyr, Beatrice d'Este, Scaife and I gossiped with Rome. The conversation turning on Pride, Scaife gave demonstrations of his foul ways and words, whereupon Tyrannus entered and in his hypocritical friendly way adjured Rome to cease. Rome with much coldness, though quite politely, dismissed him, and we continued our conversation. This evening, however, Greedy-for-Power (*Lea*) "wanted" Rome and Scaife, accused the one of filthy talk and the other of encouraging it. Rome told the story of how it happened. He was dismissed. But—and I burn to think of it—Scaife was whipt —whipt like a mere slave—that is, an oppressed fag, or lower boy, by that unutterable brute, Greedy-for-Power, for a sin of which Rome had proved him guiltless. O may all tyranny perish. May everyone be free! Let not the wretched new boy be oppressed and mishandled just for the convenience of the idle Capitalists, that is to say, the self-made priests of Athleticism, of the Public School Spirit of Imperialism.

June 27th. Peter (*Loxley*) came back to-night. Full of racing and tennis. I wish sometimes I could interest myself in such things. Of course not worship them. I have been reading the *Loom of Youth*. It is all so true in its way. Everything seems melancholy. Is life worth living?

[2] Beatrice d'Este = Raymond Coghlan
  Rome = Gibson, who was a Catholic
  Scaife = "Cully" Cox

Where can one get help? One cannot paint for ever, it only makes you into that æsthete, loose tie, velvet coat sort of thing. Poetry makes you excited, or else sadder. O to do something! But how can a Nobody do anything worth while? Help is from within. Perhaps if one saw everybody as good. It is so hard—but it is beautiful. Therefore it is meet and right to do. "Les sanglots longs" —but they do it always. "I will arise and go now, and go to Innisfree . . ." O if only I could quit this place, with its society, its "gentlemen," its absurd church. Where is a true religion? O for peace. Even this journal is hypocritical.

July 2nd. There is only one God here. Athleticism and his law is "Believe—or Be Cast out." Even now I hear the shouts and cheers, as of barbarism. Baths are banged. Boys shout. Such a display of rowdyism I have seldom heard. The Mob! The Howling of an Angry Mob. Awful. But a joyful mob is worse. The Eight have won the Ladies' Plate at Henley. Three of them are in College —"jolly boating weather—we'll cheer for the best of schools." It seems sad to think that a great crowd of boys —of cultured boys—should pour out their spirits thus. O Athleticism! Athleticism! The din is now outside my door. Horror! Horror! Baths are banged and banged—cheers —cheers. So help me!

The noise has been quelled. It is sad that N. (*Nigel*) should have been so completely corrupted by athleticism. We were quite friendly once. But now he is so devilish superior. And rude, too. What have I done? I despise Athleticism—but not Athletics, yet I have never said *he* should not worship it just because I am interested in the things that really matter. Need he be so really uncivil?

July 3rd. A boiling Sunday. The heat was most oppressive. I talked chiefly to Cyril, Peter and Farlow. These questions of fagging and of College Politics are very interesting. So is reading the Greek gospel. Belief seems to be based on such slender grounds. It is extraordinary how unchristian are the lives of all those boys who "profess and call themselves Christians" Carter, Maud, N. But there is an awful danger for us too. One is so inclined to become a Pharisee—an utter prig. The milder forms of this athleticism are not harmful for the young. They do no lasting good. But they tend to present happiness. But everyone seems to imagine that athletics mean success. Get a cricket colour and you are made for life. Half a dozen people come up to you. "I say, isn't it good for College having two Sixpennies." What could be more ridiculous? No one seems to take any interest in the fact that a Colleger has bought a Dürer, or that the Hervey English Verse Prize was won by a Colleger in C.

Carter's ignorance showed itself again yesterday. "Why Lord John Russell and not Lord Russell?" he asked. But I mustn't be a snob. The Hermit (*Martineau*)—it appears from a conversation of this evening—is an ultra-reactionary. He disapproves of boys in B playing ping-pong in Sixth Form Passage.

Last Sunday Farlow gave a tea-party in Lower Tea Room, after which the party sang songs, including a topical one by Cyril. All very pleasant, but Carter made himself somewhat objectionable to his host. On the Friday evening there had been the usual College Pop election. Cyril got in. Peter was put up three times and blackballed, I ditto twice, Carter was put up and got seven (five excludes). All this gave us much subject for conceited conversation. Peter seemed rather sad not to have got in. I was also sorry for myself. Our conceit grew vehemently. On Monday, to the general consternation of many, Carter was awarded his College Cricket. This means he will be second keeper next summer, and so in a position to make even more of himself than at present.

That summer I went abroad for the first time. My father took me to Paris and the Belgian coast. We stayed off the Rue de Rivoli and ate in restaurants with purple menus, screened from the pavement by tubs of sooty privet. I did not care for Paris, I was frightened there, it was too hot and I thought people's feet smelt, I liked only the Louvre where I felt at home, Notre Dame and Versailles which, as I wrote at the time, "suited my mood." "French revues are funnier than English," I wrote to O'Dwyer, "but after eight o'clock this town is as full of whores as camp was of wasps"—then I reverted to the interminable College politics. Carter, Nigel's great friend, in my junior election disliked me and my two cronies there, Loxley and Le Strange. There was a chance of him getting into College Pop. It was against my principles to blackball anyone yet somehow five people had to be found who would; Cazalet and Farlow, alas, had left—"You have to remember, my boy," I enjoined O'Dwyer, "that nowadays you are Cazalet, and I am Farlow."

One event in Paris upset me. On a sultry evening as I was walking back to my hotel after dinner, I was accosted outside the Café de la Paix by a pimp with a straw hat and an umbrella. He offered to take me to a music-hall. I was too nervous to refuse and he then informed me it would be "rather a rough kind of place, you understand." I was now too frightened and excited to turn back and he took me to a brothel in the Rue Colbert. I was overcome with guilt and apprehension as I sat with the pimp in the little gilded *salon* while he spoke to the Madame. The mechanical piano played, at last the girls filed in and I was asked to choose two of them. Voiceless I pointed with a trembling finger. They stayed behind and a bottle of champagne appeared. We all had a glass and then another bottle. Drink made no impression, I was paralysed with fear, partly of being hit on the head and waking up in Buenos Aires, partly of saying the wrong thing. Then it was suggested that I should go upstairs with the two ladies. It was then a new panic arose. How much was all this? In a shrunken voice I asked for the bill. *"Quoi. Déjà?" "Oui, oui, oui. Toute suite."* I explained to Madame that I did not know if I would have enough money to pay. She was astounded. "But I thought Monsieur was a gentleman!" When the bill arrived it was for almost ten pounds, mostly for champagne and with a bonus of course for the pimp. I explained that I could not pay at once, that the ladies must leave immediately, that I would give her all the money I had (about four pounds), and find the rest within the week. I gave her my card, on which I had written the address of my hotel.

My father was waiting up for me and I told him I had lost my way.

The rest of my time in Paris was spent in anguish. At any moment I expected to see Madame and the pimp arrive to ask for me. Meals in the hotel were a torture which I could not bear for I would be sure to see the pimp with his umbrella or Madame with my visiting card directed to our table by the concierge. No time of day was safe. I wrote to my grandmother who, I knew, was giving me five pounds for my birthday and asked her to send it to Paris in advance as the shops were better there than they would be in Belgium and I wanted to buy some presents for my friends. It seemed as if her letter would never arrive; my worst moment was in the Musée de Cluny, beside the iron crown of Receswinth. I went out and sat in a cold sweat on a bench in the garden.

Next day the money arrived and I rushed round to the brothel. It was eleven o'clock in the morning; no one remembered me, another Madame was on duty and listened in bewilderment while I explained, stuffing money into her hand, and wondering if it would seem impertinent to ask for my card back. At last I was safe. I bought Charles Milligan, Denis, and Freddie a few cheap presents and shortly afterwards attained my eighteenth birthday, still without having kissed anyone. The Belgian coast was a relief after this nightmare, and Bruges, with its brackish canals and Flemish primitives, like Versailles, "suited my mood," for I would try no more conclusions with the Present.

Boys do not grow up gradually. They move forward in spurts like the hands of clocks in railway stations. Most of those in College advanced in this wise though in many the sap of youth ran down after their efforts. In my own case the autumn of 1921 and spring of 1922 were a high renaissance. They were not the happiest days of my life but I was as happy then as I was able to be.

I started the new term as "a bit of a chap." I was in a "mess," that is to say I took tea in Charles Milligan's room with him and Minns and a fag to look after us, instead of having it in Tea-room. This was an advance in civilisation as one had privacy and could have masters to tea and get on better terms with them. I was also in College Pop and got my "shorts" for football, whereupon Nigel spoke to me again. We were delighted to be friends, my scepticism was now permanent but I had accepted the vanity of life and the worthlessness of human nature so fundamentally that I no longer felt bitter or with a grievance against society. "Our mess has china tea—down by the streamside" I used to sing, and we gave exclusive tea parties. Denis was in Sixth Form. All the election above him had now left except the youngest member, who was Captain of the School, a clerical reactionary held in check by Denis, Mynors, Gibson and Longden.

CHAPTER XXII: THE BACKGROUND OF THE LILIES

So far it would appear that work played a small part in our lives; this was not so, however for the first two years most boys did not enjoy their work and found it a tedious drudgery. It was not smart at Eton to work; to be a "sap" was a disgrace and to compete for prizes eccentric. Everybody used cribs though the punishments for being caught were severe. For boys at Eton wanted one thing, popularity, and the flaw in the Eton education was that work was unpopular. Indeed for twenty years I was never to grasp that the love and friendship which I sought were in this world the rewards not of seeking them but of hard work and success.

It is hard to see how such conditions arise. They are prevalent in most schools although boys are more bored and more unhappy than ever when they do not work. Even in College, among the seventy scholars, "sapping" was discredited and we were infected by the fashion from without, behind which lay the English distrust of the intellect and prejudice in favour of the amateur. A child in Ireland, a boy at St. Wulfric's, a scholar at Eton, I had learnt the same lesson. To be "highbrow" was to be different, to be set apart and so excluded from the ruling class of which one was either a potential enemy or a potential servant. Intelligence was a deformity which must be concealed; a public school taught one to conceal it as a good tailor hides a paunch or a hump. As opposed to ability, it was a handicap in life.

At Eton this was emphasised by the stigma attaching to Collegers which although an economic prejudice found expression as an anti-intellectual one and of which a ridiculous aspect was the contempt in which boys held masters,

a relic of the eighteenth century when boys brought their
own tutors to Eton and treated them, as the term "usher"
still indicated, little better than their servants. In this direction the feeling was strong; masters who were old Etonians,
who were rich like John Christie or well-born like Georgie
Lyttelton escaped, but in general the boys assumed that
most of the staff had never held a gun or worn a tailcoat,
that they were racked by snobbery, by the desire to be
asked to stay with important parents or to be condescended
to by popular boys. An Eton division consisted of thirty
boys, five of whom wished to learn something, ten of whom
wished to do what everybody else wanted and fifteen of
whom spent their time searching for the usher's weak points
and then exploiting them with the patience of prisoners of
war tunnelling out of a camp. What Proust called the
"lâcheté des gens du monde" was never so apparent as at
Eton, where the life of a teacher like Aldous Huxley was
made intolerable because of his defective sight.

The teachers in the middle parts of the school devoted
themselves to cramming and keeping order; inspired teaching, owing to the intransigence of the boys, could appear
only at the top, where there were five real teachers: the
Headmaster, Mr. C. M. Wells, Mr. G. W. Headlam, Mr.
G. H. K. Marten, and Mr. Hugh Macnaghten. They are
worth considering.

At Eton, as at other schools, there existed the ordinary
education for the average boy but there grew up as well
an inner culture, the Eleusinian mysteries of learning, to
which favoured boys were admitted and which was maintained by teachers such as these and by a few important
outside figures, the Provost, Mr. Luxmoore, Mr. Broadbent;
the pure eighteenth-century Etonian tradition of classical
humanism, which could be learnt nowhere else. Most of
the boys went through the school without knowing of its
existence, without having heard of esoteric figures like William Johnson Cory or Mrs. Warre-Cornish, Howard Sturgis
or Austen Leigh, but by 1921 (the year for me when
"modern history" begins), I was being initiated; I would
dine with the Provost and the Headmaster, or Mr. Headlam
and Mr. Marten would come to tea.

The first of the big five a Colleger came up to, when
about sixteen, was Hugh Macnaghten. Although a fine
teacher, his learning possessed the faults or rather the literary vices of his time. He was an ogre for the purple patch,
the jewel five words long, the allusion, the quotation, the
moment of ecstasy. In fact he was embedded in the Milton-
Keats-Tennysonian culture, that profuse and blooming romanticism of the "bowery loneliness,"

> The brooks of Eden mazily murmuring
> And gloom profuse and cedar arches

which had dominated English literature until the death of
Flecker and Rupert Brooke.

The Eton variety was diluted with pre-Raphaelitism.
Watts' "Sir Galahad" hung in College Chapel, Burne-Jones
and William Morris had been Eton figures, and Mr. Luxmoore painted fastidious water colours of his riverside garden in which the fair Rosamund would not have disdained
to take her medicine. He was a disciple of Ruskin, the forgotten man of the nineteenth century.

Another field for the pre-Raphaelite influence was in
translating. Homer and Virgil were the pillars of an Eton
education; it would be hard to derive more pleasure then
or now than we obtained from reading them. But we read
them with the help of two officials cribs, Butcher and Lang
for Homer, Mackail for Virgil. Lang believed that Homer
must be translated into the nearest English equivalent,
which was an Anglo-Saxon prose reminiscent of the Sagas.
He tried to manage on a Bronze Age vocabulary, and the
Mediterranean clarity of the *Odyssey* was blurred by a
Wardour Street Nordic fog. Homer, in short, was slightly
Wagnerised. Mackail, who had married Burne-Jones'
daughter, gave to his Virgil an eightyish air, the *lacrimæ
rerum* spilled over and his Christian attitude to paganism,
that it was consciously pathetic and incomplete, like an
animal that wishes it could talk, infected everything which
he translated with a morbid distress. Dido became a bull-
throated *Mater Dolorosa* by Rossetti. His translations from
the *Greek Anthology*, one of the sacred books of the inner
culture, the very soil of the Eton lilies, were even more

deleterious. They exhaled pessimism and despair, an over-
ripe perfection in which it was always the late afternoon
or the last stormy sunset of the ancient world, in which the
authentic gloom of Palladas was outdone by that attributed
to Simonides, Callimachus or Plato. Meleager was the
typical pre-Raphaelite lover.

To put it in another way, a sensitive Etonian with a
knowledge of Homer and Virgil through these translations
and a good ear, would be unable to detect in poems like
Tithonus, Ulysses or the *Lotus Eaters* any note foreign to
the work of Homer and Virgil. If he had been told that "a
spirit haunts the year's last hours" was a word for word
translation of Virgil, he would have accepted the fact. The
two classics had been "romanticised" for him, impregnated
with the cult of strangeness, of the particular rather than
the general and of the conception of beauty characteristic
of the Æsthetic Movement as something akin to disease
and evil.

Macnaghten accentuated this. He told us that the most
beautiful word in the English language was "little," he
liquidated his "r's" in reciting and intoned poetry in a special way . . .

> and hear the bweeze
> Sobbing in ver little twees.

Jolly good! He would exclaim, and to hear him chant "Ah,
poor Faun—ah, poor Faun" was a study in pity which made
his severe and even harsh discipline appear the more
surprising.

The other object of this inner cult was Plato. His humour
and sophistry were the delight of those who expounded
them to the bewilderment of those who listened. His theory of ideas and essences, his conception of body and spirit,
the romantic dualism on which he insisted formed the ruling philosophy. Platonism was everywhere, popping up in
sermons and Sunday questions, in allusions to neo-Plato-
nism, in essays by Dean Inge, at the Headmaster's dinner parties or in my tutor's pupil-room. Socrates roamed
through the classes like a Government inspector and even
Virgil and Tennyson withdrew before him. But it will be

remembered that Plato himself, in the *Republic,* turned against the poets and advocated censorship and discipline. This contradiction extended through our school life and emerged in its attitude to sex.

For there was no doubt that homosexuality formed an ingredient in this ancient wisdom. It was the forbidden tree round which our little Eden dizzily revolved. In a teaching conscious and somewhat decadently conscious of visual beauty, its presence in the classics was taken for granted; it was implicit in Plato's humour and æsthetic. Yet Eton, like all public schools, had no solution for sex. If boys had such intercourse between the ages of fourteen and eighteen, no matter with whom or with what, they had better go. The school could do nothing for them. "Created sick, commanded to be sound," the majority floundered through on surreptitious experiments and dirty jokes but there were always a number who, going further, were found out and expelled.

The extent to which sex-life is necessary and should be permitted to growing boys remains uncertain. The Eton attitude was in line with that of other authorities and with the wishes of most parents, for the dilemma is inherent in all education, lurking in the playing-fields and vinegar-scented cloisters of our seats of learning as, in the preaching of the careful Pater, beckon the practices of Wilde.

The result was that boys learnt to walk a tightrope; the sentimental friendship was permitted in some houses and forbidden in others, allowed to some boys and denied to their fellows or permitted and then suppressed according to the changing views and vigilance of the housemaster. No one could be sure on what ground they trod. There was Macnaghten who, spartan in body as he was soft in mind, would give an annual and long-anticipated lecture attacking those friendships at a point in Plato's *Euthyphro;* at the same time we were made to put into Latin verses a sentimental poem addressed by Dolben to the then Captain of the Eleven. One thing was certain; the potentially homosexual boy was the one who benefited, whose love of beauty was stimulated, whose appreciation was widened and whose critical powers were developed; the normal boy, free from adolescent fevers, missed both the perils and the prizes; he was apt to find himself left out.

There is much celibacy in public schools and, where many housemasters are not married, it is possible to say that their teaching will encourage continence officially and homosexuality by implication, sending up to the universities, from whence they will immediately rebound as masters, that repressed and familiar type, the English male virgin.

Another effect of Macnaghten's teaching was to associate English literature with Latin verses. We came to think of poetry in terms of tags and useful epithets, and to consider the best poetry as being in the form of the sonnet or sixteen-line lyric. Macnaghten would not treat Latin verses as a cross-word puzzle; he insisted that we put feeling into them, that we exercise our dreams of literary composition through the medium of another language. In his taste he was a true escapist; everything he admired reeked of the death-wish, port after stormy seas, holy quiet and romantic fatigue. No one who did his verses well could write poetry afterwards. There would be one slim Eton-blue volume with a few translations a *Vale*, and a couple of epigrams, then silence. For the culture of the lilies, rooted in the past, divorced from reality and dependent on a dead foreign tongue, was by nature sterile.

It may be wondered why I call Macnaghten a good teacher. The reason is that although he concentrated on moments of beauty, he did not neglect the encircling drudgery, and because, although his taste was uncertain, he would permit no blasphemy. To laugh at anything he thought good meant punishment. He chastened the hooligans (even Highworth could but mumble) and he insisted on the modesty, the abnegation without which great art cannot be appreciated. "Up" to him boys for the first time had the experience of literature and every now and then, in the dusty classroom, grew aware of the presence of a god.

Wells taught the classical specialists; he was a fine cricketer and a judge of claret, a man of taste with a humour of understatement in the Cambridge style. The Headmaster was theatrical, he liked knotty points and great issues, puns and dramatic gestures. He was a worldly teacher, a Ciceronian, an All Souls Fellow and we felt we were learning Divinity from a Prince of the Church. He was fond of paradoxes and we learnt to turn out a bright essay on such a subject as "Nothing succeeds like failure" or "Nothing fails like success." The exaggeration of his teaching was repugnant to the classical specialists and such was the moral weight of William Egerton, Denis, or Roger Mynors, that he became a naughty boy "showing off" in their presence although his entry into any other classroom would petrify us with fear.

His was the cult of that light verse which had always been the official poetry for despite Gray, Shelley, Swinburne and Bridges, the kind of poetry which Eton took to its heart was either the sentimental lyric, the translation (of which Cory's *Heraclitus* is the example) or the facetious. Praed, Clough, Calverley, W. S. Gilbert and the sacred J. K. Stephen were the official bards and if the Headmaster had had to include a living writer he would have added Father Ronald Knox.

Thus, although the *Eton College Chronicle* made an appeal to premature essayists and the fourth leader of *The Times* was within the grasp of its editors, critical or creative writing there was none. Humorous "Ephemerals" had a sale but in spite of tradition, and the encouragement given to them, the Arts at Eton were under a blight. Figures of the post-war world such as Aldous Huxley, and Maynard Keynes had been in College, but we would never have known it. They were not recognised, they did not wear like Maurice Baring, Arthur Benson, Percy Lubbock or J. K. Stephen, a halo in the pale-blue canon.

Into this world the history teachers introduced a note of realism. Marten was a model of clarity and enthusiasm; he was the sanest of schoolmasters but for that reason had less influence on us than a teacher like Headlam who did not aspire to be impartial.

If the Headmaster epitomised All Souls, Headlam was typical of Balliol but it was not Balliol that made him impressive, so much as the fact that in his classroom there was at last evidence of a Pre-Ruskinian culture, of the eighteenth century. His favourite writer was Horace, the book he gave to us on leaving was *Boswell's Life of Johnson.* To us he was an enigmatic figure, he seemed to go some of the way towards futility and yet while our conclusions from the axiom All is Vanity were "nothing is worth while, except art," "except friendship," "except pleasure," or "except wisdom," his seemed to be "except success—except doing a job efficiently." He appeared cynical but that may have been only because he was un-Tennysonian. Although irritable in the early morning he was more tolerant than other masters; his tolerance at times seemed apathy, a product of disillusion, yet he hated idleness, dishonesty and that frivolous complacency to which growing boys are addicted. He brought common sense and reasonable worldly values into his relations with boys with the result that his house was the best at Eton and, as he surveyed the row of Pops in it with affected vagueness, he must have enjoyed the bewilderment of other housemasters.

All the history specialists imitated him, his affectations of saying "Erse" instead of "Yes" and "Toosda" for Tuesday, his apparent lack of interest in games and exercise (although he was a good fives player and his house held the football cup), his attitude of *nil admirari.* He was a Tory in politics, where again he seemed to stand for tolerance, efficiency and a hatred of fuss. "You must learn that there is no justice in this world," he was fond of saying, perhaps setting the wrong boy a punishment to illustrate it and "You must always remember that nobody is indispensable," was another of his maxims.

Was he a Balliol careerist, with the affectation of laziness and indifference that was considered the Balliol manner and by which we were taken in or a split-man in whom an efficient and ambitious self was being watched by a cynical spectator? Or was he an evocation of the eighteenth-century Tory or of ancient Rome? In appearance he was dark, handsome and rather fat, not unlike the Roman poet whom he interpreted; his expression was blasé and judicial, his voice and smile were charming, his eyes, sombre in repose, when angry, kindled into fire.

All masters lost their tempers; there were some whose

rages were comic spectacles, others who became maniacs, fascinating to watch but dangerous if one got in the way; with the Headmaster or Macnaghten there was a sensation of panic owing to the severity of the penalties which they could enforce, but with Marten and Headlam alone did one get a feeling of shame; they were teachers whose rebukes of one boy enlisted against him the sympathy of the class, and "To do poorly" up to Headlam, or be "tiresome" with Marten, was distressing for at last we were attaining a level where it was not impermissible to work.

In the æstheticism which was gathering round me, part backwash of the nineties, part consequence of my Celtic romanticism being worked upon by the pre-Raphaelite background of the Eton lilies, Headlam's sober intellectual energy, his Roman values, offered a gleam of mental health. But, to an æsthete, what appealed in Headlam was his irony, his way of making a reference to authority sound ridiculous (due, one suspected, to an antipathy to the Headmaster which was pronounced among the senior old Etonian housemasters) and to his fondness for what he called gestures—"That would be a good gesture—the Massacre of St. Bartholomew was a bad gesture." The good gesture, the noisy piece of self-sacrifice, was one of the few lines of conduct sanctioned by my futilitarianism. It must be like Sidney Carton's, magnanimous, public, and useless.

By the time I had left Eton I knew by heart something of the literature of five civilisations. It was a lopsided knowledge since we were not taught literature and since the only literature which appealed to me was pessimistic but it is worth analysing, since, although many of the books had been read for hundreds of years and others seemed my own discoveries, taken together, they give a picture of fashionable reading-matter just after the last war.

I was fond of the Old Testament, disliked the New. My favourite books were Ecclesiastes and the Wisdom of Solomon in which I recognised the melancholy and tired distinction of an old race, the mysterious Ezekiel and that earthy mystic, the first Isaiah. Job was too much thrust upon me and the Lamentations of Jeremiah I found in faulty taste. All these I read with more pleasure in the

sonorous Latin of the Vulgate. They were among the books
I lived in through the winter evenings.

In Greek literature I had read the *Odyssey* with passion,
but not the *Iliad,* I admired Æschylus, particularly the
Agamemnon, and Sophocles, particularly *Œdipus Rex;*
Euripides and Aristophanes I disliked, and Plato, except
his epigrams and the *Symposium.* I enjoyed the lyric poets,
Sappho and Archilochus, and adored the Mackail selection
of the *Greek Anthology,* Theognis, Plato, Callimachus, Palladas, and Meleager; I knew all the sceptical epigrams by
heart and most of those about love and death and "the fate
of youth and beauty." In all my books I had written after
my name "τίς τίνι ταῦτα λέγεις." (Who are you that say
this, and to whom?) Mackail's *Anthology* (in the one-
volume edition with the long preface), might have been
described as the Sceptic's Bible. I was also fond of the
bloomy Theocritus and the *Lament for Bion.*

In Latin Literature I read Horace and Virgil but did not
enjoy them till later for Horace, except by Headlam, was
not inspiringly taught and Virgil associated with too many
punishments and in his moments of beauty with Macnaghten's vatic trances. Although I had learnt Latin all my life
I still could not appreciate it without a crib and it was the
arrival at the end of my time of the Loeb translations,
sanctioned by the authorities, that put its deeper enjoyment within my grasp. Virgil and Horace, without them,
had been too difficult, too tearstained. Horace besides was
more connected with character than with prettiness. We
were slow to appreciate him as a verbal artist

> Fortes creantur fortibus et bonis
> Est in juvencis, est in equis patrum
> Virtus

"Brave men are bred from the good and brave, there is in
cattle, there is in horses," Headlam would rasp, "the virtue
of their sires," and the history specialists, conscious that
though not poets, they were the stuff about which poetry
was written, seemed to preen themselves for a moment in
the afternoon drowse.

My favourite was Catullus, whose poetry "suited my

mood," and therefore the mood of the age. It was cynical, romantic, passionate and bawdy and I could substitute my own name for his. *"Otium, Cyrille, tibi molestum est,"* *"Sed tu, Cyrille, destinatus obdura."* I liked the world of Suetonius and Tacitus but the Latin prosewriter for me was Petronius Arbiter. I had four editions of the *Satyricon*. The best I had bound in black crushed levant and kept on my pew in chapel where it looked like some solemn book of devotion and was never disturbed. To sit reading it during the sermon, looking reverently towards the headmaster scintillating from the pulpit and then returning to the racy Latin, "the smoke and wealth and noise of Rome" was "rather a gesture."

I also liked Martial, crisp and Iberian, but resented the sanctimonious Juvenal, I was excited by the *Pervigilium*, I struggled through the convolutions of Apuleius and admired the pagan chapters of the *Confessions* of Saint Augustine.

In French I cultivated the Troubadours but was disappointed, as I was by those four old bores, Montaigne, Rabelais, Boccaccio and Burton. The deceptively simple verses of Villon I loved, with the Poussin landscapes of Chénier and the garden sadness of Ronsard and Du Bellay. Then came a few lines of Racine, all *Candide* and *Manon Lescaut* and an unrepresentative selection of Flaubert, Gautier, Hugo and Baudelaire, no Rimbaud but a close study of Verlaine, Hérédia, and Mallarmé.

I was fortunate to read French with Mr. de Satgé; he loved beauty and while working with him, I apprehended that remoteness of great poetry from life which is inherent in the exaction of the form and creates literature, *"la treille où le pampre à la rose s'allie."*

In English I began with Spenser sleeping in his coils, I knew little Shakespeare but I worshipped Hamlet, who seemed the Prince of Scepticism and Gestures ("How now, a rat in the arras!"), and of course Marlowe. Shakespeare's sonnets I absorbed. They formed, with Omar Khayyám and the *Shropshire Lad*, limited editions called "the Medici Books," which, unhealthy though they were in bulk, one could yet obtain as prizes. Webster was my favourite

Elizabethan, then came Donne and after him Marvell, Herrick and Sir Thomas Browne. Milton was the poet in whom my appreciation culminated. Then a gap until Blake, the *Marriage of Heaven and Hell*, and, still later, Tennyson and Matthew Arnold. I knew nothing of Pope, Dryden and Crabbe, and I had a prejudice against the romantics; Keats turned my stomach, Shelley was ethereal, Byron vulgar and Wordsworth prosy. What I required from an author was the authentic romantic thrill and the prestige of obscurity. After Tennyson was Housman, who came down to lecture to us on Erasmus Darwin, and then Bridges, Yeats, Brooke, de la Mare, Flecker, Masefield, *The Spirit of Man* and a repository of Georgian cliché called *Poems of To-Day*.

In prose, after Sir Thomas Browne, came Boswell, Gibbon and Sterne, then Pater (so clear in his thought, so evasive in his conclusions), in whose Sebastian van Storck, with his refusal "to be or do any limited thing," we recognised a fellow sufferer—lastly the usual modern mixture—Samuel Butler, Shaw, Compton Mackenzie, James Stephens, Belloc, Buchan, Conrad, Lytton Strachey and Aldous Huxley. Orwell lent me *The Picture of Dorian Gray*. But I could not swallow it. It was not necessary.

I was as fond of painting as of poetry and haunted the National Gallery. My taste was conservative. I knew of no French painter except Corot and it was typical of the civilisation of the lilies, the limitations of good taste, that I had such knowledge of the masterpieces of the past yet remained timidly at sea among the creations of the present.

CHAPTER XXIII: GLITTERING PRIZES

The result of scepticism, of escaping from the world via the pursuit of knowledge, was that I unexpectedly won the Rosebery History Prize. The gain was about twenty pounds' worth of books, but those available, with their horrible bindings, so shocked me that I obtained special permission to get Medici prints. The Man with the Glove, Beatrice d'Este and The Duke of Cleves now looked down on my bureau. After an intrigue with Denis I was given my "liberties," the privileges of not wearing a hat, of fagging boys, of having supper by themselves, accorded to the next six in college, after Sixth Form. When a boy not in Division One (Sixth Form and Liberty) won the Newcastle, a classical prize, he was co-opted into it; in getting the same reward for the Rosebery I had advanced the prestige of the History Specialists, a prestige which was rising at the expense of classics, languages and science. History was easier and more interesting, it was the fashion. Most of the important boys were history specialists, and Mr. Headlam's division had ended by becoming a field of the cloth of gold for the feudal chieftains. Of the eleven hundred boys about twenty-five were in Pop and eight of these were "up" to him. After I got the Rosebery they began to notice me.

In every division there is room for one boy to reconcile popularity with hard work. He is the brilliant idler, a by-product of dandyism. "Petronius deserves a word in retrospect. He was a man who passed his days in sleep, his nights in the ordinary duties and recreations of life: others had achieved greatness by the sweat of their brows—Petronius idled into fame." This archetype of scepticism came to my aid; by imitating his example and doing my work illicitly at night by candle my days were left free for

social intercourse. I had an excellent memory, I could learn
by heart easily, gut a book in an hour and a half of arguments, allusions and quotations, like a Danube fisherman
removing caviare from the smoking sturgeon, and remember them for just long enough to get down in an examination paper. I was the perfect examinee. The Oppidans
began to take me up. I answered difficult questions and discovered smutty passages for them and if I was caught reading a book in class, it would be something as spectacular as
the *Epistolæ Obscurorum Virorum*. Once a week we had
to recite a few lines of poetry that we learnt by heart; most
boys depended on poems they had learnt before.

> Thereisswee musichere thasofterfalls
> Thanpetalsof blowroseson the grass . . .
> On the grass. . . .

At the end I would stroll up with modest confusion and
recite a long Greek chorus chosen for its pessimism, for not
to be born was best of all.

My strong point was still being funny. I was working
hard enough to be permitted some licence, and I could
make jokes about our subject—for the history we studied
was the history of personalities—in which even Oppidans
could join. I was at my best when being taken up, grateful but not servile, sunny but not familiar and with the
schoolboy's knack of living in the moment. I had the advantage of beginning at the top, the only Oppidans I knew
were already in Pop, I had no inferiors with whom I had
been associated, no ladders to kick down. Antony Knebworth was the first to make friends with me. He had won
the other Rosebery prize and was a Byronic figure of over-
powering vitality who with his crony, Nico Davies, seemed
to make more noise than a whole division. He and Nico
were the most successful types of normal schoolboy; they
were in all the elevens, ran their houses, were able and
rather lazy at their work, conventional, intolerant and
sentimental; they were easily moved to laughter, rage or
tears, strict enforcers of privilege and always appealed to
by the headmaster when there was a question of Pop "using
its influence."

A less school-minded couple were Teddy Jessel and Edward Woodall; they were dandies in the pure sense, with a sober worldly gravity. Jessel had a touch of the "Arbiter" himself, he was critical of errors of taste, especially on the part of masters whom he treated, with two exceptions, as a set of lower-middle-class lunatics. He disliked Collegers, finding them dowdy and "pi" and he was fond of remarking how swiftly their cleverness evaporated. "A brilliant scholar, won the Newcastle three times running," he would exclaim, imitating a master's complacent tones, "and now he has passed second into the Office of Works." With me, however, he was more tolerant, Horace Walpole to Gray, Townley to Pontifex. The other important Pop was Alec Dunglass, who was President and also Keeper of the Field and Captain of the Eleven. He was a votary of the esoteric Eton religion, the kind of graceful, tolerant, sleepy boy who is showered with favours and crowned with all the laurels, who is liked by the masters and admired by the boys without any apparent exertion on his part, without experiencing the ill-effects of success himself or arousing the pangs of envy in others. In the eighteenth century he would have become Prime Minister before he was thirty; as it was he appeared honourably ineligible for the struggle of life.

Relations with Oppidans were more superficial than with Collegers. They were easy-going extroverts lacking in super-ego who regarded friendship as a question of equality and shared interests; only Collegers treated it as a philosophy, an end in itself. Meeting Oppidans was like going to smart luncheons where people seem more intimate than they are; returning to College was going on from lunch to spend all the afternoon with a bourgeois intellectual friend of long standing. Friendship, among Oppidans, was a luxury—a touch of failure, inequality, absence and it perished. In College it was a necessity of our strange monastic society, a religion invented by sensitive boys under hard conditions and which existed to combat them.

The term which was my happiest now drew to an end. College politics were absorbing and occupied our anxious elders outside to the extent that we christened these busybodies "The College Investigation Society" and wrote bawdy songs about them. Le Strange summed up the feeling of the minority:

> *Nov. 20th.* There are two great troubles: political and religious. What is one to believe? The religious services here are just awful. Singing absurd meaningless hymns among ugly windows and pictures, with hopeless tunes, and then the intoned droned prayers—all meaningless.
>
> If there is a God he can't be like the Yahweh of the Old Testament. Yet was Christ God? I think not. If there is no God—only a fiction of man's brain, what are we to do with life? Is there another life? Will it be a punishment or reward for this life? No! Then must we be good? Why not rest—peace is what I need. To get away from all the noise and squalor of the world out on to the hills— if there is any god it is Pan—but we cannot worship him except by letting ourselves be absorbed. He is deaf to prayers. He goes on his way regardless. There cannot be a benevolent God. It is impossible in all this squalor. Should one try to improve the squalor? *Dorian Gray* is an extremely interesting book but of course Lord Henry Wotton must be wrong. I have also just read *Potterism*. It is dreadful the morbid state into which people get whatever they do. Either they become jingoists like Kipling or else they think of a vanished golden age—like those patriot poets in Ireland.
>
> All the questions of freedom—ethnologically, and of Disarmament are so interesting, but the world is so parochial that one can never think of them.
>
> All my time is taken up with talking of: Athleticism, College Pop, and Fagging. They all run into one another.
>
> Peter and I were both elected to Coll. Pop at the beginning of this half, after being blackballed last summer. So was R. Cyril got in last half. We all arranged to keep Carter out. He was so awful, sarcastic, reactionary, etc. After all, he had his College Cricket, that was sufficient. Now he has got his Wall too. Poor R. has been turned out of that, he is a barbarian and to be foiled of his barbar triumphs must be hard. Everything here is done on an athletic standard. I am still in Lower Col-

lege with those small boys, good enough in themselves—
But O! the ignominy of it. Thank God Peter is also in
L.C. O Peter is splendid! unselfish, generous. It must be
wretched for him too. But I can't make myself think of
that.

I want to reform College when my time comes—to
make the fagging better if I can't abolish it, and corporal
punishment too. Why should this heaven be made a hell
just for the sake of old traditions and to make the British
public school type? Ought I to keep Carter out? He has
been good to me—but his influence is bad in College. He
stands for Athleticism and Good Form and all the rubbish joined with that. And still at the back of all these
questions of reform and improvement and an intellectual
rather than an athletic standard and so on, is the moral
question.

Is anything worth while?

Should one live for the greatest happiness of the greatest number, avoiding all classes and creeds—or live so as
to get the greatest peace for oneself. The second is so
easy, and yet conscience goes against it. What is conscience? Is it only some hereditary tradition to be
spurned with patriotism, etc.? The English Gentleman.
What an opprobrium that is. O pray, if you have a God,
for peace of mind. If we live for others we spoil ourselves. If we live for ourselves we harm others. The only
course is to give oneself up to art or literature or such.
But then that doesn't pay, and I suppose—*Il faut vivre*.

We shared Walter's contempt for the politics of the outside world; politicians were monsters of inefficiency and
self-interest, we underwent the general post-war disillusion
and would have been surprised and humiliated to be told
that through the medium of college politics we had ourselves become politically-minded. I was fond of quoting
Halifax: "The Government of the world is a very great
thing, but it is a very coarse thing compared with the fine-
ness of speculative knowledge."

My mother took me to Switzerland for the Christmas
holidays of 1921. We spent them at Mürren. I was mad

about skiing, the hotel was full of pretty girls. I skied, made friends and fell in love but still managed to work for some part of the day. I had often met girls in the holidays but when I was back at Eton they had failed to retain a hold on my imagination; if I had asked them to come down to see me I would then find excuses to put them off. Their reign would come later. Staying in the same hotel however was Antony Knebworth and we saw something of each other. For the first time I was aware of that layer of blubber which encases an English peer, the sediment of permanent adulation. Antony was highspirited and even when he rearranged all the shoes outside the hotel's two hundred bedrooms he could do no wrong. The meeting had consequences for me. The alpine heights, unfriendly, like too healthy climates, to all forms of art, were also unpropitious to philosophic doubt. My scepticism retreated; the shutter between myself and the rest of the world was raised and under Antony's protection, I enjoyed a social success.

It was now decided I must try for a history scholarship; at first Cambridge was indicated. Most Collegers went on to Kings, where there were safe scholarships for them and a reprieve for several more years from expulsion from the womb; Farlow was there and Rylands, Walter Le Strange was going on and eventually Nigel and Freddie. Some of us had been to Cambridge the term before to see the production of the *Oresteia,* and we had found it exhilarating and cosy, for, subject to a little permutation, the sentimental friendships from College continued unabated with undergraduates from other schools forming an audience, who, at a pinch, could contribute new blood to the cast.

On the other hand, Headlam advised Oxford of which we had caught a glimpse marching down the High on a wintry field-day, while the old Etonians waved to us from their college porches. Denis and Roger Mynors and Bobbie Longden were all going up for scholarships there and besides Oxford was "better for history." In the end out of admiration for Headlam I chose to try for Balliol and as a gesture because it was the more difficult. For the same reason I concentrated on mediæval history; we were taught European history from the Renaissance and "mediæval" history meant teaching myself, another "gesture," which also provided the escape that I wanted my work to be. In history I was on the side of the underdog; I liked the past, the personal element, the Ages of Faith, the policies with no future. Most stimulating were the Dark Ages, there was "no damned merit" about them, they were obscure, their futility a standing criticism of humanity. I admired the Childerics and Chilperics of the Merovingian dynasty, the chronicles of Liutprand, the crimes of Brunnhild and Fredegonde.

Each night, by my outlawed candle, I read all Gibbon, all Milman's *History of Latin Christianity*. I specialised in the heresies of anarchists and Albigensians but I was interested in them all, in the Manichæans, in the heresies of Abelard, of my hero Frederic Stupormundi, the Flagellants and in my favourite Neminians who believed in a religion of "No Man" because "No Man living hath seen God," and "To No Man is it given to escape Death."

Reading late by candle was bad for the nerves for it had to be hidden in one's bed or a chink of light might be seen under the door and, like many lazy people, once I started working I could not stop; perhaps that is why we avoid it.

The result of cramming was that a noise of any kind sent me into a temper and that ordinary schoolboy chatter drove me mad. I could speak only to Denis, Charles Milligan and Jackie O'Dwyer; in other company I would glower and pull out a book. With the Oppidans however my ill-humour vanished, I became engaging and witty.

I now admitted to myself my ambition to get into Pop and planned my campaign. My handicap was that I had no athletic distinctions, nor was I in Sixth Form from which a certain number of Pops invariably had to be chosen. My only hope was to be elected as a wit. Although it was but a small section of Pop who thought me funny, they were influential. My tactics were to seem as important as I could in College, so that my Oppidan friends would not feel that I was too powerless in my own fief to deserve recognition abroad. There were two Pops already in College, the lion-hearted Gibson, a fellow history specialist and Robert Longden, one of those angel-faced Athenians whom the school delighted to honour. I was very fond of both of them and had known them for a long time. I would walk away with Gibson, arm-in-arm, from divisions and seeing me with the only two "possible" people in College, the Oppidans felt they were safe in going about with me by themselves. I mention this technique in case others who wish to be elected to things may find it helpful. It was not very difficult for if the Oppidans observed me with the right Collegers, the latter also saw me with the right Oppidans and both felt pleased with their discrimination.

Deeper than this lay my friendship with Teddy Jessel which arose out of a certain boredom he felt at Eton through not being adolescent. I amused him because he stimulated me.

If I should get into Pop I told my conscience, my morbid spiritual director, I would make amends, for I should be free to talk to whom I liked, and then no one could stop me. There could be no further social ambition. Meanwhile I watched my step.

The scholarship examinations drew near. With Denis, Robert Longden and Roger Mynors I stayed in Balliol and did two papers a day, of which the most important was the English Essay. The subject was *Compromise* which was a favourite of mine for I had already written one essay on it and had quotations ready by which I could prove that compromises were failures and that, even if they were successes, it was one's duty to remain uncompromising. The ages of Faith came to life under my pen. But as Denis and I walked about the Quad or lunched with the Balliol contingent of Old Collegers, as we inspected the dingy rooms with no pictures and few books whose furniture was a dark green tablecloth burnt by cigarette ends, a blokey armchair and a small cold bedroom looking out on a neo-Gothic quad, a doubt assailed us. Here we were, urbanely pouring out the content of our well-stocked minds for six hours every day. *And for what?*

The sheets had not been aired in my bedroom. I got rheumatism in my shoulder and could hardly hold a pen during the later papers. The dons impressed me but the undergraduates I encountered made me long to return to my suspended boyhood, to Charles and Jackie and Nigel and Freddie, my books and Medici prints, the view from my window of wine-dark brick and the chestnut tree in Weston's Yard.

College spirit [I noted down] is antagonistic to Balliol spirit in its suppression of the political, lack of emphasis on conversation, hatred of "giants at play" and in its attention to reading and the reading of dead rather than living authors. It appears more akin to Cambridge, but with less emphasis on the bawdy Elizabethans.

We were all four school-sick (Oxford reminded me of Wellington) and radiant when the train brought us back down the Thames Valley. The term ended in athletics. I went in for school fives with Longden and then the scholarship results came out. Denis and Roger had got classical scholarships at Balliol, Robert at Trinity and I had won the Brackenbury History Scholarship. There was excitement, the history specialists cheered, and a whole holiday was given. Then came the last Sunday of term and the morning of the Pop election. I sat in my room with Charles. We had planned to go abroad together for Easter, our parents had given permission and in a few days we would realise our dream of a visit to Provence. I longed to see Avignon, the scandalous history of whose popes was as clear to me as the lines on my hand, for although I had now been abroad twice, to Paris and to Switzerland, I had never travelled alone before.

We knew that Gibson and Longden planned to put me up for Pop. The suspense grew heavy, our voices languished. Pop elections took hours, for the same boy would be put up and blackballed seven or eight times, a caucus of voters keeping out everybody till their favourite got in. Only the necessity of lunch ended these ordeals. Suddenly there was a noise of footsteps thudding up the wooden staircase of the tower. The door burst open and about twenty Pops, many of whom had never spoken to me before, with bright-coloured waistcoats, rolled umbrellas, buttonholes, braid, and "spongebag" trousers, came reeling in, like the College of Cardinals arriving to congratulate some pious old freak whom fate had elevated to the throne of St. Peter. They made a great noise, shouting and slapping me on the back in the elation of their gesture and Charles drifted away. I had got in on the first round, being put up by Knebworth, but after they had left only the faint smell of Balkan Sobranie and Honey and Flowers mixture remained to prove it was not a dream.

At that time Pop were the rulers of Eton, fawned on by masters and the helpless Sixth Form. Such was their prestige that some boys who failed to get in never recovered; one was rumoured to have procured his sister for the influential members. Besides privilege—for they could beat anyone, fag any lower boy, walk arm-in-arm, wear pretty clothes, sit in their own club and get away with minor breaches of discipline, they also possessed executive power which their members tasted, often for the only time in their lives. To elect a boy without a colour, a Colleger too, was a departure for them; it made them feel that they appreciated intellectual worth and could not be accused of athleticism; they felt like the Viceroy after entertaining Gandhi. The rest of the school could not understand that a boy could be elected because he was amusing; if I got in without a colour it must be because I was a "bitch"; yet by Eton standards I was too unattractive to be a "bitch"— unless my very ugliness provided, for the jaded appetites of the Eton Society, the final attraction!

When I went to chapel I was conscious of eyes being upon me; some were masters, cold and censorious, they believed the worst; others were friendly and admiring. Those of the older boys were incredulous but the younger ones stared hardest for they could be beaten for not knowing all the Pops by sight and mine was a mug they must learn by heart. Everybody congratulated me. The only person not to was Denis. He himself had been co-opted in as future Captain of the School and he could not believe that my election to such an anti-intellectual and reactionary body could give me pleasure. I thought that it was because he was envious, since he had been elected *ex officio*. My intravenous injection of success had begun to take.

Before we went abroad I visited St. Wulfric's. I was now

Old Wulfrician No. 1 whose triumphs were chronicled in the school magazine but although Flip and Sambo were charming, I was uneasy as I surveyed the eighty little boys in their green jerseys and corduroy knickers. I taught the Sixth Form, I wandered round classrooms and playing fields, the drill ground, the gooseberry bushes, the chapel. It seemed inconceivable that I could have felt so deeply, that I could have been a boy there myself, that Tony Watson had existed or the Manx shearwater. Flip was confidential; I saw her angry with one or two boys, then when they had gone, she would laugh about them and say what a lot of nonsense one had to tell them at that age, how difficult it was to keep them in order. Had I dreamt then about my favour-charts? Had I imagined it all, like a savage who believes that a tree or an old bone is ill-disposed to him? I could not be sure for it was clear that these monsters whom I had feared when I was ten had become delightful and reasonable people now I was eighteen—or would my "favour" change and Flip be revealed again as Avenging Juno? I was bewildered.

All the boys seemed happy; there were several peers and a Siamese prince; once more the school had won the shooting trophy and the Harrow History Prize. It was a mystery. I felt like the English lady at the Paris exhibition whose mother was taken ill in her hotel and who came back with a doctor to find her name absent from the register, the rooms relet, repapered, refurnished and the hotel staff adamant that mother and daughter had never been seen. I wired to Charles to fetch me a day early and we crossed to Dieppe. Sambo's farewell was vivid. "Don't forget, Tim. A Balliol scholar has the ball at his feet." Already I felt embarrassed to know what to do with it.

We stayed our first night near the Gare St. Lazare and visited the Folies Bergères. In the interval we roamed about the Promenoir and sat down at a table with two thin dark prostitutes. It was a great moment and seemed to wipe out my humiliation of the year before. We gave them drinks and were extremely polite, in the *Sinister Street* manner, for who knew, they might have as many different editions of Petronius as I? We wore blue suits, camel's hair waist-coats and dark blue overcoats with a waist at the back; we smoked cigars and drawled a little, for I was now in Pop, and Charles, in Sixth Form, was blonder and neater and vaguer than ever. He might have entertained prosti-tutes at the Folies Bergères all his life.

Suddenly Egerton and Rylands came up. We were un-easy and left our guests, for "Pussy" Egerton, now a scholar of Trinity, had been the Captain of the School and in the Eleven; he was "the hell of a chap" and the Colleger who had best fitted into the background of the lilies, correcting the headmaster, sleeping through difficult construes, to wake up and suggest an emendation with that bloom of laziness which was a trait in the "To him that hath shall be given" Eton type. Rylands, his great friend, was more exaggerated, more literary. He was going to be the Duchess in the *Duchess of Malfi* next year, he told us, and he talked of "Lytton" and "A.C.B."

Afterwards we went back to the hotel and lay awake in the dark. My face itched, and I could feel lumps under my fingers. I scratched, and heard a noise in the silence. Charles was scratching too.

"Charles."

"Yes."

"Are you awake?"

"Yes."

"So am I."

"Charles."

"Yes."

"Do you know how one catches it?"

"Yes. I think so. From shaking hands—or touching them or drinking out of the same glass."

"My God—it's come out on my face already."

"And mine."

"I shook hands with mine."

"Mine wore gloves—I felt fairly safe."

"But don't you think she wore them because she *had it there?*"

"Christ! How awful—and my face itches too."

"Have you got anything we can put on?"

"Only some Icilma."

"It's better than nothing—in the morning we can go to a doctor."

"Or should we go now?"

We put on the light and looked at each other. Charles sat up in his white Egyptian cotton pyjamas. They were mosquito bites. We joked about them with nervous vigour, and caught the morning train to Avignon.

There is the first time we go abroad and there is the first time we set eyes on Provence. For me they almost coincided and it would be hard to express what I felt that evening, in the garden above the Papal Palace. The frogs croaked, the silver Rhone flowed underneath, the Mediterranean spring was advancing. I have been back so many times, as a spring ritual, to that palace, to Hiely's restaurant with its plate-glass windows, to the Greek Theatre at Arles, the hills of Les Baux, the ruins of St.-Rémy, to the Rhone with its eddies and islands and the cypress hedges where the cicadas charge the batteries of summer, that I can no longer remember what they looked like for the first time. I know only that they are sacred places, that the country between the Mont Ventoux and the Canigou, from Avignon and Vaucluse to Figueras and Puigcerdá, is the expression of the complete south, the cradle of my civilisation.

We hired bicycles at Villeneuve-les-Avignon and visited Nîmes and Tarascon and Beaucaire. Then we had to make a decision. Should we go on to the Riviera or down the east coast of France towards Spain? Charles inclined to casinos but we chose Spain because it was cheaper and spent the next night at Narbonne. The town was gloomy, the mistral blew, Charles broke the chandelier in our room and tried to hide the pieces. At the last moment they were found and a large item added to the bill. The mistral made travelling impossible. We sat in the train going past platforms where the acacias and cypresses were plastered back by the wind and where even the names of the stations seemed fretted by the mistral; Agde, Leucate, Fitou, Palau del Vidre. The lagoons fascinated us, for it was the country of *Mariana in the South*. The strip of sand, the reeds, the sea lavender, the wind and sun brought back South Africa;

there was the Mediterranean, a dark streak beyond the lagoons like the edge of a pineta and close at hand the stakes in the water, the white beds of flaking salt, the barren rocks of the Corbières. We reached the red soil of Roussillon, the fortress of Salses, the cathedral of Elne where a Byzantine empress lay buried, Collioure with its phallic church tower, dingy Port Vendres, Banyuls and after many tunnels the frontier at Cerbère. We could go no farther without a visa.

Next morning we scrambled up to the top of the hill from the beach, blown flat against the ground by the mistral but able to feel we had looked into Spain. Below us was an identical stony hillside dotted with asphodel, Port Bou with its cove, Cullera and Llansa, the mountain peninsula that runs out to Cadaqués and the plain of the Ampurdán. For one moment we surveyed it, then we were blown off our feet. Unable to stay on in Cerbère, we retreated, still battered by the mistral, from the station with its queues of Catalans, in berets and rope-soled shoes, their rugs slung over their shoulders, to the palms and cafés of Perpignan. I was getting school-sick for Eton.

> *Où sont les gracieux galants*
> Whom I saw last a month ago?
> And here at Perpignan I want
> To see them all again, although
> 'Twas not with such an easy flow
> Of mutual intercourse enjoyed. . . .
> In fact I often was, I know,
> By ἔρις not ἐρῶς destroyed.
> And how does my dear Denis fare
> Called "proud" by Dadie, whom we met
> The prey of the Folies Bergères
> And wooed by many an Amoret
> Who said "*Dormirez-vous*, you pet"
> But Egerton, with visage *noir*
> Repulsed the sirenaic set
> Who circle in the Promenoir.

Our journeys back were unpleasant. We both ran out of money and because of our tickets had to return by different ways. I travelled by Toulouse, carried my suitcase across Paris, got to London in the evening and, rather than confess that I was penniless, spent my last five shillings on dining alone in Soho and then retired for the night to St. Martin's-in-the-Fields. It was cold and uncomfortable, the people coughing all round me, and wrapping themselves up in newspapers, kept me awake. The next morning I met Charles at Victoria. He was coming back by Avignon but had overslept and gone on to Marseille where they had tried to make him pay the difference. He had only a bag of dates on which he had been living and we took them to the Park and finished them before going round to his home in Upper Brook Street.

CHAPTER XXIV: *VALE*

When we went back to Eton the news of our travels had preceded us. We were sent for by the Headmaster and rebuked for having visited the Folies Bergères which was not the sort of place where Etonians go. Charles's visit in his sleep to Marseille was misconstrued by his tutor who asked him if he was aware that it was a centre of the white slave trade? I had been staying on my way back with my aunt and her butler had packed the magazines which were by my bed, including a copy of *La Vie Parisienne*. My tutor was horrified, it was bad enough to glance at such drawings he explained, what made it worse was that they were so "diabolically clever." He also took away *Tristram Shandy* and an uncut Rabelais.

Denis, Robert Longden and Roger Mynors now formed the principal mess. Charles and I now messed alone; Denis was Captain of the School but for the first month of my last term I lived among Oppidans. "Since God has given us the Popacy let us enjoy it," was my motto after Leo the Tenth's. I was ashamed to hire classical records now from the music shop and on summer mornings I would go down there with Edward Woodall, Robin Gurdon and Teddy Jessel to play "Say It with Music" while the fox-trot floated away on the sunlight and we commented on the looks of the passers-by.

It was a custom to walk up to a hotel in Windsor and sit in the garden, drinking and smoking. These were serious offences but the Pops took them for granted and never went about without a full cigarette case. At lunch they sat beside their housemasters, breathing port and tobacco over them and making patronising conversation. I soon discovered that my notion of being careful whom I went about with till I was in Pop and then making friends with whom

I liked was quite impracticable. The Pops like all tyrants clung together, as afraid of what the school thought of them as the rest were of the Pops; those who had nothing in common and disliked each other hurried when they met to link arms against an invisible danger.

Thus only boys in Pop were allowed to walk arm-in-arm. When I was not in Pop but was walking with Teddy Jessel or Robert Longden I would await the gesture, the arm first raised and then shot forward to bring the sleeve and cuff down within grip of the fingers and then the whole arm inserted, like a bishop laying on hands, with a sacred stealing motion through my own. It was a solemn moment when this public favour was conferred but when I was in Pop and enjoyed the same privilege I found that my arm seemed unwilling to experiment, and felt at ease only when another braided Pop sleeve reposed in mine.

Soon everybody in College began to seem insipid and dowdy for I saw them through Oppidan eyes and only the fastidious Charles and the genial Jackie were proof against that insolent fashionable stare. "How petty everything is," wrote Walter Le Strange. "Even people one would never suspect of it seem afraid of Cyril, speaking of him only in hushed whispers."

Some of the Pops had been worried about my not having a colour and the Captain of the Boats was persuaded to give me a rowing one; like any oligarchy the Eton Society went in terror of letting itself down. For a month I was a model member of that corrupt and glittering eighteenth-century clique and I forgot for the first time in my life that I was a "highbrow," and that highbrows are cut off from the world.

During this month I managed to emancipate myself from the Irish bogey through the Anglo-Irish boys at school who were cousins of mine and whom I met at my aunt's. Being in Pop was a distinction even the Anglo-Irish had to recognise and one day I realised that I was the most important boy there, that they wanted to know me, not I them, that I need not rack my brains to think of something to say about horses, it was for them to try to talk about the all-Colleger performance of *She Stoops to Conquer* in which I was play-

ing an exhibitionist role.[1] A voice told me that Clontarf,
rebuilt with livid stained glass in the Isle of Wight Gothic
of the sixties round an old ivied tower, was an ugly and
unimportant house in a Dublin suburb, that History, after
taking one look at the Vernons, had moved across the Channel and that whoever might now receive her favours, it
would not be the lately landed Anglo-Irish Gentry.

Alas, in my excursion into the ruling class I had reckoned
without an old enemy—the Thames Valley summer. Buttercups, lilac, elms and steamy evenings had returned and
were preparing their annual coup. They used a roundabout
method.

It was the privilege of College Pop not to have to stamp
their own letters. One member offered to "keep the stamps"
and to him a fag would bring the letters from the letter-box,
stamp them there and enter the amounts due in a book.
When stamps ran out, the stamp-keeper would go round
and ask people for what they owed him. At that time I
kept the stamps for College Pop but I spurned the dunning
of people for money and announced that I would pay for
the stamps myself. One or two conscientious boys gave
something, the rest accepted this typical "gesture" as a mixture of idealism, laziness and the desire to show off. "*Qui
veut faire l'ange fait la bête!*" I soon ran out of stamps and
having some letters brought to me to post, I remembered
that any placed in the letter-box in the rooms of the Eton
Society were franked in the same way. I sent the fag down
with them. That afternoon, when the letters were collected,
somebody in Pop chanced to go through them, and noticed
that several were to the parents of Collegers. The old hostility broke out. "Why the hell should those bloody bastards
in College post their letters here—why should we stamp let-

---

[1] *Mrs. Hardcastle.* The signatures on my programme at this
extreme moment of dandyism are revealing. Dunglass, Knebworth, Teddy Jessel, Robin Gurdon, Maurice Bridgman, Edward
Woodall, Greville Worthington, Guy Wainwright—all history
specialist members of Pop, Brian Howard (æsthete), Bernard
Brassey (toast of the day) and three fags, Alsop, Coleridge and
Ford to represent College with Nigel and his friend O'Connor.
Five of these and three members of the cast would meet violent
deaths before they were forty. *Quel époque!*

ters addressed to all the bloody villas in Tooting, etc., etc."

The Pops assumed that they had been posted by Denis, whom they disliked, to oblige his friends and made remarks about him. I heard of the proceedings but at some time in the St. Wulfric's or Dark Ages period my nerve had gone. I felt the old panic about "owning up," "going straight," "generality," and "being wanted"—I could not explain, only wait for it to blow over. Eventually—by elimination—they discovered who it was. Nico Davies and Knebworth rebuked me in a friendly way. I tried to apologise but was seized with a hopeless feeling of guilt. How could I explain? I had betrayed Pop; I had let down the friends who had made the experiment of electing me.

From that moment my vitality failed as I had seen it fail in others, I felt uneasy whenever I was with Pops, and could no longer face the rakes in the Hotel Garden. I made the mistake, common in youth, of not understanding that people who like one for oneself, will overlook occasional lapses. I felt that the members of the Eton Society liked me only in so far as I conformed while someone more mature would have known that the affair was trivial and that they liked me because they knew I could never conform. Driven underground for a year by success, my persecution mania had found an outlet.

In College my self-confidence still held out but even as I had fallen victim to scepticism a summer before, so now I succumbed to æstheticism. It was in the air; the season, the lime-flowered summer evenings undermined me and I fell. I wore, instead of a blazer, with my grey flannel trousers, a black dinner-jacket and a panama hat. The fashion was not followed. I read *Marius the Epicurean* and *A Rebours* which sent me on to silver Latin and *"faisandé"* prose. I studied the philosophy of Aristippus of Cyrene and smouldered with the "hard gem-like flame." I believed in living for "golden moments," in "anything for a sensation" and read Baudelaire, Verlaine, Hérédia, Moréas, and Mallarmé at French Extra Studies with de Satgé, from whom I borrowed *Limbo* and *Crome Yellow* which I got into trouble for reading.

I went to the rose-show at Windsor and had an intense

experience looking at the whitest of white roses; after that I always had some Frau Karl Druschkis in my room. Rancid with boredom, I burnt melancholy texts round the wall with a poker. "Let us crown ourselves with roses before they be withered" (*Coronemus nos rosis antequam marcescant*) from the *Wisdom of Solomon*, "*Finis venit, venit finis, evigilavit adversum te et ecce venit*" from Ezekiel, and from Mallarmé "*La chair est triste, hélas, et j'ai lu tous les livres.*"

I now admired the twelve Cæsars with their enigmatic deathbed sayings charged with power and satiety and the last king of France—"*mettons-nous à la fenêtre et ennuyons nous,*" exclaimed Louis XIII, "*Nous ne sommes pas heureux à notre âge*" added Louis XIV. Louis XV left no wisdom, but I learnt that on receiving the news of each defeat in the Seven Years' War "*Il ouvre ses grands yeux tristes, et tout est dit.*"

A favourite and succulent character was Audubon, in Lowes Dickinson's *Modern Symposium*.

> And just there is the final demonstration of the malignity of the scheme of things. Time itself works against us. The moments that are evil it eternalises; the moments that might be good it hurries to annihilation. All that is most precious is most precarious. Vainly do we cry to the moment, "*Verweile doch, du bist so schön!*" Only the heavy hours are heavy-footed. The winged Psyche, even at the moment of birth, is sick with the pangs of dissolution.

Walter Le Strange corroborated.

> *June 25th.* Seven months since I have seen you, sweet book! Cyril has had you—thank God they were no profane hands that touched you, or unholy eyes that read my heart. When I last confided to you I had sunk to depths of æsthetic affectation deeper than I realised at the time. Now I am (I flatter myself) more level-headed. Cyril has once more consented to *know* me, after some months of estrangement. His conversation is as butter and honey after bread and dripping. Unfortunately, instead of what was, for me at least, friendship, there is

now worship. For then we were outwardly (I flatter myself again) equal, now I am (to the world, not mentally, I hope) unchanged, while he has Success. Niké disdains me. I let Cyril influence me more than I mean to. I know all influence (especially an enervating one like his) is bad. But Cyril is so pleasant I cannot resist him even if I wished to try. (O Hypocrite that I am, this is written for his eyes.)

July 12th. Life should be lived, wildly and feverishly within, outwardly with absolute calm and composure. Nor ought one's true opinions to be given to anyone. Everything should bow to expediency and efficiency. How weak I am! In the evening I make huge resolves, in the morning I remember them and disregard them.

July 15th. Since last I wrote the whole world seems to have been spread before me. I have seen incense burnt on the altar of Dionysus and heard the *Antigone* acted in the original tongue of Sophocles. I have dined with the Headmaster and talked of Italian Art. Cyril has shown me the most beautiful flowers in the world. I have knelt on the floor looking at a mediæval map beside a Prince Palatine. I have had my 18th birthday. I have four ambitions of which only the third is likely to come true.

(1) To get a scholarship at Kings in December.
(2) To get my College Wall.
(3) To see Florence and Venice.
(4) To be in Pop next summer half.

To myself I appear a Messiah.

To my friends an ineffectual angel with a touch of the idiot.

To my enemies a negligible knave.

Coronemus nos rosis antequam marcescant. But I only do it because it is the thing to do.

Vain attempts to attract Maud.

The Beggar's Opera and *Dear Brutus* both tend to show "the utter futility of doing anything under any circumstances."

Le Strange at least kept his diary but all my own at-

tempts to write were doomed to failure. I didn't see how
one could well write in English, and my Greek and Latin
were still not good enough. I took to writing jingles in which
a Greek verse was brought in to rhyme with the English;
it was not till a year or two later that I was able to discard
English and express myself in Greek epigrams for to compose in a dead language was the creative activity toward
which my education was inexorably tending. Meanwhile
there was French.

> Roses blanches
> Qui se penchent
> En songes
> Elles m'ont chanté
> Des enchantés
> Mensonges.

> Que la vie est brève
> Rêve d'un rêve, etc. etc.

This was the summer's only inspiration.

Meanwhile a strange pink album had appeared called
the *Eton Candle*. It contained poems and some precious
stories, contributions from Max Beerbohm and those suspect
old Etonians, Aldous Huxley, Osbert and Sacheverell Sitwell. One day Teddy Jessel introduced me to the editor, a
boy in his house with a distinguished impertinent face, a
sensual mouth and dark eyes with long lashes. He wrote to
ask me to tea. I accepted, on Pop writing paper, and went
round one summer afternoon to find *foie gras* sandwiches,
strawberries and cream and my postcard of acceptance
prominently displayed on the mantelpiece. Seeing it up
there for the world to know that Brian Howard had had a
Pop to tea with him, I was miserable. I felt that once again
I had let the Eton Society down. It was natural for Teddy
Jessel to know Brian, who was in the same house. The question was, *Who else did?* I swallowed down my tea like a
lady who is offered a swig by a madman in a railway tunnel
and bolted.

Afterwards when I saw Brian alone I would talk to him;
when I was with other Pops I avoided him, as in the Dark

Ages Wilfrid had avoided me. I need not have worried for he soon became the most fashionable boy in the school but, as it was, though I grew to know him better, his politeness overwhelmed me. He belonged to a set of boys who were literary and artistic but too lazy to gargle quotations and become inoculated with the virus of good taste latent in Eton teaching and too disorderly and bad at games to be overburdened with responsibility and who in fact gained most from Eton because of the little they gave. There was Harold Acton, a prince of courtesy, his brother William, Robert Byron who was aggressive, and played jokes on the Corps, the two Messels; Antony Powell, the author of *Afternoon Men* and Henry Green who has since described them in his novel, *Blindness*. They were the most vigorous group at Eton for they lived within their strength, yet my moral cowardice and academic outlook debarred me from making friends with them.

College politics were now less exciting, for we were not in opposition but in office. Denis was Captain of the School; beatings stopped, fagging was light, the election system languished. College Pop had now extended the privilege of using its library to the Upper Half of College, and so to belong no longer brought that increase of privacy which, at Eton, formed the substance of promotion. Being in Liberty and in Pop but not in Sixth Form, I was in an irresponsible position, a school but not a house prefect. I looked on myself as a kind of Charles James Fox or Wilkes, a Whig to the left of the Whig position although I was more of an anarchist than a Liberal for I disbelieved in power and authority and thought them evil and believed that the natural goodness of human reason must triumph without them.

The deadly sin, since I was in Pop, was "Worldliness" and I preached against it whenever I could. As with many anarchists, there was some vanity in my make-up. I did not want to co-operate or be co-operated with and began to take umbrage with Denis, Roger, Robert Longden, the Periclean Caucus who governed College.

Thus after the reform of College Pop into a debating society, I resigned as a protest against compulsory debates although the notion, "that death was preferable to life," was one very dear to me. A blasé *grand seigneur* I called everybody in College by their Christian name and at Liberty Supper I would hold "wantings" which were parodies of the dread affairs of my youth and on occasion a mock beating in which the victims kept their gowns on, and the canes, carefully notched beforehand, broke in half at the first stroke. It was a silly way to behave, as rumours spread which made more difficult the genuine reforms of the Caucus. Anybody could play about with discipline in that way since however much one might rag "wantings" and fagging, there was no question of boys not turning up for the wanting or not running to be fagged.

I made friends with many of the fags; in my jaundiced state I enjoyed their simplicity and vitality, besides, I wanted them to be happier than I had been myself. I was sometimes suspected of other motives by my ambivalent housemaster which made me scornful and defiant. He had complained once of my "infernal pride" and I at last lived up to it. I hated history by now; it stank of success, and I buried myself in the classics. I was bored and unhappy but there was no equal in whom I could confide. I was afraid Denis would fail to understand, the virtuous Caucus might lecture me, my housemaster was antipathetic, Headlam could have helped me but I was too frightened of him. He had pointed out to me the seats which the Sitwells had occupied in his classroom but on the other hand he had condemned as morbid "Ere blowsy tediousness of summer days," the last line of a sonnet I wrote.

Urquhart came down from Balliol and had tea with me; he seemed with his easy-going good-mannered confidence and aroma of the days of Greville and Palmerston to promise release into an adult world of intellectual excitement and sensible activity—but after he had gone the white roses, the green bananas, the clove carnation soap and the dismal mottoes resumed their power, and I even engaged a fag to sing Gregorian chants outside my room, like Saul with David.

I was eighteen and a half, I had never had sexual intercourse, I had never masturbated. "Lilies that fester smell far worse than weeds," perhaps even St. Wulfric's, even the Eton authorities had not required a chastity so strict.

The end of term arrived. There was still Camp, which was one long operatic farewell for me but parting was imminent. I had a spectacular leaving tea, to which my friends were invited in platonic couples and where I played the *Après Midi d'un Faune* on my gramophone.

Cyril's leaving tea. A beautiful evening, tea and fair faces and good music [wrote Le Strange]. Then Liberty Supper, the last alas! How banal Liberty suppers will seem next half—*Cyril est épatant, mais comme toujours à la grande manière*. N. got his 22 to-day. He has gone completely off, as has Maud who used to be so very nice.

There was the last chapel where for the last time I refused to bow my head in the creed and read Petronius through the leaving hymn, walking afterwards under the limes with Teddy Jessel. The cant of leaving infuriated him, the sentimental farewells, the warnings against the prostitutes of Jermyn Street and the hypocritical anxiety of the stupider Pops worrying about their successors. The gruelling election had lasted all that morning, with partisans of one boy putting in two or three blackballs each against nominees of others until one understood why the College of Cardinals, on such occasions, was locked in and given no food. My principles still kept me from blackballing anyone but I enjoyed the excitement. Charles my old friend and mess mate was elected, and the second time round I put up Nigel to realise my insolent daydream of the year before.

In spite of the reconciliation our friendship was in abeyance, it would seem that in the quarrel I had expended all the emotion I was capable of feeling. I remembered how at one time noticing the shape of his ear in chapel had moved me and now he was only a bouncing fellow who had just missed the Eleven. He was not elected till a year later but his gratitude put me to shame.

In *College Annals* Denis wrote the account of his stewardship.

The past year has been conspicuous more for an alteration in the general tone of College than for any re-

markable achievements. It has always been the hope of
my own Election to destroy the inter-election enmity, as
it existed a few years ago, to abolish the scandals of College Pop, to reduce the number of beatings to a minimum, and generally to substitute a more harmonious
system of government for the old methods of repressions
and spite.

The actual changes that have occurred may be
summed up thus:—When I was a fag it was considered
a poor night for the "senior" if no one was beaten, and
"wantings" occurred every night, whereas this last half
it does not happen to have been necessary to use corporal
punishment at all, scarcely a dozen to twenty "wantings"
the whole half. As regards College Pop, instead of being
a miniature Eton society with exclusive right to Reading
Room, it has been reformed with the intention of making
it a debating society proper, and I have hopes that the
new rules will not allow it again to degenerate into a
selfish body of College "chaps", like School Pop. . . . It
is early yet to judge of the success of these experiments,
and the universal prediction of the "old men" *may* be
verified, but I can at least honestly record that College
has been in every way *happier* this year than at any time
in the last six years.

The verdict of subsequent Captains of the School on our
short-lived and unpopular experiment in happiness can be
found in Mr. Eric Parker's *College at Eton* (Macmillan,
1933). *College Annals* also included a short autobiography
of every Colleger, usually a list of his athletic distinctions,
but, under our decadent administration, more general in
tone. Thus Farlow added his slogan *"cui bono"* to his list
of triumphs, Charles included his gesture in resigning from
the Corps and Le Strange ended up "other minor scholastic
achievements there were too, which it would be tedious to
enumerate." I added a list of favourite authors, favourite
flower, rose (white) and my new motto, "I hate everything
public" (σιχχάινω πάντα τὰ δημόσια), concluding: "A
sentimental cynic, superstitious atheist and Brackenbury
scholar of Balliol College Oxford."

Although I affected not to care I dreaded leaving; one part of me was bored and looked forward to moving on, the other clung to the past. Once more I had built up a private civilisation of reason and love at a temperature warmer than the world outside; once again it had to be shattered. "We whose generations are ordained in this setting part of time are providentially taken off from such imaginations"—but I could not repress a dread of the future, of the uglification of life, of Oxford bedrooms and dour undergraduates. Eton is one of the few schools where the standard of comfort is almost in advance of the universities and unlike most boys, Denis and Robert and I were not looking forward to more liberty than we enjoyed already, to more interesting friendships, or to a room of our own for the first time. Also we were attached to the past and used to a world of boys, boys with a certain grace who like the portraits in the Provost's Lodge wore their eighteenth-century clothes with elegance. The world of matey young men with their pipes and grey bags, the blokeries to which we had been allotted, filled us with despair; we mourned with apprehension, "Not the dead but the ἥβας ἄνθος ἀπολλύμενον—the flower of youth perishing."

I was now entering the third hot room of English education; from St. Wulfric's I had got a scholarship to Eton, from Eton to Balliol and from thence there would, I supposed, be other scholarships awaiting me; I could not imagine a moment when I should not be receiving marks for something, when "poor" or "very fair" or "Beta plus" was not being scrawled across my conduct sheet by the Great Examiner. And yet already I was a defeatist, I remembered Teddy Jessel saying to me by the fives courts, in my hour of triumph: "Well, you've got a Balliol scholarship and you've got into Pop—you know I shouldn't be at all surprised if you never did anything else the rest of your life. After all, what happens to old tugs? If they're clever they become dons or civil servants, if not they come back here as ushers; when they're about forty they go to bed with someone, if it's a boy they get sacked, if it's a woman they marry them. The pi ones go into the Church and may become bishops. There goes Connolly, K.S., a brilliant fellow, an alpha mind, he got the Rosebery and the Brackenbury, and all the other berries, and passed top into the Office of Rears!"

There was much truth in this; in fact were I to deduce any system from my feelings on leaving Eton, it might be called *The Theory of Permanent Adolescence*. It is the theory that the experiences undergone by boys at the great public schools, their glories and disappointments, are so intense as to dominate their lives and to arrest their development. From these it results that the greater part of the ruling class remains adolescent, school-minded, self-conscious, cowardly, sentimental and in the last analysis homosexual. Early laurels weigh like lead and of many of the boys whom I knew at Eton, I can say that their lives are over. Those who knew them then knew them at their best and fullest; now, in their early thirties, they are haunted ruins. When we meet we look at each other, there is a pause of recognition, which gives way to a moment of guilt and fear. "I won't tell on you," our eyes say, "if you won't tell on me"—and when we do speak, it is to discover peculiar evidence of this obsession. For a nightmare I have often had has been that of finding myself back; I am still a boy at Eton, still in Pop, still in my old room in Sixth Form Passage but nobody remembers me, nobody tells me where to go. I am worse than a new boy, I am a new old boy. I go into Hall and search for a place to eat, I wander in schoolrooms trying to find a class where I am expected. When I first used to have this dream I had only just left Eton, I knew most of the boys and the masters and the nightmare then took the form of everyone, after my place had been filled, my gap closed over, having to pretend they were glad I had come back. As time went on nobody remembered me and the dream ended with my ignominious ejection. I have found other old Etonians who have had the same experience; some dream they are back in their old rooms while their wives and children hang about outside to disgrace them.

Once again romanticism with its deathwish is to blame, for it lays an emphasis on childhood, on a fall from grace which is not compensated for by any doctrine of future redemption; we enter the world, trailing clouds of glory, childhood and boyhood follow and we are damned. Certainly growing up seems a hurdle which most of us are unable to take and the lot of the artist is unpleasant in England because he is one of the few who, bending but not breaking, is able to throw off these early experiences, for maturity is the quality that the English dislike most and the fault of artists is that, like certain foreigners, they are mature.[2] For my own part I was long dominated by impressions of school. The plopping of gas mantles in the classrooms, the refrain of psalm tunes, the smell of plaster on the stairs, the walk through the fields to the bathing places or to chapel across the cobbles of School Yard, evoked a vanished Eden of grace and security; the intimate noises of College, the striking of the clock at night from Agar's plough, the showers running after games of football, the housemaster's squeak, the rattle of tea-things, the poking of fires as I sat talking with Denis or Charles or Freddie on some evening when everybody else was away at a lecture, were recollected with anguish and College, after I left, seemed to me like one of those humming fortified paradises in an Italian primitive outside which the angry Master in College stood with his flaming sword.

> Procul abest Fridericus, Fridericus capite rubro
> Procul abest Nigel, qui solebat mecum ire
> Procul absunt pueri qui clamant in cubiculis eorum
> Qui sedent super focos pulchri sine arte
> Pulchri sunt sed nesciunt, nec decoris eorum habent
>   scientiam—
> O Roma, urbs beata, lumen ultra mare.

Since I was unable to write in any living language when I left Eton I was already on the way to becoming a critic. My ambition was to be a poet but I could not succeed when poetry was immersed in the Georgian or neo-Tennysonian tradition. I could but have imitated Housman, Flecker, Brooke, de la Mare or Ralph Hodgson. By the time Eliot and Valéry came to save my generation from the ro-

[2] Even the Jews in England are boyish, like Disraeli, and not the creators of adult philosophies like Marx or Freud.

mantic dragon it had already devoured me. I was however well grounded enough to become a critic and drifted into it through unemployability.

In other respects I had been more deeply scarred. The true religion I had learnt at Eton and St. Wulfric's had not been Christianity nor even Imperialism but the primitive gospel of the Jealous God, of το φθονερόν—a gospel which emerged as much from the Old Testament as from Greek tragedy and was confirmed by experience. Human beings, it taught, are perpetually getting above themselves and presuming to rise superior to the limitations of their nature; when they reach this state of insolence or ὕβρις, they are visited with some catastrophe, the destruction of Sodom or the Sicilian expedition, the fate of Œdipus or Agamemnon, the Fall of Troy or the Tower of Babel. The happiness, to which we aspire, is not well thought of and is visited with retribution; though some accounts are allowed to run on longer than others, everything in life has to be paid for.

Even when we say "I am happy" we mean "I was" for the moment is past, besides, when we are enjoying ourselves most, when we feel secure of our strength and beloved by our friends, we are intolerable and our punishment—a beating for generality, a yellow ticket, a blackball or a summons from the headmaster, is in preparation. All we can do is to walk delicately, to live modestly and obscurely like the Greek chorus and to pay a careful attention to omens— counting our paces, observing all conventions, taking quotations at random from Homer or the Bible, and acting on them while doing our best to "keep in favour"—for misfortunes never come alone.

Consider Jackie; playing fives with me one afternoon he said "Damn and blast" when he missed a ball. The headmaster, who was passing, heard him and told Sixth Form. That night he was beaten. In the excitement of the game he had forgotten to prepare his construe. Others had prepared theirs but after the silence before boys are put on to construe, when all diversions have been tried in vain, it was he who was called upon. He was ploughed and given a "ticket" "Failed in Construe" to get signed by his tutor. He had not the courage to show it him, forged his tutor's initials on the bottom and handed it back. By chance the two masters met, the ticket was mentioned and the fraud discovered. Within three days of the game of fives the Praepostor came with the terrible summons. "Is O'Dwyer K.S. in this division? He is to go to the headmaster at a quarter to twelve." The wide doors are open which means a birching will take place. The block is put out. Two boys in Sixth Form are there to see the headmaster does not raise his arm above the shoulder, and an old College servant to lower his trousers and hold him down. "Call no man happy till he's dead. Next time it may be me."

Morally I was not in advance of this abject religion; I rejected Christian ethics yet was not enough of a stoic to adopt pagan standards in their place. I was a *vierge folle* full of neurotic pride and this gave to my thinking a morbid tinge.

Politically I was a liberal individualist with a passion for freedom and justice and a hatred of power and authority but I disliked politics and wished for nothing better than to talk to my friends, travel abroad, look at Old Masters and romanesque cathedrals, read old books and devote myself to lost causes and controversies of the Past.

The cause of the unhappiness I had come across I put down as Competition. It was Competition that turned friends into enemies, that exhausted the scholars in heartbreaking sprints and rendered the athletes disappointed and bitter. "Never compete" was my new commandment, never again to go in for things, to be put up and blackballed, to score off anyone; only in that way could the sin of Worldliness be combated, the Splendid Failure be prepared which was the ultimate "gesture." Otherwise when free from guilt and fear I was gay, with evening high spirits hardly distinguishable from intoxication and which rose and rose until the shutter fell, a glass which cut me off from loving friends and imagined enemies and behind which I prepared for that interview with the moment, that sacred breathless confrontation from which so little always results, and so much is vainly expected. I was also an affected lover of sensations which I often faked, a satirist in self-defence, a sceptical believer in the Heraclitan flux, an introspective romantic-sensitive, conceited, affectionate, gregarious and, at the time of leaving Eton, the outstanding moral coward of my generation.

Sometimes I imagine Eton replying to these criticisms, the voice of "Henry's holy shade" answering me with the serenity of a dowager.

"Yes. Very interesting. It was one of my masters, I think, who said, 'Connolly has a vulgar streak'—but we won't discuss that. As I understand, you blame us because our teaching encouraged æstheticism and the vices that are found with it and then punished them when they occurred. Has it ever occurred to you to blame yourself? You say winning a scholarship and getting into Pop turned your head, and set you back ten years. Well, I'm sorry for you. Other boys achieved this and more and were not harmed by it. Look at Robert Longden. The same age as you are and Headmaster of Wellington and Lord Dufferin, almost in the Cabinet. You complain that my teaching is cynical and concentrates on success. Don't forget what Jowett said. 'There are few ways in which a young man can be more harmlessly employed than in making money.' Not that I altogether approve of Pop myself, but since your time its morals have improved and its powers been restricted. The state of College has improved too, that Bolshy epoch, when some of the post-war unrest reached our little backwater, is a thing of the past.

"I think if you had been less vain, less full of the wrong sort of pride and with a little more stuffing, you would not have been attracted to the 'primrose path.' You would not have let a little success get the better of you. Don't forget we put you in a strong position. The great world is not unlike the Eton Society. Their values are the same. You could have made lasting friendships with people who will govern the country—not flashy people but those from whose lodges, in a Scotch deer-forest, great decisions are taken. You Bolshies keep on thinking the things we stand for—cricket, shooting, Ascot, Lords, the Guards, the House of Commons and the Empire are dead. But you all want to put your sons down for Eton. It's twenty years now since you came here. Even then people talked about this world being dead but what is more alive to-day? your Bolshevism or the English governing class, the Tory Party?

"But let's leave Pop, let's suppose it is no good in after life to a boy—excuse me—with your income. There was always a Balliol scholarship. Why didn't you follow that up? I see you show a tendency to sneer at the Government offices and the diplomatic service. And yet they rule the country more than ever. If "Pop" leads to the Cabinet, "College" leads to the Permanent Under-Secretaryships, the plums of the administration. It was the old Colleger type, prelate, judge or civil servant who turned out the late King (not an old Etonian) with such absence of friction. They decide who's to be given a visa or permitted to land; they open the mail and tap the telephones. I shouldn't sneer at them. You imply our education is of no use to you in after life. But no education is. We are not an employment agency; all we can do is to give you a grounding in the art of mixing with your fellow men, to tell you what to expect from life and give you an outward manner and inward poise, an old prescription from the eighteenth century which we call a classical education, an education which confers the infrequent virtues of good sense and good taste and the benefit of dual nationality, English and Mediterranean, and which, taking into account the difficulties of modern life, we find the philosophy best able to overcome them.

"You complain that Ruskin's cult of beauty and Tennyson's imagery of water and summer still predominate; but we can't help our buildings being beautiful or our elms stately. If you think boys are happier for a retarded development in unfriendly surroundings, you should have gone to Wellington. You say we are sterile and encourage composition only in dead languages. Shelley and Swinburne and Dr. Bridges wouldn't agree with you. And what matter, if the spirit is alive? Take this:

Quam breve tempus abit quod amando degitur! Instar[3] Momenti fugiens somnia vix superat.

[3] Que l'heure est donc brève
Qu'on passe en aimant

Exquisite! It is by Mr. Broadbent. Something you were too bathed in your masochist Celtic twilight to appreciate. You were never a very good classical scholar. Too lazy. You would not grasp that, as one of my masters writes, 'No education is worth having that does not teach the lesson of concentration on a task, however unattractive. These lessons, if not learnt early, will be learnt, if at all, with pain and grief in later life.' Now I expect you have found that out, as you will one day find out about character, too.

"About the civilisation of the lilies, Percy Lubbock and Santayana say very different things from you. However, we bear no ill-will. We shall be here when you have gone. Come down and see us some time. I admit we have been disappointed in you. We hoped that you would conquer your faults but we can't all be Pitt or J. K. Stephen and, in spite of what you say, we have since turned out a writer who has been able to reconcile being a 'live wire,' with loyalty to the school tradition, even on the Amazon."

I have concluded at this point, for it marks the end of my unconscious absorption of ideas, besides there was now nothing new which could happen to me. Although to the world I appeared a young man going up to Oxford "with the ball at his feet," I was, in fact, as promising as the Emperor Tiberius retiring to Capri. I knew all about power and popularity, success and failure, beauty and time, I was familiar with the sadness of the lover and the bleak ultimatums of the beloved. I had formed my ideas and made my friends and it was to be years before I could change them. I lived entirely in the past, exhausted by the emotions of adolescence, of understanding, loving and learning. Denis' fearless intellectual justice, Robert's seventeenth-century face, mysterious in its conventionality, the scorn of Nigel, the gaiety of Freddie, the languor of Charles, were permanent symbols which would confront me fortunately for many years afterwards, unlike the old red-brick box and

---

C'est moins qu'un moment
Un peu plus qu'un rêve
Le temps nous enlève
Notre enchantement.   Anon.

elmy landscape which contained them. I was to continue on my useless assignment, falling in love, going to Spain and being promising indefinitely.

Somewhere in the facts I have recorded lurk the causes of that sloth by which I have been disabled, somewhere lies the sin whose guilt is at my door, increasing by compound interest faster than promise (for promise is guilt—promise is the capacity for letting people down); and through them run those romantic ideas and fallacies, those errors of judgment against which the validity of my criticism must be measured.

For the critic's role was implicit in this Georgian boyhood.

> Beneath the hot incurious sun
> Past stronger beats and fairer,
> He picks his way, a living gun
> With gun and lens and bible
> A militant enquirer;
> The friend, the rash, the enemy,
> The essayist, the able,
> Able at times to cry.

It is too early to tell if he has been misled by the instinct for survival. It may be that, having laid the ghost of his past, he will be able to declare himself and come out in the open—or it may be that, having discarded the alibi of promise, it will only be to end up in the trenches or the concentration camp.

> Determined on time's honest shield
> The lamb must face the Tigress,

and the Tigress may win for in spite of the slow conversion of progressive ideas into the fact of history, the Dark Ages have a way of coming back. Civilisation—the world of affection and reason and freedom and justice—is a luxury which must be fought for, as dangerous to possess as an oil-field or an unlucky diamond.

Or so now I think; whom ill-famed Coventry bore, a mother of bicycles, whom England enlightened and Ireland deluded, round-faced, irritable, sun-loving, a man as old as his Redeemer, meditating at this time of year when wars break out, when Europe trembles and dictators thunder, inglorious under the plane.

July 1937–Aug. 1938
    "Post fanum putre Vacunae."

GERMANE STUDIES

NINETY YEARS OF NOVEL-REVIEWING

The reviewing of novels is the white man's grave of journalism; it corresponds, in letters, to building bridges in some impossible tropical climate. The work is gruelling, unhealthy, and ill-paid, and for each scant clearing made wearily among the springing vegetation the jungle overnight encroaches twice as far. A novel-reviewer is too old at thirty; early retirement is inevitable, *"les femmes soignent ces infirmes féroces au retour des pays chauds,"* and their later writings all exhibit a bitter and splenetic brilliance whose secret is only learnt in the ravages on the liver made by their terrible school. What a hard-boiled, what a Congo quality informs their soured romanticism! Invalided out only in February, my memory is still fresh with the last burgeoning of prolific and uniform shrubs and bushes. Those leathery weeds, so hard to kill, at first attract through the beauty of their flowers—the blurb or puff "splurging," as a botanist has described it, "its gross trumpet out of the gaudy wrapper." Wiry, yet insipid, characterless, though bright, these first-flowering blooms of Girtonia or Ballioli are more oppressive in their profusion, most reviewers will agree, than the forest giants, the Galsworthys and Walpoleworthys, whose creeper-clad trunks defy attempts to fell them.

An unpleasant sight in the jungle is the reviewer who goes native. Instead of fighting the vegetation, he succumbs to it, and, running perpetually from flower to flower, he welcomes each with cries of "genius!" "What grace, what irony and distinction, what passionate sincerity!" he exclaims as the beaming masterpieces reproduce themselves rapidly, and only from the banned amorphophallus, "unpleasant, dreary, difficult, un-English," he turns away his eyes.

Another sight for the cynic is the arrival of the tenderfoot who comes fresh from the university and determined "above all, to be just—to judge every book on its merits—not to be led astray by the airs and graces of writing, the temptations to score off a book in reviewing, but primarily to try and help the author while advising the reader as well." "The great thing," he begins, "is never to forget one's standards—and never to grow stale." I remember very well sitting round the camp fire one night when Tenderfoot and "Goo-Goo" (who was then going native) were "doing" a book. The date escapes me, but it should be easily traceable, for I remember there was some talk of the *Mercury* falling off, and the *Criterion* getting dull.

"This book," said Goo-Goo, "has genius, and not only is it a work of genius—of passionate intellectual sincerity and emotional directness—but it comes very near to being the best novel of the month, or at least of the latter part of it."

"Although I would willingly give an earnest," interrupted the Tenderfoot, "that this is Miss Bumfiddle's first novel, she seems to be a writer of very delicate intention, and has brought to a difficult subject a restraint, a distinction, that, to my thinking, makes *Goosegrass or Cleavers* remarkable not only as a novel, which, if not of the very first order (remember my standards), does at least attempt to state the series of reactions which a young woman of keener sensibility and more vulnerable perception than the common must inevitably receive in the conflict between genius —I use the word in all circumspection—and what, for want of a better definition, we must call life. I should like, however, to suggest to Miss Bumfiddle, in all fairness——"

"*Goosegrass or Cleavers*," broke in Goo-Goo, beaming tipsily, "is modern, as the name implies—as modern as Matisse or Murasaki. It is bold, and confronts the critic in all the perishable flamework of youth—of post-war youth burning fitfully in all its incandescent ardour. Take the scene where Alimony leaves her parents:

Midway between springsummer and summerautumn falls the old-fashioned month of August-come-July—season of gross yellow moons, brown grass, and lousy yearn-

ings. Alimony lay awake counting the slats of the blind
that seemed to scab viciously across the rich broth of
evening sunlight like the splayed fingers of a crucified
neargod, a flayed Marsyas. She hated bed by daylight.
Through the windows came the noise of the party and
her parents' voices. "Now try and rush the red down to
the next hoop—with luck you might perhaps push her
through it. O dear! You should have poked her more."
"But I did poke her." Alimony cringed involuntarily. To
think she ever would be one with the ungainly old—and
yet to-morrow was her birthday! It was hot, stifling—out
in the fields perhaps. . . . She opened the introduction
to a novel beside her. "A short while ago a friend of mine
put into my hands an object which I had little difficulty
in recognising—Sir James Buchan and Mr. John Barrie,
whom I consulted, soon confirmed me. 'Yes,' they said,
'it is a book, but only identifiable as such by a few discriminating people.'" Idly she turned the pages. "Girt
slough of cloud lay cast upon the jannock mere. Weaver,
be th'art there—weaver, I'm drained with love of you
among the drule scrobs, though in the village they call
me a hard woman." "Ah, to write—to write like that,"
thought Alimony—"to write like Mary Webb. But how,
without experience? Out in the fields perhaps." . . .
She rose and collected a few scattered belongings. Tiptoeing down the stairs, she saw it was not yet past seven.
Suddenly she imagined herself tiptoeing through life, a
broken stalk embalmed of this day's roses—like her own
equivocal youth, now cast behind for ever. "Alimony!
go back to bed." It was her mother. Something in Alimony seemed to snap. She turned, her face transfigured.
"For crap's sake leave me alone, mother. I will not be run
by people; all my life people have been trying to run me
and all my life I've been escaping them. I damn will continue to. I guess my life is my own, even if it is a mess,
isn't it? And you presume to speak to me when I have to
listen to you and Poppa fighting on the lawn like a pair
of alley cats. Hell and all it gripes me so I guess I could
upchuck." "Dearest mine o' mine, my own ownest, my
octopet." "Oh, go sit on a tack, mother—can't you see

I've had enough of it?" She flung out, past the front door, with its friendly knocker, on to the gravel, by the dining-room windows. She turned to look through them. Her birthday presents were there for the morning; on the table was the solemn cake with its eleven candles. The click of croquet balls sounded faint on the lawn. "Weaver," she sighed again; and something told her the old Alimony was dying—would be dead, perhaps, before the night was past—before even the moon of metroland had risen on the filling stations.

"A strong book," resumed Goo-Goo. "This is no work for those who prefer——"

"One has to be on one's guard, of course," said Tender-foot, "against being too sympathetic to a writer simply because she provides a restatement of one's own problems."

"One of the few modern masterpieces," continued the other, "a book for the library rather than the linen room—for those who like to find, between a Bradshaw and a breviary, between a gold and a glister, a modern-ancient trifle that will fulfil Milton's definition of the novel as something slow, sinuous, and sexy. A work, in fact, a work of—— But be it not mine to deface our lovely currency by stressing that most distressful word. Simply I will say—slowly, sinuously, but not, I hope, sexily, 'Welcome, Miss Bum-fiddle! welcome, Alimony!'"

And yet, looking back on those evenings when the fates of so many unreadable books, and so many more unread ones, were brilliantly decided, I can't help feeling regret and tenderness rather than relief at being free of them. It is easy to forget the nerve-strain and the nausea, the cynical hopelessness with which we strove to quench the indefati-gable authors. There is something so clean and surprising about a parcel of review copies that one cannot but feel pleasure in opening them. The sense of getting something for nothing, though short-lived, is pleasant while it lasts, and the early expectations one had of discovering a new writer are perhaps less keen a pleasure than one's later hopes of being able to discredit an old one. The real fault of English fiction is that it has ceased to be readable. If novels were only this, it would matter much less that they were bad. American writers are readable; in general, a second-rate American book carries a reader along with it. He may resent this afterwards, but it is desirable at the time. The English novel doesn't, and never will so long as it consists either of arranged emotional autobiography or a carefully detached description of stupid people to show that the author is too clever to be clever. But I am getting into my stride again. Meanwhile a new generation of novel-reviewers is growing up, and this thought brings me to the real tragedy of reviewing—to that ironical and irrevocable law of poetic justice which ennobles the humdrum work and allows the broken journalist to feel in his very ruin something of the divine. For all the novels that he scotches the novel will in time scotch him; like the King at Nemi, the slayer shall himself be slain. Brave and agile, the reviewer enters the ring. He rushes blindly at the red wrappers. He disembowels a few old hacks. But his onsets eventually grow futile, his weapons are blunted, his words are stale. He may go under nobly, a Croker facing his Keats; he may simply wear out in praising or abusing—it matters not which—the never-ceasing flow of second-rate and worthy productions—but eventually the jungle claims him.

What advice, then, would I give to someone forced—for no one could be willing—to become a reviewer? Firstly, never praise; praise dates you. In reviewing a book you like, write for the author; in reviewing any other, write for the public. Read the books you review, but you should need only to skim a page to settle if they are worth reviewing. Never touch novels written by your friends. Remember that the object of the critic is to revenge himself on the creator, and his method must depend on whether the book is good or bad, whether he dare condemn it himself or must lie quiet and let it blow over. Every good reviewer has a subject. He specializes in that subject on which he has not been able to write a book, and his aim is to see that no one else does. He stands behind the ticket-queue of fame, banging his rivals on the head as they bend low before the guichet. When he has laid out enough he becomes an authority, which is more than they will. And had I

stood the climate, this was what I might have been! The
problem of the retiring age has long bewildered economists.
Wandering, as I now do, among other finished critics,
broken in health and temper by the rigours of the service,
or the censure of authors, publishers, and public, I can't
help wondering, in the shabby watering-places, the *petits
trous pas chers* near Portsmouth or the Riviera that the
retired inhabit, if we are really down and out. Can a reviewer come back? Is he too old at twenty-five? Could he
find a place, with younger men, in the front lines where
they stem the advance of autumn novels—and die in har-
ness? I know it is foolish to dream, to think on these possibilities. I should face facts as bravely as I once faced fiction.

> miser Cyrille desinas ineptire
> et quod vides perisse perditum ducas—

And yet these secret heartburns are only human. The other
day, languishing among the back numbers in a French
hotel, I received a letter from New York which almost
gave me hope again. "When," demanded the writer—"when
will you tell the public that Mr. Compton Mackenzie, in
his last three novels, has not only recaptured the prose style
of Congreve, but also Congreve's attitude to life?" "When,"
I breathed—and there were tears in my eyes—"when shall
I?"

August 1929

MORE ABOUT THE MODERN NOVEL

Sixty books out of every hundred published are novels, nine out of those sixty are here, three out of that nine are readable, none out of the three worth seven and sixpence. This type of remark is a reviewer's platitude by now. There are several obvious but impracticable remedies. One author thinks that novels, like poetry, shouldn't be reviewed any more. Then only the best work would struggle occasionally into print. But if novels are not reviewed, then the publishers complain (for sixty books out of every hundred, etc.), and if they complain they will not advertise, and consequently there wouldn't be a paper left in which to review the good ones. I would prefer to have a closed season, no new novels to be published for three years, their sale forbidden like that of plovers' eggs. And nobody under thirty should be allowed to write one—it is amusing to apply this age-canon and see how well it works out, how little would be lost to us. But above all, I should like to see an enormous extension of the censorship—not simply libel and obscenity would be taboo, but whole landscapes, whole strata of our civilization would become unmentionable. Schools and universities, all homes with incomes of between three thousand and three hundred a year, words like Daddy, love, marriage, baby, birth, death, mother, buses, shops—I particularly dislike both the shopping expedition ("she looked at her list, let me see, two bars of soap, three bars of chocolate, but already the huge store had overwhelmed her with its Oriental mystery—it was an Arab bazaar, Eunice decided rapidly as she paused before a chinchilla mantilla. Seven yards of demi-rep the list continued") and those horrible bus rides, when the stars are so close, and the young man treads on air ("he was getting nearer, Pimlico was a forgotten dream, Fulham and West Brompton

passed unheeded—supposing she should be out? 'Fares
please,' shouted the conductor for the third time. 'Four-
penny to heaven,' he answered unthinking"), and picnics,
and going for walks, and conversations in pubs, and all
novels dealing with more than one generation or with any
period before 1918 or with brilliant impoverished children
in rectories or with the following regions, which I understand are going to be preserved from novelists by the
National Trust: the Isle of Wight, the Isle of Purbeck,
Hampshire, Sussex, Oxford, Cambridge, the Essex coast,
Wiltshire, Cornwall, Kensington, Chelsea, Hampstead,
Hyde Park, and Hammersmith. Many situations should be
forbidden, all getting and losing of jobs, proposals of marriage, reception of love letters by either sex (especially if
they are hugged closely and taken up to attics or the familiar seat in the apple tree), all allusion to illness or suicide
(except insanity), all quotations, all mentions of genius,
promise, writing, painting, sculpting, art, poetry, and the
phrases "I like your stuff," "What's his stuff like?" "Damned
good," "Let me make you some coffee," all young men
with ambition or young women with emotion, all remarks
like "Darling, I've found the most wonderful cottage"
(flat, castle), "Ask me any other time, dearest, only please
—just this once—not now," "Love you—of course I love you"
(don't love you), and "It's not that, it's only that I feel so
terribly tired."

Forbidden names: Hugo, Peter, Sebastian, Adrian, Ivor,
Julian, Pamela, Chloe, Enid, Inez, Miranda, Joanna, Jill,
Felicity, Phyllis.

Forbidden faces: all young men with curly hair or remarkable eyes, all gaunt haggard thinkers' faces, all faunlike characters, anybody over six feet, or with any distinction whatever, and all women with a nape to their neck
(he loved the way her hair curled in the little hollow at the
nape of her neck).

Really good novels excepted, the rest fall into two kinds,
English and American; the one will probably be written
by a woman, the other by a man. The English novel certainly, the American probably, will begin with childhood.
This insistence on childhood is the radical defect of most

ordinary novels of to-day. There are three reasons for this. Childhood is not in itself interesting, the great accounts of childhood are of abnormal childhoods, and the reader is now too wary to be caught with this familiar bait—which permits the novelist to meander about among the past, confident of hiding his egotism under a thin coating of squalid charm, and behind a tender appeal to the universal experience of the race. Secondly, childhoods are nearly all wholly irrelevant to any plot; memoirs, essays, poems are the proper place for accounts of childhood; at the beginning of novels they only hold up the action, while giving a very poor idea of the characters. And lastly, the novelist is usually clever, and the childhoods of the clever are invariably unpleasant, a record of grievances and snubs, of too brutal perception and too smart replies. Then the childhood theme is often introduced to show up the parents, a dreary device. Formerly the most touching feature of Victorian novels lay in such a situation as "Mother, why have those men taken father away?" "There has been a dreadful mistake, my darling, but he will soon come back, for the law will put it right." This has changed, however, to the child complaining with all the pained malice of the habitual eavesdropper or commenting brutally, with the penetration of self-pity, on the defects of the parents' conjugal relations.

The American novel will only not begin with childhood if the hero is a group hero (a family, a factory, a small town, a business, or the American nation). In these cases it usually begins several generations farther back with matter which is as irrelevant as childhood, but which yields that dazzling sequence of births and deaths which enables the book to appear an "epic." The typical 100-per-cent American novel has almost invariably a group hero, and is usually a monument of wasted energy, sentimentality striving after realism, and an admirable talent for description being thrown away on life that is quite unworthy to be described. This vigorous material confidence provokes many exceptions, and these in turn fall into three classes, for the romantic revolt against success in life and realism in literature has but a very narrow path of escape. If the novelist hates business, births and deaths and prosperity, he falls a victim to minority worship and writes about Indians, Mexicans, Negroes, or subject populations of America, finding in them the idealism which is his goal. If he is too reflective for those, he falls back on the past—tales of a grandmother, the old days on the farm, the novel of the orchard. If he is interested as well in style, he is swallowed up by Europe. This type of American is invariably a culture snob. These uprooted self-exiled Americans, however, are mostly taking refuge from a life for which they were unfitted rather than seceding in passionate rebellion; hence a limpness in all their work, for the soft spot that caused their failures in their native land becomes a defiant timidity when they are landed on an indifferent Europe; hence the tepid quality of the expatriate American novel, which has escaped vulgarity to become insipid instead. Many more American novels are halfway towards Europe, with a dullness about things American similar to that in caterpillars, which, when about to enter their chrysalis, go off their feed. The culture applauded in these American novels is nearly always the French literature of the end of the last century, the art for art's sake movement which reveals the timidity rather than the defiance at the heart of these emigrants religiously escaping for the sake of their style. Flaubert, Verlaine, Huysmans, Baudelaire, Pater, Henry James, and George Moore are alluded to most frequently by these intending fugitives, and a mention of one of them should place the book at once for the reader, just as that of an American real-life writer will betray the fake epic, the ruthless saga about the most commonplace world.

With the English novel we are in a different universe, the realm of the egotist, and of the most dangerous kind of egotists, those who, for self-protection, have developed the gland of charm. Having so often bewailed the glut of feminine autobiographies, there is little more to say about this except to warn the reader against the daydream which, always abused in these novels, leaves a sickening taste behind. The daydream is an immense discovery for the novel's technique, but an innate capacity for luxurious wish-fulfilment makes it an instrument to be handled with the greatest reluctance and care. The daydream should be crisp, terse, and relevant to the plot, or else an exquisite and impersonal lyric like a simile from Homer or *Paradise Lost*. When the reader experiences a muzzy and unpleasantly tipsy feeling, it means the passage is autobiographical, and probably the most trying form of autobiography, the arrangement which self-worship dictates of how something might have happened could we have it all over again. These English autobiographies, however, at least end in marriage, while the American epics seldom end at all. They are, moreover, tender, graceful, and humorous books, and their zeal for understatement saves them from the terrible American faults of style ("powerful" passages in the epic, rhetorical epigrams in the Europeanized form). The English cake is plain and eatable except for the dank spots where the mildew of childhood daydreams and school friendships has left its shadowy web; while the American is either massively stodgy and commemorative, thick with icing, or, like tea-cake on a railway train, cut into thin, tasteless slices, not indigestible, but a little stale. If the reader can apply this classification to the main body of novels he will need no reviewer at all; only he must keep in mind the possibility of the grace of England, the vitality of America, or the enterprise of the Rive Gauche, producing at any moment a great work.

1935

REVIEWERS

Reviewers can be divided into two classes. For one literature cannot be too esoteric, too much a preoccupation with
style and imagination. I like only two kinds of novel, the
work of art or slim volume, and the novel of entertainment.
The other kind of reviewer prefers didactic fiction; for him
the novels I admire most are merely full of pretty writing,
frivolous, amusing, or egotistic. The novel, he feels, is not
an end in itself, but a means to redress injustice, to present information or tabulate theories. *Wuthering Heights*
may claim thousands, but *Uncle Tom's Cabin* claims tens
of thousands. The novel of political propaganda, more than
any other, I find as unpalatable as a cannon ball in a plum
pudding.

After struggling with such a book it was sad to read Mr.
Sean O'Casey's attack on reviewers in *Time and Tide's*
"Notes on the Way." He considers all reviewers, except
those on the Sunday papers, to be timid and contaminated
to the last degree. It is possible, with hard work and a bit
of luck, for a highbrow reviewer to earn fifteen pounds a
month, but nine to eleven would be more like it. And on
that he expects them to give as spirited a performance as
that of the Sunday novel-reviewers, who have always been
famous for their savage and incorruptible assaults on author
and publisher! And anyhow, "reviews never sell a book,"
as the publishers are never tired of telling us. No, it is
farther than that that he must look for the causes of the
decline of the novel, even if the sycophantic torpor of
reviewers contributes to it. There is, for instance, the indigence of authors who are forced through journalism or
over-production to deny themselves the gestation which
their talent demands; and the intransigence of libraries
and of all other book-societies which cater to the public,

and which in turn use pressure on the publisher to make him exact the longest and dullest contribution from the safest writers, an omnibus if possible, and failing an omnibus a saga; and failing a saga a hundred-and-twenty-five-thousand-word cavalcade. And then there is the ignorance of the publishers themselves, their lack of standards. Of how many books can you say "It must be good—So-and-so published it"—as you could say it of the work of architects or painters or film-producers? And then their hopeless ambition to publish a best-seller which will pay for the masterpiece—which results in confusion: the verdict of posterity obsessing the popular writer; the writer of masterpieces dreaming of Hollywood; the publisher himself combining vague leanings towards creation with the desire to double his capital; a middleman of talent anxiously deleting words like "rape" in novels that are in any case unreadable. And one might add the imbecility of collectors, who (caring only for rarity, condition, and some incomplete experience of their childhood) take one look at *Howard's End, Prufrock,* or *Inclinations,* and go hurrying on in search of Mary Webb, and *Winnie the Pooh, Beau Geste,* and *The Tale of the Flopsy Bunnies.*

One might conclude by mentioning the ox-like indifference of the reading public which cannot bring to its activity even the discrimination of the chewing one, and thus we have six interlocking causes of the dullness of our current fiction. They do not seem easy of remedy, and meanwhile the English novel must descend to the barathrum of incompetence in company with those twin horrors, the English hotel and the English nursing home.

Reviewing is a whole-time job with a half-time salary, a job in which our best work is always submerged in the criticism of someone else's, where all triumphs are ephemeral and only the drudgery is permanent, and where no future is secure except the certainty of turning into a hack. There are days when a reviewer approximates more and more to that robot figure on Brighton pier, who wheedles the passers-by in a brassy subhuman voice, and when they put down a coin hands out a cardboard square of commonplace and irrelevant criticism. He can say of his books like

the sundial of the hours, *"vulnerant omnes; ultima necat."*
Who would not rather than the best of reviewers be the
worst of novelists and contrive between November and
April a novel from the excesses which he has committed
from May to October?

1935–36

MR. MOSSBROSS TAKES THE CLASS

And now for Mr. Linklater's *Ripeness is All.*

"What are the characteristics of middlebrow satire?"

"Sanity, sir."

"Not bad; MacDonnell?"

"Being Scotch, sir."

"That's not funny; Collier?"

"Topicality." "Ribaldry." "Tolerance."

"Don't speak at once, one at a time—you, Agate?"

"Splendidly virile, robust, immensely readable, sir."

"Mackenzie?"

"Full-throated laughter, sir, a rousing bumper."

"And you, Priestley?"

"Zest and gusto, sir, the high spirits of a clever man."

"Very good, all of you, you avoided the trap. And you are quite right—for if you put irony, indignation, feeling—in short, wit—into this sort of thing you overdo it, like Swift, or merely irritate the public, like Joyce and Lawrence. You must be careful not to offend anybody. How are you going to manage? First: don't let your characters come to life—they must be types, you can abuse them freely. How do you create a type? You take a character and say he is a bridge bore or a golf bore or a poet or a colonel—and then whenever he appears he talks about bridge or golf or poetry or the army. Then you create a comic situation. You shut the poet and the colonel up in a stuck lift, you put the bridge bore on the golf links, or you let loose a pig at the vicarage garden party, like Linklater here. And then you put in the satire."

"How do you do that, sir?"

"The golden rule, I find, is to avoid the personal. Go in for something you really feel about and you endanger sanity. Endanger sanity and where is gusto? And, without gusto, what are royalties? No! Read the newspapers,

and satirize what they satirize. Foreigners, Americans,
D.O.R.A., Fascists, and spinsters. Never write a word you'd
be ashamed to write for the *Daily Express*."

"And zest, virility, sir?"

"Get that eighteenth-century feeling. Study sturdy common sense. Become a good trencherman. Make a few jokes
about the way of a man with a maid. Remember—the
frankness of Fielding with the slyness of Sterne! And plenty
of generalization about humanity! Style? That will come
with *Tom Jones* and practice. Show them, Linklater."

"Bugler Bliss's tongue was imperfectly taught, and
that poignant call, that may summon the heart to a loneliness like the outer stars, brayed with his breath like a
tinker's moke.

"Major Gander's life had not been happy, and the ceremonies attendant on his death were correspondingly mis-
managed."

"Got the knack? If the major's life had been happier
would the bugler have known the Last Post? No—but don't
you smell the eighteenth century? Now once more, please,
here's the chalk—and put some poetry into it."

"But the Silver Trumpets sang:

> Blow, northern wind,
> Send thou me my sweeting

and a pizzicato, like the pin-prick pattern of April rain,
softened all hearts and all desired that Daisy and Katherine and Bolivia should have twenty pink-bottomed
babies a-piece, a festoon of them, wreaths of them, troops
of them, with no thought of prizes but simply to match
May and fulfil the turning of the year. The triumph of all
who'd begotten, and the travail of all who'd borne, were
as warp and weft in their lot, and flute and fiddle, brass
and drum, would join in a great cry, 'Ripeness is All.'"

"Thank you very much. Time's up. Good night, boys.
Happy Pens!"

"Yes, sir." "Thank you, sir." "Happy Pen, sir!"

1935

FELICITY

As there seems a little space left over, I am utilizing it to thank those correspondents who have submitted unfinished manuscripts to me for advice and help. I am afraid they cannot be returned; for instance, I have lost all of Kip Streatham's novel, except the page beginning, "It felt pretty good to be out there under the moon with the gin running round in me like an electric hare and my arm as far as it would go round Myrtle." He will have to write another.

Hedda Bedales, who is "five feet ten and a half in her hikers," she tells me, has sent in a tale of primitive passion on a Hertfordshire farm somewhere up near the North Circular. Thirza, the heroine, refuses to take her bicycle out in the rain, and narrowly escapes a larruping. The second two hundred pages show a falling off.

But it is with real joy that I print some of the manuscript of Miss Aglae ("three syllables please, but it's not my real name anyhow") Oakenshaw's unpublished novel, *Absent from Felicity*—publishers, those lean subfusc creatures with rolled umbrellas and little blue engagement books, must keep a look-out for Aglae $(-\smile\smile)$:

Felicity was dressing for dinner. A cosy gas-fire burned in the grate towards which she held out her bare foot while she held out (in her hand I mean) a slinky open-mesh gold stocking. She loved to crinkle her toes in the firelight. Her foot didn't seem to belong to her, it was a little pink animal or something. She loved her bedroom, which had been her nursery, with its dado of beasts and its view out on the Hampstead garden. There was a knock at the door. "Come in." It was Dads! "Hello, old chap," he said. "How's tricks?" She looked up lovingly at the curly head, tanned face, and open smile of her father. Dads was wonderful, only he worked so terribly hard. He was a blurb-writer, and April was coming on so that he was absolutely indispensable.

"Not been overdoing it, skipper?" she asked anxiously. "Only the Golding omnibus," he smiled back, but she thought he looked worried all the same. "Don't fret about me—I'm strong as a Steen." He laughed. It was one of their favourite jokes. "May there be no Cronin' at the Bar," she capped. "Hurry up now, old boy," he cried. "Don't keep your mother waiting." For Felicity's mother, Mrs. Arquebus, was a very special person. She pulled on her stocking and took a last look at the room. A bowl of hyacinths, her white bed with the green eiderdown, and very few pictures. A small oil by Barribal called "Green Chartreuse" hung over the mantelpiece, with its plaster gargoyles from the little shop near Notre Dame, and there were one or two etchings with masts and a choice Steggles of Rosebery Avenue that she had got, in an austere mood, out of the Picture Library when she took the Edward Wolfe back. And her books! She loved the little cabinet with its glass doors. There was just room for her favourite authors, Phyllis Bentley, Phyllis Bottome, Helen Waddell, Helen Simpson, G. B. Storm, Beverley, and Theodora Benson—and poetry, too, Humbert Wolfe of course, and some of the new writers who left one rather breathless, and whose books had lovely cold names like *Open the Sky* and *Armed October*. The door opened again. This time it was Mums. "Hurry up, daughter o' mine, there's a good fellow!" she cried. "Fellow" was Felicity's favourite nickname. She had brown curly hair, rather special brown eyes, and a nose with the weeniest tilt to it, "just room for a deck quoit," as Dads put it, and a very pretty figure. She loved green, smoked lots of cigarettes, adored dancing, but knew there were other things beside it, and was altogether a heathery honeyish brackeny kind of Hampstead Piskie, alternately the joy and tribulation of her family, servants, nanny, teachers, friends, and taxi-drivers, in fact of everyone whose delight and misfortune it was to know her. Phew! She was just grown up. As Dads had said the other day, "Fellow used to be a drawing by Shepperton. Now she's a Gouache by Lewis Baumer." She repeated it to herself on her way down to the hall and cocktails. To-night it was a party. There were two other successful blurb-writers and their wives,

Mr. Goulash the publisher, and two very nice young men for Felicity. A "poet" and a "thinker." "Mr. Beastly may drop in afterwards," said Mums, who looked almost regal. "I'm thinking," said the thinker, "he has the root of the matter in him." "I've always found him charming myself," said Mr. Goulash; "the only realist in Flask Walk," said a blurb-writer. "Is his new book *John Hanbury, Ironmaster,* or *John Hanbury, Ironmonger?*" whispered the other—"in writing the blurb that's going to be rather important; one used to be able to go by the picture on the wrapper, but with these beastly yellow-jacks one never can tell." They had out the silver fish-knives and napkin rings "with two k's!" as Dads put it. That meant one of their grand parties.

Outside in the spring night the laburnums were hanging their golden bodkins over the wall, and the laurustinus loomed evilly out of the shadow. "Scrumptious, Sacred, and Profane!" cried one of the blurbies. "The moment I saw it I said, 'This is NOT a detective story.'" "I don't know what you mean by that word," said Miss Gibbon, who was a stickler for etymology. "And I don't know which word you mean either," riposted the blurbie. "And does Miss Felicity," he laughingly added, "inherit the family talent for 'appreciation'?" "Don't talk cocker," laughed Fellow—and she smiled secretly to herself at the idea of *Her* writing blurbs. For she was going to do something creative. A biography of her father, perhaps, with all the family jokes in it. Not that she wanted—she looked across at him, handsome, healthy, shaggy, smiling—still, you never knew, these athletes cracked up sooner than you expected, and blurb-writing carried with it, she had heard, a high mortality. First the dedication—*to the memory of the dearest of Dads* —then the preface, "*I have not hesitated to set down the other side of the picture. Gilbert Arquebus was, in many ways, a very tiresome man. . . .*" Good heavens, what was she thinking! She smiled brightly at him, and reassuringly he smiled back. "Absent thee from Felicity," he reflected, "awhile." Yes. But why not for ever? More money all round. Conceited little bore. Expensive, too. Trying that grin on me now. All right! This evening she should have her first glass of port. More money all round! And then, maybe, he could get at that actress, the one who was playing the governess, a big fat bouncing creature who looked as if she had a temper. He began to hum "Singing in the Rain" to himself. Macking in my whack, I'm whacking in my mac, 'cos I'm glad to be back. . . . "Elia," he cried suddenly. "My adorable Elia! Who reads him now?" "Oh, Dads!" and Mums beamed loyally down the table. Special Person indeed! he thought. If they knew what a drag a writer's wife can be. The woman who shares your early struggles is very different from the one you would choose to share your later success. And why the hell should she? Port for her too. "I saw the first caterpillar to-day," Mums went on, "it was a looper." "You might really be in the depths of the country," said Mr. Goulash. The poet was telling a story, " 'And what do *you* do?' I asked her. 'Paint.' 'And what do you paint?' 'Fans.' 'What fun—like Conder, I suppose; do you get a lot of fan-mail?' 'Not fans, you idiot, vans. I don't paint silly fans, I paint useful vans.' She's a girl from the Tottenham cell." Tiresome young cub, thought Dads—and that dreary thinker, with his Scotch face hanging over the savoury. A glass of port all round. "A very special bin," he said, when the time came. "Not a has-bin, I hope," said Mr. Goulash. Dads scowled. "I want you all to drink a health," he said. "It's my birthday, don't forget!" The blurbies were still whispering. "Who wrote the last Charles Morgan?" said one —"I don't know who did the front; as a matter of fact, I did the back." "I did the front," said Dads, "if you still want to know." They didn't, for the cyanide was doing its work. "You were quite right not to like the laurustinus, Felicity," laughed Dads—"but my biography will have to wait." The way they fell they reminded him of a skittle alley, only quieter; each seemed to knock against the next one, there would be a wobble, and over they'd go. Last went the thinker, and Dads drummed impatiently on the mahogany with his cigar-cutter while he was "passing." Soon all, with varying grace, had made the fatal exit, and it was a very lonely man indeed who, five minutes later, was speeding down Haverstock Hill on his way to the stage door.

June 1936

THE NOVEL-ADDICT'S CUPBOARD

"Other people's hobbies," as one book-collector has remarked, "are always ridiculous," so I will do no more than say that about two years ago the printed words "Second edition, second issue, seventh thousand, first published in . . . reprinted in . . ." suddenly became to me the most horrible stains and blots on a book imaginable. And cheap editions, travellers' libraries, anti-travellers' libraries; ghastly! There is some point in collecting ancient first editions, for in the seventeenth and eighteenth centuries they differed often very considerably from succeeding texts, and were, also, lovely objects. But I collect modern ones, the seven-and-sixpenny poisons. They are cheaper and one has the pleasure of backing one's judgment, generally wrongly, against the whole weight of middlebrow, sentimental, childhood-loving, and pedantic opinion represented by booksellers' catalogues. I still do not collect books unless I think I shall enjoy reading them, but I do not expect that phase to last. Reading, in book-collectors, is replaced by a kind of fidgeting motion, balancing the book in the left hand, opening it and shutting it with the right, and exclaiming "But that's not really his first book at all, you know," or some other holy rubric. But as a good many of my books are novels, it may be of interest to recall a few in the hope of suggesting some new titles for the novel-addict or reminding him of some old ones. Incidentally, it will be proof that there was once a time when I enjoyed fiction. Where the authors are American, I try to get the American editions, as the English are so often altered, but there is no book I am going to mention that is not in some form cheaply and easily procurable. I can't afford *South Wind*, *The Way of All Flesh*, *Of Human Bondage*, or the *Old Wives' Tale*, so you must imagine them filling shadowy blanks to begin with, and there are some publishers whom I refuse to collect, because all their novels look exactly alike, and destroy my conception of a book-shelf, which should be a mass of gaudy variety.

E. M. Forster, *Howards End, A Room with a View* (Arnold). *Howards End,* written in 1910, introduces the first post-war young highbrow, with a post-war name (Sebastian), and a simplified form of writing in full revolt against Henry James. But an artist's revolt—not a philistine's, like Wells'. The themes of Forster's novels are always the breaking down of bridges and barriers—between English and Indian, between the intelligentsia and the bourgeoisie (*Howards End*), between soldier and scholar (*The Longest Journey*)—he is really anti-highbrow, in the sense that he dislikes nothing more than intellectual presumption and spiritual pride. He is consequently a revolutionary writer, one of the first to attack the individualism of the nineties, to find the crack in the ivory tower; his heroes are plain men and plainer women, his motto "only connect"—yet as a writer he is an artist always. I think *Howards End* is his best book, *The Longest Journey* (which started the Wiltshire trek) second. He has written only one book since 1910, and is still waiting for English fiction to catch up.

Henry James, semi-complete. I get an inconceivable pleasure from a Henry James book when I am able to finish it, but too often I can only flounder out a few yards and then have to retreat. For others in this plight I recommend his long short stories, particularly *The Lesson of the Master, The Aspern Papers,* and *The Death of the Lion.* They enshrine the subtlest vanities and disappointments of the pursuit of letters for all time. Another remedy is to read anecdotes of Henry James. He is the last of the great writers to be a great man, and even the dirtiest pens take on a new quality when they write about him—enough to send one back to his books again. Or read his letters—that one in which he so pathetically reminds Gosse that he is "insurmountably unsaleable" and says of his collected edition, like Ozymandias, "look on my works, ye mortals, and despair."

A great critic has described Mrs. Wharton as the Sargent of the modern novel, and it is on her accomplished, rich interiors that it gives me most pleasure to gaze. She has been fortunate enough to belong to a class—the super-rich, the super-philistine, the super-cosmopolitan—that can as a rule be observed only from outside and consequently is misrepresented. Therefore the studies of these jewelled and inaccessible analphabetics by one who is pre-eminently a serious and intelligent writer may become valuable documents. *The Custom of the Country* and *Glimpses of the Moon* are the brightest.

Maurice Baring, semi-complete. *Passing By* and *Daphne Adeane* seem to me his best books, which are all variations on a theme—the rivalry of sacred and profane love. One knows that sacred love will always win, and profane love be always on the point of winning, and the consequent order, regularity, and logic of the treatment, resembling a Greek tragedy, is his greatest power. Like those Spanish *aficionados* who watch a series of dancers repeating the same steps, singing the same song, one resents any alteration in structure as keenly as one derives pleasure from the variations of the performers in tempo, grace, and style. "It seduces one. And then it seduces one again."

Aldous Huxley, complete. David Garnett, complete. Lawrence, *passim*. Mr. Huxley tells a story of Firbank meeting him in the Café Royal: "He gave his usual agonized wriggle of embarrassment and said, 'Aldous—always my *torture*.'" I think I feel the same way about him. At school I borrowed *Limbo* from one master only to have it confiscated by another, while the Frenchman who let me read Mallarmé's *L'Après-Midi d'un Faune* for extra studies had to turn repeatedly to Huxley's translation to find out what it meant. I bought *Crome Yellow* out of some prize money. After that his novels and stories continued to dominate my horizon, so enormously competent, so clever, sympathetic, and on the spot. During the twenties it was almost impossible for the average clever young man not to imitate him—just as he once had imitated Norman Douglas, Firbank, and Eliot. Now that I have been free for a few years I see *Crome Yellow* as his best book, backed up by *Limbo, Antic Hay*, and his short stories. His early work had a natural gaiety, his satire lacked the heavy hand of the moralist;

Science, with its horrible plausibility, had not yet walked
off with Art. The first forty years of Aldous Huxley's literary career have been marred by over-production, for which
the present economic system is to blame. Conventionality
of thought and diction, fatigue of style result—but his long
silence since *Brave New World* is the most hopeful augury
for the remaining threescore. David Garnett's books remain a standing argument in favour of the short novel, for,
though equally bound to his publisher by golden cords, he
has resisted Aldous Huxley's temptation to long novels, pamphlets, essays, and philosophical journalism. As for Lawrence, I really believe he is asleep at last, and I think nothing
should be done to disturb him. If you must approach him,
do it lightly, and by way of his early books, those like *The
White Peacock*, with its creamy pastoral descriptions of the
English countryside, full of a sentiment that has not yet
been muddied by dogma.

Firbank, complete. Every critic, however roughly he may
seem to wisecrack away the achievements of his enemies,
the creators, will sooner or later shyly unlock his playbox
and produce his few treasures. Then woe betide the reader
who does not express a proper admiration. For my part, I
am secretly a lyricist; the works to which I lose my heart
are those that attempt, with a purity and a kind of dewy
elegance, to portray the beauty of the moment, the gaiety
and sadness, the fugitive distress of hedonism; the poetry of
Horace and Tibullus, the plays of Congreve, the paintings
of Watteau and Degas, the music of Mozart and the prose
of Flaubert affect me like this, and of recent books, the
novels of Ronald Firbank. That doesn't mean I think he is
as good as Mozart, I hasten to say, but that in him more
than in any contemporary writer I find that taste. He and
the early Eliot seem to me the pure artists of the twenties,
Lawrence and Huxley the philosopher-artists, the explain-
ers. His thin black books are incidentally some of the few
which it is a pleasure to collect. Of course, it is quite useless
to write about Firbank—nobody who doesn't like him is going to like him, and he can be extremely aggravating and
silly—but he was a true innovator, and his air of ephemeral-
ity is treacherous in the extreme.

Hemingway, complete. Waugh, complete. Powell, complete. Scott Fitzgerald, complete. Now we are among the Firbank derivatives. Great Hemingway is under a cloudlet, partly owing to the increasing truculence of his subject matter, partly owing to the spate of imitations of him, and his boom. Yet he has created the American style: no other transatlantic novelist so combines native force with mastery of form. Scott Fitzgerald represents a more literary compromise between the American qualities (generosity, courage, open-mindedness, and immoderation) and the English technique. His *The Great Gatsby* and *Tender Is the Night* (Chatto) are also, incidentally, two of the novels most typical of the Boom, as is the charming *Gentlemen Prefer Blondes*. Evelyn Waugh, as a novelist, seems also to me to be in a predicament. I regard him as the most naturally gifted novelist of his generation (the round-about-thirty). He has a fresh, crisp style, a gift for creating character, a mastery of dialogue, a melancholy and dramatic sense of life—but his development has taken him steadily from the Left towards the Right, and Right Wing Satire is always weak—and he is a satirist. The anarchist charm of his books (of which *Black Mischief* is the best example) was altered in *A Handful of Dust* to a savage attack on Mayfair from a Tory angle. And though there on safe ground, it is going to be difficult for him to continue, since Tory satire, directed at people on a moving staircase from a stationary one, is doomed to ultimate peevishness [Example, Beachcomber]. *A Handful of Dust* is a very fine novel, but it is the first of Evelyn Waugh's to have a bore for a hero.

The novels of Antony Powell are unaffected monochromes of realism. Anything which might heighten the colouring is scrupulously omitted. They deal in nuances of boredom, seediness, and squalor—"the artist is recognizable by the particular unpleasantness of his life" is his creed, and since he gaily accepts it his novels have a delightful quality, containing much of the purest comedy that is now being written. I recommend especially *Afternoon Men* and *From a View to a Death* (Duckworth). Then there is that other comedian, Compton Mackenzie, whose *Vestal Fire* and *Extraordinary Women* are among the few modern novels that make the most of that wonderful subject, money, and which bring the Mediterranean lapping round our doors and the smell of cistus through the fog-bound windows. One day I want to do a dossier of the characters in those two books, and their mighty begetter, *South Wind*, with photographs of them all and pictures of their villas. And while still on satirists, there are *Cakes and Ale* and *The Moon and Sixpence* of Maugham. *Cakes and Ale* belongs to that group of satires on literary shop that form one of the most remarkable achievements of the English novel. Max Beerbohm's *Seven Men* belongs also, and Osbert Sitwell's *Dumb Animal* with that admirable short story "Alive, Alive-Oh!"

It would seem that I do not collect any women writers, but that is not the case. I have the books of Miss Compton-Burnett, though I cannot read them, and Mrs. Woolf complete to *The Waves*, which holds one of the key positions of modern novels, inferior only to *Ulysses* (no first edition, alas!), and all Miss Elizabeth Bowen's ironical and delicate studies, and all Rosamund Lehmann, another natural writer, and *Frost in May* by Antonia White, *Orphan Island*, the best novel of Miss Macaulay, *Voyage in the Dark* (Constable) by Jean Rhys, a short and tragic book—and even shorter, *My Mortal Enemy* and *A Lost Lady*, the two best books of Willa Cather, and *Winter Sonata* by Dorothy Edwards. Gay but less haunting are *Country Places*, Christine Longford, and Julia Strachey's *Cheerful Weather for the Wedding*. This leads one on to those novels that one feels are little known or underrated, that are never followed by a successor, or whose effect on people is unpredictable and subversive. Such are Clifford Kitchin's two books, *Mr. Balcony* and *The Sensitive One*. Nathanael West's *Miss Lonelyhearts* (a defiant masterpiece of futility), George Beaton's *Jack Robinson* and his *Almanack*. Or *How Like a God* by Rex Stout (Kennerley); *Blindness* and *Living* by Henry Green (who *is* he?), published by Dent; and *Murder, Murder* by Laurence Vail (Peter Davies), which begins so well and ends so badly. And *Arm's Length* by John Metcalfe, *Futility* by Gerhardi, *Some People* by Harold Nicolson (great period interest), and *Café Bar* by Scott

Moncrieff (gloomy!). The *Four Just Men* by Edgar Wallace, and that strange sadistic highbrow thriller, and analysis of the Paris Commune, *The Werewolf of Paris* (John Long) by Guy Endore. And *Extra Passenger* by Oswald Blakestone, and *Tropic of Cancer* (Obelisk Press), a gay, fierce, shocking, profound, sometimes brilliant, sometimes madly irritating first novel, by Henry Miller, the American Céline. Anyone interested in the problem of American genius, whether it can ripen or ever achieve real freedom and honesty in its home surroundings, should try to get this book which would appear completely to justify expectation. Apart from the narrative power, the undulating swell of a style perfectly at ease with its creator, it has a maturity which is quite unlike the bravado, the spiritual ungrownupness of most American fiction. Miller's writing is more in the nature of a Whitmanesque philosophic optimism which has been deepened and disciplined but never destroyed by his lean years in a city where even to starve is an education. And there are books for the *sottisier*, such as the *Berry* volumes of Dornford Yates. Sometimes, at great garden parties, literary luncheons, or in the quiet of an exclusive gunroom, a laugh rings out. The sad, formal faces for a moment relax and a smaller group is formed within the larger. They are admirers of Dornford Yates who have found out each other. We are badly organized, we know little about ourselves and next to nothing about our hero, but we appreciate fine writing when we come across it, and a wit that is ageless united to a courtesy that is extinct. Or books for collectors which remind one of all the glass cases full of boring limited editions of Coppard, Collier, Hanley, Hampson, Powys, and Potocki de Montalk. And there are parodies like *The Oxford Circus* (Miles and Mortimer) and more American books, Dreiser, Glenway Westcott, Faulkner, O'Hara, Saroyan—and I see I have the complete works of Wyndham Lewis. But that should be enough.

January 1936

TOLD IN GATH

(With apologies to Mr. A*d*us H*xl*y)

"Vulgarity is the garlic in the salad of charm."
                                        St. Bumpus

It was to be a long week-end, thought Giles Pentateuch apprehensively, as the menial staggered up the turret stairs with his luggage—staggered all the more consciously for the knowledge that he was under observation, just as, back in Lexham Gardens, his own tyrannical Amy would snort and groan outside the door to show how steep the back-stairs were, before entering with his simple vegetarian break-fast of stinkwort and boiled pond-weed. A long week-end; but a week-end at Groyne! And he realized, with his in-stinct for merciless analysis that amounted almost to tor-ture, that in spite, yes, above all, in spite of the appre-hension, because of it even, he would enjoy all the more saying afterwards, to his friend Luke Snarthes perhaps, or to little Reggie Ringworm, "Yes, I was at Groyne last week-end," or "Yes, I was there when the whole thing started, down at Groyne."

The menial had paused and was regarding him. To tip or not to tip? How many times had he not been paralysed by that problem? To tip was to give in, yes, selfishly to give in to his hatred of human contacts, to contribute half a crown as hush-money, to obtain "protection," protection from other people, so that for a little he could go on with the luxury of being Giles Pentateuch, "scatologist and eschatologist," as he dubbed himself. Whereas not to tip . . .

For a moment he hesitated. What would Luke Snarthes have done? Stayed at home, with that splayed ascetic face of his, or consulted his guru, Chandra Nandra? No—no tip! The menial slunk away. He looked round the room. It was comfortable, he had to admit; a few small Longhis round

the walls, a Lupanar by Guido Guidi, and over the bed an
outsize Stuprum Sabinarum, by Rubens—civilized people,
his hosts, evidently.

He glanced at the books on the little table—the *Odes of
Horace, Rome 23 B.C.*, apparently a first edition, the
Elegancies of Meursius (Rochester's copy), *The Piccadilly
Ambulator, The Sufferings of Saint Rose of Lima, Nostra-
damus* (the Lérins Press), *Swedenborg, The Old Man's
Gita.* "And cultivated," he murmured, "too." The bath-
room, with its sun-lamp and Plombières apparatus, was
such as might be found in any sensible therapeutic home.
He went down to tea considerably refreshed by his lavage.

The butler announced that Lady Rhomboid was "serving" on the small west lawn, and he made his way over the
secular turf with genuine pleasure. For Minnie Rhomboid
was a remarkable woman.

"How splendid of you to come," she croaked, for she had
lost her voice in the old suffragette days. "You know my
daughter, Ursula Groyne."

"Only too well," laughed Giles, for they had been what
his set at Balliol used to call "lovers."

"And Mrs. Amp, of course?"

"Of course!"

"And Mary Pippin?"

"Decidedly," he grimaced.

"And the men," she went on. "Giles Pentateuch—this is
Luke Snarthes and Reggie Ringworm and Mr. Encolpius
and Roland Narthex. Pentateuch writes—let me see?—like
a boot, isn't it?" (Her voice was a husky roar.) "Yes, a
boot with a mission! Oh, but I forgot"—and she laughed
delightedly—"you're all writers!"

"Encantado, I'm sure!" responded Giles. "But we've all
met before. I see you have the whole Almanach de Gol-
gotha in fact," he added.

Mary Pippin, whose arm had been eaten away by
termites in Tehuantepec, was pouring out with her free
hand. "Orange Pekoe or *Chandu*, Giles?" she burbled in
her delicious little voice. "Like a carrier pigeon's," he
thought.

"*Chandu*, please." And she filled him a pipe of the consoling poppy, so that in a short while he was smoking away like all the others.

"Yes, yes," continued Mr. Encolpius, in his oily voice which rose and fell beneath the gently moving tip of his nose, "Man axalotl here below but I ask very little. Some fragments of Pamphylides, a Choctaw blood-mask, the prose of Scaliger the Elder, a painting by Fuseli, an occasional visit to the all-in wrestling, or to my meretrix; a cook who can produce a passable 'poulet à la Khmer,' a Pong vase. Simple tastes, you will agree, and it is my simple habit to indulge them!"

Giles regarded him with fascination. That nose, it was, yes, it was definitely a proboscis. . . .

"But how can you, how can you?" It was Ursula Groyne. "How *can* you when there are two million unemployed, when Russia has reintroduced anti-abortionary legislation, when Iceland has banned *Time and Tide*, when the Sedition Bill hangs over us all like a rubber truncheon?"

Mary Pippin cooed delightedly; this was intellectual life with a vengeance—definitely haybrow—only it was so difficult to know who was right. Giles, at that moment, found her infinitely desirable.

"Yes, and worse than that." It was Luke Snarthes, whose strained voice emerged from his tortured face like a cobra from the snake-charmer's basket. "Oh, decidedly, appallingly worse. The natives of Ceylon take the slender Loris and hold it over the fire till its eyes pop, to release the magic juices. Indicible things are done to geese that you may eat your runions with a sauce of *foie gras*. Caviare is ripped from the living sturgeon, karakul fur torn from the baby lamb inside its mother. The creaking plates of the live dismembered lobster scream to you from the *Homard Newburg*, the oyster winces under the lemon. How would *you* like, Mr. Encolpius, to be torn from your bed, embarrelled, prised open with a knife, seasoned with a few drips of vitriol, shall we say, and sprayed with a tabasco as strong as mustard-gas to give you flavour; then to be swallowed alive and handed over to a giant's digestive juices?"

"I shouldn't like it at all!" said Mr. Encolpius, "just as I shouldn't, for that matter, like living at the bottom of the sea and changing my sex every three years. Not that it might not"—and he twitched his nose at Mary Pippin—"have its compensations."

"S-s-s-s-s-s-s-s-s-s-s-s-s-s-s-s-s-s-s-s-s-s-s-s-suppose,"   said Reggie Ringworm, who stammered, etc., "vat ve thilly oythter is weally weady and villing to be ab-s-s-s-orbed, I mean ab-th-th-th-th-th-thorbed, by our fwend, vat vat is in f-f-f-fact exactly ve end for which it has been cweated. Vat th-then?"

"What are we to think then," snarled Snarthes savagely, "of the Person or Purpose who created creatures for such an end? Awful!" And he took out his notebook and wrote rapidly, "The end justifies the means! But the end *is* the means! And how rarely, how confoundedly rarely, can we even say the end justifies the end! Like Oxenstierna, like Ximenes, like Waldorf, we must be men of means"—he closed the book with a snap—"men of golden means."

"I know what you mean," cried Mary Pippin from her dovecot. "That if Cleopatra's nose had been half an inch longer Menelaus would never have run away with her!"

Luke's face softened, and he spread out his splayed fingers almost tenderly. "And I don't mind wagering, if we can believe Diodorus Siculus, that, the nose unaltered, she bore a remarkable likeness, Mary, to you!"

"Ah, but can we believe old Siculus?" The other nose quested speculative. "Any more than we can believe old Paterculus, old Appian, Arrian, Ossian, and Orrian? Now a Bolivar Corona or a nicely chambered glass of sparkling Douro—even a pretty tea-gown by Madame Groult, I opine"—and he bowed to Mary—"these convince me. They have a way with one. Oh, yes, a way, decidedly! And just because they have that way it is necessary for me to combine them, how often, how distressingly often, with my lamentable visits to the Ring at Blackfriars, or to my meretrix in Holland Park. Why is it that we needs must see the highest though we loathe it? That happy in my mud—my hedonistic, radio-active, but never-the-less quite genuine nostalgic *boue*, I should be reminded of the stars, of you, Miss Pippin, and of Cleopatra?" And he snuffled serio-comically, "Why can't you let Hell alone?"

A gong rang discreetly. The butler removed the pipes and Mrs. Amp and Roland Narthex, who were still in a state of kif, while the others went away to dress. Giles, who found something stimulating in Mr. Encolpius' nose, took out his notebook and wrote:

"Platitudes are eternally fresh, and even the most paradoxical are true; even when we say the days draw in we are literally right—for science has now come largely to the rescue of folk-lore; after the summer and still more after the equinoctial solstice the hours do definitely get shorter. It is this shortness of our northern day that has occasioned the luxuriance of our literature. Retractile weather—erectile poetry. No one has idealized, in our cold climate, more typically than Shakespeare and Dryden the subtropical conditioning. But we can consider Antony and Cleopatra to have been very different from their counterparts in the Elizabethan imagination, for on the Mediterranean they understand summer better and, with summer, sex.

"What were they really like, those prototypes of Aryan passion, of brachycephalic amour? Were Cleopatra's breasts such as 'bore through men's eyes' and tormented those early sensualists, Milton, Dante, Coventry Patmore, and St. John of the Cross? We shall never know.

"Professor Pavlov has shown that when salivation has been artificially induced in dogs by the ringing of a dinner bell, if you fire simultaneously into them a few rounds of small shot they exhibit an almost comical bewilderment. Human beings have developed very little. Like dogs we are not capable of absorbing conflicting stimuli; we cannot continue to love Cleopatra after communism and the electro-magnetic field have played Old Harry with our romantic mythology. That characteristic modern thinker, Drage Everyman, remarks, 'Destroy the illusion of love and you destroy love itself,' and that is exactly what the machine age, through attempting to foster it through cinemas and gin-palaces, deodorants and depilatories, has succeeded in doing. Glory, glory halitosis! No wonder we are happier in the present! If we think of the 'Eastern Star,' in fact, it is as advertising something. And when we would reconstruct those breasts of hers, again we are faced with the diversity of modern knowledge. What were they like? To a poet twin roes, delectable mountains; to a philanderer like Malthus festering cancers; to a pneumatogogue simply a compound of lacticity and heterogeneous pyrites; to a biologist a sump and a pump. Oh, sweet are the uses, or rather the abuses, of splanchnology! No, for details of the pathological appeal of these forgotten beauties we must consult the poets. The ancients were aware of a good thing when they saw it, and Horace knew, for instance, with almost scatological percipience, exactly what was what.

"There are altitudes, as well as climates, of the mind. Many prefer the water-meadows, but some of us, like Kant and Beethoven, are at home on the heights. There we thermostatically control the rarefied atmosphere and breathe, perforce, the appropriate mental air."

In another room Luke Snarthes was doing his exercises. Seated in the lotus position, he exhaled deeply till his stomach came against his backbone with a smart crack. After a little he relaxed and breathed carefully up one nostril and down the other and then reversed the process. He took a nail out of the calf of his leg, and after he had reinserted it, it was time to put the studs into his evening shirt. "I was there," he murmured, "when it started, down at Groyne."

When he had dressed he unlocked his despatch-case and took out a sealed tube. It was marked, "Anthrax—non-filterable virus, only to be opened by a qualified literary scientist." "Jolly little beggars," he thought, and the hard lines on his face softened. "I'll take them down to amuse Miss Pippin. She looked the kind of person who'd *understand*."

"Snuff, peotl buds, hashish, or Indian hemp, sir?" said the butler. Dinner was drawing to an end. It had been an interesting meal. For Giles and Luke (on the "regime"), grass soup and groundsel omelette, washed down with a bottle of "pulque"; for Mrs. Amp, whose huge wen, like Saint-Evremond's, made her look more than ever like some heavily wattled turkey, a chicken gumbo; for the rest Risibisi Mabel Dodge, bêche de mer, bear steak, and Capri pie.

"There's some *bhang* on the mantelpiece," said Minnie Rhomboid, "in poor Rhomboid's college tobacco jar."

"Delicious." It was Mr. Encolpius. "Common are to either sex artifex and opifex," he continued. "But, golly, how rare to find them contained in the same person—qualis opifex, Lady Rhomboid! I congratulate you—and this *barask*—perfection!" And he poured himself some more, while the snout wiggled delightedly.

"And you can drink that when Hungary is deliberately making a propaganda war for the recovery and re-enslavement of a hundred-thousand at last sophisticated Slovakians!" It was Ursula Groyne.

Poor Ursula, thought Giles, she carries her separate hell about with her like a snail its carapace! Not all the lost causes, all the lame dogs in the world could console her for the loss of her three husbands, and now she was condemned to the hades of promiscuity—every three or four years a new lover. Poor Ursula!

"And if you knew how the stuff was made!" The phrase was wrung from Luke Snarthes on his tortured calvary. "The apricots are trodden by the naked feet of bromidrosis-ridden Kutzo-Vlachs who have for centuries lived in conditions far below the poverty line! The very glass-blowers who spun that Venetian balloon for you are condemned to the agonies of alembic poisoning."

"Doubtless," answered Mr. Encolpius urbanely, "that is why it tastes so good. It all boils down to a question of proteins. You, my dear Ursula, are allergic to human misery; the sufferings of Slovaks and Slovenes affect you as pollen the hay-fever victim, or me (no offence, Minnie) a cat in the room. To ethics, mere questions of good and evil, I am happily immune, like my cara doncella here—am I right, Mary? Let Austin have his swink to him reserved, especially when it is a swink of the Rhomboid order. Go to the slug, thou ant-herd! If you could make up to kings (you remember what Aristippus said to Diogenes, Snarthes), you would not have to live on grass!"

"B-b-b-b-b-b-b-b-b-b-b-b-b-b-b-b-but   all   flesh   is gwath, so ve pwoblem is only sh-shelved." It was Reggie Ringworm!

"Sit down, everybody, it's time for the séance," commanded Lady Rhomboid. "We have persuaded Madame Yoni."

In darkness they took their seats, Mr. Encolpius and Giles on each side of Mary Pippin, while Snarthes elevated himself to a position of trans-Khyber ecstasy suspended between the table and the laquearia. The *bhang*-sodden bodies of Mrs. Amp and Roland Narthex they left where they were.

The darkness was abysmal, pre-lapsarian. Time flowed stanchlessly, remorselessly, from a wound inenarrable, as with catenary purpose. Madame Yoni moved restlessly, like Bethesda.

In her private dovecot Mary Pippin abandoned herself to the eery. What a thrill, to be here at Groyne, and for a séance! There had been nothing like it since she had joined the Anglican Church, to the consternation of her governess, Miss Heard, because of the deep mystical significance (as of some splendid sinner repenting on the ashes of lust) of the words, "for Ember Days." All the same, she was not quite sure if she liked Mr. Encolpius. But what was this? —another thrill, but positive, physical. With moth-like caresses something was running up and down her arm— 1, 2, 3, 4, 5,—spirit fingers, perhaps: the tremulous titivation continued, the moths were relentless, inexorable, 86, 87, 88. Then on her other side, along her cheek, she felt a new set of moth antennae playing. From the chandelier above came the faintest ghostly anticipatory tinkle—someone was on the move as well, up there! 98, 99 . . . Suddenly Madame Yoni screamed—there was a crash, as of three heads bumping together, and the lights went up to reveal Pentateuch and Mr. Encolpius momentarily stunned by the Ixionic impact of the fallen Snarthes. His power had failed him.

"W-w-w-w-w-w-w—" stammered Reggie Ringworm, but he was interrupted by a shout from Luke. "My God—the anthrax!" He took from his pocket the fragments of the broken tube. "At the rate of multiplication of these bacilli" —he made a rapid calculation—"we shall all be by morning,

Lady Rhomboid, dead souls." His splayed face had at last found its justification.

"Death!" said Mr. Encolpius, "the distinguished visitor! One bids good-bye, one hopes gracefully, to one's hostess, and then, why then I think one degusts the Cannabis Indica. Well, cheerio, kif-kif!" And he picked up the Brasenose jar.

Imperturbable, schizophrene, the portraits of Groynes and Rhomboids by Laurencin and the excise-man Rousseau looked down from the walls. So Miss Heard had been right, thought Mary. The wicked *do* perish. Than this there could have been no other conceivable termination to a week-end of pleasure!

> They say of old in Babylon
> That Harlequin and Pantalon
> Seized that old topiary, Truth,
> And held him by Time's Azimuth. . . .

Why had the nursery jingle recurred to her?

Luke removed a nail or two disconsolately. They would be of little use now. He tried to reassure Minnie Rhomboid. "After all, what is anthrax? What, for that matter, are yaws, beri-beri, dengue or the Bagdad Boil, but fascinating bio-chemical changes in the cellular constitution of our bodies, a re-casting of their components to play their new cadaverous roles? Believe me, Lady Rhomboid," he concluded, "there are more things in heaven and earth than are dreamt of in the British Pharmacopoeia!"

Giles took out his notebook. "La Muerte, Der Tod, Thanatos," he wrote.

"Your C-C-C-Collins perhaps?" stammered Reggie.

Giles began again: "It was at Groyne, during one of Minnie Rhomboid's most succulent week-ends, that it all happened, happened because it had to happen, because it was in the very nature of Luke Snarthes and Mary Pippin that exactly such things should happen, just as it was character not destiny, character that *was* destiny, that caused Napoleon . . ." He paused and looked up. The menial was regarding him reproachfully.

WHERE ENGELS FEARS TO TREAD

From Oscar to Stalin. A Progress. By Christian de Clavering. (The Clay Press.)

At last the authentic voice of a generation! "You are all a lost generation," remarked Gertrude Stein of us post-war age-groups, and now, thanks to Mr. Christian de Clavering, we know who lost us. Let me try and tell you all about this book while I am still full of it. First thing you know you have opened it, and there is the dedication:

"TO THE BALD YOUNG PEOPLE"

Then comes a page of fashionable quotations all in German. The middle part by Kafka, the fringes by Rilke and Hölderlin. The rest by Marx. Impeccable! And the introduction.

"Why am I doing this, my dears? Because I happen to be the one person who can do it. My dears, I'm on your side! I've come to get you out of the wretched tangle of individualism that you've made for yourselves and show you just how you can be of some use in the world. Stop worrying whether he loves you or not; stop wondering how you will ever make any money. Never mind whether the trousers of your new suit turn up at the bottom; leave off trying to annoy Pa. We're on to something rather big. The Workers' Revolution for the Classless Society through the Dictatorship of the Proletariat! Yes! It's a bit of a mouthful, isn't it! We're used to words of one syllable, words like Freud, Death, War, Peace, Love, Sex, Glands, and, above all, to Damn, Damn, Damn! Well, all that's going to be changed. Morning's at seven, and you've got a new matron.

"I'm told Mr. Isherwood is writing a book about the twenties. Mr. Isherwood is a Cambridge man, and we who made the twenties do not wish them looked at through the wrong end of a cocoa-tin. Through either end. My precious twenties! He shan't have them! Avaunt. Avanti!"

(And so the autobiography starts. I will quote a few of the dazzling vignettes. For the reasons with which the author concludes, I have refrained from comment.)

Home. Background. Mother.

"Mother, who is that horrible old obesity with the black chin? I believe he's following us."

"Hush, that's Daddy."

And so dawned my second birthday.

Home.

"Mother, where is home this time? Heliopolis? Hammamet? Ragusa? Yalta?"

"Guess again."

"I know. Prinkipo."

"Warm."

"Monte Carlo."

"Very warm."

"Has it got a clever coastline? I know! Cannes!"

And home for the next two months it was.

"Mother—what does Father do?"

"He has his business, boy o' mine."

"And what is that?"

"He's a sort of accountant."

"On 'Change?"

"On the Turf!"

"Poor Mother, poor darling Mother—but we needn't see him, need we?"

"Of course not, precious, but I thought you were old enough to know."

I pulled the hood down and for a moment it was very stuffy inside the pram. . . .

Children's Party.

"What is your father, Christian?"

"He's interested in racing—my mother is the Honourable. What is *your* father, Edelweiss?"

"A mediatized prince. What sort of racing?"

"Oh, never mind now—let's ask Mother to play some *Rimsky.*"

But I realized I couldn't stay on in Montreux Territet.

My mother an angel. My father a bookie!

"And don't forget, my boy, a tenner for every little nob you bring home with a handle to his name."

Eton. Henry's holy shade. An impression, above all, of arches, my dears, each with its handsome couple, and study fireplaces always full of stubs of Balkan Sobranie. And the naughtiest elms! While the battle of Waterloo was being fought all round me, I just sat still and watched my eyelashes grow. There were books, of course. Pater, Alma Pater, with his worried paragraphs. His prose reminded me of stale privet—and Petronius, who made me long to know more Latin. (I only learned two words, *curculio* and *vespertilio*, a bat and a weevil, but they got me everywhere, afterwards, on Mount Athos.) And Compton Mackenzie as he then was, and Huxley, before he had acquired his Pope and Bradley manner, and Verlaine of course; Rimbaud, Mallarmé, Baudelaire.

"What is that book, de Clavering?"

"*Les Chansons de Bilitis,* sir."

"And what is this lesson?"

"You have the advantage, sir."

"What do you mean, boy?"

"Ah, sir, fair's fair. I told you what my book was. You must tell me what's your lesson."

"Elementary geometry."

"But it sounds fascinating! Then this delicious piece of celluloid nonsense is—I know, sir, don't tell me—a set-square?"

"I have been teaching it for twenty years, and never met with such impertinence."

"Twenty years, and still at Elementary! Oh, sir, what a confession." And it was a very purple face one glimpsed behind the blackboard. Ah, those Eton masters! I wish I could remember any of their names, for I was really sorry for them. What tragedies went on under their mortarboards! Some of them were quite young, and one often got the impression that they were trying, inarticulately, to communicate; would have liked, in fact, to share in the rich creative life that already was centring round me. They used to teeter round my Baksts, and once I caught my house-master sniffing at a very special bottle made up for me by Max of Delhez, and gingerly rubbing some on his poor old pate. Worldlings, yet deprived of all worldly grace, of our rich sex-life how pathetically inquisitive! They are all there still, I suppose, and I often wonder, when I motor through Switzerland in summer, if one will not find a bunch of them spawning round some mouldy *arête*, in their Norfolk jackets, like eels in the Sargasso Sea.

The boys of course took up most of my time. I soon found that it was easy to get on with them by giving them presents, and making them laugh. A dozen of claret here, a humidor of Coronas there, a well-timed repartee, and persecution was made impossible. It was easy to find the butts and make rather more skilful fun of them than anybody else. In fact, I give this advice to those of my readers who are still at school. In every group there are boys whom it is the fashion to tease and bully; if you quickly spot them and join in, it will never occur to anyone to tease and bully you. Foxes do not hunt stoats. But always defer to the original teasers, and hand your prey over to them for the *coup de grâce*. And boys like expensive presents, though they are genuinely embarrassed by them. All the same, they were a provincial lot. I never felt very safe unless I had several of them round me, in coloured caps and gaudy blazers, puffing away at my cigarettes and looking for dirty jokes in the *Vie Parisienne*. By cultivating all the Captains of Games in this way I found my afternoons were left free. I would watch them troop away with their shinpads to some mysterious district on the way to Slough, then saunter up to Windsor with a book—on the bridge I would wave to any who seemed to be pushing a particularly big boat underneath it. Happy river of Eton-Windsor! I have always been very vague about its name, but I often pictured it winding away past Reading Gaol and into the great world somewhere—the world of the Ballet and the Sitwells, of Cocteau and the Café Royal.

"Hello, Faun, what a way to spend your *Après-midi*."

It was Harold, my most uneasy disciple.

"I was just thinking that summer made a noise like the rubbing together of biscuits."

"Yes, it is hot," he replied. "If it goes on like this I shall have to buy some FLANNELS."

"And be mistaken for Peter Fleming?"

"Oh, you're cruel. But seriously, what *shall* we do?"

"Well, there's Tull's, and I haven't eaten a lobster patty since this morning—or one might buy a gramophone record —or a very cool Braque of half a dozen ash-blond oysters —then there's that place one goes to London from."

"You mean the G.W.R.?"

"Thank you—and by now the school library will probably have heard of William Morris—or one might try the arches and see what one could pick up."

"Or the Castle."

"I'm bored with bearskins—but, my dear, that man—he's touched his cap—so familiar."

"You mean the Headmaster?"

It seemed an evil omen.

Then there was the Corps. I quickly joined the signal section. You didn't have to carry rifles. It was there that I first met intellectuals, dowdy fellows mostly, who went in for Medici prints and had never heard of Picasso. I realized for the first time what a gap separated cultured and cosmopolitan art lovers like myself, people who cared equally for music, painting, and literature, from those whose one idea was to pass examinations; literature is a very different thing to a poet and to someone who has to make a living out of it. "What do you think of Apollinaire?" I asked one of them. "Good God, we won't get a question on that—he's well outside the period." "On the contrary, he's very much of it. His book on Sade is vital." "I thought you meant Sidonius Apollinaris." I could make no contact with them. But signalling was delightful. One sat for hours beside a field-telephone while little figures receded into the distance with the wire. "Can you hear me?" "No." "Can you hear me now?" "No." "Well, try this." "This" was the Morse code machine, and nimbler fingers than mine would fill the air with a drowsy song. Iddy iddy umpty umpty iddy umpty iddy . . . However, all things come to an end, and there were tiresome scenes—long waits in red-brick classrooms looking at huge sheets of paper—"write only on one side of the paper." But which side? and the precious minutes were wasted. Suddenly a lot of people I had always been willing to avoid seemed to have no object in life but to want to meet one. They would cluster round some old cannon outside New Schools, gowns fluttering and tassels wagging. One afternoon, when the place was looking more Raphael Tuck than ever, I went upstairs, and unforgivable things were said. It seemed one was suspected of all the alluvial vices, in fact one was not getting the best out of the curriculum. For the last time I crossed the bridge over the mysterious river, past Tom Browne's, where rather a good pair of "sponge bags" were being created for me for Ascot, past Hills and Saunders, who had turned out some passable groups of my tea parties. "These people are my friends," I would implore the photographer, "I want them to look fresh and good-looking and aristocratic and rich." "But, sir." "Remember, they are not the Shooting Eight, or Mr. Crace's Old Boys, and I don't want to sit in the middle with folded arms and a football. I shall stand rather over to the side and at the back, and the only way you will know I am the host is by this enormous cocktail shaker."

"Oh, my boy, my boy, 'ere am I sweating away on the Turf to edicate you, and just when I 'ope you'll bring the nobs in you go and get sacked. Sacked from Eton!"

"Not sacked, Pater—supered."

But my father could never appreciate an academic distinction.

Before one can understand Oxford one must have lived in Capri, and it was there that I spent the next few months, cramming. Mother had taken a quiet villa with a view of the funicular. At seventeen it was rather odd to figure fairly recognizably in five novels in three languages. But Monty and Norman were insatiable. "No one would think it absurd if you sat to five painters," they remonstrated, and I retorted that I had a jolly good mind to—but I was too busy at that time, sitting for Fersen.[1] It was my first introduction to *les paradis artificiels* (not counting Tidworth), and with all a boy's healthy craving for novelty I flung myself down on the Count's couches and sampled poppy after poppy through his amusing collection of Chinese pipes. When the time came for my Oxford vivâ, I was older than the rocks and my eyelids were definitely a little weary. I could not decide. Magdalen and *Sinister Street*, Merton and Max, Balliol and Gumbril? or the House—Peers and Peckwater? Max had praised my eyelashes. Harold said Balliol was perfect for case-histories like mine, but I realized I should find it madly ungay. That Buttery! Finally it was the House I chose, two vast eighteenth-century rooms which I did up in pewter and cinnamon. Harold supplied wax fruit, and antimacassars for the Chinese Chippendale chairs, I added incense, brass trays and Buddhas, and Robert a carpet from the Victoria and Albert (the yacht, not the museum).

My father had become reconciled to me. "'Appiest days of your life, my boy, and don't forget, a pony for every youngster you bring 'ome with a 'andle to his name. Good for the business." I was worried about my father. "Mother," I said, "don't you think Daddy is looking definitely *blafard?*" "Is he?" she replied. "You're sitting on the Continental Bradshaw."

Most of my Eton friends had also come up to the House, and, as my father had taken a flat in Bicester, "ponies" and "monkeys" came rolling in. I spent them on clothes and parties, on entertaining and on looking entertaining. Parties! "Are you going to de Clavering's to-night?" and woe betide the wretch who had to say no. Nothing much happened at the time, but he soon felt he was living on an icefloe, drifting farther and farther from land, and every moment watching it melt away. De Clavering's to-night! The candles burn in their sconces. The incense glows. Yquem and avocado pears—a simple meal—but lots and lots of both, with whisky for the hearties and champagne for the dons. "Have a brick of caviare, Alvanley? More birds' nest, Gleneagles? There's nothing coming, I'm afraid, only avocado

[1] The Marsac of *Vestal Fire*.

pear and hot-pot." "Hot-pot!" "Christian, you're magnificent!" "Caviare and hot-pot—Prendy will be blue with
envy!" And then dancing, while cannons go home across
the quad, and David stomps at the piano. I took care at
these parties to have a word and piece of advice for everyone.

There was an alert young man in a corner, looking rather
shy. "I know—don't tell me," I said to him, "it's your first
party." "Yes." I pinched his cheek. "*Si jeunesse savait!*" I
laughed. It was Evelyn Waugh.

Another merry little fellow asked me if I could suggest a
hobby. "Architecture," I gave in a flash. "Thank you." It
was John Betjeman.

"And for me?"

"Afghanistan."

It was Robert Byron.

"And me?"

"Byron," I laughed back—it was Peter Quennell.[2]

And Alvanley, Gleneagles, Prince Harmatviz, Graf Slivovitz, the Ballygalley of Ballygalley, Sarsaparilla, the Duc
de Dingy, the Conde de Coca y Cola—for them, my peers,
I kept my serious warnings.

"These bedroom slippers, Dingy? I flew them over from
my *bottier*."

"You ought to look a little more like a public school prefect, Alvanley. The front cover of *The Captain*, it's rather
more your *genre*. There! Wash out the 'honey and flowers,'
and try a fringe effect. I want to see a pillar of the second
eleven."

"Good jazz, Gleneagles, is meant to be played just a little bit too slow."

"Graf Slivovitz, this isn't the *Herrenclub* in Carpathian
Ruthenia, you must take off your hat. Yes—that green
growth with the feudal feathers."

"Sarsaparilla, only the King rouges his knees when he
wears a kilt, and then only at a Court ball."

"Harmatviz, I can smell that Harris a mile away. What
on earth is that terrifying harpoon in the lapel?"

[2] All of whom, I am told (autumn 1937), still keep afloat.

"That, de Clavering, is a *Fogas* fly."[3]

"More Yquem, Ballygalley?"

"What's that?"

"That—if you mean the thing under your elbow—is how I look to Brancusi; the other is a kind of wine. Stand him up, will you, Ava?"

"Before the war we heard very little of the Sarsaparillas —he would not dare wear that tartan in Madrid."

"Before the war I hadn't heard of you, Coca y Cola, either; Count, this is a democratic country."

"I am democrats, we are all democrats. *Vive le roi.*"

"Thank you, Dingy, you must have been reading *Some People*. Now I want all the Guinnesses and Astors to go into the next room and get a charade ready. Alvanley, Gleneagles, Harmatviz, and Slivovitz—you will drive quickly over with me for a few minutes to Bicester to say good-night to father."

"No I don't think."—"My price is ten guineas."—"Jolly well not unless we go halves."—"Where is my hat and gotha?"—and madcap youth was served.

My crowning moment. The Summerville Grind. Peers and their mothers and sisters in mackintoshes and shooting-sticks. My mount. A huge animal whose teeth need cleaning. For the first time in my life I wear a bowler hat. And my racing colours. White silk shirt with a broad blue stripe—but zigzag! Alvanley and Gleneagles on each side of me—off! I was petrified, my dears; the first fence was enormous and my animal seemed hours getting over it. There was time for me to get down, and I rolled over. On it thundered, its great ugly stirrups banging together. A man leant over me. "Not hurt, are you?" he said. And then, *plus fort que lui,* "Where *did* you get that shirt?" It was on a sigh that I answered, as I lost consciousness, "Sire, at Charvet's." It was the Prince.

And there was talk—all kinds—the banter of my friends.

"Ah, de Clavering, if you were only of the nobility. I would ask you to stay at Dingy. What a pity you are not a real goodfellow."

[3] An amusing fish from the Balaton.

"Apfelstrüdel! He is coming to Schloss Slivovitz with Pryce-Jones, is not that good enough for you?"

"Slivovitz—how picturesque it must be. But at Dingy we have to consider the *convenances,* my aunt Doudeauville, my uncle Sagan. . . ."

"She 'appens to be *my* aunt Doudeauville too.[4] Her mother was of the German branch."

"I can find no Harmatviz on Madame Sacher's table-cloth."

"Rosa Lewis says the Claverings are an old Scotch family."

"Sarsaparilla would know that."

"Before the war we heard very little of the Sarsaparillas, now it appears . . ."

"Ah, bonjour, Coca y Cola, how is the Alvis?"

"Very well, would you like to look under the bonnet?"

"Haw, haw, haw, what a suggestion."

"But seriously, de Clavering—you are rich, you are intelligent, why have you no titles? Have you spoken to the King?"

"He may have no title, but I would trust him with my waistcoats."

"And I shake him by the hand—and say—'Well, what the hell, who cares?'"

"Bravo, Harmatviz, it's a democratic country. *Vive le roi!*"

Then there was brilliant conversation at Balliol, where the food makes long journeys to the dowdy sitting rooms, under tins.

"We were discussing, de Clavering, whether it was more correct to say Theophylactus Simocattes or Simocatta—"

"You should consider yourself very lucky, Sparrow, to be able to say either."

"And what the collective noun is for a group of pelicans; there is a gaggle of geese, of course, and a pride of lions."

"A piety of pelicans, I suggest."

"Thank you—how delightfully Thomas Browne. I shall repeat that."

---

[4] By the marriage of Graf Hubertus Mary von and zu Slivovitz-Slivovitz with Katarina Auburn-Cord.

"I don't know which I dislike most, people who repeat my epigrams or people who copy my ties—and, by the way, I hope you don't mind. I've brought Raymond Radiguet."

"Where's he up?"

"He's not up. He lives in Paris."

"Paris! If I get an All Sogger I am determined to go there. It's right on the way to the British School."

"I know a very nice little hotel near the *Bibliothèque Mazarine.*"

"I can't see why they don't build an arcade from Brick Top's[5] to the Ritz." Nobody laughs. As usual, one can find no contact with them.

My twenty-firster. Fifty people in fancy dress. The orchestra from the *Grand Ecart.* A large silver waste-paper basket. "To Christian de Clavering, the Great Commoner —Alvanley, Alba, Ava, Abercorn, Andrassy, Aberconway, Argyll, Auersperg"—you can imagine the signatures. As the college barge, which I had taken for the occasion, glided up the Cher, life's goblet seemed full to brimming. But Nemesis pursued me. The dons descended. I suppose they hadn't had enough invitations. It appears that those afternoons which I spent under some hot towels in Germers were full of goings-on, lectures, tutorials, Heaven knows what. Divinity seemed a prominent element in the City of Lost Causes. I went down. Oxford, like Eton, had never really "given."

London at last.[6] The twenties. Parties. Parties. Parties. And behind them all an aching feeling.—Was it worth it? What is it all for? Futility. . . .

"Christian—you must dine with me to-night!"

"Gawain—I can't—I've engaged myself to the *'Derries.*"

"Are you the manager?"

"Yes, sir."

"My name is de Clavering. I should like to say I have never eaten such a disgusting meal. *Même à la Cour.* But haven't I seen you before?"

---

[5] Always my favourite nightbox.

[6] A London then where everybody knew everybody and we all squeezed into one telephone book!

"Oui, monsieur, je vous connais depuis l'Eldorado."

❊   ❊   ❊

"Es usted el cuadro flamenco?"
"Si."
"Si."
"Si."
"Si."

❊   ❊   ❊

"Beverley, my dear, such a gaffe! I've just gone up to the old Dowager of Buck-and-Chan and mistaken her for the old Dowager of Ham-and-Bran!"
"Christian!"

❊   ❊   ❊

"She's got what the Americans call 'that.'"
"What?"
"What the Americans call 'that.'"
"What's that?"
"'That'—that's what she's got."
"But what the Americans call what? I don't even know that."
"Oh, my dear Duchess!"
For it was sometimes my privilege to give instruction to a very great lady.

❊   ❊   ❊

"M. Picasso—Mr. Hemingway. M. Hemingway—Señor Belmonte. Mr. Nicolson—Mr. Firbank—and now shall we begin without Miss Stein? I'm starving."

❊   ❊   ❊

"I can't decide whether to stay with Lorenzo in Taos or Crowley in Cefalu—where *does* one go in August?"

❊   ❊   ❊

"Dear Evelyn, *of course*, put me into it!"

❊   ❊   ❊

"Voulez-vous téléphoner à Mr. Proust de venir me trouver dans les bains de la rue de Lappe?"

❊   ❊   ❊

"Herr Reinhardt ist zuschloss?"

❈   ❈   ❈

"You know Diaghilev, of course, Dingy?"

❈   ❈   ❈

"I've found the title for you, Breton—*Surréalisme*."

❈   ❈   ❈

"And for this rather brusque poem, Osbert, I shall need the 'meg.' "[7]

Parties. Futility. You can read of most of them in old gossip columns. I still remember my tropical party, when a punkah was heard for the first time in Egerton Crescent. Palms and bananas decorated the rooms. The central heating (it was in July) provided the atmosphere. Some stewards from the P. & O. worked away at the punkahs, or at distributing *reistafel* and planters' punch. The guests wore shorts, sarongs, stingah shifters, or nothing at all.

"But this is *me*," I remember saying, holding up a slim volume. "Why haven't I been told about this before, Dadie? Who is this T. S. Eliot?"

"He works in a bank, I believe."

"Works in a bank—and writes *The Waste Land!* But he should be here, at my Tropical Party! Go and fetch him."

But there is a new disturbance, and Bolitho, our butler, is at my elbow.

"Some young people, sir."

"Their names?"

"The *Blackbirds*."

"Ask them to come up. We shall want some more room. Patrick, help me spread Elizabeth somewhere else. Ronald, come out from under that sofa, you're hunching the springs.[8] Fallen out of the window, you say, with Brenda? Never mind, for the moment. I want to be alone. I want to read this book."

And then the blow fell. A summons, next day, to the Royal Automobile Club. "I'm ruined, my boy. I'm ruined.

[7] A megaphone, and such small ability as I may have acquired with it, now constitute my "platform manner."

[8] Firbank's shyness was proverbial.

'Aven't got a penny left. Those pals of yours, Alvanley and
Gleneagles. They've skinned me. You'll 'ave to earn your
own living from now on. Oh, your poor mother!" "It's poor
me, you old banana. I've no intention of earning my own
living, thank you."—"Ow, wot a boy, wot a boy." And I
flung out. Tears. Consultations.

"I can always sell my Gris." "But what will you do then?"
"Oh, write—paint—don't fluster me."

"And we were to have gone to the Londonderry del Vals!"
"Poor mother."

One thing stood out with terrible clarity in those dark
days. The old life was over. I could never associate any
longer with those friends who had been used to look to me
for advice, loans, old clothes, and entertainment. They
would see to that. The Ritz, the Blue Lantern, must know
me no more.

Exile. A few months in Paris—but Montparnasse, now,
my dears, *Montparnasse;* a few offers for my memoirs; then
Berlin, Munich—and finally, Greece. There, "in the worst
inn's worst room," I existed, miserably, on fried goat and
raki. To write or to paint—to work—but how? Write only on
one side of the paper. But which side? It was the old dilemma. A wandering exile, the quays of the Piraeus knew
me, the noisy bars of Terreno, the Dôme and the Deux
Magots, Bohême and Silhouette, and that place in the
Marokaner Gasse. I ate rose-leaf jam with the good monks
of Holy Luke, and fried locusts with the dervishes of
Moulay Idris. And one crazy Fourth of June, lobster salad
with my housemaster! My slim figure lingered, winter-
bound, in dim cathedrals, and there were beaches where
summer licked me with its great rough tongue. Ah, summer! There's a crypto-fascist for you! The spring I never
cared for. It held nothing but a promise, and I, too, was
promising. The autumns I adored; they smelt of cassia. But
poverty was crippling. To whom life once had been a bed
of roses—no, of *Strawberry-leaves,* there remained only the
"Welcome" at Villefranche, the old Boeuf in the Boissy
D'Anglas, the Pangion. It was not good enough. I came
back to live with my mother.

It was then that I saw the light. One day I wandered into

a little book-shop near Red Lion Square. It was full of slim
volumes by unfamiliar names—who were Stephen, Wystan,
Cecil, and Christopher? Madge? Bates? Dutt? These blunt
monosyllables spoke a new kind of language to me. I looked
at the books. Not at all bad, and some of these young poets,
I realized, had even attended my university! One quatrain
in particular haunted me.

> M is for Marx
> and Movement of Masses
> and Massing of Arses
> and Clashing of Classes.

It was new. It was vigorous. It was real. It was chic!

> Come on Percy, my pillion-proud, be
> camber-conscious
> Cleave to the crown of the road

and

> It was late last night when my lord came home
> enquiring for his lady O
> The servants cried on every side
> She's gone with the Left Book
> Study Circle O!

And everyone was called by their Christian names! So cosy!
From that moment I've never looked back. It's been pylons
all the way. Of course they didn't want me, at first. The
meetings behind the Geisha Café—they suspected me of all
sorts of things, I'm afraid—I said quite frankly: "I realize I
shall never understand eclectic materialism but I'm terribly
terribly Left!" And I showed them one or two things I'd
written for the weekly reviews, all among the waffle-receipts
and the guest-house advertisements.[9] And I called myself
Cris Clay. Then—on a drizzling February morning—came
my first Procession! It was for me a veritable *Via Crucis,* for
we had to march up St. James's Street—past Locks, and
Lobbs, and Briggs, and Boodles. All my past was spread
out before me. There weren't very many of us, and it was
difficult to cheer and shout our slogans

[9] Soon to be published under the title of *I Told You So.*

One, two, three, four
Pacifism means War.

I raised my eyes to White's bow-window.

Yes, there they were—Alvanley and Gleneagles, with their soiled city faces and little moustaches, their bowlers and rolled umbrellas—and, good heavens, there were Peter, and Robert, and Evelyn! I never felt more ridiculous. When suddenly something made me look round. "De Clavering, old horse!" "Well, I'm spifflicated." "You old *finocchio!*" "*Spinaten!*" It was too good to be true.

"But, Harmatviz—I see you don't know the first thing about the cut of a corduroy."

"Not a red shirt, Slivovitz—a red tie if you must."

"And you, Coca y Cola—you look like a scarecrow."

"These are good workmen's pants, de Clavering, real dungaree!"

We gave a boo to the bow-window that made the *Tatlers* rattle in their holders.

"But how did you get here?"

"I was expelled for plotting against the Regent in favour of the traitor Otto."

"I was turned out for lack of enthusiasm for the present regime and communicating with the traitor Wilhelm."

"I wanted to annoy Sarsaparilla."

"Anyhow, we're all good anti-Fascists," cried Comrade Graf Slivovitz.

I wanted to say something more—that I had even been told by the Party that I should be more useful outside it, but I couldn't speak. Old friends had met, travelling a stony road, coming to the same hard conclusions, and together.

And that's about all. There are one or two things I've left out, the war, the slump, the general strike, and my conversion to Catholicism, because I'm so vague about dates. But I think this will remain—A Modern Pilgrimage. And now for the reviewers. I think they'd better be careful. They'd better be very careful indeed. A line is being drawn. I'm going to say it again, and very slowly. A line is being drawn. Quite quietly at present—just a few names jotted down in a notebook—one or two with a question mark after them. They have another chance. And the rest don't. Those lines mean something. Tatatat! Yes, my dears, bullets—real bullets, the kind of bullets they keep for reviewers who step across the party line. One day you're going to see something rather hostile. It will make you feel, perhaps, a little uneasy. It's heavy—and stubby—and rather pointed. Guess? Yes. A machine-gun. POINTED AT YOU. And behind it, with his hand on the trigger, Comrade—no, COMMISSAR—Cris Clay. Did you write such and such an article? Yes (No). It doesn't matter which. Tatatat. It's no good then bleating about how you voted in the last election, or where your sympathies have always been. We don't want your sympathy. We don't want you at all.

You subscribed to the *News-Chronicle*, did you? I am afraid you will be under no necessity to renew that subscription.

You wrote for the *New Statesman*? What did you write about? "Gramophone records."

"To sit on the fence is to be on the wrong side of it—line him up, Gollancz."

"Yes, Commissar."

"And you—what were you?"

"Turf-Accountant."

"Your face seems vaguely familiar—but that doesn't make it more pleasant—line him up, Stephen."

"It was no accident, Pryce-Jones, that you have lived near three royal palaces."

"But—"

But I am anticipating. There are two ways to review a book like mine, a right and a wrong. The wrong way is to find fault with it, for then you find fault with the book clubs behind it, in fact, with your advertisers. And if I seem too clever it's because you're too stupid. Think it over. The right way is to praise it, and to quote from it in such a way that you can all learn my lesson. I stand no nonsense. Remember, my dears, a line is being *drawn*. Tatatat. See you at the Mass Observatory.

> Something is going to go, baby,
> And it won't be your stamp-collection.
> Boom!

And that I think could particularly be meditated by the
Fascist Connolly.

CRIS CLAY

PARIS—BUDAPEST—PARTON ST.
　　　1936–1937

THE FATE OF AN ELIZABETHAN

Antony. By his Father the Earl of Lytton. Peter Davies, London.

This is a remarkable book, extremely interesting from three points of view—as a portrait of contemporary youth, as a study of the relations between parents and children, and as a picture of the governing class—not of the delightfully eccentric upper classes, but of a small knot of powerful aristocratic families. First we are presented with an adorable child, living in the world of the Homeric heroes, driving a pony-cart like a chariot, standing up in his Greek costume and galloping about the park at Knebworth with a spear in his hand. At his private school he is first introduced to the world where for fifteen years games and popularity are to matter more than anything else—and there are lectures on the last war. "He is talking all about bombing, glorious! We have got a God in the room, it is great fun. He is talking so well that he makes you think you are in the trenches. Goodbye." Already he wrote vigorous natural letters which he signed "someone," and already his father remarks: "He lost something of his originality, as all boys do at school." At fourteen he writes from Eton a brilliant description of an interview with his tutor about making friends with a boy from another house who cribs:

> "He is a boy with a very bad past record and he is not the sort of boy I like my little children to be friends with. . . . He seems to me to be a boy with a great lack of honour. What sort of a boy do you think he is?"
>
> "I think he is a very nice boy."
>
> "How can you think that a boy who cribs is a very nice boy?"
>
> "I don't see that it makes any difference to a boy whether he has had the bad luck to be *caught* cribbing or not." (I did not tell him that there wasn't a boy in his house, or for that matter in the school, who hadn't

cribbed, and it was bad luck on anyone who happened
to be caught.)

And so the battle rages.

The letters from Eton suffer because they are all written
to his parents and consequently dwell on triumphs rather
than disappointments, and on functions, which are the natural copy of schoolboys' letters home, while their real life
is a series of friendships, conversations, intrigues, and awak-
enings in which an event like the Fourth of June is as unimportant as the Lord Mayor's show. What matters is getting
popular and winning colours, tasting the joys of power for
the first time, acquiring knowledge and avoiding punishment; in fact, growing up. I remember very well that Eton
of fifteen years ago, it was still almost entirely pre-war in
feeling. After a pathetic year or so of serfdom, when fear
was the dominating emotion, one emerged gradually into
the full blaze of feudal sunlight. The masters represented
the Church, praising, cajoling, blaming, pointing the way,
with the Headmaster as a kind of terrible Pope; the boys,
with their great hierarchy of colours and distinctions, were
the rest of the population, while the prefects and athletes,
the captains of houses and self-elected members of "Pop,"
were the feudal overlords who punished offences at the request of the Church (and in return were tacitly allowed
to break the same rules themselves); in those days they
could beat almost anybody for almost anything at sight, and
it seemed to a droll, idle, timorous little beetle like myself
that most of the staff were deeply in awe of them. Work
was generally deplored as too drastic a remedy for our un-
employment; games oddly enough were not in themselves
a sure passport to popularity; for the last time in our lives
money didn't matter, and if one had to say what really
counted one would have had to admit that it was a curious
blend of elegance and vitality to which the addition was
much appreciated of a certain mental alertness and the gift
of being amusing. The times when I am really transported
back to Eton are when I read the memoirs of Grammont, or
La Princesse de Clèves. But there were two serious influences that stood out above the general gaiety and magnifi-

cence, Mr. Headlam and Mr. Marten. Both taught history to the history specialists, from whom the feudal princes were recruited. Otherwise the atmosphere was eighteenth-century and political, much as in the days of Gray and Walpole. It was assumed that in after life ravens would feed us; science and most contemporary knowledge was taught but discredited, and we continued to be happier than we could have conceived possible and to acquire a wide, but (for me) on the whole rather useless, knowledge of the way to govern an empire or a board.

Supreme among these thousand boys were a small group of powerful dandies, who were looked on with an awe that luckily in most of us atrophies, or we should be miserable still: Nico Davies and Edward Woodall (to whom the best letters in the book are written), Antony Knebworth, the exquisite Mr. Edward Jessel, the languid Lord Dunglass. Lord Knebworth was remarkable for his vitality, which was often boisterous, his fits of melancholy, his ability and his charm. He was a beautifully built and slightly stooping athlete, an incarnation of that adventurousness and courage which is so alluring to intellectuals and which usually ends in them breaking their legs. The group transplanted itself in a body to Oxford and was disappointed at first, as are all boys who are happy at Eton, by the dismal emptiness and ugliness of Oxford and the difficulty of starting life all over again.

> I dare say Oxford is a good interesting place for old men of forty, but for boys, why I'd rather be at a girls' school for knitting. It would be better exercise. . . . I want an incentive to do something. I have ambition, but no goal and therefore nothing to work for. Money? I want it, but it doesn't thrill me. God? I don't understand him and he doesn't fill me. Passion? Yes, but what does it mean? How do I get it? What do I do? Strength? Yes, but what good is physical strength? Power is perhaps the only light I can see clearly, but that is very dim and very far and the obstacles are incredible and the pleasures which distract one from getting it too good."

To this questioning his father replied with words of golden wisdom, recommending the pursuit of happiness and drawing a distinction between happiness and pleasure. But his son is already bitten with the idea of political realism.

> I think the most fatal thing of all is the general tendency everywhere to be good. It is such a mistake and so unnatural. I mean by "being good" things like disarmament, upholding the integrity of smaller nationalities, prohibition, League of Nations. . . . It's these drivelling idealists like Woodrow Wilson and Bob Cecil (is that libel?) who want to try to make people do everything for the peace of the world at the expense of nationality. It is fundamentally communism and a fatal thing for everyone.

To which his father replies: "You may not agree with idealists like Bob Cecil, and you are fully entitled to disagree with them, but if you call them 'drivelling' you betray a want of confidence in your own case."

For the moment skiing solves the problem, for Lord Knebworth was one of the fastest and most enterprising skiers of his generation, but it only made him more dislike Oxford and the idea of an office to follow—but other places are worse; of the sailors at Dartmouth he says: "They are so concentrated on modesty, ignorance, and manhood as to be almost unnatural." Then *Don Juan* revives him with its appeal to the blend of cynical and romantic which shows in his own rather histrionic nature. At twenty-one the "career" seems to burden him more than ever.

> I have a dread of becoming just one of many young men living miserably in London and working hopelessly in the city. . . . But I suppose really the conventional life is the right one or it would not be the conventional one. . . . I hate the thought of Parliament, or the City, or of London, or of anything except something quite peculiar.

He is saved by going out as A.D.C. to his father in India, where he plays polo, climbs to Tibet, skis in the Himalayas ("Believe me, the plains of Tibet are horrid. They are all like a desert to look at; only the yak, who lives on rocks and sands and snow [poor sweet] can subsist there—they're so high you can't breathe, eat, or move without being sick,

and you have headache all the time.") In India he is bliss-
fully happy: "It is Eton. Play, sport, games are the thing;
work the odious duty, the side-show!" He wishes to stay on
there, but is not permitted to. The prison-house is now closing rapidly round him—he works first at Conservative
Headquarters, then in the Army and Navy Stores, still
hopelessly rebelling.

This method of life persistently carried on for about
forty years eventually produces wealth, dignity, power,
position, and universal respect. It is called Christian
civilization. . . . I see in these things only the same piece
of green blotting-paper every morning.

He became a Conservative member of Parliament in
1931, but was already turning entirely against democratic
government. He worked in the Army and Navy Stores,
went to the House, and spent his spare time flying, finding
in aviation that escape from daily routine (his description
of flying to Milan reads like the Airman's journal in Auden's
Orators) which for most of us becomes all we can hope for
in the way of real self-expression. He more and more hates
the liberty which he has had to abandon, and his last letters
are devoted to fascism, Roman Catholicism, and a crusade
against the decadent influence on English debutantes of the
works of Mr. Noel Coward.

They are going to make us promise not to use bombs
in the next war. It is all too fantastic and futile for words.
. . . My political and philosophical and social war is a
revolt from Liberty and Liberalism. . . . That is why I
admire the Catholic Church.

In his last letter to him he quotes a saying of his friend
Windham Baldwin, whom he had known at Eton:

"Only gods can stand freedom; we turn bad on
it." . . . I have been lucky and rich and happy and
prosperous and have felt, as a boy, like a god. Then I
have had no hemp, himp, homp [work in steel mill] like
you, no clutch of circumstance, and I have gone bad,
that's all.

Three months later he was killed, flying, obeying an officer in an impossible manœuvre. He was then twenty-nine.

Well, there is the picture, the picture of a young Elizabethan, gifted with a good deal of brain, a strong character,
and a wonderful body, and aided by every advantage of
birth and education, and every help that a devoted family
life, and the wisdom of one of the few obviously perfect
fathers in literature, could give. One should think of him as
a terrible loss to his country, as an example to other young
people of the scope for physical adventure and moral
energy that exists in the world—and yet one can't, one can
see him only as the victim of a system, as a young man
crowned with too early success and afterwards struggling
hopelessly to disentangle himself from it, noting down in his
letters with the amazing alertness and self-criticism that
were so typical of him the alternative lives that, always
presenting themselves, are yet always forbidden. We hear
a lot of criticism of public school education from those who
were failures at school—but is there anything in reality more
dangerous than early success? I was myself a success at
school, and it seems to me that only recently have I recovered my balance. Early laurels weigh like lead, and
looking back at Antony Knebworth's school days, I see now,
not only all the envy and irritation which his successes must
have caused his rivals, but the effect of the competitive
system on him; always to be going in for something and
always having to win it, and then to find that there are no
more competitions, just a slight dazzle from the conflagration of his early successes to remind him of the small school-
universe where he had been most fully alive. If competition
is carried into after life with similar violence it becomes a
kind of piracy, and a kind at which Antony Knebworth was
too high-spirited and romantic to succeed. Hence his dis-
content, his regret at not having fought in the last war—for
temperamentally he was Edwardian; intolerant, egotistic,
and bred to consider the world his oyster and politics his
game. He lacked the idealism which alone could dominate
the fatal inherited family facility, and without which all
natural gifts must spoil. But any system of education derives from the class which bring it into being, and it is this
governing class, I feel, which is really to blame for the

transition of Elizabethan into Fascist that we have watched
take place. For, although there are exceptions, of which
Lord Lytton is obviously one, it is a class which has persistently underestimated the intellect, which regards it as a
source of evil and not a source of pleasure; where ability,
self-interest, and shrewdness, heavily coated with good-
fellowship and charm, are what matter, and from which
an intellectual or artistic member must often drag himself
out with ignominy or without success, distrusted by his old
friends, and discontented with the new. "Power makes men
stupid," it has been said, and the power of the governing
classes is cumulative and hereditary. Had Lord Knebworth
belonged to another class, had he been like Lawrence a
miner's son, he would have risen by his intellect rather than
been kept down by his athletic accomplishments. He would
have met his intellectual equals instead of remaining all his
life with his intellectual inferiors, and might have become
what he wanted to become, a writer. "I know I could write
a great book," he says, "that I could make my living with
my pen, that I could be really great in that line, and then
I should be happy. But I know, too, that I never shall." As
is to be expected, his writing has great ability but no
standards. The writers who were at Oxford with him, Evelyn Waugh and Peter Quennell, for instance, were impossible—they were aesthetes—and so instead we see someone
whose intellect (as opposed to his intelligence) remains the
same as at his private school, who never looks at a picture
or a building, who mentions no music but Gilbert and
Sullivan, who mentions no living writers but Belloc, Chesterton, Philip Guedalla, and Maurice Baring, and who enjoyed Mark Antony and *Wuthering Heights* at school, but
afterwards read and re-read *The Constant Nymph*. What
did he gain by cutting himself off from the life of the mind,
from all genuine aesthetic experience? He did not write
better or ski better or box or fly better; he only missed
entirely the two great conceptions of our day: that of artistic integrity, the life of the spirit, and that of social justice,
"the palpable and obvious love of man for man."

December 1935

THE POSITION OF JOYCE

James Joyce has brought out a new book. It is a fragment of a longer one, and is called *Anna Livia Plurabelle*. We are used to the reputations of authors fluctuating from year to year, but Mr. Joyce's also fluctuates from place to place. He is resented in Ireland, neglected in England, admired by a set in America, and idolized by another in France. In every nation there is a general public and a literary public. In Ireland the general public is provincial and priest-ridden. It cannot forgive Joyce his blasphemy nor his contemptuous parodies of Irish jingoism. The other, the smaller public, has chosen escape in a romantic return to the past, characterized by a special lyric note of easy and indefinable melancholy born of self-pity. Joyce is a realist, and out of touch intellectually with that generation. "Michael Roberts remembers forgotten beauty. He presses in his arms the loveliness which has long faded from the world. I desire to press in my arms the loveliness which has not yet come into the world." Thus Joyce's only disciples in Ireland are the young realists of the post-rebellion period. In England the literary public is governed by good taste. Cautious as the cenotaph, the critics decide the value of a book in terms of "delicious" and "charming." The general public is equally conservative, and the fate of a book like *Ulysses* (so hopelessly unpresentable when submitted to the Chelsea canon) is decided in advance. It is in America, where there is a large and less sophisticated general public, and in Paris, where there are a great many young writers anxious to experiment in literary form, that the "*Ulysses* generation" has grown up.

Mr. Forster, in his lectures on the novel, states perfectly the English attitude to Joyce, the bad bogey-man of letters. "*Ulysses*," he writes, "is a dogged attempt to cover the universe with mud, an inverted Victorianism, an attempt to make coarseness and dirt succeed where sweetness and light failed, a simplification of the human character in the interests of Hell." It is also an "epic of grubbiness and disillusion . . . a superfetation of fantasies, a monstrous coupling of reminiscences . . . in which smaller mythologies swarm and pullulate, like vermin between the scales of a poisonous snake." "Indignation in literature," adds Mr. Forster, "never quite comes off," and the passage I have quoted does little except to express the general attitude of English culture towards novelty, and to prove that the vocabulary of scandalized vituperation is drawn from the reptile-house in every age.

"Indignation" is not a quality of Joyce's work, but "the raging of Joyce seems essentially fantastic, and lacks the note for which we shall be listening soon," continues Mr. Forster, who proceeds to classify *Ulysses* as belonging to the period of *Zuleika Dobson*. Let us get a clear idea of *Ulysses* before we try to estimate the later work of its author. James Joyce is, by temperament, a medievalist. He has always been in revolt against his two greatest limitations, his Jesuit education and his Celtic romanticism. Each of his books reveals a growing fear of beauty; not because life is not beautiful, but because there is something essentially false and luxurious in the "Celtic Twilight" approach to it. This tinsel element is very strong in Joyce's early poems, and is contrasted with an equally pronounced repulsion from it in *The Portrait of the Artist*. In *Ulysses* he has got it in hand, and is experimenting in other approaches to beauty; the pagan simplicity of Mrs. Bloom's reverie, the mathematical austerity of the catechism which precedes it. Only Stephen Dedalus, the Hamlet young man, thinks automatically in the diction of the Celtic Twilight; but in him the remorse, the guilty sense of loneliness which attacks brave but weak men who destroy the religious framework of their youth, has fused with his minor poet melancholy, and gives to his reverie the quality of a Greek chorus. Stephen Dedalus, in fact, equips the *Ulysses* generation with a fatalism, a dramatization of their own forebodings, and with the medieval quality so rare in America, so reduced

in England, so rife in Europe—the Tragic Sense of Life. This
is the great link between Joyce and Proust, otherwise so mis-
leadingly compared. Both the Irishman and the Jew possess
the tragic intelligence; the idea that life can only be appreciated, can only be lived even, if the intelligence is used
to register all the beauty and all the intimacy which exist
in ironic contrast to the unrelieved gloom of squalor and
emptiness, mediocrity, disease, and death.

> For all our wit and reading do but bring us
> To a truer sense of sorrow.

The whole climax of *Ulysses* is a single moment of intimacy,
when Bloom, the comic character, rescues Stephen in a
drunken brawl. Bloom had a son who died, Stephen a father who is alive; but for this instant of spiritual paternity
all the swelter of that urban summer, all the mesembrian
pub-crawls of Bloom and Stephen, the "vermin" and the
"scales" and the "serpents," move into place. The central
emotion of *Ulysses* is not indignation, but remorse; and remorse, though perhaps second-rate in life, is an emotion
which usually succeeds in literature. Expiation and the
sense of doom, which form the essence of Greek tragedy,
are only a variation of this feeling; and though in real people remorse seems so feebly static, its very tranquillity and
remoteness from action lend it a glassy literary beauty. In
Ulysses Stephen dwells in the consciousness of having has-
tened his mother's death by his atheism, Bloom feels obscurely his father's suicide and the troubled history of his
people, while all Ireland seems listlessly aware of its destiny.
Perhaps the most typical scene in *Ulysses* is that in which
Stephen, who has run away from the squalor of his father's
house, comes across his young sister also trying to escape
her environment without the help he might have given:

> He turned and halted by the slanted book cart. Two-
> pence each, the huckster said, four for sixpence. Tattered
> pages. *The Irish Beekeeper. Life and miracles of the
> Curé of Ars. Pocket Guide to Killarney.*
> "I might find there one of my pawned school prizes."
> "What are you doing here, Stephen?"

Dilly's high shoulders and shabby dress.

Shut the book quick. Don't let see.

"What are you doing?" Stephen said.

A Stuart face of nonsuch Charles, lank locks falling at its sides. It glowed as she crouched feeding the fire with broken boots. I told her of Paris. Late lieabed under a quilt of old overcoats, fingering a pinchbeck bracelet; Dan Kelly's token.

"What have you there?" Stephen asked.

"I bought it from the other cart for a penny," Dilly said, laughing nervously. "Is it any good?"

My eyes they say she has. Do others see me so? Quick, far and daring, shadows of my mind.

He took the coverless book from her hand. Chardenal's *French Primer*.

"What did you buy that for?" he asked. "To learn French?"

She nodded, reddening and closing tight her lips.

Show no surprise, quite natural.

"Here," Stephen said, "it's all right. Mind Maggie doesn't pawn it on you. I suppose all my books are gone."

"Some," said Dilly, "we had to."

She is drowning. Agenbite. Save her, Agenbite. All against us. She will drown me with her, eyes and hair. Lank coils of seaweed hair around me, my heart, my soul. Salt green death.

We.

Agenbite of Inwit. Inwit's Agenbite.

Misery.

This quotation reveals many other aspects of the book; the old word for remorse, for instance, becomes one of those snowball phrases with which *Ulysses* is packed. Appearing continually in the characters' daydreams, they gather momentum from each association, echoing through the chapters till by the end they are charged with as much personality as the thinkers themselves. Then the drabness of the scene, the halting, trite dialogue, illustrate the other side of *Ulysses*: the attempt to create beauty out of city life, and style out of the demotic English which is spoken in therein. Every year more people's lives are passed in towns than in the country; but while there is a whole vocabulary of rural beauty, there is so far only the slenderest aesthetic of cities, the roughest technique in appreciating them. What Baudelaire and Laforgue did for Paris, or Mr. T. S. Eliot for modern London, Joyce has done for Dublin: and at a time when Yeats and Synge had monopolized the Gaelic side of the Irish, he was able to create a language out of the demotic commercial speech of the anglicized burghers of Dublin itself. Literary English has become very hackneyed, as a glance at any book of essays or a preface to an anthology at once will show, and Joyce in *Ulysses* set out to revive it by introducing the popular colloquial idiom of his own city, by forming new words in the Greek fashion of compound epithets, by telescoping grammar, by using the fresh vocabulary of science manuals, public-houses, or Elizabethan slang. Here, for instance, are two quotations, one to illustrate the city aesthetic, the note of Celtic melancholy introduced into the descriptions of an urban summer sunset by the Hill of Howth, where Bloom had once made love; the other, an example of Joyce's highly latinized English, which produces an effect of austere rhetoric and elaborate original rhythm.

A long-lost candle wandered up the sky from Myrus' bazaar in search of funds for Mercer's hospital and broke, drooping, and shed a cluster of violet but one white stars. They floated, fell: they faded. The shepherd's hour: the hour of holding: hour of tryst. From house to house, giving his everwelcome double knock, went the nine o'clock postman, the glow-worm's lamp at his belt gleaming here and there through the laurel hedges. And among the fine young trees a hoisted linstock lit the lamp at Leahy's Terrace. By screens of lighted windows, by equal gardens, a shrill voice went crying, wailing, "*Evening Telegraph*—stop press edition! Result of the Gold Cup races!" And from the door of Dignam's house a boy ran out and called. Twittering the bat flew here, flew there. Far out over the sands the coming surf crept, gray. Howth settled for slumber, tired of long days, of yumyum rhododendrons (he was old) and felt gladly the night breeze lift, ruffle his fell of ferns. He lay but opened a red eye unsleeping, deep and slowly breathing, slumberous but awake. And far on Kish bank the anchored lightship twinkled, winked, at Mr. Bloom.

*　　　*　　　*

What play of forces, inducing inertia, rendered departure undesirable?

The lateness of the hour, rendering procrastinatory: the obscurity of the night, rendering invisible: the uncertainty of Thoroughfares, rendering perilous: the necessity for repose, obviating movement: the proximity of an occupied bed, obviating research: the anticipation of warmth [human] tempered with coolness [linen], obviating desire and rendering desirable: the statue of Narcissus, sound without echo, desired desire.

Besides this he directed a campaign of parody against the whimsy and archaism latent in English prose style. It is indeed as an enemy of "literature" that Joyce really might appear to Mr. Forster as working "in the interests of Hell." Though he did not originate the "stream of consciousness" as a form of writing, he saw that by recording the thoughts of each character he could take shorthand liberties with their syntax as well as get nearer to their selves. He too, among those who have used this method, is the only one to have grasped that people, besides thinking differently, think at a different pace. Mrs. Woolf, whose *Mrs. Dalloway* is in many ways a feminine adaptation of one idea of *Ulysses* to English good taste, tends to make all her characters think in the same tempo. She gives us anatomical slices; not human beings, but sections of them, which portray the doubts, the tendernesses, the half-hopes and half-fears of the human mind all conceived in the same mood of genteel despair. Bloom, Mrs. Bloom, Stephen, however, and the nameless Cyclops narrator possess mental processes which are quite incomparable with each other. Bloom's mean, good-tempered, second-rate, scientific curiosity colours all his commonplace meditations. Stephen's bitterness, imagination, and petulant intellect quicken feverishly the pulse of his thought. The racy, cynical and shamelessly prejudiced gusto of the Nameless One transforms his narrative into the whirl of the winds of Aeolus that it is meant to symbolize, while elaborate journalese retards the speed of the book for those chapters when the action is at a standstill. Lastly, the even breathing of Mrs. Bloom times with her steady physical reverie, her pagan meditation so free from Stephen's medieval anguish, Bloom's scepticism, or the problems which faced the morning of the one, the evening of the other, and their common night.

The link between the new work of Joyce and *Ulysses* is chiefly one of language; though both are united by the same preoccupation with the aesthetic of cities, with the absurdity of our Jewish-American democracy, and with the capacity for being beautiful which this democracy yet retains.

Here are two quotations, one showing the Hill of Howth again treated in a symbolic manner, the other the praise of Dublin, rhetorical as cities are—Earwicker (the Danish castle) is bragging to his wife, the Liffey, of all he has done for her. I have annotated the text so that the complexity of the portmanteau language may be gauged:

"Old Whitehowth is speaking again. Pity poor Whiteoath! Deargone mummeries, goby. Tell the woyld I have lived true thousand hells. Pity please, lady, for poor O.W. in this profoundest snobbing I have caught. Nine dirty years mine age, hairs white, mummery failing, deaf as Adder. I askt you, dear lady, to judge on my tree by our fruits. I gave you of the tree. I gave two smells, two eats: my happy blossoms, my all falling fruits of my boom. Pity poor Haveth Children Everywhere with Mudder. That was Communicator a former Colonel."

". . . And I built in Urbs in Rure for mine elskede, my shiny brows, an earth closet wherewithin to be quit in most convenience from her sabbath needs: did not I festfix my unniverseries, wholly rational and got alike [three Dublin universities national and godlike with Trinity to suggest the holy]; was not I rosetted on two stelas of little Egypt, had not rockcut readers, hieros, gregos, and democriticos [the Rosetta stone]; and by my syvendialed changing charties Hibernska ulitzas made not I [allusion to superimposing a street map on an older one and rotating it to find what streets lie along a Roman road. Ulitza is the Slav for a street, but in this case is also a prophecy of Ulysses and his labours] to pass through 12 Threadneedles and Newgade and Vicus Veneris to cooinsight. [Allusions to Ulysses, to Newgate prison on the Roman Road.] Oi polled ye many, but my fews were chosen: and I set up twin-minsters, the pro and the con [Christchurch and the pro-Cathedral] woven of peeled wands and attachattouchy floodmud [Italian root, "sticky"] arched for the convenanters and shinner's rifuge; all truant trulls made I comepull, all rubbeling gnomes I pushed, go go; and thirdly for ewigs I did reform and restore for my smuggy piggiesknees her paddy palace on the cross-knoll [St. Patrick's restored] and added there unto a shallow laver to put out her hell fire and posied windows for her oriel house and she sass her nach, chilly-bombom and 40 bonnets, upon the altar-stane, may all have mossyhonours!

"I hung up at the Yule my pigmy suns helphelped of Kettil Flashnose [electric lights introduced in Dublin under Kettle, the chief of the electricians and descendant of Kettle Flatnose, an original Dane settler] for the supper hour of my frigid one, coulomba mea, frimosa mia, through all Livania's volted ampire from anods to cathods, and from the topazolites of Mourne by Arcglow's sapphire seamanslure and Waterford's hook and crook lights to the polders of Hy Kinsella [old Danish beacons]."

The ordinary man of letters, when faced with modern civilization, plays the ostrich with its head in the sand. A very whimsical, arch, mock apologetic, and well-subsidized ostrich too. In fact, they are the paid entertainers of democracy, the jesters who are allowed the licence of bewailing the rattle of hansom cabs, of beginning every sentence with "I must needs avow that I have never seen eye to eye with those who," and ending "nevertheless, to my thinking, when all is said and done. . . ." Of course, there is no law compelling anyone to belong to his period; but not to belong to it is to take sanctuary, to eke out a whimsical existence and an archaic style in a half-timbered Utopia, visited, like an Elizabethan teashop, by the most insipid of the public one would wish to avoid. If *Ulysses* is largely a parody of literary manners, a dissatisfaction with style, the new work of Joyce is a parody of language, an attempt to create a new vocabulary for literature itself. And both, which readers are unwilling to see, are meant to be funny. After all, the ballad of the Jabberwock has passed into the accepted treasury of English humour; yet when the method Carroll used to reinforce words with double meanings is applied to contemporary prose, which surely needs it, the result is that we label the originator mad.

Literary language in England has become very far removed from conversation, nor is it able to profit, like American, from a rich background of polyglot slang. All literary words in addition tend to be used, especially by Georgian poets, without a due conviction of their meaning, and this depreciates the currency so that most epithets become like the dead notes on an old piano, which go down when they are sounded, but do not come up. The best instance of this is the penultimate passage of *The Oxford Book of English Prose*. The new language of Joyce is only a kind of piano-tuning, whereby he tightens up certain words by grafting fresher foreign equivalents on to them, approximates them to other words to strengthen their own vigour, above all puns with them freely, and gives words a synthetic meaning, with which either to express life, or simply to make a series of academic jokes. The experiment may be a failure, just as Esperanto or phonetic spelling may be a failure, but there is nothing that is contrary to reason in the idea itself. The chief defect of Mr. Joyce's new language is that, so far, it has swamped the lyrical quality of his other prose writings; he has not attempted purple patches in it so much as rhetorical imitations of them. Here is the close of a fable called "The Mookse and the Gripes," which can be compared with Bloom's city sunset, quoted above:

The shades began to glidder along the banks, dusk unto dusk, and it was as glooming as gloaming could be in the waste of all peaceable wolds. The mookse had a sound eyes right but he could not all hear. The Gripes had light ears left yet he could but ill see. He ceased. And he ceased and it was so dusk of both of them. But still one thought of the deeps he would profound on the morrow and still the other thought of the scrapes he would escape if he had luck enough.

The new book is full of fables, because the whole of the first part is really a *surréaliste* approach to the prehistory of Dublin, the myths and legends of its origin, Duke Humphrey and Anna Livia, the mountain and the river, from a black reach of which the city took its name. The first words "river-run brings us back to Howth Castle and Environs" suggest the melodies to follow. All the urban culture of Ireland is by origin Scandinavian; and, to emphasize this, Joyce has introduced the greatest possible amount of Norse words into his description of it. There are four parts to the new work of Joyce: the first is a kind of air photograph of Irish history, a celebration of the dim past of Dublin, as was *Ulysses* of its grimy present; the second is an interlude in a barn near Chapelizod; some children are playing, and react unconsciously the old stories of the first (Iseult of Ireland linking in the suburb's name); and the third part, jumping from the "past events leave their shadows behind" of the first, to "coming events cast their shadows before," deals in four sections with the four watches of one night. As this is literary criticism, I cannot go into the metaphysics of Joyce's new book, which are based on the history of Vico and on a new philosophy of time and space; but two other things emerge, the same preoccupation of the author with his native town, his desire to see all the universe through that small lens, and his poetic feeling for the phases of the dusk, for that twilight which originally gave the Celtic revival its name. The book opens in a museum with a mummified description of the battle of Waterloo:

"This the way to the museyroom. Mind your hats goan in! Now yiz are in the Willingdone museyroom. This is a

Prooshious gun. This is a ffrinch. Tip. This is the flag
of the Prooshious, the Cap and Soracer. This is the bullet
that byng the flag of the Prooshious. This is the ffrinch
that fire on the Bull that bang the flag of the Prooshious.
Saloos the crossgun! up with your pike and fork! Tip.
(Bullsfoot! Fine!) This is the triple-won hat of Lipoleum.
Tip. Lipoleumhat. This is the Willingdone on his same
white harse, the Cokenhape."

Monotonous as the tap of a lecturer's pole, rusty, archaic,
the old contraptions of history reveal themselves, the past
lumbers slowly into being under the touch of the chirpy
guide. The museyroom, the sightseers, moving dustily
among the dregs of the forgotten battle, clank into place
in the uncouth language; we are looking at the earth from
a long way away, perhaps as one might look at it by over-
taking the light rays—by turning a telescope on the Dark
Ages, from some planet so far that it still could watch them
going on. "Only a fadograph of a yestern scene."

So, now idler's winds turning pages on pages, annals
of themselves timing, the cycles bring fassilwise to pass
how. 1132 A.D. Men like to ants or emmets wondern
upon a groot hwide Whallfisk which lay in a Runnel.
Blubby wares up at Ublanium.

Figures emerge from the chronicle: in this early Dublin,
Irishman meets Norseman, typical of all misunderstanding
since the days of Babel. The Irishman begins:

"Hop! In the name of Anem this carl on the kopje a
parth alone who the Joebiggar be he? Forshapen his pig-
maid hoagshead, shroonk his plodsfoot, me seemeth a
dragon man. . . . He is almonthst on the kiep fieg by
here, is Comestipple Sacksounn, be it junipery or febrew-
ery, marracks or alebill, or the ramping riots of prouriose
and froriose. What a quhare soort of a mahan. It is evident the minchindaddy. He can prapsposterous the pil-
lowy way to Hirculos pillar. Scuse us, chorley guy! You
tollerday donsk? N. You tolkatiff scowegian? Nn. You
spigotty anglese? Nnn? You phonio Saxo? Nnnn. Clear all

so! Tis a Jute. Let us swop hats and excheck a few strong
verbs weak oach eather yapyazzard abast the blooty
creeks."

Jute: Yutah!

Mutt: Mukk's pleasurad.

Jute: Are you jeff?

Mutt: Somehards.

Jute: But you are not jeffmute?

Mutt: Noho. Only an utterer.

Jute: Whoa! Whoat is the matter with you?

Mutt: I became a stun a stunner.

By and by other heroes appear, Shaun the Rabelaisian
postman, sly Shem, his writer brother, H. C. Earwicker
(here comes everybody) (alias the Hill of Howth), the
typical great man of the new democracy, and his bride,
the lovely Anna Livia.

Writers are on safest ground when they confine themselves to what interests them, and the key to this obscure
and difficult book is the author's *pietas* for his native city.
Joyce's life has been nearer to the classical tradition of great
writers than to the Victorian comfort of the men of letters
of to-day. His existence resembles that of the old Greek
poets, a youth spent in city politics and local revels, then
banishment to foreign places, the publication of a masterpiece after ten years, as Dedalus promised, with his weapons "silence, exile and cunning." Now his whole art is applied to celebrating his native town, though his feeling for
Dublin, its squares and stews and beery streets, its hills and
foreshore, seagoing Liffey and greenbanked Dodder, is very
different from the provincial quality of Irish patriotism and
is more akin to the pagan sentiment of birthplace. There is
nothing flamboyant in his tender attitude to the "poor little
brittle magic nation, dim of mind."

Anna Livia is an episode from this book describing the
legend of the Liffey. Two old washerwomen stand on each
side of the stripling river and gossip away as they pound
the clothes. ("O tell me all about Anna Livia.") They talk
of Earwicker's affair with her under his other identity, of

Duke Humphrey, and gradually their language breaks into
a melody of water music, a kind of paean, like the praise
of the brook Kishon, into which the names of every conceivable river are brought in as onomatopoeic train-bearers.

> . . . She sideslipped out by a gap in the devil's glen
> while Sally her nurse was sound asleep in a shoot, and
> fell over a spillway before she found her stride and lay
> and wriggled in all the stagnant black pools of rain un-
> der a fallow coo and she laughed with her limbs all aloft
> and a whole grove of maiden hawthorns blushing and
> looking askance upon her. . . . And after that she wore
> a garland for her hair. She pleated it. She plaited it. Of
> meadow grass and river-flags, the bulrush and the water
> weed, and of fallen griefs of weeping-willow.

Occasionally the charwomen break in with their own
troubles:

> "O my back! my back! my back! I'd want to go to
> Aches-les-Pains . . . spread on your bank and I'll spread
> on mine. It's wat I'm doing. Spread! It's turning chill.
> Der went is rising."

Gradually the widening stream carries them apart as the
night falls, for they are standing on the two banks of the
infant river as on a moving stairway, and the gap between
them has widened as the Liffey leaps, in the words of her
song, "to the slobs of the Tolka and the shores of Clontarf
to hear the gay aire of my salt troublin' bay and the race
of the saywint up my ambushure." When night falls, the
old women shouting across in the dark cannot understand
each other; still gossiping, they are transformed into an elm
and a stone, the strange obscurity of the old myths from
which they have emerged gathers about them, and the
motif of the past of Ireland is re-echoed in their dumb
block-like language; for the Mookse and the Gripes had
suffered the same fate, mortal beside the immortal river:

> ". . . and it was never so thoughtful of either of them.
> And there were left now only an elm tree and but a stone.
> O! Yes! and Nuvoletta, a lass."

The end of the *Anna Livia* marks another of Joyce's extraordinary descriptions of dusk:

"Whawk? Can't hear with the waters of. The chittering waters of. Flittering bats, fieldmice bawk talk. Ho! Are you not gone ahome? What Tom Malone? Can't hear with the bawk of bats, all the liffeying waters of. Ho, talk save us! My foos wont moos. I feel as old as yonder elm. A tale told of Shaun or Shem? All Livia's daughtersons. Dark hawks hear us. Night! Night! My no head halls. I feel as heavy as yonder stone. Tell me of John or Shem? Who were Shem and Shaun the living sons and daughters of? Night now! Tell me, tell me, tell me, elm! Night night! Tell me tale of stem or stone. Beside the rivering waters of, hitherandthithering waters of. Night!"

The best way to read Joyce's new book, apart from this rare reprint of *Anna Livia,* is in a quarterly called *Transition,* edited by Americans living in Paris. The contents are often as grotesque as the idea is enterprising. But we have no paper for literary experiment in England, and literature is, after all, as technical a business as medicine or engineering. *Transition* is sometimes a silly magazine, and sometimes intensely amusing, for, like most rebel journals, its satire is on safer ground than its originality; but it is the only one which publishes the honest, sometimes fascinating, often incoherent research of those who take new literature seriously in every country. Of course, it is not possible to pronounce a verdict on Joyce's work while it is still fragmentary. The best that this article can hope to prove is that the new work of Joyce is respect-worthy and readable. There is nothing insane in its conception nor bogus in its execution. Though to many a spinster fancy it probably will continue to lack the "note for which we will be listening soon," to others it promises amusement and a most interesting and strange approach to life and beauty. In short, it is an experiment. We are content to accord the wildest tolerance to the latest unintelligible—even uncommercial—pamphlet of Einstein—can we not admit a little of the same tolerance to something in writing which we do not under-

stand? It must be remembered that Joyce, besides being a
lover of words, is an Irishman under no obligation whatever
to rest content with the English language, and also that,
while our literature, unaware of a decline of the West or a
defence of it, grows daily more bucolic and conservative,
Continental Letters are nourished on an exhilarating sense
of an uncertain future which makes the liberties of their
volcano dwellers permissible—and which we are entirely
without. Literature is in essence a series of new universes
enforced on a tardy public by their creators. This one may
be a fake, but it is not from a writer who has previously
given us fakes; it may be a failure, but it is surely an
absorbing one, and more important than any contemporary
success. I, personally, am biased as a critic by nationality,
and by the same feeling for geography and Dublin, but still
more by the enthusiasm which comes to everyone when
they discover themselves through a book—a service which
Joyce, Proust, and Gide have rendered generally to almost
all our thinking generation; for me any criticism of *Ulysses*
will be affected by a wet morning in Florence, when in
the empty library of a villa with the smell of wood-smoke,
the faint eaves-drip, I held the uncouth volume dazedly
open in the big armchair—Narcissus with his pool before
him.

April 1929

ONUS VALLIS VISIONIS

Arthur Rimbaud. By Enid Starkie. Faber and Faber, London.

This is the most complete and best-informed life of Rimbaud that I have read. Miss Starkie has had access to new material and brought a critical sense unhampered by preconceived ideas to the understanding of it. Everyone has his "theory" about Rimbaud. That of Miss Starkie is that Rimbaud was a mystic who for a period really thought that he was God, that he had found the key to existence, had reconciled good and evil, and risen superior to life; this was the period of *Bateau Ivre, Les Illuminations*, of his friendship with Verlaine, and of his missing work, *La Chasse Spirituelle*. But Rimbaud had, in imitation of Baudelaire, used too many short cuts, and his relations with Verlaine made it hard for him to sustain the illusion. In the "dark night of the soul" which followed, the *Saison en Enfer*, he wrestled with doubt about his inspiration, about the nature of his influence on Verlaine (*Délires* I) and of his "alchemy of the word" (*Délires* II). Unlike other mystics, he did not emerge from the "dark night" more conscious of the authenticity of his vision. There was no one to cry "This is my beloved son in whom I am well pleased" —on the contrary, he was shattered by it, and the victory which he thought he had won was only the acceptance of his position in life, the return to reality, *"Esclaves, ne maudissons pas la vie"*—a victory which was impoverishing and worthless to the victor. From that moment his life, in so far as it was possible, became based on conventional values, or his conception of them. He became an adventurer determined to grow rich, kind to his subordinates, quarrelsome with his superiors, anxious for news of home,

ambitious to save money, to return to France, to marry and
settle down—and his life was a double tragedy—because
in the material struggle he failed as completely as in the
spiritual. The long agony of his last illness, when, after the
amputation of his poisoned leg, he tried in vain to return
to Abyssinia, seems to parallel the anguish of the *Saison en
Enfer* when he tried to return to childhood purity and adolescent omnipotence, despite common sense. Miss Starkie
does good service in discrediting the accepted idea that
Rimbaud, after Verlaine stabbed him and went to prison,
wrote *Une Saison en Enfer* as his farewell to literature
and then at once rushed off to Abyssinia to make money,
never putting pen to paper again and hating all his old
associates. What is the truth? Rimbaud took great pains
over *Une Saison en Enfer;* it is the only considerable work
of his which he saw through the press and carefully re-
vised. He sent off presentation copies and regarded it as
the beginning of his literary career, not as the end of it.

There is no evidence that Rimbaud intended to say
a final and definitive farewell to art; it was only to be a
farewell to frenzied inspiration, to the *Théorie du Voyant*,
to *L'Alchimie du Verbe*. *"Cela s'est passé,"* he said at
the end of *L'Alchimie du Verbe*, referring to his previous
attitude to art. *"Je sais aujourd'hui saluer la beauté."*
Delahaye tells us that Rimbaud had spoken to him during the winter of 1872–3 of the new prose poems he was
going to compose, not the short prose poems of the
previous year, but poems on a grandiose scale, something
more vivid than Michelet. The general title was to be
L'Histoire Magnifique, and it was to open with scenes
called *Photographies des Temps Passées*.

It is clear from this (*Photographies* is the operative word)
that Rimbaud was moving towards a less personal form, a
literary realism. Disappointment at the reception of *Une
Saison en Enfer might*, but the life he led during the next
six years *must* have made it harder for him to go on. For
it was six years before he abandoned Europe—six years in
which he lost his looks, began to grow grey at twenty-five,
in which he lived in London with Germain Nouveau,

threatened Verlaine, became interpreter to a circus, and
year after year set out for the East, only to be repatriated
by a French consul, back to Charleville. "Verses of his?"
wrote Delahaye to Verlaine in 1875. "His inspiration has
long run dry." The Rimbaud of these six years is still the
Rimbaud of before, the boy genius, the *"époux infernal,"*
but now abandoned by the Muses, with only his faults remaining; while Rimbaud of Harar, proud of his business
reputation, his word, his efficiency, his industry and parsi-
mony, is no longer the dead husk of inspiration, but the
new kernel of reality. Miss Starkie goes very fully into Rimbaud's Abyssinian life and shows how, in the rude society
of Harar, Rimbaud was still famous for his wit, his erudition, and his anecdotes. The intellect which made him the
prize pupil of Charleville continued to mature, as his hand-
writing showed, independently of the vicissitudes of genius.
If his leg had not been poisoned, he might easily have become an important figure, a wielder of French influence
in the complicated struggle for Abyssinia, a great adminis-
trator. The letter from Ras Makonnen to Rimbaud's sister
on his death shows his hold on one great chieftain. Miss
Starkie has chapters on Baudelaire's influence on Rimbaud,
on Rimbaud *"le voyant"* and Rimbaud *"le voyou,"* on the
Cabbala, and the mysticism of Ballanches, and on the curious moving poem, *Le Cœur Supplicié*, which she claims
was the result of an unfortunate experience in the barracks
of the National Guard which was to colour his whole life.
Its symbolism substantiates this. There are some interesting illustrations, one a photograph of the young Rimbaud
which we can compare with Fantin-Latour's delicious *Coin
de Table*. The Rimbaud in the painting looks like a pensive
Botticelli angel beside Verlaine's correct, weak, ninety-ish
schoolmaster figure; the Rimbaud in the photograph is a
spiritual Dillinger. There is a full bibliography. The faults
of the book, besides a misquoting of the title of Mr.
Waugh's *Remote People* and *le* for *la* on page 182, are
iteration, amplification, and digression—a lack of distinction
in the writing and a somewhat harsh summing-up. At the
age when English writers are still qualifying for the school
magazine, Rimbaud had created at least six works of ab-

solute genius and raised problems which critics of all nations are still trying to answer. Miss Starkie has most intelligently stated them.

But everyone, as I said, has his theory about Rimbaud; I continue with some reflections after reading Miss Starkie, and rereading him.

The three great artist-writers of the nineteenth century, Baudelaire, Flaubert, Rimbaud, are all French. Beside them, as beside Tolstoy, Dostoievsky, Tchekhov, English authors—Tennyson, Browning, Thackeray, Dickens—appear amateur; incomplete and immature talents hamstrung by respectability. Keats, Shelley, Byron were the last European geniuses which England produced. They represent the romantic heyday. English literature of the nineteenth century could not improve on them. They were to dominate our poetry. English writers were not prepared to sacrifice their lives to the dictates of their artistic conscience, to be celibate like Flaubert, or to be debauched like Baudelaire and Rimbaud: they would not stand up to the matador. They represented romanticism in decay, shielded from its logical consequences by good mixing, Anglican ethics, Victorianism. Baudelaire, Rimbaud, and Flaubert are important because they made a synthesis out of romanticism and realism. Thus a hundred years after Keats we have Rupert Brooke, who is still blending a washy Keatsian romanticism with a dash of Byron. English poetry in the nineteenth century did not, except for Hopkins, in any way *progress*—but in French poetry Baudelaire had carried the romantic movement a step beyond Hugo and Lamartine, and Rimbaud taken it a step beyond Baudelaire.

Romantic poetry is the poetry of the Fall, poetry in which childhood represents a state of grace, a period of innocence, of the apprehension of beauty, and hence maturity a period of disillusion, when the sense of guilt, the knowledge of good and evil, of the conflict between soul and body, poisons everything. Romanticism is an aesthetic consequence of Platonism and Christianity, and Romantics who accept the Fall but reject Redemption take refuge in Satanism as their defeatist cult. Baudelaire tried *"les paradis artificiels,"* Rimbaud saw that it was necessary to get out-

side Christianity altogether, and so introduced the cult of
the Negro, who was untarnished by the sense of sin; his
original title for *Une Saison en Enfer* was *Livre Païen ou
Livre Nègre*. And the blame for his romanticism he placed
on his forebears, the servile Gauls, easy prey of the Church,
and on *"cette sale éducation de mon enfance."* He saw the
true nature of the problem. Romanticism is a state of mind
which has been suggested to humanity by Christian morality and which is tragic when not supported by Christian
belief, for it is the idea of Eden and the Fall, without
Paradise to round it off. It is aesthetic Calvinism. Why go
through life looking always back to childhood, why tolerate
a philosophy which envisages life as a paradise before pu-
berty, a series of ecstatic moments in early youth, and a
disastrous anticlimax, a gradation of decay after the age
of twenty-six? Why carry a burden of guilt for sins never
committed, why split oneself up into two people, an angel
and a baboon? Who cares about the childhood of Voltaire?
Of Horace, Lenin, Newton, or Julius Caesar? Why reject
maturity, and be afraid to grow up? The English pre-
Romantics, Vaughan, Traherne, Jeremy Taylor, balanced
their love of childhood by their hope of heaven. To accept
the Fall and reject Redemption is to be a scapegoat of
Christianity, victim of a confidence trick. Aware of this,
and of the need for a religion, Rimbaud had staked everything on his personal vision, and worn himself out in the
process. Had he possessed *any* money with which to miti-
gate his hardships and privations, or the leisure to gain
disciples without the necessity of admitting defeat by returning home—home where his failure to rise above his
surroundings was always rubbed in—he might have lasted
out longer, and so have made contributions to realistic literature as valuable as *Les Illuminations* have been to romantic. One cause of Rimbaud's silence was that he was
literally too poor to write, for the poverty that is tolerable
to a boy becomes for a young man a cause of self-reproach.

Technically, the English writer who most resembles
Rimbaud is Blake. How curious is the parallel between
Rimbaud's poetry and the *Songs of Innocence* and *Songs of
Experience;* between some of his prose and *The Marriage of*

Heaven and Hell, between Swedenborg and the Cabbala!
How alike their attitudes to Christianity! Even their poetic
beginnings are similar, one starting at the age of fifteen with

> How sweet I roamed from field to field
> And tasted all the summer's pride;

the other with

> Par les soirs bleus d'été j'irai dans les sentiers
> Picoté par les blés, fouler l'herbe menue.

Another cause contributing to Rimbaud's rejection of his
art which could be more deeply gone into is his use of
drugs. We know he and Verlaine experimented with drugs,
but how much, and when? Did he use opium as well as
hashish? Has some competent opium-poet, like Cocteau,
ever gone over Rimbaud's work, noticing what images and
what poems suggest the influence of the drug to him? I
have heard that opium-smokers develop an exquisite lyrical
sense, that they are capable of writing short lyrics of great
beauty, but of no sustained effort—opium-smoking painters,
for instance, tend to produce fashion-drawings. Cannot one
detect three kinds of effect in the later work—the Hit, when
the drug has liberated some subconscious memory of childhood, and the artificial paradise held the key to the *"vert
paradis"*; the Miss, when the drug sets up images which,
as communication, are meaningless, like jokes in dreams;
and thirdly, the conscious effort, written without external
stimulus, the descriptive prose poem, in which one is more
conscious of talent than of magic? Examples:

(1) *Hit.* "*Une matinée couverte en juillet. Un goût de
    cendres vole dans l'air;—une odeur de bois suant
    dans l'âtre,—les fleurs rouies—le saccage des prom-
    enades—la bruine des canaux par les champs.*"
(2) *Hit.* The whole of *Enfance*—which seems, espe-
    cially sections 2, 3, 4, to be influenced by opium
    or hashish. "*O les calvaires et les moulins du
    désert, les îles et les meules!*" "*Il y a enfin, quand
    l'on a faim et soif, quelqu'un qui vous chasse.*"
    "*Des fleurs magiques bourdonnaient,*" etc.

(3) *Miss.* All such poems as *Nocturne Vulgaire* with its clinical comment, *"Un vert et un bleu très foncés envahissent l'image"*—or such impressions as *"Oh —le pavillon en viande sanglante sur la soie des mers et des fleurs arctiques; (elles n'existent pas)—"*

(4) *Straight.* The longer prose poems, *Villes, Conte,* etc., which seem written in a different language.

If the *Illuminations* were written under the influence of drugs, then *Une Saison en Enfer* might have been written during a disintoxication, for Rimbaud could hardly obtain such things at Charleville. The depression of the cure would then form an ingredient in his despair, and the disgust at a clumsy and fallible stimulant contribute to his disillusion with the inspiration which it produced.

Verlaine and Rimbaud, the caterpillar and the ichneumon!—Verlaine's face: authority waiting to be depraved, *"que de larmes! et que de larmes encore plus tard, j'espère!";* Rimbaud's, the destroying angel. There is an element of masochism in cultured liberal society—from time to time it generates such high-powered scavengers, and when they have done their work and eaten out the decaying tissue, it turns on them.

Rimbaud's influence. Alas, it has been tardy and misdirected! If only the *jeune ménage* of Howland Street had been presented with letters of introduction in the early seventies to young Mr. Gosse, or Pater of B.N.C., how much ink and paper would have been saved! There might have been no Georgian poetry.

For the lesson to be learnt from Rimbaud is that, after him, romanticism can go no farther, a reaction is necessary, inevitable. Rimbaud himself knew this, hence his plan for the *Photographies.* Those who have been influenced by him, being romantics, have refused to see it, and used him to sanction their short cuts and excesses. They accept the lovely ejaculations and suspiria of *Les Illuminations* and ignore the concentrated realism of *Une Saison en Enfer,* like guests who look away when the bill arrives. Thus the conception of the poet as the seer opens the field to the charlatan. Surrealist poetry ignores the conclusions which Rimbaud drew from this theory, and in consequence it has not produced anything to equal him. However much Rimbaud raided the subconscious and the world of dreams, it must be remembered that he was a first-rate intellect and a ruthlessly conscious artist; his alchemy of the word was paid for in a gruelling apprenticeship, and if he took short cuts they were afterwards repudiated. Those whom he has influenced, with hardly an exception, have only ended where he began, instead of beginning where he left off. Baudelaire, Flaubert, Rimbaud, were romantic writers who were intelligent enough to purge their medium. Though occupied with problems of guilt and sin, they eliminated romantic traces from their technique, they permitted no luxuriance, vagueness, inflation, or verbosity; their sentiment is never false. To jot down nostalgic dreams, to flaunt a private damnation, a Delphic obscurity, will no more make a Rimbaud than an arrangement of dots will produce a Seurat. What must remain supreme in Rimbaud is the fusion of romantic imagination, militant thought and verbal mastery into, in his best passages, a precision of inspiration.

C'est le repos éclairé, ni fièvre, ni langueur, sur le lit ou sur
    le pré.
C'est l'ami ni ardent ni faible. L'ami.
C'est l'aimée ni tourmentante ni tourmentée. L'aimée.
L'air et le monde point cherchés. La vie.

August 1938

THE ART OF BEING GOOD: A NOTE ON MAUGHAM AND FORSTER

I. *The Razor's Edge.* By W. Somerset Maugham. Heinemann.

This is Mr. Maugham's best novel since *Cakes and Ale,* and, appearing at a time when the decline in literary quality is fairly matched by the decline in literary taste, it breathes the atmosphere of another world.

The novel is a considerable addition to the literature of non-attachment, and ranks with Huxley's *Grey Eminence* and Heard's *Man the Master* as powerful propaganda for the new faith or, rather, new version of an old faith, which is called by various names—neo-Brahmanism, or the Vedanta of the West—and which has made its home in somewhat macabre proximity to Hollywood. This does not mean that Mr. Maugham "has been converted by Gerald Heard" and so forth, for in all his previous work there has always been a strong inclination to mysticism and an ill-concealed sympathy for those who turn their back on the world. Mr. Maugham's gallery of bums and beachcombers, his sanguine study in *The Moon and Sixpence,* his interest in the Spanish mystics in *Don Fernando* and in various Eastern types of holy man, proclaim this obsession through all his work. He is the worldliest of our novelists, and yet is fascinated by those who renounce the world, whether to do nothing, to become artists, to be a Communist as in *Christmas Holiday,* or a saint as in *The Razor's Edge.* The book is indeed a study in pre-sanctity in the early years of a man whom the author hints is capable of saving the world, if it will ever listen—and it is part of his sanctity that Larry should be in many ways very like everybody else, a delightful, simple, single-minded Krishnamurti from the Middle

West. Since he is to be tempted, we have also pictures of the World and the Flesh: the world in the form of Elliot Templeton, most perfectly drawn of all the characters; the genial, infinitely painstaking romantic snob, with Catholic and discreetly homosexual leanings, whose magnificent but empty career of social success Mr. Maugham paints with lingering tenderness, right down to the wonderful death-scene which is a kind of farewell offering to his old corrupt world of Paris and the Riviera, whose eclipse he would seem here both to acknowledge and to regret.

The flesh appears in the guise of three women: Isabel, Elliot's niece, an admirably drawn American girl, charming and sensitive when first engaged to Larry, but moulded by the conditions of moneyed American life into a chic, beautiful, greedy, heartless woman, typical of all well-dressed, noisy, yet withal warm and honest, machine-tooled cosmopolitans. It is Isabel's tragedy to know that Larry, whom she rejected as a suitor because he was poor, is the only man who really attracts her and can bring out her own potentialities. The two other women are Sophie Macdonald, the type of American girl gone to the bad—drink, drugs, sailors—out of the violence of her disappointment with life; and Suzanne Rouvier, Mr. Maugham's familiar female character, the honest whore. She represents the charm and common sense, the fundamentally worth-while values of French civilization, as contrasted with the depravity of American, as typified by the worldly Elliot, the savage Isabel, the nymphomaniac Sophie, and Isabel's simple, money-making husband Gray. These are the material the young saint (who, however, is also an American) must get to work on. On the whole, he is not a success, for in this presanctity stage, in his commonplace, somewhat priggish, larval form, he is chiefly concerned with getting away from people like these and trying to find the truth by reading and travel, manual labour and meditation. He is enlightened by a holy man in southern India, and the lovely descriptions of this country make some of the pleasantest reading in the book. They also present Mr. Maugham with his hardest problem, that of conveying the mystical experience, that explosive which has so far defied all rational analysis. I think that, on the whole, for a writer who is not a mystic, he has managed to do this: he conveys well the passionate quest for truth which consumes Larry's whole life and which originates in his experiences as a pilot in the last war, when he made the discovery that "the dead look so terribly dead when they're dead." Thus the moment of faith to which it leads up comes as no surprise. But of what faith? This seems to me the real difficulty: to a sceptical mind it seems doubtful whether human beings actually possess the apparatus which can discover truth, and when they pin it down in a doctrine there is always a sense of disappointment. Now, the neo-Brahmans of Hollywood have a doctrine, and that doctrine embraces a considerable amount of Hindu religion and Yoga mysticisms, so Larry has to believe in the transmigration of souls, in Brahma, Vishnu and Siva, and Mr. Maugham's attempt to make this convincing seems far more disastrous than his penetrating criticism of Christianity or the mystical experience which he previously described. A ridiculous hypnotic trick, an example of suggestion, is made use of as a "sign" of power, and the vision of Larry's previous selves also fails to convince. It would have been better for the novel not to have confined Larry to any known religious system: to let him have his revelation and then leave it at that.

The Razor's Edge shows a great technical improvement on the author's recent novels. He handles his four or five characters to perfection, and includes himself—not as a fictional character—but as the flesh-and-blood Willie Maugham of real life, with complete mastery. Here is a novelist right inside his own novel—not a mere stooge or onlooker, or larger than life, as a *deus ex machina,* but on the same plane as all the other characters, not more real nor less—a brilliant feat, carried off with quiet mastery. The too short staccato sentences which often mar his style have also been expanded; there is less of "I have a notion," and the writing is delightfully flexible, vivid and easy. Everything appears haphazard, yet everything is to the point. Maugham is the greatest living short-story writer, and so one expects his handling of plot to force one into a breathless, non-stop reading from the first page to the last, and his character-drawing and observation to be in the fine tradition—but one would not expect to be so captivated by the brilliant fluency of the writing. Here at last is a great writer, on the threshold of old age, determined to tell the truth in a form which releases all the possibilities of his art. His comments and asides excite us in their justice and sometimes by their rancour. He has, for example, a note of particular asperity whenever there is any question of the standing of writers in the social world. If there is one thing to regret about this novel it is that it is written not for us but for Americans: one detects a considerable amount of playing down to the transatlantic common man and a faintly disapproving attitude to Europe and this country. Mr. Maugham has never been a master of words; he has always preferred the *mot moyen* to the *mot juste;* he is incapable of those flights of vocabulary which we find in the great living stylists: Logan Pearsall Smith, E. M. Forster, Max Beerbohm; but even he should know better than to use "exquisitely gowned" or various slangy expressions (not in dialogue but in the author's musings) which are already out of date. Yet if his book is written for Americans, it is certainly a tract for them! Never have their weak points been so tactfully yet remorselessly suggested—Mr. Maugham never forgets the spiritual dust-bowl which every American carries within him, and which he vainly tries to irrigate with alcohol, statistics, or labour-saving devices. "I have a notion," Mr. Maugham seems to say, "that the new Messiah is going to have his work cut out." Here is his final judgment:

> Larry has been absorbed, as he wished, into that tumultuous conglomeration of humanity, distracted by so many conflicting interests, so lost in the world's confusion, so wishful of good, so cocksure on the outside, so diffident within, so kind, so hard, so trustful and so cagey, so mean and so generous, which is the people of the United States.

It has puzzled me, considering the sheer delight that I and all my friends have received from this novel, that it has been so uncharitably reviewed. Are we becoming incapable of recognizing excellence when we see it? I think prejudice is to blame—prejudice against any book which so perfectly recaptures the graces that have vanished, and against any writer who is so obviously not content with the banal routine of self-esteem and habit, graced by occasional orgies of nationalism and herd-celebrations, with which most of us, from the lovely Isabels and exquisite Elliot Templetons, down to the tame gravel-throwing apes of Fleet Street, fidget away our one-and-only lives.

II. The Undeveloped Heart.

"To write simply," says Mr. Somerset Maugham, "is as difficult as to be good." One might add that to write badly is as natural as to do evil, if we accept Baudelaire's definition: *Le mal se fait sans effort, naturellement, le bien est toujours produit d'un art.*

But supposing the connection is even closer—supposing it were true, as the Victorians and some of the ancient Greeks believed, that to write simply it is necessary to be good; that virtue has the best style—what a burden of right conduct would be laid on the already overburdened tribe of authors! Yet that, I think, is what Mr. Forster believes, and certainly it is the secret of his art. For Mr. Forster, whose great-grandfather was a pillar of the Clapham Sect, is in everything he writes a moralist, a militant tractarian who in all his novels and stories not only blatantly rewards the good and punishes the wicked, but (in a long series of personal asides) distributes marks and awards points on his characters' behaviour and actions.

So much is clear; here in an age whose values are blurred is a writer with a creed—not a creed, like Mr. Maugham's, of Oriental fatalism—but a vigorous and clear-cut ethical system. What is not so clear is how it may be defined. But it is through such a definition of this creed that we can best understand Mr. Forster, and a very clear one has just been advanced by Dr. Trilling, an American professor of English literature and author of a book on Matthew Arnold, whose

E. M. Forster is now published in England by the Hogarth Press.

> Sawston-Tonbridge [he writes] may have made Forster miserable, but it gave his thought its great central theme. This is the theme of the undeveloped heart. In his essay, "Notes on the English Character," Forster speaks of the public school system as being at the root of England's worst national faults and most grievous political errors. For, he says, the faults of England are the faults of the middle classes that dominate it, and the very core of these middle classes is the English public school system, which gives its young men a weight out of all proportion to their numbers and sends them into a world "of whose richness and subtlety they have no conception," a world into which they go "with well-developed bodies, fairly developed minds, and undeveloped hearts."

> The theme is almost obsessive with Forster. It is not the unfeeling or perverted heart that absorbs him, but the heart untrained and untutored, the heart checked too early in its natural possible growth. His whole literary effort is a research into this profound pathology.

Bearing this interpretation in mind let us continue our inquiry into Mr. Forster's religion. Here is the first sentence of one of his early stories, a sentence which also illustrates what is meant by writing simply and writing well.

> Few things have been more beautiful than my note-book on the Deist Controversy as it fell downward through the waters of the Mediterranean. It dived, like a piece of black slate, but opened soon, disclosing leaves of pale green, which quivered into blue. Now it had vanished, now it was a piece of magical india-rubber stretching out to infinity, now it was a book again, but bigger than the book of all knowledge. It grew more fantastic as it reached the bottom, where a puff of sand welcomed it and obscured it from view. But it reappeared, quite sane though a little tremulous, lying decently open on its back, while unseen fingers fidgeted among its leaves.

"It is such a pity," said my aunt, "that you will not finish your work in the hotel. Then you would be free to enjoy yourself and this would never have happened."

What can we conclude from this passage? First let us notice the rapid vivid impressionist character of the writing. This is typical of all his work. Then the exactness of his observation and the felicity of his imagery—"like a piece of black slate"—"magical india-rubber stretching out to infinity"—and so on. Then a kind of ascetic delight which is the particular hall-mark of his sensibility: Mr. Forster sees the world not so much as a child but as a poet who is in training, who neither drinks nor smokes nor obscures his vision with any form of self-indulgence; his eyesight is extraordinarily good, whether he is looking at the Blue Grotto or at the hypocrisy which lurks concealed in a cluster of mixed motives. Now we come to the ethical content. What happens in this sentence? A notebook (full of obsolete academic information obtained in a northern university) falls into the blue southern sea and becomes, for the first time in its existence, an object of beauty. The owner of the notebook experiences a sense of release and exhilaration in which the author obviously shares; an Anglo-Saxon aunt, however, misses the point and immediately makes a reproving remark.

Here already is much of Mr. Forster's religion. The notebook is Culture (Culture not so much for its own sake as for some academic preferment), the sea is Life, the owner of the notebook is English Youth, and the Aunt is English governing-class authority. On the next page the naked Italian boatman dives for it, and he will then represent the pagan element of beauty and natural desire. Forster is always on the side of life; always against authority, puritans, prigs, and pedants—he is continually making clear to us the choice between life and the cultivation of class or money, comparing the spontaneous and living with the neatly fossilized dead. For culture-prigs, those who exclaim *"procul este profani!"* or "oh, what a good boy am I!" he reserves his most vibrant arrows.

His religion, in fact, in its early stage is an Hellenistic

paganism in which there are no dualities; death is a friend
—beauty and goodness and impulse are one. Youth, helped
perhaps by a sensitive old lady, is right, and age, convention, privilege and success are generally wrong. The Aunt
(or Uncle), the Italian Diver, the Youth torn between the
South and the demands of his family, constantly reappear.
One might say that Mr. Forster's religion is a primitive
pantheistic paganism to which has been afterwards added
an Oriental preoccupation with non-attachment and abnegation, all worked upon by his inherited moral temperament. Pan is led by conventional English standards of
decency to the Krishna of the Bhagavad-Gita; the Greek
religion whose origins were in the East is traced back to its
source.

Dr. Trilling writes at length of one of Forster's short
stories, *The Eternal Moment*, which is also one of his most
perfect works, stamped throughout with his moral insight,
his lyricism, and ascetic vitality. It is an attack on our civilization; on its well-meaning destructiveness and its money-
values. Miss Raby, a successful novelist, with an admiring
and sensitive friend, Colonel Leyland, returns to the village
in which she had once been made love to by her Italian
guide. The village, now grown popular through her book,
has become a tourist-ridden and corrupt Dolomite capital.
The Italian guide has evolved into the concierge of the big
hotel: she realizes that, for an eternal moment in the past,
she had loved him, and tries to tell him so. The concierge is
deeply embarrassed and alarmed by her. Colonel Leyland,
even more shocked at her class betrayal, opens his wallet,
taps his head and so connives in the idea that she is mad.
If we think how Proust, or Maugham, or Hemingway, or
other male novelists would have treated this story we see
that they would all really have thought such an elderly
lady insane, victim of a temporary sexual aberration, and
that none of them would have seen anything vile in the
colonel's gesture, nor anything inherently ignoble in the
concierge's position. To Proust a concierge was a kind of
fashionable cardinal. But to Forster, who is a moralist, a
concierge is a wicked thing. Miss Raby, who by writing her
best-seller has made it possible for the mountain guide to

become a plump concierge, has indeed betrayed life, and
has every reason to take the blame.

> He opened the windows, he filled the match-boxes, he
> flicked the little tables with a duster, always keeping an
> eye on the door in case anyone arrived without luggage,
> or left without paying. . . . She watched the man
> spreading out the postcards, helpful yet not obtrusive,
> alert yet deferential. She watched him make the bishop
> buy more than he wanted. This was the man who had
> talked of love to her upon the mountain. But hitherto he
> had only revealed his identity by chance gestures be-
> queathed to him at birth. Intercourse with the gentle
> classes had required new qualities—civility, omniscience,
> imperturbability. It was the old answer: the gentle classes
> were responsible for him. It was absurd to blame Feo for
> his worldliness—for his essential vulgarity. He had not
> made himself.

This leads us on from Forster's ethical to his political
sense. For he is a political writer who prefers unpolitical
themes: his two best novels, *Howards End* (which Dr.
Trilling says is about "who shall inherit England") and *Passage to India*, are, for all their romantic interest, tales of the
barricades and the class war, and Forster, acutely though
he sees the weaknesses of the under-privileged, remains un-
questionably on their side. What Miss Raby hated about
Feo's hostelry, the *Grand Hôtel des Alpes*, were "the ostentatious lounge, the polished walnut bureau, the vast
rack for the bedroom keys, the panoramic bedroom crock-
ery, the uniforms of the officials, and the smell of smart
people—which is to some nostrils quite as depressing as the
smell of poor ones."

"The uniforms of the officials, and the smell of smart people"—all his life Forster will detest these, for he is somewhat
more than a liberal in politics: he is a libertarian. Though
he believes in original sin and feels the contempt of those
who share this belief for those who don't, he also believes
in human dignity, courage and freedom—given the right
conditions. "Death destroys a man," he says in *Howards
End*, "but the idea of death saves him—that is the best ac-

count of it that has yet been given." As a philosopher Forster may be sceptical about progress; as a political being he is much more than sceptical about reactionaries, militarists, millionaires, pharisees, and bureaucrats. We are lucky to possess what amounts to the creed of this artist-philosopher, in his pamphlet *What I Believe* (Hogarth Press, 6d.). He "doesn't believe in Belief," but he does believe in (1) Personal Relations; (2) Democracy; (3) Aristocracy, "an aristocracy of the sensitive, the considerate, and the plucky. Its members are to be found in all nations and classes, and all through the ages, and there is a secret understanding between them when they meet. They represent the true human tradition, the one permanent victory of our queer race over cruelty and chaos."

In his golden pamphlet Forster also mentions what he does *not* believe in—heroes, great men, leaders, Christianity, autocracy, asceticism, intolerance, and the State—and here too he enounces his slogan—his act of faith. "The people I respect must behave as if they were immortal and as if society were eternal. Both assumptions are false: both of them must be accepted as true if we are to go on working and eating and loving, and are to keep open a few breathing holes for the human spirit."

In a world of masters and slaves both Maugham and Forster have escaped to the minority of the free. Maugham, the cynic, is sentimental about his hero's goodness; Forster, the progressive liberal, sees virtue warily as something which, so lax have we become, has to be punctiliously enforced, like vaccination. Maugham has bought his freedom through hard work and popular success. "The value of money," he remarks, "is that with it we can tell any man to go to the devil." It is "the sixth sense which enables you to enjoy the other five." Forster's freedom is based on money also, for he has never had to earn his living, but he has also learnt to make do with very little, to purchase freedom through an exacting conscience, a detached passion for the life of the spirit and (this is common to Maugham also) an attitude to the State which can best be described as one of quiet effrontery. Long life to them!

THE ANT-LION

The Maures are my favourite mountains, a range of old rounded mammalian granite which rise three thousand feet above the coast of Provence. In summer they are covered by dark forests of cork and pine, with paler interludes on the northern slopes of bright splay-trunked chestnut, and an undergrowth of arbutus and bracken. There is always water in the Maures, and the mountains are green throughout the summer, never baked like the limestone, or like the Southern Alps a slagheap of gritty oyster-shell. They swim in a golden light in which the radiant ebony green of their vegetation stands out against the sky, a region hardly inhabited, yet friendly as those dazzling landscapes of Claude and Poussin, in which shepherds and sailors from antique ships meander under incongruous elms. Harmonies of light and colour, drip of water over fern; they inculcate in those who stay long in the Midi, and whose brains are addled by iodine, a habit of moralizing, a brooding about causes. What makes men divide up into nations and go to war? Why do they live in cities? And what is the true relationship between Nature and Man?

The beaches of the Maures are of white sand, wide, with a ribbon of umbrella-pines, below which juicy mesembryanthemum and dry flowers of the sand stretch to within a yard of the sea. Lying there amid the pacific blues and greens one shuts the eyes and opens them on the white surface: the vague blurred philosophizing continues. Animism, pantheism, images of the earth soaring through space with the swerve of a ping-pong ball circulate in the head; the woolly brain meddles with ethics. No more power, no aggression, no intolerance. All must be free. Then whizz! A disturbance. Under the eye the soil is pitted into a conical depression, about the size of a candle extinguisher, down whose walls the sand trickles gently, moved by a suspicion of wind. Whizz, and a clot is hurled to the top again, the bottom of the funnel cleared, in disobedience to the natural law! As the funnel silts up it is cleared by another whirr, and there appears, at the nadir of the cone, a brown pair of curved earwig horns, antlers of a giant earwig that churn the sand upwards like a steam shovel.

Now an ant is traversing the dangerous *arête*. He sidles, slithers, and goes fumbling down the Wall of Death to the waiting chopper. Snap! He struggles up, mounting the steep banking grain by grain as it shelves beneath him, till a new eruption is engineered by his waiting enemy. Sand belches out, the avalanche engulfs him, the horny sickles contract and disappear with their beady victim under the whiteness. Mystery, frustration, tragedy, death are then at large in this peaceful wilderness! Can the aggressive instinct be analysed out of those clippers? Or its lethal headpiece be removed by a more equitable distribution of raw materials? The funnels, I observe, are all round me. The sand is pockmarked with these geometrical death-traps, engineering triumphs of insect art. And this horsefly might be used for an experiment. I shove it downwards. The claws seize on a wing, and the struggle is on. The fight proceeds like an atrocity of chemical warfare. The great fly threshes the soil with its wings, it buzzes and drones while the sand heaves round its propellers and the facets of its giant projectors glitter with light. But the clippers do not relax, and disappear tugging the fly beneath the surface. The threshing continues, a faint buzzing comes from the invisible horsefly, and its undercarriage appears, with legs waving. Will it take off? The wings of the insect bomber pound the air, the fly starts forward and upwards, and hauls after it—O fiend, embodiment of evil! A creature whose clippers are joined to a muscle-bound thorax and a vile yellow armour-plated body, squat and powerful, with a beetle set of legs to manœuvre this engine of destruction. The Tank with a Mind now scuttles backwards in reverse, the stern, then the legs disappear, then the jaws which drag its prey. Legs beat the ground. A fainter wheeze and whirr, no hope now, the last wing-tip vanished, the air colder, the pines greener, the cone empty except for the trickle, the sifting and silting down the funnel of the grains of pearl-coloured sand.

Nature arranged this; bestowed on the Ant-Lion its dredging skill and its cannon-ball service. How can it tell, buried except for the striking choppers, that the pebble which rolls down has to be volleyed out of the death-trap, while the approaching ant must be collected by gentle eruptions, dismayed by a perpetual sandy shower? And, answer as usual, we do not know.

Yet the relationship between the Ant-Lion and the curving beaches of Pampelone suggests a parallel. This time at Albi. Here Art and Nature have formed one of the most harmonious scenes in Europe. The fortress cathedral, the Bishop's Palace with its hanging gardens, and the old bridge, all of ancient brick, blend into the tawny landscape through which the emancipated Tarn flows from its gorges to the Garonne. Here again one wanders through this dream of the Middle Ages, by precincts of the rosy cathedral where the pious buzz like cockchafers, to be brought up by a notice on the portcullis of the Bishop's Palace. "Musée Toulouse-Lautrec." Tucked in the conventional Gothic of the fortress is a suite of long rooms in which the mother of the artist, using all her feudal powers, forced the municipal authorities to hang the pictures of her son. Less fortunate than those of Aix, who refused Cézanne's request to leave his pictures to the city, the fathers were intimidated by the Countess into placing them in this most sacred corner, lighted and hung in salons whose decoration has concealed all traces of the unsightly past.

The concierge turns proudly to the Early Work—pastoral scenes and sentimental evocations of Millet—these he likes best; they are what the Count was doing before he left his home and was corrupted by the Capital. Then come the drawings, in which emerges the fine savage line of the mature artist, that bold, but not (as in some of the paintings) vulgar stroke, which hits off the brutality of his subjects, or the beauty of those young girls doomed to such an inevitable end. In the large room beyond are the paintings, a morgue of End of Century vice, a succession of canvases in which there is hardly daylight, and where the only crea-

ture who lives by day is the wizened little Irish jockey.
The world of the hunchback Count is nocturnal, gas-lit,
racy, depraved and vicious; the shocked Albigeois who pass
through the gallery are riveted by the extraordinary picture of the laundress who checks over with the *sous-
maîtresse* the linen from her Maison. As one goes from picture to picture the atmosphere intensifies, Valentin le
Désossé and La Goulue become familiars, and the lovely
girls blur into the dark of the Moulin Rouge, where one
distinguishes a favourite figure, the long, sad, nocturnal,
utterly empty but doggedly boring face of "L'Anglais,"—
some English habitué to whom constant all-night attend-
ance has given the polish of a sentry at his post.

At the end of the gallery is a door before which the
concierge smiles mysteriously, as if to prepare us for
Pompeian revelations. He opens it, and we emerge on a
small terrace. The sun is shining, the sky is blue, the Tarn
ripples underneath. Beyond the ancient brick of the bishop's
citadel and the arches of the bridge stretches the landscape
of the Albigeois—foothills of green corn delicately crowned
by pink hill villages, which merge into the brown of the
distant Cévennes under the pale penetrating light of the
near-south, the transitional-Mediterranean. A lovely and
healthy prospect, in which fields and cities of men blend
everywhere into the earth and the sunshine. One takes a
deep breath, when obstinately, from behind the closed
door, one feels a suction; attraction fights repulsion as in
the cold wavering opposition between the like poles of a
magnet. Deep in his lair the Ant-Lion is at work; the hunchback Count recalls us; the world of poverty, greed, bad
air, consumption, and of those who never go to bed awaits,
but there awaits also an artist's integration of it, a world in
which all trace of sentiment or decadence is excluded by
the realism of the painter, and the vitality of his line. In
the sunlight on the terrace we are given the choice between
the world of Nature and the world of Art. Nature seems
to win, but at the moment of victory there is something
lacking, and it is that lack which only the unnatural world
inside can supply—progress, for example, for the view from
the Palace has not altered, except slightly to deteriorate,

for several hundred years. The enjoyment of it requires no more perception than had Erasmus, while the art of Lautrec is modern, and can be appreciated only by those who combine a certain kind of aristocratic satisfaction at human beings acting in character, and in gross character, with the love of fine drawing and colour.

Not that Lautrec was a great artist; he is to Degas what Maupassant is to Flaubert, one who extended the noble conception of realism by which a great master accepts the world as it is for the sake of its dynamism, and for the passive, extraordinarily responsive quality of that world to the artist who has learnt how to impose his will on it. The world of Lautrec is artificial because it excludes goodness and beauty as carefully as it excludes the sun. But it is an arranged world, a world of melancholy and ignorance (figures melancholy because ignorant, patient in the treadmill of pleasure), and so the artist drags us in from the terrace because force and intelligence dominate that arrangement. And once back, we are back in his dream, in a hunchback's dream of the world; the sunlight seems tawdry, the red brick vulgar, the palace ornate; the crowd who stand in their tall hats gaping at the blossoming Can-Can dancers are in the only place worth being.

Now I understand the Ant-Lion. It is in Nature and with a natural right to its existence. There is no conflict between them; it is an advanced gadget in the scheme which includes the peaceful hills and the beach with its reedy pools of brackish water. Nor is there any opposition between Lautrec and the landscape of Albi. Albi was the oyster, and the contents of the museum are the Pearl. The irritant? The action of a physical deformity on an aristocratic, artistic but unoriginal mind which was happiest in the company of its inferiors, and which liked to be surrounded by the opposite sex in places where the deformity could be concealed by potency, or by the distribution of money. The result, a highly specialized painter, one of Nature's very latest experiments. And yet even that peaceful landscape was the home in the Middle Ages of a subversive doctrine, the Albigensian heresy; a primitive anarchism which taught that men were equal and free, which disbelieved in violence and believed in a chosen priesthood, in the Cathari who attained purity by abstinence, while they encouraged the Count's royal ancestors to come through excess and indulgence to heavenly wisdom. It was they who believed that the human race should cease to procreate, and so solve the problem of evil, who were massacred at Muret and Lavaur, and whom Simon de Montfort slaughtered with the remark, "The Lord will know his own." And the Heretics were right. Had a revolt against procreation spread outwards from Albi the world would have become an empty place, nor would such obstinate human beings who survived have been driven to kill each other for living-room, victims, for all we may know, of some deeper instinct of self-destruction which bids them make way for a new experiment, the civilization of the termite or the rat.

Much has happened since the summer. To-day the Maures are out of bounds, the Museum closed, and many generalizations based on incorrect assessment of the facts fallen to pieces, but (since the operations of the Ant-Lion have now been extended) it seems worth while to recall that the statements on the life of pleasure which Lautrec took from his witnesses at the Tabarin and the Moulin de la Galette, and which he so vigorously recorded on canvas, are still available to the traveller of the future, and assert their truth.

December 1939

RECONSIDERATIONS

ON REREADING PETRONIUS

I first read Petronius when I was at school, and though I had no idea what most of it was about I had two editions by the time I left, two more a year later and two more since then, but it was only the other day I read him for the first time since that elm-heavy summer thirty years ago. I was perfectly right. It is a very great book.

Not great, perhaps, magical is a better word and, something even rarer, it is a humane book. Imagine that nothing at all survived of our literature but one or two poems and histories and a long novel like Proust's of which only a few disjointed fragments reached posterity and formed the only record of how we talked or loved or ate or felt about poetry or painting or friendship or money. Imagine a few remarks of the Duc de Guermantes or some head waiter as all that was known about our pronunciation, together with a dinner party at Mme. Verdurin's coming down intact, with a crepuscular glimpse of Swann and Odette, Marcel and Albertine; how our posterity would pore over every sentence. Yet, though in Petronius we possess a fragmentary Roman Proust, how few have studied him; how little known to generations of boring novelists is the secret of his rapidity of style, of his visual clarity, biting dialogue, intellectual fastidiousness or of the haunting fugacity of the picaresque —that art which keeps characters on the move from waterfront to waterfront, brothel to palace, adventure to adventure. "I dimly saw Giton standing on the curve of the road in the dark and hurried towards him." Thus we are introduced to one of the principal characters. I think a study of such a book could help many young writers to give movement and montage to their characters, the lilt of transience which is the breath of readability.

There are at least four Petroniuses whom for convenience

we have rolled into one. 1) The historical Petronius of Tacitus, 2) the author of the *Satyricon*, 3) the author of the prose fragments and 4) the writer of some separate poems. The fragments (preserved by grammarians) indicate that he came from Marseille, a place, as Tacitus said, "where Greek refinement and provincial puritanism meet in a happy blend" but the fragments are all dated very much later, and one of the puzzles about this extraordinary book is that it would seem, even in antiquity, to have been very little known. The *Satyricon* itself tells us nothing about the author except that he is looking at low life from a standpoint which is above it and that he is very interested in a poet who must be Lucan. Trimalchio tries to sing a song by Menecrates whom Nero greatly admired. The Petronius of Tacitus is a historical figure, the artist in extravagance, the dandy who idled into fame and who after being an efficient proconsul in Bithynia became the arbiter of Nero's pleasures until he aroused the jealousy of Tigellinus. When he found the plot against him had succeeded, he committed suicide at Cumae, "the finest death" according to Saint-Evremond "in all antiquity." "The reflection arises at once," writes his editor, Mr. Michael Heseltine, "that, given the *Satyricon*, this kind of book postulates this kind of author."

We then have a picture of a great nobleman such as haunted Versailles or perhaps like Charles II's Lord Rochester, poet and lover of low life who finds time between governing Asia and amusing his Imperial master to write an enormously long work of which we possess fragments only of Books 15 and 16. There may have been twenty-two like the *Odyssey*. He belongs to a strange world: to the little group of writers who effect the transition between the Augustan age and silver Latin. The next generation, Tacitus, Suetonius, Juvenal, Martial, the younger Pliny and Quintilian came through the tunnel of the terror into the prolonged sunlight of the Antonines, but our group all come to violent ends. Seneca, Petronius and Lucan were forced by Nero to kill themselves, Persius died very young, and the elder Pliny perished in the eruption of Vesuvius. As far as the arts are concerned the Rome of the Julio-Claudian emperors was only at the very beginning of decadence.

There is nothing *fin-de-siécle* about Petronius, rather an enormous gusto. What was the *Satyricon's* real subject? Is Trimalchio's banquet a parody of Nero's entertainments or is it written especially to amuse him together with the hostile criticism of Lucan? Is it a *roman à clef*? I think myself that like James Joyce's *Ulysses*, it had something to do with Greek literature; the fragments we possess all deal with Greek-speaking cities, especially those which are on, or near, the sea. There are lecturers called Agamemnon and Menelaus, a charmer called Circe with a maid called Chryseis. The four main characters and a great many minor ones have Greek names and a theme runs through it like a parody of epic doom: The Wrath of Priapus. Encolpius (whose name means "cuddlesome") is the narrator, a young man with literary ambitions and all the physical graces; high-tempered but quick to forgive and with a deep and constant affection for his young companion Giton and some kind of tie with a rival, Ascyltos, who might be described as a neurotic hearty. There are also men of learning who gravitate around the three adolescents and several insatiable ladies of fashion. Though the tone is homosexual, the *Satyricon*, as Saint-Evremond remarked, is the only classical work where "*galanterie*" appears in the relation of the two sexes, as in the delicious exchange of letters between Circe and Polyaenus. Encolpius has been in trouble at some time: "I fled from justice, I cheated the arena, I killed my host," he moans, and Ascyltos calls him "a filthy gladiator who was kicked out of the ring, one who strikes people in the dark." He has robbed a shrine of its sacred images, and he is constantly profaning the mysteries of Priapus, who punishes him by a psychological impotence which he remedies with difficulty only to infringe the sacred rites once more. When the story opens we find him at Cumae, near Naples; later on, the three learned scallywags sail round to Croton on the instep of Italy. Fragments allude to Marseille and Egypt and there is a reference to a quarrel in the Porch of Hercules which indicates Rome. Encolpius, I think, was an Epicurean: Epicurus is mentioned as "divine" and as the "very father of truth." And when Encolpius has to take another name he chooses

Polyaenus, a disciple of Epicurus, while only an Epicurean could proclaim "at all times and in all places I have so lived that I have spent each day as if it were my last." I think we were meant to appreciate a conflict between the sunny reasonable sceptical attitude of Encolpius and the Dark God whom he provokes, and the God's priestesses with their superstitious rages and horrible medicines.

The novel is written in alternate passages of prose and verse which produce a peculiar effect rather like a staccato recitatif which leads up to an aria, but the verse arias are not as memorable as the prose recitatif; they are less tense and vivid; good minor poetry and nothing more. I would like to give an example of the prose which holds, I think, something of the magic of this novel. Encolpius is speaking:

I came into a gallery hung with a wonderful collection of various pictures. I saw the works of Zeuxis not yet overcome by the defacement of time, and I studied with a certain terrified wonder the rough drawings of Protogenes, which rivalled the truth of Nature herself. But when I came to the work of Apelles the Greek which is called the One-legged, I positively worshipped it. For the outlines of his figures were defined with such subtle accuracy that you would have declared that he had painted their souls as well.

I cried out as if I were in a desert, among these faces of mere painted lovers, "so even the Gods feel love. Jupiter in his heavenly home could find no object for his passion, and came down on earth to sin, yet did no one any harm. The Nymph who ravished Hylas would have restrained her passion had she believed that Hercules would come to dispute her claim. Apollo recalled the ghost of a boy into a flower, and all the stories tell of love's embraces without a rival. But I have taken for my comrade a friend more cruel than Lycurgus himself."

Suddenly, as I strove thus with the empty air, a white-haired old man came into the gallery. His face was troubled but there seemed to be the promise of some great thing about him; though he was shabby in appearance, so that it was quite plain by this characteristic that he was a man of letters, of the kind that rich men hate. He came and stood by my side . . .

"I am a poet," he said, "and one, I hope, of no mean imagination. . . ."

"Trimalchio's supper" is rather topheavy for the book as we possess it. I think the important character is Encolpius and he has to be kept in constant motion. What a prose writer he is—of a fine lady's tears "when this designing rain had ceased." *"Tam ambitiosus detumuit imber"* and his Existentialist reflection on the drowned merchant who happens to be the only virtuous character. "Make a fair reckoning and you find shipwreck everywhere" (*si calculum bene ponas, ubique naufragium*).

Petronius died in A.D. 66 and Herculaneum was engulfed in A.D. 79. There was just time for the *Satyricon* to get into one of those libraries in the "Sirenland" which its author loved. If the world cared anything for literature, we might live to see a sustained effort of the United Nations to excavate all that the lava has buried—buried and not always burned—and perhaps then the missing volumes will turn up. I know that I would sacrifice any cargo the space-ships bring back from Venus or all the mineral on the moon for a sight of those rolls in their charred cases, and a few more episodes of these aesthetes in adventure. In the picture gallery Eumolpus said that in an age that worshipped drink, sex and money there could be no more great art; people would no longer take the trouble to write well and would rather earn a gold ingot than own an Old Master. Like many whose gaze is fixed with longing on the past, he was apt to find himself looking into the future.

FRANÇOIS VILLON

Poems of François Villon. Translated by Norman Cameron. Jonathan Cape.

An obstinate sadness hangs about the death of the Middle Ages as about the end of winter; something harsh and rude lingers on, a bank of blackening snow while primrose and violet bloom elsewhere. So it is with the France of Louis XI: Chaucer has long since flourished, and Petrarch and Boccaccio; across the Alps the high Renaissance is in full bloom, but no whisper of it has reached murky Paris, a frost-pocket of feudal strife and academic obscurantism; there, in 1438, fourteen people were devoured by wolves in one night, secret police and inquisition burrowed and perjurers were boiled in oil.

A hundred years of war had impoverished it and another hundred were to elapse before the laughter and grace of Rabelais and Ronsard; yet from this indigence of flesh and spirit rose one of the great lyric poets of all time.

First of us all and sweetest singer born
Whose far shrill note the world of new men hears
Cleave the cold shuddering shade as twilight clears . . .

Several qualities distinguish François Villon from all other poets; he is not, like some aesthetes, *"l'ami du criminel,"* but in his own right a robber and a murderer, a member of the dreaded rogues' fraternity of "La Coquille." Hence the note of genuine ferocity in his scenes of low life, the sincerity of his visions of goodness and his moments of remorse. When a poet has three times been condemned to death and has bitten on the *"poire d'angoisse"* (the gag which is thrust on those who wait for torture) he will speak of grief and passion with authority. Villon is an absolutely personal poet, his best work is all autobiographical and when we open him, he is with us in the room:

Finally as I sat here writing
at nine o'clock this night, alone
and merry, these bequests inditing,
I heard the bell of the Sorbonne,
as always at this hour, intone
the angel's message of salvation:
whereat I laid my labours down
to pray at my own heart's dictation.

Yet this most Catholic poet reflects the decline of the
Age of Faith, the Dance of Death is in all he writes; the
corruption of the Church, the fires of justice and man's
mortality seem to blot out the fair Christian vision. No poet
has so loved the underworld, the underdog, the old, the
outcast and the poor. In spite of his personal and romantic
attitude this inspired gangster has a dominating sense of
form. His poetry is ornate, classical to perfection, riddled
with elaborate rhyme and acrostic; his feelings bubble
forth with divine simplicity, but his wit is intricate with
double meaning and his compression is the translator's despair. Notice the exquisite line, three from the end of this
verse, which telescopes the brief glory of old courtesans
with the cheap fires they sit by. *"C'est d'humaine beaulté
l'issue . . ."*

Ainsi le bon temps regretons
Entre nous, povres vieilles sottes
Assises bas, à crouppetons
Tout en un tas comme pelotes
A petit feu de chenevottes
Tôt allumées, tôt éteintes;
Et jadis fûmes si mignottes
Ainsi on prend à mains et maintes.

So we make moan for the old sweet days
Poor old light women, two or three
Squatting above the straw-fires' blaze,
The bosom crushed against the knee.
Like fagots on a heap we be,
Round fires soon lit, soon quenched and done;
And we were once so sweet, even we!
Thus fareth many and many an one.

Thus Swinburne, now for Mr. Cameron:

> Tis thus we mourn for good old days,
> Perch'd on our buttocks, wretched crones,
> Huddled together by the blaze
> Of some poor fire of forest cones,
> That dies as quickly as our moans,
> A briefly-lit, brief-living flame—
> We who have sat on lover's thrones! . . .
> With many a man 'tis just the same.

Notice how well Swinburne recovers from a sentimental start, how each fails at *"mains et maintes"* and deviates from literal meaning over *"pelote"* and *"chenevotte"* to suit their rhyme.

In translating these ballads Swinburne has the better of it, but the value of Mr. Cameron's book (value which would be double were the French included) lies in his translation of the whole of Villon's work from the difficult archaic original into a living seventeenth-century diction. In England we know the ballads well, but are much too ignorant of the exquisite chains of stanzas in which these jewels are set. Villon's eight-line narrative verse, with its rich rhymes, its changing moods and sighing caesuras is like the monotonous music of raindrops in the lulls and gusts of the southwest gale, and in the long lament for his youth it reaches the heights of great poetry:

> I mourn the season of my youth
> (in which I revell'd more than most
> Before old age had brought me ruth).
> Youth drank with me no final toast;
> It did not march on foot, nor post
> Away on horse; how did it go?
> Suddenly in the sky 'twas lost,
> And left no parting gift below . . . .

Mr. Cameron's translation is generally admirable; his achievement is a most timely benefit and should bring many back to an artist by whom our favourite poets have been inspired, and whose secret of fire, melody, wit and pathos is so disastrously lost.

ADDISON REVISITED

The Life of Joseph Addison. By Peter Smithers. Oxford.

Fifteen years ago I called Addison some harsh names. Now, with the deeper humility and wider tolerance of middle age, and with what I dare to hope is riper judgment, I have returned, under the spell of Mr. Smithers' monumental biography, to take a second look at the statesman essayist in his serene ascent from Addison's Walk to Addison Road.

He is worse than I ever remembered. "A parson in a tye-wig," a tea-table philosopher, a crazy-pavement Montaigne, a money-loving placeman and devotee of good form, good sense and good salesmanship, and creator of the armchaired, affluent, decorous and dim-witted bourgeoisie of letters, this premature Forsyte has wielded an influence as mediocre as it is fatal. Tangential to three men of genius, Swift, Pope and Congreve, the arc of his ambition was circumscribed by a talent eminently genteel and, like that of so many soft-voiced careerists, quietly ruthless.

Mr. Smithers has devoted many years and a splendid book to his honour. Let me say at once that it is a labour of love and will long remain the standard life. Unlike most people who have written about Addison, Mr. Smithers has grasped the central situation. His hero had set himself the Roman ideal of being a complete man; a Cato or Cicero who served the state, made his fortune, and cultivated the urbane art of letters. He was a young don who went into politics at a time when a new party had vacancies for talent.

Seen from this angle his whole career falls into place. Nothing whets the appetite for power like being a clergyman's son. A Fellow of Magdalen at an early age, Addison forsook Oxford, went abroad as a tutor and fitted himself for the diplomatic service, profiting from his influence and abilities to become an Under-Secretary for Foreign Affairs while his party was in power, and afterwards Chief Secretary for Ireland (twice), and finally Secretary of State.

Voltaire and the French (and many English since) considered the rise to power of Addison as proof of our enlightened love of literature. The truth is otherwise. For a very few years both parties had need of highly educated pamphleteers, and Addison, like Prior, was a diplomatist rather than a poet by profession. He was cautious, discreet, hard-working, high-principled, astute, loyal to his superiors, devoted to his friends and underlings and a great success in several delicate undertakings.

It is only when applied to the literary life that such qualities are shown in a bad light, as in Pope's lines on Atticus. There, talent, integrity, charm and influence are not enough. "Every name which kindness or interest once raised too high," wrote Johnson of him, "is in danger, lest the next age should, by the vengeance of criticism, sink it in the same proportion"—and Addison was not merely flattered but wrongfully praised by his contemporaries for poetry which is in fact singularly uninspiring and essays which seemed original but contained largely the new tricks and truisms of literary journalism.

The problem of Addison's prose style deserves a chapter to itself. "Whoever wishes to attain an English style familiar but not coarse, and elegant but not ostentatious," wrote Johnson, "must give his days and nights to the volumes of Addison," and Mr. Somerset Maugham tells us that he formed his own style on Addison's cadences. On the other hand Mr. Eliot and Mr. C. S. Lewis regard him with a kind of horror. The truth is that his style is simple, fresh and musical and his essays are constructed on a classical pattern of reason, grace and measure. The content is, however, somewhat thin, the product of an engaging fancy but not of a first-rate mind, and tinged with priggishness. At times, as in the famous passage on the Abbey tombs, it does strike out a genuine music, though more often it imitates itself. Mr. Smithers does not go into this deeply, preferring to consider the political career, the success of *Cato* and *The Spectator* and the absorbing flux of Augustan politics. He deals admirably with the literary quarrels, and I only hope the year will bring other biographies of such richness and lucid intellectual detachment.

COLERIDGE

Coleridge. By Humphrey House. Rupert Hart-Davis.

Somebody should write an essay on the cult of Coleridge, one of the strangest phenomena of modern times. Here is a man who was accounted a failure and who accounted himself a failure, sick, neurotic, frustrated, author of some lovely but fragmentary poems, mouthpiece of German metaphysicians, eclipsed by Wordsworth during his lifetime, by Keats after his death, a whale stranded on the nineteenth-century sea-front: and now, owing to the devotion of editors and critics, emerging as the greatest of them all, almost the subject of a new religion.

Sir Herbert Read hails him as the founder of modern scientific criticism—the true inventor of existentialism, *"Gestalt"* and Jung's Collective Unconscious, as well as the greatest of transcendentalists and precursor of Freud: large volumes are written about the genesis of his poems, the implications of his prose; every scrap is treasured, every erasure annotated.

"One of the great seminal minds of the nineteenth century," Mr. House calls him, and he is coming into his own as our national sage, a worthy antagonist to Goethe and Voltaire. His failure clothes him in refreshing mists like a fog-ridden mountain of problematic altitude, whereas every stone on their summits is numbered and worn threadbare. "There is something inherently mean in action," he wrote. "The Almighty more or less made a mistake in creating the universe." There is consequently nothing mean about Coleridge. He is the least vulgar of writers; every hint of accomplishment disappears in that great lachrymose, self-pitying eye. His failures are on a giant scale, as if he failed for our sakes that we might raid his huge quarries and carry off the half-finished blocks without guilt of plagiarism:

> Hitherto, I have laid my eggs with ostrich careless-
> ness and ostrich oblivion—the greater part indeed have
> been crushed underfoot; but some have crawled to light
> to furnish feathers for other men's caps and not a few
> to plume the shafts of the quivers of my calumniators.

When I try to analyse my own strong prejudice against Coleridge, I find that it springs from my inability to under-stand metaphysics and consequent dislike of them, an im-patience with his dilapidated existence which betrays a fear of it and above all from my horror of *The Ancient Mar-iner*. I cannot believe that this is a good poem. I cannot believe that the sensitive ears which are ravished by the prose melodies of Coleridge or the delicacy of some of his blank verse can support this barbarous jingle. Yet they do.

"This is made fully apparent," writes Mr. House, "in that wonderful pair of stanzas in which the thought and verse are in shape identical, but with opposite content":

> And I had done a hellish thing
> And it would work 'em woe:
> For all averred I had killed the bird
> That made the breeze to blow.
> Ah wretch! said they, the bird to slay
> That made the breeze to blow!
>
> Nor dim nor red, like God's own head,
> The glorious Sun uprist:
> Then all averred, I had killed the bird
> That brought the fog and mist.
> 'Twas right, said they, such birds to slay,
> That bring the fog and mist.

The first four lines seem to me like the patter of a comedian, the beginning of the second stanza contorted and ambigu-ous and the opposing sentiments of the sailors equally life-less. Surely such a stanza (which was to lead Oscar Wilde astray in *Reading Gaol*) belongs to the small change of poetry and enforces too many rhymes and repetitions to sustain a long poem? How can it be compared with a contemporary expression of the same sentiments like Wordsworth's *Hart-Leap Well?*

Mr. House's lectures, however, have been converting me to Coleridge and are completing the good work begun by Sir Herbert Read's eulogies. It is through the notebooks and the letters that one begins to love him, and Mr. House is an authority on these notebooks, most of which have never been published:

> I write melancholy, always melancholy: you will suspect that it is the fault of my natural Temper. Alas! no —this is the great Cross in that my Nature is made for Joy—impelling me to Joyance—and I never—never can yield to it—I am a genuine Tantalus.

Coleridge in fact stands head and shoulders above all other guilty men, patron saint of those artists (and they include the most exquisite) who are prevented not so much by vanity and sloth from committing themselves to masterpieces as from a deep horror of enjoying themselves. Perfection is the Albatross they fear to slay:

> I was followed up and down by a frightful pale woman who, I thought, wanted to kiss me, and had the property of giving a shameful Disease by breathing on the face.

This is a guilt dream, it is Coleridge who pursues his Muse, fearful of contaminating her with the sickness of being himself.

In one fragment I might hazard a conjecture. "O Sara wherefore am I not happy," he writes in his notebook one stormy night, "why for years have I not enjoyed one pure and sincere pleasure! one full joy!—one genuine Delight, that rings sharp to the Beat of the Finger!—all cracked, and dull with base Alloy—*Di boni! mihi vim et virtutem vel tu . . . ehue! perdite. . . .* But still have said to the poetic Feeling when it has awakened in the Heart. 'Go! Come tomorrow.' " The dots represent erased Latin words—did he perhaps write *"Perdidi musam tacendo,"* "I have lost the

Muse by my silence," quoted from the *Pervergilium Veneris?*

But not all these fascinating notes are depressing:

> Fowls at table—the last dinner at Gallow Hill, when you drest the two fowls in that delicious white sauce which when very ill is the only idea of food that does not make me sicker.

Mr. House is the most understanding of critics, and his interpretation of *Frost at Midnight* and of the first version of the *Ode to Dejection* increases the stature of the poem and the poet. What can one say of this magnificent romantic youth, who carries intuition and lucidity with him into the long years when he has been deserted by inspiration, and who so perfectly dissects his own condition?

> Instead of a covey of poetic partridges with whirring wings of music or wild ducks shaping their rapid flight in forms always regular (a still better image of verse) up came a metaphysical bustard, urging its slow, heavy, laborious, earth-skimming flight over dreary and level wastes . . .

"Do not call him poor Coleridge!" Lamb was right. "Call him Coleridge."

STENDHAL'S LETTERS

To the Happy Few. Selected Letters of Stendhal. John Lehmann.

There should be a pale blue wrapper round certain books meaning, "You can read your way out of anything with this. It is another world and a better." A red wrapper would mean, "Another world, but a sadder." Thus the letters of Flaubert are magnificent but harrowing, the correspondence of Baudelaire slow torture—only in the world of Stendhal do we sail away to forty years of good-humour. "Apart from this everything goes well: we have not seen a woman since the postmistresses of Poland, but by way of compensation, we are great connoisseurs of fires"—so he begins the retreat from Moscow. "I, too, have had a grapple with the void. It is only the immediate experience which is disagreeable, and the horror of it comes from all the silly nonsense that is put into our heads at the age of three" —so he announces his last illness, with the strange prophecy of his end: "There is nothing ridiculous about dying in the street, provided one does not do it on purpose."

Though he considered himself an unhappy man, and felt boredom as only artists can, he had a sunny and optimistic disposition, and he had imbibed from his grandfather (like George Sand) something of the rational art of happiness of the eighteenth century. Of the three writers in the age of transition who grew up under Napoleon and led the way to modern literature, Stendhal is the most solid and indestructible. Constant could not fertilise a whole generation by *Adolphe* alone, Chateaubriand formed a delicate, sombre leaf-mould round Flaubert and Baudelaire. The writers influenced by Beyle's *"On me lira vers 1880"* are still emerging.

"My habitual state of being is that of one unhappily in love who adores music and painting. I have set an exquisite sensibility to seek out beautiful landscapes. That has been the only object of my travels. I have valued contemplation above everything else, even a reputation for wit." Such is the romantic Stendhal's definition of himself. But there are two others: the realist and the man of action. The realist could observe the unhappy love affairs of the romantic while conducting the consulship of Civita Vecchia, enjoying Roman balls, analysing political trends and satirising social follies. The man of action had the makings of a hero and fell with Napoleon in 1815.

In every work by Stendhal we can perceive the fusion of these personalities, which exist in rather different proportions in Balzac and Delacroix. On the whole, the realist predominates, and gives a somewhat flinty aroma, a whiff of the garrulous and lonely old bachelor to the correspondence: but the inclusion of many love letters in this book redeems the *coté boulevard* by a *coté salon*, and Stendhal was fortunate to live at a time when love still had its dangers and drawing rooms their magic, so that the abandonment of the pursuit of glory was not embittering. He wrote very few letters about his books, and the three drafts of his acknowledgment of Balzac's great tribute to the *Chartreuse de Parme* are almost an autobiography. His correspondents were chiefly worldly and beautiful women or worldly and cynical men. It is regrettable that the superb exchange with Merrimée published by "Fontaine" is not included, but in the letters to Di Fiore we find a charming relationship, with a cultivated younger man, which went on until his death.

I am not a Beylolater, I need a *fond noir à contenter* in my hero, but of all those without one, the seed of Epicurus, Stendhal is the least stupid. We can never dismiss him as insensitive or shallow. He has the quality, which Norman Douglas inherited from him in his travel books, of a serene acceptance of himself and of the universe, coupled with a prickly wit, critical curiosity and a deep reverence for love and youth and courage. He deserved to know Byron, to dig up Etruscan tombs and find a bust of Tiberius. Could

Horace have said good-bye better? "I have great hopes of recovery. Nevertheless I want to say farewell to you, in case this letter may be the *ultima*. I truly love you, and you are not one of a crowd. Farewell, take events cheerfully as they come."

BALZAC IN ENGLISH

Lost Illusions. Honoré de Balzac. Translated by Kathleen Raine. John Lehmann.

There has been no translation of the *Comédie Humaine* into English in this century. Every generation requires its own rendering of the great books of the past. These three volumes in one make an excellent beginning. Kathleen Raine's translation is smooth, readable, vivid and accurate.

The book has one serious defect. The third volume of the trilogy is a dull anticlimax. "I recommend the reader to take this section as fast as he can," writes Mr. Raymond Mortimer in his introduction. But why include it? The third volume should have been *Splendeurs et Misères* and deal with the hero's return to Paris, not with the undeserved misfortunes of a provincial printer. Pace and interest need not have been sacrificed.

Having made this complaint, let us abandon ourselves to the marvellous talent of Balzac. At first we set out slowly and quietly on our magic voyage. Gradually the enchanted universe of the *Comédie Humaine* grows nearer and clearer; ultimately we are engulfed by it. Once more we live through the great theme of the French romantic novel (whether by Balzac, Flaubert or Proust), the conquest of Parisian society, glittering and poisonous as a moonlit *datura*, by the handsome young poet and lover who one day will turn and trample on it.

* * *

What separates Balzac completely from other novelists of the period, like Thackeray, Scott, Dickens, Dumas, is that he is a great and conscious artist who cares intensely about the writer's situation. Lucien de Rubempré, coming to Paris in 1821 when a little younger than the century, with a bourgeois father and a noble mother, penniless and consumed with literary and social ambition, is faced at once with the same predicament which many a young writer who wishes to live by his pen and go out in the evenings is tackling today. Shall he invest in a dinner jacket? Or the big Oxford Dictionary? How can he write if he does not learn about society? How can he go out in society without more money than writing can bring in?

The greatness of Balzac lies in his having, like all romantics who survive, both experienced and surmounted every temptation. His account of journalism is of something more evil and corrupting than we have to face, even as his picture of the great world describes rewards which are now beyond our reach. *A Provincial Celebrity in Paris*, the second of these volumes, seems even now a work of pure genius, a marvellous morality for all who have inhaled, as age creeps on, the miasma of their wasted time. The indictment deepens through the book: "I know Lucien! He wants the harvests without the toil—that is his nature. Social duties will eat up his time and time is the capital of those whose intelligence is their only fortune. . . ." "Every writer goes about with a parasite in his heart, a sort of tapeworm which eats up his feelings as they hatch. Which will survive, the parasite or the man? As talent increases the heart dries up. Any man who is not a colossus is left at the end, either without heart or without talent. You are fragile and delicate: it will break you."

> Lucien walked home, turning over in his mind that terrible verdict, whose profound truth seemed to him to throw light on the literary profession.
> "Money!" a voice kept crying. . . .

The passage illustrates Balzac's intuitive knowledge of damnation. The insoluble dilemma, the death of the heart, is sketched out in two or three sentences; and then the abrupt transition—not to repentance but to a new kind of crime—as "the beat of that great pendulum money struck like a hammer, blow after blow, on his mind and heart."

The retribution which overtakes Lucien is perhaps over-indulged in. The misery he causes those nearest him is over-coloured even as the insincerity of his own remorse is most subtly portrayed. Alas for great novelists—one and all they are dominated by evil: Lucien, Charlus, Emma Bovary, Becky Sharp, infallibly the active and wicked steal the lime-light from the virtuous. Balzac's good characters may love virtue; their creator is obsessed by vice. Greed, lust, re-venge, treason: a gong seems to sound in his prose when they are touched upon. The illusions which are lost are those of first love and poetic glory, the ones which remain are of vanity and worldly success. For great novelists have need of society and so must re-create it, and cannot allow it to perish entirely in the flame of their satire.

The supreme greatness of Balzac resides in his grand romantic conception of life, which is never weakened but rather illuminated by his own intellectual disillusion. Lucien seems entirely destroyed by his trip to Paris; but, after all, he is but twenty; the illusions re-form in clearer focus; for him life is only just beginning. The romantic's last word is never said.

DELACROIX

The Journal of Eugène Delacroix. Introduction by Hubert Wellington; translated by Lucy Norton. Phaidon Press.

It was Baudelaire who compared Delacroix in society to the crater of a volcano artificially concealed by a clump of flowers, even as it was he who seized the fundamental nature of his genius. *"Une passion immense doublée d'une volonté formidable, tel était l'homme."* This was, of course, the passion of the Romantics, but the will power sprang from the cold and intellectual desire for perfection which led him to reject almost every quality of the French Romantics except their sense of pageantry and drama. He was the first to suspect their idea of progress and belief in inspiration, as Flaubert and Baudelaire were afterwards to do, and thus to affirm the particular note of the nineteenth century with which we are in harmony.

Finding Voltaire shallow and Hugo pompous he had to create an ideal companion—himself—even as, disliking at the beginning of his life the classicism of Ingres and at the end the realism of Courbet, he became the one painter to bridge the gulf between them. He is one of those artists whom one cannot call A or B because they belong to the genus AB. He worships not only Rubens, Michelangelo, and Shakespeare but also Raphael, Racine, Mozart and Voltaire.

His heredity is revealing: his mother belonged to a family of royal furniture-makers, the Oebens and Rieseners; his putative father was a lawyer who signed the death warrant of Louis XVI; his real father is supposed to have been Talleyrand. The great minister certainly used some of his influence to help the family and made things easy for the unsuspecting young painter by that secret assistance, the providing of which, according to Balzac, is one of the few

pleasures we can share with the gods. Besides a strong
physical resemblance, some of the qualities of the diplomat
are certainly present—scepticism, dandyism, detachment,
sensuality, contempt for human nature and tact; but no
two worlds remain mutually more exclusive than the
power-haunted political society of the father and the vision
of the lonely artist who could write of his studio, "All my
ambition is bounded by these walls."

The "Journal" of Delacroix consists of one very early section, which might have been kept by any art student of
high fancy, and a long interior monologue from which the
year 1848 is unfortunately missing. The present edition,
admirably introduced and translated, reduces the three
French volumes to four hundred pages of India paper
which fit in the pocket. The notes could be fuller: thus it
would help to be told that Clesinger's "daguerreotype in
sculpture" was the famous nude of Mme. Sabatier, that the
Duc de Morny was a natural grandson of Talleyrand, that
it was Gounod's *Faust* which the painter disliked, and so
on. But after this charming edition it is unlikely that it will
be necessary to translate or abridge these journals again.

And what of the journal itself? It is a painter's, not a
writer's diary, two-thirds of it technical, and so it lacks the
tragic brilliance of Baudelaire's journals or the wrought-iron
gossip column of the Goncourts. It is a painter's record of
his impressions and difficulties, the self-portrait of a proud
and aloof artist who opposes the times in which he lives
and who regards mechanical inventions as disasters and the
desire for change as a disease of the human spirit. The message of the journal is stoical: "The practice of an art demands a man's whole self." Work, work, work, he proclaims,
and meditate on the great ones. All else is vanity and boredom. "Evening party at the Tuileries. I came home feeling
even sadder than after poor Visconti's funeral. The faces of
these rogues and worthless women make me sick; their
flunkeys' souls hidden under their embroidered uniforms."

Like many great and isolated figures, Delacroix builds a
kind of Pantheon for himself: for Mozart's music he has to
emerge, for his worship of Rubens there is an occasional
pilgrimage to Belgium, for the sea there is Dieppe, but the

true life is within. "I have been saying to myself and I cannot say it too often for my happiness and tranquility (they are one and the same) that I must and can live only through the mind; the food it needs is more necessary than bodily food."

Nature, however, is a consolation to him which makes up for society, and he recommends looking at the sea as the perfect cure for boredom. "Water, water of which I never grow tired: I feel a continual longing to plunge into it, to be a bird, a tree whose roots are steeped in it, to be anything except an unhappy, sick, bored old man."

In pursuit of music, Delacroix would have to go out at night. Unfortunately for us he describes his friends too briefly. A combat between a fly and a spider or some ants and a beetle is minutely rendered, but what can we infer from such an entry as "went to call on Madame Sand. That good-natured fellow Chopin played for us," or "M. Baudelaire called just as I was starting work. . . . His views seem exceedingly modern and progressive."

Yet it was Baudelaire, had Delacroix known, who was to draw a far more life-like portrait of the artist than the diaries furnish, depersonalised as they are, by the artist's classical reserve and by that deep reverence for the masterpieces of the past which inhibited the display of his own accomplishments. Beneath the endless bouquets for Mozart and Michelangelo, Rubens and Racine, the volcano rumbles. Sometimes there is an explosion. "He's always scheming to make money out of small pictures. He's finished! He's beginning to say: 'It's too late now' like all lazy people who have been in the habit of saying confidently, 'I've got plenty of time.'"

A BAUDELAIRE CONUNDRUM

The cult of French literature during the war was a feverish gesture of solidarity, a protest against isolation. Since then a reaction has set in and I doubt if more interest is shown in contemporary French writing here than our neighbours take in ours. The war names—Sartre, Malraux, Camus, Genet, Michaux, Paulhan—are always sure of a hearing, but we no longer keep up with the new magazines or grapple with the young poets, any more than we read and re-read the once consoling and endangered classics or travel with Racine or Rabelais in our pocket. At the same time we must go on reading French; the habit is unbreakable, for we need a literature whose authors do not live on Green Line bus routes or lunch at their clubs, whose civilization is observed through a sheet of glass. We have never experienced anything like the vivarium of Versailles, the salons or the Terror, the battle of *Hernani* or Mallarmé's Tuesdays; we have no café life. When we read too much English literature we grow depressed by the unalterable bourgeois scene which has survived so many literary groups, even as it will outlast our own. Oxford common-rooms, London squares, Sussex cottages, sausages, landladies, publishers' cocktail parties, Sunday afternoons—one can fit almost every English writer into the familiar mould; tea is being served behind the house with the blue plaque as expertly as when the great man lived there, be he Addison or Gosse, Colley Cibber or George Moore. Thackeray or Gray or Pater are not so far removed from us in manners and habits as Valéry or Gide or Proust. My favourite writers are those whose sensibility is more modern than their surroundings, who, like Baudelaire or Flaubert, died just before it became necessary to wear a collar and tie and whose floppy cravats are almost the last we see before the universal dinginess of modern neckwear enforces equality.

* * *

Both are authors whom one can read and indeed write about for ever. Among the strangest phenomena of French literature today are the lives dedicated to nineteenth-century authors by their twentieth-century disciples. Crépet on Baudelaire, Dumesnil on Flaubert, Martineau on Stendhal, Mondor on Mallarmé—they are not so much latter-day Boswells as projections into the present of the personalities of these old masters, the genius of the dead artist appearing to re-create itself into a devastating arrangement of consciousness which seizes hold of the living mind and invests it like a fortress. When we study how a dead writer was occupied every day of his life we know him better than he knew himself, and such knowledge can be dangerous. We know now why Mme. Schlesinger could not permit herself to love Flaubert. (Her worthless husband had legitimized her child by marrying her and gained a moral hold of which Flaubert had no inkling.) We know now that when Baudelaire resolves to visit Flaubert at Croisset, his will is not equal to the voyage; we know, with each move into some cheap hotel, exactly how many other cheap hotels lie ahead of him.

A scholar's life is a lasting concern, and when it is entirely devoted to the study of one man the few outstanding mysteries attain an exaggerated importance. A lacuna in Baudelaire's adolescence, his attempted suicide, the true nature of his relationship with Jeanne or of her lost letters to him obsess and harry the patient investigators to whom all the rest is daylight. That three-letter dedication of *Les Paradis Artificiels*, how it torments them! "À 'J.G.F.'" "It's quite impossible to suppose for a moment that it could ever have been intended for such a vulgar creature as Jeanne Duval, one so completely indifferent to poetry," writes M. le Dantec (editor of the "Pléiade" Baudelaire) when referring to the appearance of these strange initials over the poem *Héautontimorouménos* in the second edition of the *Fleurs du Mal*. Others have pointed out that the preface to the *Paradis Artificiels* would be entirely above Jeanne's head from the very first sentence. *"Ma chère amie—Le Bon Sens nous dit que les choses de la terre n'existent que bien peu, et que la vraie réalité n'est que dans les rêves."* What is needed in fact is a refined and cultivated muse with a philosophical turn of mind who has shared some of the poet's extra-sensory expeditions into the world of hashish and opium. The existence of such a paragon was established by a letter to M. Porché (another Baudelairian) from a M. Robert Jacquet, who said he was both the grandson of a painter and the nephew of a lady who had been entrusted with the confidences of a Mme. Juliette Gex-Fagon, to whom Baudelaire had been introduced in the Louvre by the sculptor Pradier. Pradier (who had also presented Flaubert to Louise Colet) died in 1852. Mme. Gex-Fagon lived on the Île St. Louis, on the quai d'Anjou, while Baudelaire was near at hand in the Hôtel Pimodan; she had copper-coloured hair, a rose carnation skin, a mind avid of sensations and a naïve affection for the poet. It was not, however, a love affair but a romantic friendship. She hoped to save his soul and, in gratitude for her care in the opium dens, he reminded this Electra in the dedication of de Quincey's friendship for Anne: *"tu devineras la gratitude d'un autre Oreste dont tu as souvent surveillé les cauchemars et de qui tu dissipais d'une main légère et maternelle le sommeil épouvantable."* When the *Paradis* appeared in 1860 and the new *Fleurs* in 1861 bearing the mysterious dedications, Mme. Gex-Fagon may have been dying. We learn that the dedicatee was ill, one *"qui tourne maintenant tous ses regards vers le ciel, ce lieu de toutes les transfigurations."*

❋   ❋   ❋

It would seem that the mystery is now solved were it not for the odd fact that M. Jacquet gave no address and that M. Porché was unable (by 1943) to verify his assertions or even his identity. Let us now examine the evidence for Jeanne. In the *Héautontimorouménos* (which was originally intended as an epilogue to the *Fleurs du Mal*, and whose title is taken from *Terence*, by de Quincey) Baude-

laire tries to explain his sadomasochistic temperament to
his victim and to justify the suffering he has inflicted. *"Je
suis la plaie et le couteau,"* and the dedication to *Les
Paradis* also concerns a woman whose love has been of the
deepest significance to him, *"C'est à une qui, quoique
malade, est toujours active et vivante en moi."* Now Jeanne
had indeed been very ill and taken to the hospital with a
stroke in 1859, and M. Crépet is convinced that the two
dedications were acts of reparation on Baudelaire's part,
protestations of a new friendship, remorseful courtesies for
the ruined, ailing quadroon whose disintegration he records
at the same time in the marvellous sonnet sequence, *Un
Fantôme*. As is often the case the dedication is a kind of
epitaph, though Baudelaire was to continue to live with her
"en papa et tuteur." In that case to write above her head,
to pay her classical compliments, to assume that she was
of the élite who "find happiness an emetic," is to honour
her, to treat her on a level with Gautier and the other dedi-
catees and thus to rebuke the friends who considered her
an evil and stultifying influence:

> Les stupides mortels qui l'ont jugée amère.

And he writes to his mother at this moment (October
1860) that for eighteen months he had only been kept from
suicide because he could not bear to leave Jeanne penniless,
"cette vieille beauté transformée en infirme." If the J.G.F.
of *Les Paradis* is indeed Jeanne (and the publisher Poulet-
Malassis thought so), it remains but to solve the meaning
of the initials. Here again there are two schools. M. Crépet
suggested that they referred to the initials of her real name
or else *"À Jeanne, généreuse, grande, ou glorieuse femme,"*
while M. Mouquet and M. Pommier have opted for *"À
Jeanne, gentille femme,"* a romantic archaicism employed
in an early dedication used either by Baudelaire or his
friend Privat d'Anglemont. To this solution M. Crépet eventually rallied.

*   *   *

But *"À Jeanne, gentille femme"* seems hardly worth so
much mystification and appears to lack the aroma of se-

crecy which initials usually possess. I should like to make
one more suggestion.

Letter to Poulet-Malassis, 3 May, 1860

Maintenant, je ne blague pas. Une terreur me prend,
relativement à la note pharmaceutique de la fin. Ré-
fléchissez-y-bien. Il suffit de la malveillance d'un méchant
bougre, dans quelque sale journal, pour nous créer un
embarras. [Reference to a chemist's advertisement on the
preparation of opium or hashish which was to terminate
the *Paradis Artificiels* and for which he might be
prosecuted.]

Je pense à la tireuse des cartes, qui m'avait prédit que
j'allais recontrer une fille très grande, très mince, très
brune, agée de . . . . Or, je l'ai rencontrée.

Vous connaissez son autre prédiction. Il est encore
temps. La dédicace, c'est J.G.F. Préparez donc C à ma
visite.

To the Same. No date.

Mon cher,

Voici le billet D; j'espère que vous avez écrit aujourd'-
hui un mot à C que j'irai voir demain. Ne vous moquez
pas de moi, à cause de mes histoires de tireuse de cartes.
Qu'y aurait-il d'étonnant dans ce fait qu'un agent trop
zélé trouvât immoral qu'à la suite d'un livre sur l'opium
et le haschisch on indiquât les différentes préparations
des substances et les différents avantages ou incommo-
dités attachés à chacune d'elles?

It would seem that a fortune-teller had once made two
predictions: that he would go to prison (?), as might happen were he to be prosecuted again for an immoral book,
and that he would meet *"une fille très grande, très mince,
très brune."* An exact description of Jeanne Duval. "J.G.F.,"
then, refers to his private destiny: *"À Jeanne, ma grande
fille"* (in a letter of December, 1859, he addresses her as
"ma chère fille"), and the initials can also be traced in the
last line of the dedicatory sonnet which brought her cycle
to an end (*"Je te donne ces vers"*):

Statue aux yeux de jais, grand ange au front d'airain.

The fortune-teller may even be the *"vieille hydropique"* whose evil-scented pack contained the "handsome knave of hearts and the queen of spades" whose sombre talk of their dead love in his most splenetic sonnet symbolized their decaying passion.

But there is still a possibility that the visit was quite a recent one, that the prediction referred to yet another dark, tall, thin beauty whom he had met since Jeanne's illness in 1859, a name in the carnet, an Aglae or Agathe, a Negress like the Laure whom he brought to sit for Manet and that irony, the *"poison noir"* of the *"victime-bourreau"* in J.G.F.'s poem has triumphed over his commentators: *"Il importe d'ailleurs fort peu que la raison de cette dédicace soit comprise,"* he writes in Les Paradis, and in a rough draft he is even more explicit: *"Je désire que cette dédicace soit inintelligible."*

ARNOLD BENNETT

Works of Arnold Bennett: *The Old Wives' Tale; Clay-hanger; Anna of the Five Towns; Riceyman Steps; Grand Babylon Hotel; The Journals.* Penguin Books.

By the enterprise of Sir Allen Lane,[1] who has published five representative novels and a selection of the diaries, all introduced by the faithful Mr. Swinnerton, Arnold Bennett has been exhumed, like a mammoth in an ice-pack, a quarter of a century after his death. It is now the turn of the critic to pronounce on the remains. Are they indeed those of the fabulous, fearsome monster on whose like we shall not look again, or do we but perceive the amiable, bun-weary eye of an old circus-performer?

If we may take note of the significant way in which names are grouped together we notice that while Meredith, Conrad, Hardy, Henry James are somehow on one side, Shaw, Wells, Bennett, Galsworthy, Maugham are of another. An invisible watershed runs between them, as between poverty and riches, introvert and extrovert, aesthete and publicist, novelist-poet and novelist-playwright. The first group are mammoths, the second are people like ourselves who happen to be very much more talented, or industrious or successful. Realism was then in the air and the unpalatable fiction of Maupassant and Zola became magnificently anglicised in long leisurely saleable novels, half-autobiographical, half-documentation, which the Edwardian reader trundled through as if he were playing the pianola.

The Old Wives' Tale, The Way of All Flesh, Of Human Bondage, The Forsyte Saga, Mr. Polly, all depict the revolutionary transition from Victorian society to modern

[1] The publisher of Penguin Books.

times. I had never read *The Old Wives' Tale* before, nor had I realized the extent of Bennett's debt to the French naturalist school (or to George Moore's English adaptations of it). I should like to feel it was a great book, but I cannot. Words, words, words—two hundred thousand of them to be precise—all the clumsy paraphernalia of the family chronicle: the death of old Mr. So-and-so, the arrival of the first bicycle, tram, motor-car, aeroplane, the little jokes of Great-Aunt Such-and-such, the boys going up in the world, the old devoted servants, the younger, less devoted servants, the full-length dog-gallery, the apoplexies and elopements, the wars and revolutions filtered through the provincial gaslight, the white hair and sunken cheeks slapped on the principal characters from time to time to age them up a bit, the startling, fatal symptom which precedes the inevitable death scene.

Two executions, two strokes, one pneumonia, one rheumatic fever, one exhaustion and some senile decay—canine —enliven *The Old Wives' Tale* as against only one birth.

Against this must be set the high conception and general readability of the whole; the subtle, warm, impersonal charity of the author and the magical appeal of those two unfailing sources of good fiction, a provincial childhood and a passion for Paris. The Victorian "genre" scene which forms the first part is a delicious word-portrait and the Maupassant short novel which fills the second, with its unforgettable description of the execution, is a brilliant and macabre success. Once the two husbands are removed from the two sisters something goes out of the book as well as out of their lives. Bennett is at his best as a novelist of the conflict between men and women, and without that conflict we detect a certain woodenness in his major characters.

After this overdose of the Midlands I decided to postpone *Clayhanger* and *Anna of the Five Towns*, and turned to *Riceyman Steps*. This gave me great pleasure. Its best is nothing like as good as the best in *The Old Wives' Tale*, but it is an unusual and well-constructed novel, with no fat on it. I love to read about a good miser and much prefer the terrible death-figure of Mr. Earlforward to the oversentimentalised life-giving Elsie, while the ambience of the second-hand bookshop in Clerkenwell is pure Sickert.

The *Grand Babylon Hotel* is a very early and very improbable thriller, full of loose ends, but announcing, as early as 1902, that passionate preoccupation with the running of such establishments which was to stay with him all his life and lead up to his last and most unreadable book. It is gay and warm and full of food and wine and money, a period piece to which much can be forgiven.

The Journals, of course, should hold the clue to the whole man—but they don't. They are interesting and agreeable but no more. To be young in Paris between 1890 and 1914 and engrossed in life and letters, and to have kept a diary— what more can one ask? And Bennett's is a good diary; but it is the diary of a professional novelist with many other irons in the fire—a one-man newsreel, not a *journal intime*.

And so the verdict emerges. Not a great writer, not a genius, no artist in words, no poet, not even a creator of character, but an immensely industrious, painstaking, observant craftsman, a first-rate comic, a genuine novelist who applies a well-tried formula, adult, unshockable, life-enhancing; in fact, one who passes the main test, that of providing his reader with a world that has more vitality, coherence, and warmth than prevail outside—and also more luxury:

> An artist works only to satisfy himself (1897).
> . . . Bought a car, a yacht and arranged to buy a house (1912).
> One small light burning in the bedroom. Beaverbrook's pyjamas second-rate (1918).

He certainly deserves his Penguins, and even one or two more might be added, such as *Lord Raingo*. Of course, as with most of his group, the plutocratic neo-Georgian self is of much less interest than the uncorrupted Edwardian personality, but the objective honesty acquired in Paris always remained uppermost in this flamboyant, affable, helpful, particularly nice man, who remarked as early as 1897 that he "would not care a bilberry for posterity."

F. SCOTT FITZGERALD: THE LAST ROMANTIC

The Far Side of Paradise. By Arthur Mizener. Eyre & Spottiswoode.

Here comes a full-length biography of Scott Fitzgerald, the Valentino of American fiction and Rupert Brooke of the Riviera. *The Far Side of Paradise* is a very good book indeed. The central episode of Mr. Schulberg's recent novel, *The Disenchanted,* the disastrous trip to Dartmouth, is here recorded in two pages, and, instead of the author having to imagine Fitzgerald's past, it is carefully reconstructed from a wealth of original sources.

This is an admirable biography which refuses every opportunity for fireworks and concentrates on a scholarly and sympathetic understanding of its subject and the unfolding of his sad story. Whatever standing Fitzgerald will possess as an author, he is now firmly established as a myth, an American version of the Dying God, an Adonis of letters born with the century, flowering in the twenties, in the Jazz Age which he perfectly expresses and almost created, and then quietly wilting through the thirties to expire—as a deity of spring and summer should—on December 21, 1940, at the winter solstice and the end of an epoch.

❋ ❋ ❋

The myth encloses three ingredients: Fitzgerald the American success, the author whose first novel, *This Side of Paradise,* with its title taken from Rupert Brooke and its content from *Sinister Street* had yet become an extremely American thing, selling forty thousand copies and giving to the penniless young man just down from Princeton the wherewithal to capture his eighteen-year-old southern belle with whom he was in love; this myth was sustained by his stories of romantic young men and bobbed-haired young women which brought him in up to forty thousand dollars a year.

Then we have the Dying God, the reverse of the medal, the American failure, taking to drink, having his stories rejected, sinking into debt, expiring penniless at forty-four in the "Garden of Allah" as an obscure Hollywood script writer. And suddenly the rehabilitation, the publication of his last unfinished novel and the memorial volume of his essays and letters.

The third ingredient is his marriage, the immensely happy marriage which made the Fitzgeralds seem one of the most charming, impulsive, devoted and glamorous couples in all the gay places of the world, the very spirit of the twenties made flesh. Incredibly handsome, successful, fêted, rich, he rose from his first popular success to *The Great Gatsby* in 1925, one of the landmarks of the American novel, an achievement of which any author might be proud, his beautiful wife Zelda (to whom it was dedicated) standing beside him, and New York and New-York-in-Europe at his feet. About 1928 the decline begins. "They arrived in Paris in a haze of alcohol," writes their biographer. "They had a bitter quarrel during which unbelievable charges were made by both of them." They were broke, though Fitzgerald's income was still around thirty thousand dollars a year. A quarrel with Hemingway, his devoted protégé, follows, and the four admirable friends (of which any author could be proud), Edmund Wilson, Ernest Hemingway, John Dos Passos and Gerald Murphy, begin to recede into the stern father postures which his alcoholic remorse has designated for them.

Despite the important failure of his grandly conceived but too patchily carried-out novel of Americans in Europe, *Tender Is the Night*, the last years are a tale of mounting tragedy. Schizophrenia develops in Zelda, precipitating and precipitated by the alcoholic illnesses of Scott. Even in the early days of the marriage a fatal spirit of competition was born, and the myth which poor Scott illustrated best of all has perhaps something to do with the sex-war. "Zelda constantly making him drink because she was jealous of his working well," wrote Hemingway, looking back; "money

went through her fingers like water," said his publisher.
"She wanted everything; she kept him writing for the magazines." "They clung to each other like barnacles cling to
rocks, but they wanted to hurt each other all the time,"
wrote Carl Van Vechten, and I remember Joseph Herges-
heimer once explaining the situation to me and calling
Zelda "a very deleterious woman."

A careful reading of Mr. Mizener, however, reveals a
permanent strain of exhibitionist, neurotic and anti-social
behaviour in both of them, and a more than normal addiction to drinking. They were always "undressing in public or
diving into fountains." "Fitzgerald got in fights with waiters
and Zelda danced on people's dinner tables." With a basic
sense of social insecurity, an aggression liberated by drink
or cruel practical jokes, they must often have been disastrous company even in the very beginning.

The human tragedy is appalling, since Fitzgerald, though
drinking himself to death, retained a brilliant insight into
the process, its effect on himself and on his friends, and
fought stoically all the while to pay his debts and recapture
his genius, while Zelda, in her asylum, was capable of
heart-rending lucidities. Fitzgerald was forced to watch the
disintegration of someone he had loved as part of himself
in the knowledge that he had contributed to her destruction, and that her death-in-life involved him in emotional
bankruptcy. He died in 1940; and in 1947 Zelda perished
in a fire in the asylum where she was confined in Mont-
gomery, the little southern town of which she had once
been the belle.

Yes, the human tragedy is almost unbearable, but in the
world of art, the kingdom of these pages, we must acknowledge other standards. In art there is no tragedy except in
the failure of great spirits to communicate their vision of
the world before death or illness mows them down. The
untimely deaths of Keats or Shelley or Lorca are tragic; or
Joyce sacrificing his eyesight and his great gifts on a
twenty-year onslaught on the impossible; but not this feverish scramble for dollars, this round of parties, this bingo-
bango on a bookless Parnassus. The Muses have seen too
many young writers with more talent than vocation wear

themselves out on illusions, and too many quarrelsome night-club couples who won't read, the man tearing off his coat, the woman peeling off her skirt, to be very hopeful. The strains of Gatsby's "neat sad waltz" will be heard when the sorrows of its composer are long forgotten. As Balzac said to the young man who had lost his father, "and now to serious things. Who's going to marry Eugénie Grandet?"

OPPOSITE NUMBER: EDMUND WILSON

Classics and Commercials. By Edmund Wilson. W. H. Allen.

Mr. Wilson and I seem fated to write about each other; we are like passengers in two trains which are running along-side; we stare, we smile, and finally we make a face. Let us hope a time will come when we are both too distinguished to be required to point out each other's failings. Meanwhile, "Mr. Connolly is not quite a first-rate critic," explains Mr. Wilson, and *"Classics and Commercials,"* retorts Connolly, "is not quite a first-rate book."

The reason is easy to state. Fifty of these collected articles appeared in *The New Yorker* and are somewhat too regular in length and tone, "the solicitous care of the editors to eliminate anything unexpected in the way that the writers expressed themselves" demands a veneer of urbanity which is not really suited to such a teutonically thorough, naturally belligerent and deeply original critic as Edmund Wilson. His best work (which certainly is first-rate) con-sists of articles such as these incorporated into much longer general studies of the authors in question, and linked to-gether, as in *Axel's Castle, To the Finland Station,* or *The Wound and the Bow,* by some new and compelling idea. But for those who enjoy a critic's table-talk of the highest quality, who rather like it to hop about from topic to topic, I can recommend no more entertaining introduction to what Americans are now thinking of their literature and of our own. Mr. Wilson's mind purrs away like a dynamo, some-times humorously, sometimes with a note of anger, but al-ways alive and intelligent to a high degree, "very flexible . . . very definite and firm in its judgments, and very direct and courageous in registering unpopular opinions," as he himself writes of Sir Max Beerbohm.

Edmund Wilson was born at Red Barn, New Jersey, in 1895 and educated at Princeton. He saw himself as a critic in the American Renaissance of the twenties with a dual role—to bring writers like Eliot, Joyce and Proust home to the new generation, and to explain to the bourgeois intellectual the most recent developments in Marxism. So we find in all his criticism a note of political engagement, and also the buoyancy of one who feels himself participating in an ideological revelation.

Thus he maintains that Mr. Aldous Huxley "was never particularly intelligent" because "his interest in the great intellectual movements that were bringing most light in his own time was on exactly the same level as his interest in a twelfth century heresy . . . the connoisseur of abstract painting does not appear any more interesting than the fancier of Victorian bric-à-brac." But Mr. Wilson can write "the longing for mystic experience seems always to manifest itself in periods of social confusion when political progress is blocked," which would seem equally superficial to Mr. Huxley.

With his Freud-Marx skeleton key, however, he is able to uncover a great many skeletons, and because of his deep love of literary form the results are often admirable. His essays on Peacock, Jane Austen, Thackeray, Wilde, Saintsbury, Firbank are searching and original and increase our understanding of the subjects. He is also excellent, if sometimes severe, on his own contemporaries and, unlike the professional critics at American universities, never diffuse. "Mrs. Wharton was always quite rich. Where did her money come from? Was it her own or was it her husband's? And why did she marry Edward Wharton? . . . What precisely was the matter with him when he became deranged and Mrs. Wharton finally divorced him?" His dislikes are of a piece; mystery thrillers, detective stories, Maugham, Bromfield, MacLeish, Kafka, survivors of the twenties who became secret communists, "a pathetically easy prey to the two great enemies of literary talent in our time, Hollywood and Henry Luce," and brash Californians who somehow seem to defy the skeleton key, like Steinbeck and Saroyan.

But these anathema are infrequent, and a Parisian love of literature tempers the Mencken-bred ferocity of analysis. Mr. Wilson modestly describes himself as a journalist "whose principal heroes among journalists have been de Quincey, Poe, and Shaw"; he has lived to see the United States emerge from the provincial pandemonium which drove its artists into exile and become the civilised capital of the humanities, but he has never forgotten that his country was basically philistine from the Civil War to the Slump, and he knows that the enemies of the Enlightenment never disappear. Even when they seem, like Firbank or Peacock, to bask in the sun, his favourite writers are all aware of the lengthening shadow.

This makes him one of us, a European who happens to be an American, perfectly at home in the literature of England, Russia, America and France, and yet too independent a thinker ever to fall a victim to the polyglot's melancholy.

ENVOI

AMERICA AND EUROPE

When I was young I was fond of exploring remote parts of Europe by mule. Greek monasteries, villages of the Alpujarras, ruined sanctuaries of Calabria . . . how delicious it was to escape from the American tourists down below and follow the stony trail which led up into the hills. And there, in nearly every village, one would be welcomed by the returned expatriate, the "Say Mister," the *Americano*. The Greeks were the worst, then the Italians—"Why you come to a little place like this, say Mister? Waddya wanna see?" And meanwhile, back at my base, another Buick-load would have driven up with Poppa, Momma, Lois, and Junior, with their cameras, dark glasses, Oshkosh, and dust coats.

I became a great hater of Americans for they seemed to be destroying my Europe at both ends—my Europe being the picturesque and poverty-stricken legacy of the feudal system which the English traveller felt he had a right to expect. It never occurred to me that there could be any connection between the "Say Mister" up the mountain and the pink-faced family in the Buick, both of whom were contributing so much more generously than I to the revenues of the countries I loved. The Buick family were Europeans who had been away for a hundred and fifty years, whereas the *Americano* had only stayed thirty or forty years in the land of opportunity. I failed to understand that America had been created by Europeans who didn't like Europe and that the things they didn't like were intolerance, injustice, and inequality; poverty, in fact, but the poverty of those who inherit not only a poor soil but a poor spirit, who have an apathetic inability to fight their way out of the rut.

All these conditions exist in the United States, too, because human beings create them wherever they go, but

Americans like to pretend they do not occur in their own land since their absence is a feature of the American dream. However vulgarized by El Dollarado, the "Say Mister" had none the less returned to his backward native village; the Buick family, despite their impervious complacency, their spic-and-span mediocrity, were making the fight of their lives not to be sucked back into the Europe from which their ancestors had escaped, determined to exorcise the antique demon of solitude and neurosis by chewing up the kilometres and clinging to wholesome Baedeker, the holy book.

There is, of course, no such thing as American influence considered as an unrelated phenomenon; European peasants become immigrants and, ultimately, Americans who are privileged to get away from America, and who pour back into Europe the money which finds its way down to more workers and peasants to pay for their passages. All American influence on Europe, however vulgar, brings with it an improvement in the standard of living and dissipates certain age-old fears. The problem eventually takes the form of whether the passage to America and back can be eliminated; whether Europeans can turn into Americans without having to move at all, like the Italian children who were looked after by the G.I.s.

It is interesting to study this relationship geographically. Thus Morocco and California are two countries on about the same latitude with a long seacoast, two harbour-cities, San Francisco and Casablanca, and high mountain ranges parallel with the coast; inland, a hot desert climate, and near the coast, palms and oranges, mild winters and summers made bearable by a cold sea current. Two hundred years ago they must have been very alike, but how different now! California means wealth, exuberance, Hollywood, motels, Coca-Cola, William Randolph Hearst, while Morocco is fanatical Islam, the Middle Ages fossilized, the Glaoui in his kasbah, slavery, harems, fighting Berber tribesmen, the Foreign Legion, Fez.

But let us look closer—Fez while the gates are closed at dusk is still impregnable, but Casablanca is very like a third-rate American city, with Arabs sleeping out in rows on the street through the summer night, and the girls, their Turkish trousers discarded for blue jeans, smoking American cigarettes and pinning up some Hollywood Handsome on the wall of the clean white brothel—and the Coca-Cola advertisements—for Coca-Cola is a great boon to thirsty, teetotal Islam. It's all very like the Mexican quarters of downtown Los Angeles. The two cities might almost be said, below a certain income level, to be turning into the same place (which geographically they so nearly are). At the top are the palaces of the film stars on one side, the kasbahs of the Atlas chiefs on the other, the religious and academic worlds which remain poles apart; but down below, among the little businesses and the bums on the waterfront, everything is going into the American melting pot.

Should Europe oppose this influence? Europe which has destroyed so many exotic civilizations without even providing them with the democratic optimism which America brings in with her films, her gadgets, and her lingua franca, the demotic language which obliterates all class distinction? We cannot oppose this infiltration on the economic level, nor on the feudal level—there are not enough sultans to go round who can outlaw shorts and banish bubble gum—nor will the high priests be listened to. The intellectuals? Ah! They are the true custodians of Europe, the last élite; they say "refrigerator" instead of "fridge"; they stand for quality not quantity, for pure scholarship, aesthetic integrity, unapplied science. But I seem to be describing all my friends in America. In fact, I can think of no country in which there is a more impressive "state within a state," where there are more people swimming against the current, living without venality, fighting for ideals, existing for ideas, liberal, humane, disinterested, and generous; this country possesses more hostile critics of its own than any other has been able to show since the France of the Encyclopædists.

And all this they have learnt from Europe: novelists like Hemingway and Faulkner, Dos Passos and Steinbeck, critics like Edmund Wilson and Lionel Trilling, humourists like Thurber are, in the best sense, Europeanised Americans who, through their books, are now Americanising, in the best sense, Europe. They have brought a new quality to the language, vivid, astringent, and exhilarating—and some of those who seemed at first only to inject an awareness of the utter futility, absurdity, and misery of life into our dignified European smugness have come round now to a belief in life. Despair is often an antidote to decay, and Faulkner's Nobel Prize Address is a positive declaration of faith: "I believe man will not merely endure, he will prevail." "The single secret will still be man," wrote E. E. Cummings, but younger American writers like Tennessee Williams, Truman Capote, Paul Bowles, or Norman Mailer are trying very hard to isolate that part of man in which the mystery resides, to learn how to look for it with more persistence and vitality than their European contemporaries who are apt to be more limited by a conventional upbringing, less ranging and curious, and too inbred culturally.

As for jazz, gangster stories, bad films, tales of violence, the *Reader's Digest*, science fiction, and other products for which we reproach America, why has Europe so enthusiastically welcomed them? Jazz because our own folk music has perished, thrillers because we are bored, films because we can't stay home in the evening, the *Reader's Digest* because we can neither digest nor read, and the gangster because he represents the anarchic adolescent conception of liberty which in times of peace we are forced to stifle. Since Edgar Allan Poe, Europe has always preferred the morbid and eccentric by-products of American culture to that respectable nineteenth-century humanism which is an imitation of its own, and now, I am afraid, it may only be in America that the European races will grow to the full moral and mental stature of which they are capable. We are fond of making a wrong historical analogy; we like to talk fatalistically of Europe as about to be taken over by America, as if it were Greece on the eve of surrender to Rome or Macedon, in order to make the point that, with our superior civilization, we shall soon civilize our conquerors. But I am more inclined to see Washington as Byzantium. We are like the aged Roman Empire, threatened by the barbarians, internally vulnerable, leaded with debt. So the empire is divided; the new capital, for security reasons, is moved west, not east, and, like Constantinople, Washington may pre-

serve the culture of the West for a thousand years in some
rigid form by its strong armies and admirable civil service,
its full treasure and rich hinterland. This is the America
which the philosopher Santayana has envisaged:

> If material life could be made perfect, as (in a very
> small way) it was perhaps for a moment among the
> Greeks, would not that of itself be a most admirable
> achievement? . . . And possibly on that basis of per-
> fected material life, a new art and philosophy would
> grow unawares, not similar to what we call by those
> names, but having the same relation to the life beneath
> which art and philosophy amongst us ought to have had,
> but never have.

Americanisation, in fact, may be something we must go
through, like nationalism, in order to find something better,
as so many Americans are trying to do.

The most dazzling of European intellectuals, the late
Paul Valéry, wrote: "Europe will be punished for her politics; her wines, her beer, and her liqueurs will be taken
away from her—and a great deal more. Europe is simply
asking to be governed by an American Committee. All her
political activities are leading up to it. Because we don't
know how to get rid of our own past, we will be liberated
only by new and happy peoples without one or almost
without one. It is these happy nations who will impose on
us their own felicity."

Who will *impose* their happiness on us! Ah, there is the
crux, and it indicates the only valid European protest, the
one way in which our torn and self-destructive continent,
left with but a few miserable pieces on the board, can try
to draw the game. It is too late to make an appeal to our
mineral resources, our inventive genius, our political em-
piricism, our industrial potential, even to our scholarship,
our traditions, our moral intractability, our gardens, and
museums. On all these points America has caught up
with us. All except one. When the French man of letters,
M. Léautaud (aged seventy-six), was being interviewed
on the Paris wireless—interviews, I may say, which could
have been broadcast in no other country, combining as they

did so much free speaking with such a regard for the minutiae of literature, he expressed himself as follows:

"I wrote once: 'Death is more beautiful than Life, Poverty is more lovely than Riches, Solitude is more fair than Society. A writer of talent who is unknown is a finer thing than a writer everyone has heard of.'"

"Why this panegyric," broke in his interviewer, "of what is in fact suffering?"

"No, not suffering. Melancholy—melancholy is a noble feeling. Happiness is mediocrity."

There we have it, the one reply which the old continent of "If only" can make to the new world of "Why not." There is very little melancholy in America; it is not a country of long twilights; it doesn't appreciate Oscar Wilde's definition of gloom as a wet Sunday afternoon in the Cromwell Road. "Be happy." (It is commanded by the American constitution.) "If you can't be happy, be busy. They come to the same thing. If you can't be busy, be gregarious—for the alternative with us is not the poet's fine melancholy, but the drunkard's oblivion." Let us put it another way. Suppose a secret society were to be formed of Europeans who are intensely proud of the European heritage and of the European spirit—from the Parthenon or the painted caves of Lascaux to the Amalienberg and the Café de Flore—diehard aesthetes who are sworn to protect it by every possible means, as the early Jesuits defended the faith, against the materialism and uniformity of America and the materialism, uniformity, and tyranny of Russia; let us imagine it to be called the "Brotherhood of the Tragic Sense of Life." Is there one European who could be trusted not to betray? Never to open a food parcel or look at *The New Yorker?* How soon would it be before one of the brotherhood had sold an article on their aims to *Life* magazine, before the whole organization, in fact, was being subsidised by Americans, many of whom were enthusiastic to join? No, there is no cure. It is too late. No one need be influenced against his will. All that Europe can do now is to try to facilitate the infiltration of the good America, of the other America, rather than of the bad—in other words of the America which has improved on European virtues rather than that which has mass-produced our own vices. For we are in no position to resist or blame. European wars are all of them wars which are made and lost by Europe, and the fallen Samson can only apostrophise the American Delilah in Milton's words:

"I led the way, bitter reproach, but true;
I to myself was false ere thou to me."